The New Disability History

The History of Disability Series

GENERAL EDITORS: Paul K. Longmore and Lauri Umansky

The New Disability History: American Perspectives
Edited by Paul K. Longmore and Lauri Umansky

The New Disability History

American Perspectives

EDITED BY

Paul K. Longmore and Lauri Umansky

NEW YORK UNIVERSITY PRESS
New York and London

NEW YORK UNIVERSITY PRESS
New York and London

Library of Congress Cataloging-in-Publication Data
The new disability history : American perspectives /
edited by Paul K. Longmore and Lauri Umansky.
p.   cm. — (The history of disability series)
Includes index.
ISBN 0-8147-8563-8 — ISBN 0-8147-8564-6 (pbk.)
1. Handicapped—United States—History. 2. Sociology
of disability—United States—History.   I. Longmore,
Paul K.   II. Umansky, Lauri, 1959–   III. Series.
HV1553 .N48 2001
305.9′0816—dc21   00-011661

New York University Press books are printed on acid-free paper,
and their binding materials are chosen for strength and durability.

Manufactured in the United States of America
10 9 8 7 6 5 4 3 2 1

Contents

Introduction

Disability History: From the Margins to the Mainstream

Paul K. Longmore and Lauri Umansky

If controversy is any measure, disability has arrived on the American scene. Passage of the Americans with Disabilities Act (ADA) in 1990 has provoked public dispute ever since. Newspaper headlines shout the battles: "Four Insurers Accused of Bias against Disabled"; "Advocates for Disabled Sue Movie Theater Chain"; "Disabled Golfer's Lawsuit to Use Cart Challenges PGA Tour's Right to Make Its Own Rules"; "Disabilities Act Abused? Law's Use Sparks Debate"; "Disabilities Act Dilemma: Job Rights vs. Job Safety; Bias Suits Pose Public Risk, Employers Say."[1] If nothing else, disability has, it seems, at last won a place in the "national conversation."

While hardly a panacea, the ADA proposes to ensure the right of Americans with disabilities to move from the margins of society into the mainstream. It promises them equal access to the public sites where their fellow citizens conduct their everyday lives: subways and snack bars, offices and auditoriums, jury boxes and gymnasiums. When it passed the act, Congress declared, "Historically, society has tended to isolate and segregate individuals with disabilities." When he signed the ADA into law, President George Bush proclaimed, "Let the shameful wall of exclusion finally come tumbling down."[2] The unavoidable public presence, the surprising political participation of citizens with disabilities are both the ADA's cause and its consequence. Claiming and exercising their rights of access, disabled people have compelled their country to move away from that historical isolation, segregation, and exclusion. Ramps and blue wheelchair-access symbols and Braille markers seem to have sprouted everywhere. Sign-language interpreters seem now to interpret every public event. Though compliance studies report that, to a significant degree, U.S. society continues to restrict or exclude people with disabilities, many Americans, disabled and nondisabled alike, feel that a vast social transformation is under way. George Will, conservative syndicated columnist and father of a disabled child, has called it "the last great inclusion," the culmination of the civil rights era.[3] So it seems that *disability* is no longer hidden and taboo; that disability issues will get, must get, public attention; that people with all sorts of disabilities have presently emerged from the shadows to assert their citizenship.

But in fact, disability has always been central to life in America. From before the antebellum debates about the qualifications of democratic citizenship recounted in the first two essays of this volume, to the current controversies over access and "reasonable accommodations," disability has been present, in penumbra if not in print, on virtually every page of American history. Taken together, the essays here show that Americans have long grappled with issues of disability in both their personal lives and the public arena. And people with disabilities themselves, as individuals and in organized associations, have, in all eras, struggled to control definition of their social identities, to direct their social careers. As Douglas Baynton observes in the opening essay, "Disability is everywhere in history, once you begin looking for it, but conspicuously absent in the histories we write."

Two examples illustrate the pervasive presence of disability and its conspicuous absence from the historiography. Baynton has reminded us elsewhere, as he does in his essay here, that since colonial times "the exclusion of disabled people has been one of the most fundamental and least controversial aspects of American immigration law." Over time, immigration laws increasingly "lowered the threshold for exclusion and expanded the latitude" of immigration officials in turning away aliens with every sort of disability. Historians have typically overlooked this major theme of immigration history, except when they noted that restrictionists attributed disability to various ethnic groups. Apart from decrying that ascription as a slur against would-be immigrants, scholars have not asked what these policies reveal about cultural values regarding disability or about prejudice and discrimination against people with disabilities.[4] To take another striking example, because occupational injury and illness have happened frequently among laborers, disability has been a common experience in American working-class families. Medical historians have studied these occurrences under the aegis of industrial medicine and legal historians in terms of the development of tort law. Meanwhile, labor historians have shown how cultural constructions of masculinity infused male workers' class consciousness. But as John Williams-Searle observes, scholars have failed to examine "the ideological relationships" among "risk, gender, disability, and capitalism" in shaping labor union, business, and governmental responses to disability or workers' understandings of disability's meaning. Labor historiography seldom recognizes the experience and perception of disability in laborers' lives or in working-class subcultures.[5] Thus, in two major fields of historical inquiry in which disability was significant, as lived experience and social phenomenon, historians have largely ignored it. Their accounts have rendered people with disabilities invisible and have neglected disability themes that were of central concern to their subjects.

The essays in this collection begin to fill the historiographical gaps. They show us that disability has a place not only in immigration and labor history but also in the histories of African Americans, business, citizenship, education, family, gender, politics, policy, popular culture, social reform, war, and women; in biographical studies, intellectual history, and southern history, even in medical history. These essays direct attention to the frequency, the virtual commonplaceness, of disability as personal yet also public experience, social problem, and cultural metaphor. In these pages, people with various kinds of disabilities appear in the popular press as well as in specialized periodicals, on lecture platforms as well as on sideshow stages. They lobby legislators and advocate their interests in petitions and letters to public officials. They claim their rights as full and equal citizens to vote, to work, to marry, to receive veterans benefits and to secure civil rights protections, to gain access and to get respect. They disclose their thoughts, hopes, and fears in diaries and private letters. They work on the railroad and they bake in the kitchen. They gather at local meetings of the American Legion and in the annual conventions of the American Blind People's Higher Education and General Improvement Association. The children attend residential schools, day schools, and "hospital schools," while the adults defend the right of those children to education but debate just what sort of education best meets the children's needs. Many of them demand a voice in their own lives. Some of them join with other physically disabled veterans, with other blind Americans, with other members of the Deaf community, to oppose government bureaucrats or sighted professionals or hearing educators and to claim the legitimacy of their collective view of their situation and their right to a say in it. Sometimes they gain a measure of power, often they lose. Some of them are murdered, and their killers are acquitted. Some are blind and some are Deaf.[6] Some walk with crutches and some are missing limbs. Some are paralyzed; a few have multiple disabilities. They are celebrated as cultural icons, exploited as cultural metaphors, devalued as cultural failures. They are men and women, adults and children, black and white, Southerners, New Englanders, and Midwesterners, patrician, middle-class, and poor.

The lives, the actions, of the men and women who traverse these pages evidence the enormous diversity of disability. While public policy has sought to fashion *disability* as a generic category and attempted to impose that classification on people with an assortment of conditions, disability has never been a monolithic grouping. There has always been a variety of disability experiences.

At the same time, the experiences outlined above—experiences of cultural devaluation and socially imposed restriction, of personal and collective struggles for self-definition and self-determination—recur across the various disability groups and throughout their particular histories. Whether they were blind or deaf or physically disabled, the people whose experiences these essays recount faced comparable social perils. In many ways, they marked parallel historical paths.

Twentieth-century public policy contributed to the emergence of both disability-specific political efforts and cross-disability alliances. For example, the chartering by the state legislatures of residential schools for deaf children and blind youngsters resulted from and encouraged the further development of constituencies that supported each of those types of schools. In her account here of the struggle for control of early twentieth-century Deaf education, Susan Burch reports how various state associations of Deaf people and organizations of oralists vigorously lobbied state lawmakers. Contemporaneous to those political campaigns, as K. Walter Hickel and Richard Scotch show in their essays, disabled–veterans benefit programs drew together veterans with a variety of disabilities, thereby generating cross-disability advocacy early in the century. Late in the century, the Americans with Disabilities Act and a number of preceding federal laws resulted from even more extensive alliances. Over time, policy definitions significantly influenced how people with disabilities themselves understood disability. Even when public policies, programs, and funding affected only particular disability groups, they helped politicize those groups. Other policies providing social-insurance or social-welfare benefits or banning discrimination and ensuring access gathered many diverse disability groups under a generic categorization. Those policies helped promote—and in the case of the civil rights laws, also grew out of—a sense of disability as a collectively

Paul K. Longmore and Lauri Umansky

shared status and experience. That slowly developing understanding fostered among disabled people a growing perception of common political interests. It also spurred the formation of cross-disability coalitions. Throughout the twentieth century, public policy contributed significantly to the transformation of disability from a series of pathological medical conditions to a politicized status, identity, and set of interrelated interest groups.

The long-term impact of public policies and the similarities in the experiences of various disability groups suggest the need for a comparative historical approach. Those features also warrant us in speaking of a general disability history that encompasses the particular histories of those groups.

The political themes in disability history call attention to the material interests at stake. We can readily see the economic concerns in John Williams-Searle's account of friction among railroaders over jobs or financial aid for disabled trainmen. Similar interests appear in K. Walter Hickel's report of both white and black disabled veterans' eligibility or disqualification for vocational retraining and pensions. Once alerted, we recognize the issues of power underlying the disagreements between blind advocates and sighted professionals or between Social Security administrators and disability rights activists over "work disincentives," respectively discussed by Catherine Kudlick and Richard Scotch. In its campaign for sign language and against "pure oralism," the Deaf community, Susan Burch tells us, fought fiercely for control of the content of Deaf children's education, for command of the core institutions in American Deaf life, and, not least, for jobs. Another contest for power, this one to shape rehabilitation, occurred as orthopedists displaced what Brad Byrom calls "social rehabilitationists." Byrom prompts us to consider the issues of class and professional power evident when rehabilitationists indentured "crippled" working-class children to prevent their parents from coddling them into "dependency"; the new "experts" institutionalized those youngsters in programs of medical, vocational, and moral training to forestall their becoming beggars. The gendering of identities and roles reflects and reinforces another dimension in the structuring of power. Byrom notes the placement of "crippled" girls in hospital-schools, on the assumption that they needed vocational training because they would never marry. Likewise, Kudlick contrasts images of desexualized girls in a domestic-science class with a profile of a blind wife and mother. Those placements and images reflect the material options made available or denied to women with disabilities. That relations of gender, class, and race or between professionals and clients are relations of social, economic, and political power is obvious. That relations involving disability entail similar dynamics requires a new way of thinking. The new disability history scrutinizes struggles not just over identities and discourses but over power and access to material resources.

Although these experiences are quintessentially American, we have largely screened them out of our collective historical memory. Why have historians generally left people with disabilities out of the account?

One major practical reason may be that historians assume a paucity of primary sources for disability history. How can one write the history of a subject if one cannot gather much evidence about it? The essays that follow demonstrate that, in fact, the primary materials of disability history exist in abundance. The contributors tap many sources to generate many types of evidence. They find the data of disability history in mass-circulation newspapers such as the *New York Times* and in magazines for specific audiences such as the venerated *Deaf Worker* and the virtually forgotten *The Problem*. They uncover it in predictable sources such as *Outlook for the Blind* and in such unexpected places as the *Locomotive Engineers' Monthly Journal*. They glean it from the files of the Veterans Bureau and they gather it through oral history interviews. They explicate it in the diary of Alice James, an L. L. Bean catalog, the provisions of Social Security Disability Insurance, and the manuscript letters between a Civil War–era North Carolina family and their brother, a student and later teacher at the New York School for the Deaf. The documentation supporting these essays indicates the variety and volume of primary source materials for disability history. Historians might have predicted the quantity of material in professional journals and perhaps even public documents; they will surely express surprise at the extent of evidence in a wide array of periodicals. And, contrary to what they might expect, a great deal of that material was produced by or conveys the perspectives of people with disabilities themselves. Given the plethora of evidence—given that, as Baynton says, "disability is everywhere in history, once you begin looking for it"—historians' oversight seems all the more puzzling.

The elision of disabled people from the historiography also surely reflects the "existential anxiety" that disability often evokes. A considerable literature in psychology verifies that the presence of individuals with disabilities stirs dis-ease in many individuals who view themselves as *normal*.[7] A more recent literature in cultural studies of disability strongly suggests that those nervous reactions stem from more than individual temperament. To a significant degree, they arise from the most basic of modern, and particularly

American, cultural values and social training. Amercians often perceive disability—and therefore people with disabilities—as embodying that which Americans fear most: loss of independence, of autonomy, of control; in other words, subjection to fate.[8] The culturally conditioned psychological response to disability may help explain disabled peoples' absence from historical accounts. That which we fear, we shun.

At an intellectual and theoretical level, historians may have neglected disability history because they view the experience of disability from a medical perspective. This outlook has dominated modern policymaking, professional practice, and societal arrangements regarding people with disabilities. It defines disability as caused primarily by any of a series of pathologies located in the bodies or minds of individuals. From this perspective, these physiological impairments produce personal limitations in performing the "major life activities" ordinarily "expected" of people in particular age groups: for children, attending school and engaging in play; for working-age adults, holding jobs or keeping house; for older adults, managing their households and caring for themselves. This approach personalizes disability, casting it as a deficit located within individuals that requires rehabilitation to correct the physiological defect or to amend the social deficiency. Given this framing, the study of disability has traditionally been regarded as an appropriate subject only in medicine, rehabilitation, special education, and other applied professional fields. Research and teaching about disability still appear primarily in those academic sectors and continue to be based on medical models. On the rare occasions when the liberal-arts fields broach the topic of disability, Simi Linton notes, "the deficit paradigms remain, and the focus is on the individual as deviant subject, rather than on the social structures that label difference as deviance and pathology."[9]

With regard to historical study, the medicalized perspective may cause scholars to view disability as involving individual case histories, rather than as the stuff of social, cultural, or political history. From this viewpoint, if disability has a place in historical analysis, it belongs in medical history. In recent years, medical historians have increasingly addressed the sociocultural experience of illness and public discourse about disease, health, and health care. Even so, most works have focused on professional and societal responses to epidemics, the critical phases of diseases, the functioning of health care institutions, and the interactions between patients and various medical professionals. If people with disabilities appear in these narratives, they surface typically as "patients," "afflicted" with disease or undergoing treatment for injuries.[10]

The explanation of disability as pathology individualizes and privatizes the causes of alleged social incapacity. It largely precludes recognition of cultural, social, and political factors in the construction of "disability" experiences. Thus, we expect to find people with disabilities in medical institutions, but we neglect to look for them in other social settings. The essays in this anthology show that few people with "disabilities" spent more than a portion of their lives—if they spent any time at all—in medical institutions or interacting with medical professionals. Medicalized interpretations of their situations and needs did impact them, but usually through the brokerage of schools and social service agencies rather than health care institutions, of educators and social workers rather than doctors and nurses. *The New Disability History* contributors point historians to the places we have failed to look.

Moreover, because older works in disability history operated from the perspective of medical pathology, they typically presented people with disabilities as passive. The real historical actors were professionals, philanthropists, and policymakers, few of whom had disabilities. Traditional histories of "the blind" or "the deaf" offered stories of hearing and sighted heroes bringing enlightenment or speech to the objects of their beneficence; blind people and deaf people remained inert and effectively invisible.[11] In another arena, though policy historians have recounted the formulation of the "disability category" in public policy, people with disabilities commonly appear as historical agents only when the narrative arrives at the late twentieth century and disability rights activism becomes highly visible.[12] Even in those fields of historical study in which disability has received attention, then, it seems that the paradigm of medical pathology has caused historians to neglect disabled persons as historical actors.

Historical examination of disability based on medical pathology misinterprets or filters out a great deal of evidence. It distorts our understanding. The contributors to this collection offer a new approach that examines social, cultural, and political factors; they accord people with disabilities an active role in their own history.

Finally, at an ideological and political level, the new disability history has encountered the same resistance that has often denied disability studies courses a legitimate place in academic curricula outside the medical and applied fields. Some critics of diversity regard disability studies, in its scholarly and curricular aims, as further evidence that helps discredit all such innovations and reforms. They dismiss disability studies research and teaching as an instance of identity politics expropriating academic legitimation and resources to promote the personal self-esteem and parochial political agenda of a narrow interest group. They accuse the disability studies project of further fragmenting both intellectual exchange and the larger society. Besides, they claim, perhaps associating it with the shortcomings of rehabilitation research, the project lacks rigor, validity, and wider intellectual significance. Ironically, supporters of diversity who propose to make teaching and research more comprehensive, more accurate and representative, often marshal the same accusations in opposing the inclusion of disability studies in that project. Some even add the distinctive argument that incorporating disability would "water down" diversity requirements. As a result, "progressive" proponents of attention to issues of race, class, and gender and "conservative" critics of multiculturalism at times unconsciously join forces to limit examination of disability in intellectual discourse. Meanwhile, academics invested in the traditional "disability" fields such as rehabilitation and special education, alongside humanists and social scientists who simply do not consider disability an appropriate, worthy, or significant area of scholarly inquiry outside the applied fields, often effectively restrict the study of disability to the medical and quasi-medical disciplines. Finally, "the extraordinarily low representation of people with disabilities in academic settings" as students, faculty, and administrators, as well as the general failure to recognize them as an underrepresented minority, has excluded their perspectives from both current discussions of curricular reform and ongoing intellectual discourse.[13]

Taken together, a range of factors in the academy combine to define disability as pathological rather than political, clinical and not cultural, fundamentally different from race, class, and gender. That perspective, in turn, confines the study of disability to parochial academic arenas and intellectually narrow approaches, while it unknowingly robs broader academic discourse of significant modes of analysis. The past generation of intellectual controversy has taught us to ask why some forms of knowledge are privileged and others marginalized. We have learned to examine the implicit political content of each position, to inquire into the specific interests at stake. We have been instructed to recognize that all intellectual discourse benefits when it is critiqued and to pay particular attention to critiques from the margins. Disability history, like disability studies in general, speaks from one of the margins to both the old centers of authority and the new.

The new centers of authority arose under the stimulus of the social, cultural, and political transformations outside the academy. Just as the Second Reconstruction prompted a wholesale revision of African American history, just as the modern feminist movement spurred a vast excavation of women's history, so the new disability history has arisen in response to contemporary social changes.

The ADA capped a generation of innovative lawmaking regarding Americans with disabilities. That legislative process began with the federal Architectural Barriers Act of 1968, a result of activists' campaign to make public places and public transportation accessible. Five years later, Section 504 of the Rehabilitation Act of 1973 outlawed discrimination against "otherwise qualified" handicapped individuals in federally funded programs; it was the first civil rights statute extending protection to such persons. In 1975, the Education for All Handicapped Children Act (since renamed the Individuals with Disabilities Education Act) guaranteed children with disabilities the right to attend public schools for the first time in U.S. history. In all, some fifty acts of Congress passed between 1968 and 1990 represented a major departure in lawmaking and policymaking regarding persons with disabilities. This body of legislation did not propose to provide more "help" to persons regarded as disadvantaged by disability. Instead, it reflected and sought to implement a fundamental redefinition of what disability is, of what it means to be disabled in American society.[14]

Congress did not invent this redefinition. It largely responded to the campaigning of disabled people and their nondisabled allies. The two decades of transformative lawmaking grew out of disability rights activism that reached back for generations, as the following essays reveal, but achieved new levels of political effectiveness in the last third of the twentieth century. Some groups, such as the National Association of the Deaf and the National Federation of the Blind, had long labored for the rights and interests of their members. Others, such as the United Cerebral Palsy Associations and the National Easter Seal Society, still mainly offered services but increasingly expanded their legislative lobbying efforts. Still others, such as the American Diabetes Association and the Epilepsy Foundation of America—traditional funders of medical research and treatment—began to take legal action on behalf of their constituents. Parents of disabled children, particularly of children with developmental disabilities, joined by some special educators, mobilized throughout the latter half of the twentieth century in organizations such as The Association for the Severely Handicapped (TASH) and the Association for Retarded Citizens (the ARC) to win deinstitutionalization, community-based living, and access to public education. Most startling to a society steeped in decades of devaluation, cognitively disabled Americans began

Paul K. Longmore and Lauri Umansky

to speak out for themselves in advocacy groups like People First. Beginning in the 1970s, many of these varied constituencies joined forces in cross-disability political campaigns such as the American Coalition of Citizens with Disabilities and, later, the presidentially appointed advisory body the National Council on Disability.[15]

Advocates lobbied against discrimination. They demanded "equal access" to public transportation, public accommodations, and telecommunications, to school and work, to "independent" or "congregate" living in the community rather than in institutions. Lobbying in the national and state legislatures and filing suits in the federal and state courts, organizations of and for people with various disabilities adopted a civil rights approach. Militant groups such as ADAPT (American Disabled for Accessible Public Transit, since renamed American Disabled for Attendant Programs Today) borrowed the tactics of earlier social justice movements by engaging in civil disobedience. In the 1980s, ADAPT activists dramatized the inaccessibility of public transit by sliding down out of their wheelchairs to block buses. In the 1990s, to draw attention to federal funding priorities that perpetuated the incarceration of disabled people in nursing homes, they picketed the annual meetings of nursing-home industry corporate leaders and chanted, "Free our people!" In the mid-1990s, the cleverly named Not Dead Yet challenged as expressions of lethal disability bias the assumptions of the "right-to-die" movement and the celebration of Jack Kevorkian as some sort of eccentric folk hero. More than at any other moment in this activist history, for five days in March of 1988 the entire world watched as Deaf students at Gallaudet University in Washington, D.C., backed by the Deaf community, seized their campus to protest the appointment of yet another hearing person as president of the premier institution of education for deaf people. They demanded a "Deaf President Now!" and they won.[16]

The mounting activism of these various groups reflected their intent to redefine disability just as the new laws and policies were doing. Indeed, their activism aimed principally to promote passage of that legislation, which mandated new policies and practices. But deeper than the political agenda, the advocacy expressed a shift in self-perception, through which millions of Americans with disabilities redefined their identities. By the mid-1980s, survey research began documenting the emergence of a minority-group consciousness among a generation of younger adults with disabilities.[17]

Various politicized disability communities today press disability-related issues as never before. Disabled youngsters and their parents make increasing demands of the educational system as they push for education as a civil right. The expanding elder population's public activism also highlights issues of disability. The crises in the health care and health financing systems generate policy and ethical discussion about who has a right to how much medical treatment, while innovations in medicine spark legal cases regarding both the right to treatment (for example, for disabled newborns) and the "right to die." Demands to ban discrimination, along with calls to ensure "equal access" and "reasonable accommodations" in everything from hiring practices to hotel services, restaurants to rental cars, professional licensing exams to professional golf playing, incite debates about equality, convenience, and cost.

All these controversies compel serious rethinking about disability. The complicated, sometimes bewildering issues prompt profound questions: What is disability? What is equality? What constitutes discrimination? What is a minority group? How are individual and group identities shaped and altered? What does it mean to be an American? What makes someone human? The quest for answers reaches into public law and policy. More fundamental, it extends into social, professional, and institutional values and practices regarding persons with disabilities. It was perhaps inevitable—it was certainly necessary—that scholars in many academic disciplines would take up these questions.

As with disability rights legislation and activism, the new academic field of disability studies has arisen in response to the medical model's deficiencies in explaining or addressing the social marginalization and economic deprivation of many people with disabilities. Disability studies takes as its domain the intricate interaction among cultural values, social arrangements, public policy, and professional practice regarding "disability." For the medical model it substitutes sociopolitical or minority-group models of disability. Utilizing a multidisciplinary approach, it "centers the study of disability on its social construction," explains Simi Linton, "the processes that have accorded particular meaning to disability and that have determined the treatment and positioning of people with disabilities in society."[18] Viewed from this perspective, people with a variety of conditions, despite considerable differences in etiology, confront a common set of stigmatizing social values and debilitating socially constructed hazards.

The first wave of disability studies emerged in the 1980s in fields such as political science, policy studies, and sociology. It directed its efforts toward providing an analytical research base for the reform of public policies and professional practices, seeking ultimately to reconstruct society. That approach continues to have profound implications for many areas of academic inquiry and professional training. It increasingly influences not just the obvious fields that deal directly with people with disabilities, such as education, medicine, policy studies, and social services, but also the numerous fields that affect disabled people in important ways directly or indirectly: business, computer science, industrial and consumer-product design, engineering, law, public administration, and urban planning.[19]

A second wave of disability studies in the 1990s comprised scholars in the humanities. Writing in the *Chronicle of Higher Education* in 1997, literary scholar Michael Bérubé noted the philosophical significance and the societal consequences of "the cultural representation of people with disabilities." He urged his colleagues in the liberal arts to incorporate the study of disability into their work.[20] In fact, a growing number of scholars had already begun to examine disability from the distinctive perspective of the humanities. Humanistic disability studies has rapidly developed as a vibrant area of inquiry.

Disability studies in the humanities has built on recent work in the various humanities disciplines. It adopts from literary theory and rhetorical studies the critical inspection of representation and of discursive constructions of reality. It extends the new social history's attention to marginalized groups, while it espouses cultural studies' contention of the implicit political orientation of research and pedagogy. Just as humanities scholars have probed the complex cultural construction of such assumedly natural representational systems as race and gender, some have begun explicating the creation of "disability" through the interactions of material practices and cultural representations regarding different modes of functioning.

The analytical tools of the humanities disciplines furnish the means to address questions about disability that the traditional, impairment-oriented medical and quasi-medical disciplines cannot treat. These tools transform the study of disability from a specialized field within medicine, rehabilitation, or social work. But humanistic disability studies does not limit itself to analyzing and redressing the disadvantaged status of people with disabilities, though that agenda remains central to the project. In addition, it presents disability as a subject important for, indeed essential to, wide-ranging intellectual inquiry. As Linton notes, disability studies "goes beyond cataloging discrimination and arguing for social change." It also "deepens the understanding of gender and sexuality, individualism and equality, minority group definitions, autonomy, wholeness, independence, dependence, health, physical appearance, aesthetics, the integrity of the body, community, and notions of progress and perfection that pervade every aspect of the civic and pedagogic cultures." At bottom, disability studies explores "fundamental epistemological issues" that reach into all spheres of intellectual inquiry.[21]

As disability studies scholarship and professional activity surge, disability topics appear with growing frequency on the programs of scholarly conferences and in the meetings of the major professional scholarly associations. The leading disciplinary journals publish more and more articles; the major academic presses issue an increasing number of critical studies and even book series.[22]

While historians have contributed to the conferences, anthologies, and periodical literature of disability studies, their work has appeared less frequently and more haphazardly than it should. Yet many of the questions being examined by disability studies scholars in the humanities and social sciences, in policy studies and applied professional fields, are questions of history.

Reminders of the immediate relevance of history to contemporary issues of disability confront us daily. In but the latest example, as we write these words, the United States Supreme Court has accepted appeals from several states which claim that Congress exceeded its constitutional authority in imposing the ADA on the states. Congress lacked evidence to prove that state governments had engaged in a historical pattern of discrimination against persons with disabilities, this argument claims in part; without evidence of state discrimination, the federal government overran its jurisdiction. The essays gathered here indicate that evidence of discrimination against disabled people reaches well beyond our living recollection. Until we can document the past with the evidence and rigor that solid historical research necessitates, the absence of disability from our written history, its suppression in our formal collective memory, jeopardizes the current quest of Americans with disabilities for full citizenship. This history matters, and not in the abstract.

That historians have only recently begun to take fuller notice of the prominence of disability in American life reflects both the marginalization of people with disabilities and the power of their recent political activism. The deep excavation necessary to retrieve for the record lives shrouded in religious, then medical, and always deep-seated cultural misunderstanding requires not only massive historical digging but a conceptual revolution in historiographical thinking. At the same time, thirty-five years of "new" scholarship in gender, race, and ethnic studies testifies to the centrality of historical research to fresh interdisciplinary enterprises in the humanities. Like women like people of color, people with disabilities have complex and often hidden histories; these need to be found and explained. Like gender, like race, disability must become a standard analytical tool in the historian's tool chest. That is the goal of the new disability history: to join the social-constructionist insights and interdisciplinarity of cultural studies with solid empirical research as we analyze disability's past. The essays in this volume return to the traditional discipline of history with the tools and insights garnered from the humanities-based disability studies movement.

The emerging field of disability history also parallels, and builds on, the new social histories of the past forty years in significant ways. Consider the development of U.S. women's history as a case in point. In the 1960s, spurred by their own feminist involvement, a few historians and activists essayed to put women "back into history." In the roughest sense, this meant scouring the annals of history as they already existed and finding places where women had made significant contributions to public life. This type of compensatory history revealed its limitations quickly, even as a pantheon of historical heroines rose to an arguably well deserved prominence as the first or only or truly exceptional women to accomplish various feats.[23]

More to the point, historians noted, women's absence from history reflected precisely the fact and the nature of their disempowerment. Retrieving women's experience for the historical record required that we redefine what "doing history" meant. The private as well as the public, the ordinary as well as the elite, absence from the record as well as presence—all these now mattered. This phase of investigation yielded horrific evidence of oppression, in Victorian parlors as in Lower East Side sweatshops, by law as by custom.[24]

An activist impetus to scholarship continued to shape the field, as scholars pressed beyond men's prescriptions for women's behavior to understand what sense women themselves had made of their lives. In an academic corollary to the radical 1960s sensibility that "the people" should and do have a say in their own fate, historians sought to comprehend how women in the past had defined themselves and their circumstances. In labor, leisure, love—in all aspects of their lives—women had created cultures through which they had asserted their own will and had acted on history.[25]

Meanwhile, women's historians incorporated the findings and insights of numerous other historians, regarding race, ethnicity, class, sexuality, and more. By the 1980s, the field had burgeoned into a major branch of historical inquiry, with scores of books published each year and a strong presence in all the historical journals and conferences. In fewer than twenty years, women's history had moved—to borrow a phrase from historian Joan Scott—from "the margin to the center" of the historical profession.[26]

Even so, in 1986, Scott urged that we alter our approach still further. Rather than treat women's history as a discrete subtopic, albeit an important one, of a larger historical project, she proposed that we consider gender as a principal constituent factor of all historical analysis. Visible or not, gender has played a role in every historical situation; therefore, scholars must include gender in the calculus of any thoroughgoing historical examination.[27]

To some extent, we can accurately substitute "disability" for "gender" in the foregoing schema. The new disability history certainly derives from the disability rights movement in crucial ways, as does the interdisciplinary project of disability studies. As we detail above, disability rights activists since the 1970s have applied a minority-group analysis to the situation of disabled people in order to fight for legal, social, and economic rights and to nurture community. Just as feminists pointed out that "sex," as a physiological marker, differed from the vast social meanings assigned to women in the name of "gender," disability activists have stressed that social, and not biological, definitions of disability determine the makeup of the minority group and account for its oppression. In each of the academic disciplines, disability studies scholars have been attempting since the early 1980s to use social models to piece together the complex meanings of disability as a personal and group identity, a cultural signifier, and a theoretical paradigm.[28]

The quest to recapture the history of people with disabilities has taken several forms. A celebratory and compensatory initiative appeared among activists and advocates beginning in the late 1970s. As with any group denied a significant place in history, people with disabilities claimed heroes: Beethoven was deaf! Milton was blind! Franklin Delano Roosevelt had polio! Deaf football players at Gallaudet College invented the huddle! This heritage hunting often unwittingly reinforced oppressive mainstream heralding of disabled people who had "overcome" their disabilities to almost miraculous effect. If Beethoven was, arguably, the greatest of the classical composers, and if FDR led us through both the Great Depression and World War II, why could not, why should not, the average person with a disability also, through strength of character, overcome his or her "problems"? Nonetheless, for groups that have been denied an important role in recorded history and have also gone unrecognized as communities, this reclamation of common pasts peopled with heroes as great as any the dominant culture can marshal carries great weight. While the assignment in hindsight of an

Paul K. Longmore and Lauri Umansky

"identity" to people who would not have recognized the category in its modern form poses problems for historians, these problems are by no means unique to disability history, nor do they eclipse the stirring effect of historical heroes.

If a degree of hagiography still suffuses popular disability culture, most historians have branched off to other approaches. Much as historians of women and of African Americans had done earlier, historians of disability by the 1980s concentrated largely on the myriad patterns of abuse, discrimination, and oppression in the history of people with disabilities. Examples abound in every disability category, every subfield of history, and every era. From the prevalence of eugenics and euthanasia themes in American film to the imposition of oralist education on Deaf children from the late nineteenth to the late twentieth century, historians began to uncover the powerful ways in which deaf and disabled people's lives have been defined and circumscribed directly by the state, by "experts" of various sorts, and more generally by an "audist" or ableist sociocultural milieu.[29]

More recently, historians have turned their attention to the cultures, values, and activism of disabled people themselves. As participatory agents in their own lives, people with disabilities have often resisted the definitions and "cures" imposed on them by others. Residential schools, for example, have been autonomous "places" of culture for Deaf people for almost two centuries. R. A. R. Edwards reports in her essay on Horace Mann and mid-nineteenth-century Deaf education that the self-created Deaf communities alarmed some hearing educators, including manualists, who saw themselves as benefactors of the deaf. Two and three generations later, during oralism's early twentieth-century heyday, as Susan Burch shows in "Reading between the Signs," Deaf resistance to the elimination of sign language from Deaf children's education persisted, with the schools serving as epicenters of cultural memory and continuance. Meanwhile, Catherine Kudlick's "The Outlook of *The Problem* and the Problem with *The Outlook*" recounts how, in another turn-of-the-century arena of contest, blind advocates asserted their own perspectives about blind people's education and social roles, disagreeing with one another and especially with sighted professionals in the emerging field of "work with the blind."

Disability historians are also increasingly folding nuanced readings of gender, class, race, sexuality, age, and region into their analyses. The essays in this book reflect this state of the scholarship vividly. Hannah Joyner links a North Carolina slaveholding family's negotiations over the autonomy of one of its Deaf members during the Civil War to notions of southern white honor, able-bodiedness, and independence. Natalie Dykstra examines Alice James's final years to show how gendered understandings of work played out in terms of disability for this woman of the upper crust. John Williams-Searle charts the ambivalent reactions of late-nineteenth-century railroaders to what they perceived as the demasculinizing and declassing effects of economic dependency on disabled trainmen. K. Walter Hickel inspects disabled veterans policy from the World War I era; he finds that ideas about race factored heavily into official decisions concerning who did and who did not "qualify" for compensation, who was and who was not appropriately "disabled." Kim Nielsen looks at the political ineffectuality of Helen Keller's rhetorical conflation of gender and disability oppression. Catherine Kudlick reveals how early twentieth-century understandings of blindness could turn the feminine ideals of that era on their heads. Susan Burch documents the inimical positioning of Deaf and hearing women that occurred as a by-product of debates over oralist education in the first half of the twentieth century. Janice Brockley shows how mother-blaming in the 1930s mingled with prejudice against people with physical and mental disabilities, to deadly effect. David Gerber explores how blinded World War II veterans sublimated a period of organizational and personal struggle to make sense of blindness acquired during adulthood into a smoother group memory of racial and ethnic tolerance. Indeed, each of the articles in this collection scrutinizes the complex intersections of disability and other axes of analysis or identity.

In addition, historians of disability have begun to paraphrase and engage the overarching question Joan Scott posed to historians: In what ways does disability function as a primary construct, an underlying structure in all of history? As Douglas Baynton remarks in these pages, we need not rummage far for instances of disability's historical presence. He, for one, finds that understandings of disability framed the three great citizenship debates of the nineteenth and early twentieth centuries—slavery, women's suffrage, and immigration—even when the ostensible focus of controversy seemed remote from the actual experience of disability. Meanwhile, Rosemarie Garland-Thomson discusses how photography has constructed particular "visual rhetorics" that influence how "modern America imagines disability and disabled people"; as she shows, these rhetorics reveal more about the culture that valorizes "the stare" than they do about the disabled people the photographs depict. Unraveling the underlying meanings of disability's ubiquity as an organizing concept or symbolic structure promises to become as much a goal of disability history in the future as charting the specific pasts of people with disabilities.

The comparison between women's history and disability history yields differences as well as likenesses. Whereas women's historians have grappled with diversity among women based on race, class, and other factors, they have not had to argue too forcefully for the validity of gender as a signifying category. Disability, on the contrary, as an identity and an analytical category gets tugged at from several directions. What does it mean, after all, to link the histories of people who did not—and often still do not—necessarily feel connected? Does present-mindedness contaminate the application of a social model to historical periods when disability would have been understood very differently? Disability historians must hold these questions in the balance as they also resist capitulating intellectually to the prevailing, if unstated, understandings of disability held by their historical subjects.

Also unlike women's historians, who in the first instance wrote about people other historians had ignored, historians of disability often tread where others have gone before. Medical history at least appears to parallel disability history in its concentration on people with various "conditions." In reality, the divergences between these two fields in many ways define disability history's parameters. The new disability history, like disability studies generally, rejects the medical model by examining the social experience of disability as not the exclusive and inevitable sequelae of disease or physiological conditions but a product of the interactions between individuals with such conditions and the arrangements of sociocultural, policy, and architectural environments. "Disability," in other words, is not simply located in the bodies of individuals. It is a socially and culturally constructed identity. Public policy, professional practices, societal arrangements, and cultural values all shape its meaning.

And yet, disability historians must grapple with the significance in the lives of their historical subjects of physiological states that depart from typical human experience. Those conditions result in different bodily configurations and different modes of functioning. Disability rights activism and law affirm these differences by insisting on alternative means of access and "reasonable" alternative accommodations. Those differences also stand at the core of the lived history we need to reconstruct. For example, the Deaf community came into existence partly because the residential schools drew together significant numbers of geographically dispersed deaf people who then formed themselves into social networks, ultimately a community and subculture. At the same time, the condition of deafness itself made sign the most effective, the necessary, mode of communication; the "natural language of signs" in turn helped bring the Deaf community into being. A physiological condition led to a different mode of functioning that in turn interacted with a social milieu to create an entirely new social, cultural, and political context. Throughout the history of what we have come to call "disability," physiological states and social contexts have acted on one another. The interplay of modes of functioning with social milieus has shaped the historical experience of disability.

Just as bodies are mediated and interpreted by their surroundings, so, too, does the social construction of disability manifest in part through felt and perceived embodiedness. Some of the history of disability has to do simply with differences in appearance or modes of functioning. Some of it has to do with bodily limitation. Further, as many disability activists acknowledge, impairment can bring pain, and loss, and difficulty in its own right. Using a social model of disability ought not mean negating the significance of physiological, cosmetic, or functional differences, or of impairment, injury, or illness in disabled people's lives. At its best, the new disability history recognizes the corporeal dimension of human experience and its consequences for daily functioning, while striving continually to understand the contingencies that shape, reflect, express, and result from that dimension. By probing this tension rather than ignoring the role of difference, historians can reveal disability's complexity.

In another way, the differences involved in and among disabilities have structured the history of disability. Various disabilities result in various modes of functioning. For example, blindness and paraplegia both necessitate alternative modes of mobility, but using a white cane or dog guide is not the same as riding a wheelchair. Each of these modes involves a different way of negotiating the environment and requires different forms of access and accommodation. As Richard Scotch points out in his historical overview, "American Disability Policy in the Twentieth Century," the first U.S. accessibility statutes were the state and local laws adopted in the 1930s that ensured the right of blind people to use white canes and dog guides in public places. The first laws mandating construction of ramps for wheelchair riders came three decades later. Particular conditions produce not only specific needs but specific interests. Education and training, services and treatment, political organizing and advocacy historically have been developed around and within disability-specific groups. At the same time, the medicalization of disability has promoted organization of programs and funding according to diagnostic categories.

As a result, the differences among disabilities and the medicalization of all of them have produced a set of disability-specific histories. Both older works based on a medical model and more recent research operating from a social model, including most of the essays in this anthology, focus on particular disability categories: blindness and blind people, deafness and Deaf people, and so forth. It could be argued that historians of disability have simply gone where their sources have taken them. The historical trail necessarily leads through archives of blindness, deafness, mental retardation, polio, war, and workplace injury. The dispersal of the records through disability-specific channels and institutions reflects the historical reality.[30]

The differences among disabilities, the medicalization of disability, and the location of sources have combined to influence the intellectual content of disability history scholarship. Seldom have the various historical studies overlapped or offered comparative analyses. Two principal exceptions to this framing of disability have appeared. Policy historiography has necessarily looked at disability in general, because, with some exceptions, public policies have frequently gathered the range of disability groups into a generic disability category. More recent literary and cultural studies that analyze disability's cultural deployment have often examined societal discourses of disability in general or of disabilities in comparison, rather than focusing on only one type of disability.[31]

As the new disability history unfolds, we need to interrogate the disability-specific approach. While we assemble the many separate histories of people with particular conditions, we can begin to note patterns that individuals in the past might not have had the perspective or privilege to perceive. Although we must not falsely impute cross-disability consciousness or inaccurately delineate a general historical experience that ignores the particularities, neither should we overlook their incipient presence in ideological and social contexts grounded in particular disability experiences or steeped in medical ideation. In this way, disability history, like any historical inquiry done well, will both record and analyze the material it uncovers.

In a similar way, the periodization of disability history does, and must, incorporate the very worldviews that have defined, and often oppressed, people with disabilities. The essays in this book illustrate disability historians' grapplings with the slippery task of charting and interpreting change over time. New focus on the various disability groups reveals chronologies that sometimes intersect and sometimes diverge, forming a web of increasing complexity.

One period of disability history draws particular attention. The essays in the middle section of this anthology, some essays in other sections, and previous work in disability-specific histories all point to the half century from around 1880 to 1930 as a moment of major redefinition. In that era, public policies and laws; emerging medical, educational, and social-service professions; and the institutions those policies and professions created either questioned the competency of people with virtually all types of disabilities for full citizenship or declared them disqualified. As a result, various state-sanctioned institutions brought many disabled people under professional supervision either to mend them into fit citizens or to sequester them permanently for society's safety. The regime fashioned during this era continued to shape the lives of many people with disabilities throughout the twentieth century. Contemporaneous advocacy resisted it; later activism sought to dismantle it. The era of that regime's establishment requires historians' sustained investigation from a cross-disability perspective.

In some ways, the list of forces that have molded the histories of blind people, Deaf people, and people with physical disabilities into similar shapes and that have become historians' interpretive markers still reads like an index of nemeses to the self-determination of disabled people. The authors here document the power of superstition, religion, liberal individualism, medicalization, the rise of the expert, and more. As distasteful as these signposts might be to those of us schooled in histories told from the bottom up, they remain important to our understandings of disability history. At the same time, however, as historians uncover more detail about the actual lives of people with disabilities, they unveil intervening forces that signal the multiple valences on which Americans' interpretations of disability have hung, in every era. Thus, for example, we can see that the "medical model," powerful though it has been in shaping the life experiences of people with disabilities, has never gone uncontested.

The fourteen essays here are arranged both chronologically and thematically. The timeline runs from the early nineteenth century to the present, with a majority of the pieces situated in the late nineteenth to early twentieth centuries. We have titled the thematic groupings "Uses and Contests," "Redefinitions and Resistance," and "Images and Identities." While these overarching themes appear in each of the historical periods in question, they seem to emerge with particular force in the nineteenth century, at the turn of the century, and in the mid-to-late twentieth century, respectively.

The works of synthesis that signal the full maturity of a field remain to be written. This anthology seeks rather to *open up* a history that has largely been hidden. Some of these essays discuss prominent figures and major historical processes. Others look at briefer moments and "ordinary" people. Alone and together, they explore significant issues and interlocking themes. In offering fourteen glimpses into the American past, the collection suggests new ways to think about disability, new ways to understand the American experience. If, in the present moment, America is truly engaged in "the last great inclusion," then the new disability history must provide that moment with a usable past.

NOTES

1. Caroline E. Mayer, "Four Insurers Accused of Bias against Disabled; Housing Group's Suit Alleges U.S. Law Violated," *Washington Post*, July 9, 1997, final ed., D8; David Segal, "Advocates for Disabled Sue Movie Theater Chain," *Washington Post*, December 18, 1997, final ed., D2; Marcia Chambers, "Just How Level a Playing Field? Casey Martin Says He Needs a Cart to Play; the PGA Says No," *New York Times*, January 15, 1998, late ed.—final, C1; Thomas Bonk, "Disabled Golfer's Lawsuit to Use Cart Challenges PGA Tour's Right to Make Its Own Rules," *Los Angeles Times*, January 26, 1998, C1; Stephanie Armour, "Disabilities Act Abused? Law's Use Sparks Debate," *USA Today*, September 25, 1998, final ed., 1B; Kirstin Downey Grimsley, "Disabilities Act Dilemma: Job Rights vs. Job Safety; Bias Suits Pose Public Risk, Employers Say," *Washington Post*, April 8, 1997, final ed., A1.

2. National Council on Disability, *Equality of Opportunity: The Making of the Americans with Disabilities Act* (Washington, D.C.: National Council on Disability, 1997); G. Tysse, ed., *The Legislative History of the Americans with Disabilities Act* (Horsham, Pa.: LRP Publications, 1991).

3. Stephen L. Kaye, *Disability Watch: The Status of People with Disabilities in the United States* (Oakland: Disability Rights Advocates, 1998).

4. Douglas Baynton, "Defectives in the Land: Disability and Federal Immigration Policy, 1882–1924" (paper presented at American Historical Association Annual Meeting, Seattle, 1998).

5. John Williams-Searle, "Courting Risk: Disability, Masculinity, and Liability on Iowa's Railroads, 1868–1900," *Annals of Iowa* 58 (Winter 1999): 28–31. See also Karen Hirsch and Jerrold Hirsch, "Paternalism and Disability: Rethinking the History of the Southern Mill Village" (paper presented at American Historical Association Annual Meeting, Seattle, 1998).

6. Here and elsewhere, we and the contributors observe the well-established practice of using "deaf" to designate an auditory condition and "Deaf" to refer to membership in a linguistic and cultural community.

7. Harlan Hahn, "The Politics of Physical Differences: Disability and Discrimination," *Journal of Social Issues* 44 (1988): 39–47; G. Albrecht, B. Walker, and J. Levy, "Social Distance from the Stigmatized: A Test of Two Theories," *Social Science Medicine* 16 (1982): 1319–27; K. Dion, E. Berscheid, and E. Walster, "What Is Beautiful Is Good," *Journal of Personality and Social Psychology* 24,3 (1972): 285–90; R. W. English, "Correlates of Stigma towards Physically Disabled Persons," *Rehabilitation Research and Practice Review* 2, 4 (1971): 1–17; Erving Goffman, *Stigma: Notes on the Management of Spoiled Identity* (Englewood Cliffs, N.J.: Prentice-Hall, 1963); M. Horne and J. Ricciardo, "Hierarchy of Response to Handicaps," *Psychological Reports* 62 (1988): 83–86; R. L. Jones, "The Hierarchical Structure of Attitudes toward the Exceptional," *Exceptional Children* 40 (1974): 430–35; Robert Kleck, Hiroshi Ono, and Albert H. Hastorf, "The Effects of Physical Deviance upon Face-to-Face Interaction," *Human Relations* 19 (1966): 425–36; R. Olkin and L. Howson, "Attitudes toward and Images of Physical Disability," *Journal of Social Behavior and Personality* 9, 5 (1994): 81–96; S. A. Richardson, "Attitudes and Behaviors toward the Physically Handicapped," *Birth Defects: Original Articles Series* 12 (1976): 15–34; C. Schneider and W. Anderson, "Attitudes toward the Stigmatized: Some Insights from Recent Research," *Rehabilitation Counseling Bulletin* 23, 4 (1980): 299–313; J. L. Tringo, "The Hierarchy of Preference toward Disability Groups," *Journal of Special Education* 4 (1970): 295–306; Harold E. Yuker, ed., *Attitudes toward Persons with Disabilities* (New York: Springer, 1988).

8. David T. Mitchell and Sharon L. Snyder, eds., *The Body and Physical Difference: Discourses of Disability*, (Ann Arbor: University of Michigan Press, 1997), in particular Paul K. Longmore, "Conspicuous Contribution and American Cultural Dilemmas: Telethon Rituals of Cleansing and Renewal," 134–58.

9. Simi Linton, "The Disability Studies Project: Broadening the Parameters of Diversity," in Elaine Makas and Lynn Schlesinger, eds., *End Results and Starting Points: Expanding the Field of Disability Studies* (Portland, Maine: Society for Disability Studies and Edmund S. Muskie Institute of Public Affairs), 323–25.

10. See, for example: Roy Porter, "The Patient's View: Doing Medical History from Below," *Theory and Society* 14 (March 1985): 175–98; Susan Reverby and David Rosner, eds., *Health Care in America: Essays in Social History* (Philadelphia: Temple University Press, 1979); Charles E. Rosenberg and Janet Golden, eds., *Framing Disease, Studies in Cultural History* (New Brunswick: Rutgers University Press, 1992); Morris J. Vogel, "Patrons, Practitioners, and Patients: The Voluntary Hospital in Mid-Victorian Boston," in Daniel Walker Howe, ed., *Victorian America* (Philadelphia: University of Pennsylvania Press, 1976), 121–40; Morris J. Vogel and Charles Rosenberg, eds., *The Therapeutic Revolution: Essays in the Social History of American Medicine* (Philadelphia: University of Pennsylvania Press, 1979).

11. John Vickrey Van Cleve, ed., *Deaf History Unveiled: Interpretations from the New Scholarship* (Washington, D.C.: Gallaudet University Press, 1993), ix; Floyd Matson, *Walking Alone and Marching Together: A History of the Organized Blind Movement in the United States, 1940–1990* (Baltimore: National Federation of the Blind, 1990), iii–iv.

12. Edward D. Berkowitz, *Disabled Policy: America's Programs for the Handicapped* (New York: Cambridge University Press, 1987); Deborah Stone, *The Disabled State* (Philadelphia: Temple University Press, 1986); Claire H. Liachowitz, *Disability as a Social Construct: Legislative Roots* (Philadelphia: University of Pennsylvania Press, 1988); Theda Skocpol, *Protecting Soldiers and Mothers: The Political Origins of Social Policy in the United States* (Cambridge: Harvard University Press, 1992). For an exception to the usual policy historiography, see Richard K. Scotch and Edward D. Berkowitz, "One Comprehensive System? A Historical Perspective on Federal Disability Policy," *Journal of Disability Policy Studies* 1 (Fall 1990): 1–19.

13. Linton, "Disability Studies Project," 323–25; Lennard J. Davis and Simi Linton, "Introduction: Disability Studies," *Radical Teacher*, no. 47, special issue (Fall 1995): 2–3; Simi Linton, Susan Mello, and John O'Neill, "Disability Studies: Expanding the Parameters of Diversity," *Radical Teacher*, no. 47, special issue (Fall 1995): 4–10.

14. National Council on Disability, *Equality of Opportunity*; National Council on Disability, *Back to School on Civil Rights: Advancing the Federal Commitment to Leave No Child Behind* (Washington, D.C.: National Council on Disability, 2000); Richard K. Scotch, *From Good Will to Civil Rights: Transforming Federal Disability Policy* (Philadelphia: Temple University Press, 1985); Joseph Shapiro, *No Pity: People with Disabilities Forging a New Civil Rights Movement* (New York: Times Books, 1993); H. R. Turnbull, *Free Appropriate Public Education: The Law and Children with Disabilities* (Denver: Love, 1990); Margret A. Winzer, *The History of Special Education: From Isolation to Integration* (Washington, D.C.: Gallaudet University Press, 1993).

15. Berkowitz, *Disabled Policy*; Epilepsy Foundation of America, *The Legal Rights of Persons with Epilepsy: An Overview of Legal Issues and Laws* (Landover, MD: Epilepsy Foundation of America, 1992); Matson, *Walking Alone*; Fred Pelka, *ABC-Clio Companion to the Disability Rights Movement* (Santa Barbara: ABC-Clio, 1997); Scotch, *From Good Will to Civil Rights*; Shapiro, *No Pity*; James W. Trent, Jr., *Inventing the Feeble Mind: A History of Mental Retardation in the United States* (Berkeley: University of California Press, 1994); Peter L. Tyor and Leland V. Bell, *Caring for the Retarded in America: A History* (Westport, Conn.: Greenwood Press, 1985); John Vickrey Van Cleve, ed., *Deaf History Unveiled*; John Vickrey Van Cleve and Barry Crouch, *A Place of Their Own: Creating the Deaf Community in America* (Washington, D.C.: Gallaudet University Press, 1989).

16. Renee Anspach, "From Stigma to Identity Politics: Political Activism among the Physically Disabled and Former Mental Patients," *Social Science and Medicine* 13 (1979): 765–73; Robert Funk, "Disability Rights: From Caste to Class in the Context of Civil Rights," in Alan Gartner and Tom Joe, eds. *Images of the Disabled, Disabling Images* (New York: Praeger, 1987), 7–30; Fred Krueger, "Transportation: Organization Is

the Key," *Mainstream* 10, 10 (March 1986): 8–13; P. Lee and T. Fagan, "New Social Movements and Social Policy: A Case Study of the Disability Movement," in Michael La Valette and Alan Pratt, eds., *Social Policy: A Conceptual and Theoretical Introduction* (Thousand Oaks, Calif.: Sage, 1997); Paul K. Longmore, "Disability Rights Activists and Assisted Suicide," *Cornell Journal of Law and Public Policy* 7, 2 (Winter 1998): 280–85; Jean Flatley McGuire, "Organizing from Diversity in the Name of Community: Lessons from the Disability Civil Rights Movement," *Policy Studies Journal* 22, 1 (1994): 112–22; Pelka, *ABC-Clio Companion*, passim; Richard K. Scotch, "Disability as the Basis for a Social Movement: Advocacy and the Politics of Definition," *Journal of Social Issues* 44, 1 (1988), 159–72; Richard K. Scotch, "Politics and Policy in the History of the Disability Rights Movement," *Milbank Quarterly* 67, supp. 2, part 2, (1989): 380–401; Shapiro, *No Pity*; Trent, *Inventing the Feeble Mind*; Tyor and Bell, *Caring for the Retarded*; Jack Gannon, *The Week the World Heard Gallaudet* (Washington, D.C.: Gallaudet University Press, 1989).

17. International Center for the Disabled, *The ICD Survey of Disabled Americans: Bringing Disabled Americans into the Mainstream* (New York: International Center for the Disabled, 1986), 112–15. Louis Harris and Associates surveyed adults with disabilities late in 1985; the responses to two questions documented a generational shift toward a minority-group, civil rights–oriented consciousness. (1) "Do you feel that disabled persons are a minority group in the same sense as are blacks and Hispanics, or not?" The percentage of respondents who said yes decreased with age. A majority of younger adults expressed a minority perspective: 54 percent of those aged sixteen to thirty-four, 53 percent of those thirty-five to forty-four, 48 percent of those forty-five to fifty-four, 45 percent of those fifty-five to sixty-four, and 37 percent of those sixty-five and over. (2) "Do you think that the civil rights laws that cover minorities against discrimination should also cover disabled persons, or not?" Substantial majorities in every age bracket said yes, but the two youngest age groups presented the biggest majorities: ages sixteen to thirty-four, 82 percent; thirty-five to forty-four, 83 percent; forty-five to fifty-four, 77 percent; fifty-five to sixty-four, 72 percent; sixty-five and above, 68 percent.

18. Davis and Linton, "Introduction," 2.

19. Davis and Linton, "Introduction," 1–2; Vic Finkelstein, *Attitudes and Disabled People: Issues for Discussion* (New York: World Rehabilitation Fund, 1980); Harlan Hahn, "Disability Policy and the Problem of Discrimination, *American Behavioral Scientist* 28 (1985): 293–318; Linton, "Disability Studies Project," 323–25; Simi Linton, Susan Mello, and John O'Neill, "Locating Disability in Diversity," in Elaine Makas and Lynn Schlesinger, eds., *Insights and Outlooks: Current Trends in Disability Studies* (Portland, Maine: Society for Disability Studies and Edmund S. Muskie Institute of Public Affairs, 1994), 229–33; Linton, Mello, and O'Neill, "Disability Studies."

20. Michael Bérubé, "The Cultural Representation of People with Disabilities Affects Us All," *Chronicle of Higher Education* (May 30, 1997): B4–5.

21. Linton, Mello, and O'Neill, "Disability Studies," 5.

22. For example: G. Thomas Couser, *Recovering Bodies: Illness, Disability, and Life Writing* (Madison: University of Wisconsin Press, 1997); Lennard Davis, *Enforcing Normalcy: Disability, Deafness, and the Body* (London: Verso, 1997); Lennard Davis, ed., *The Disability Studies Reader* (New York: Routledge, 1997); Nancy Eiesland, *The Disabled God: Toward a Liberatory Theology of Disability* (Nashville: Abingdon, 1994); Rosemarie Garland Thomson, *Extraordinary Bodies: Figuring Physical Disability in American Culture and Literature* (New York: Columbia University Press, 1997); Rosemarie Garland Thomson, ed., *Freakery: Cultural Spectacles of the Extraordinary Body.* (New York: New York University Press, 1996); Sander Gilman, *Seeing the Insane* (Lincoln: University of Nebraska Press, 1996); Diane Price Herndl, *Invalid Women: Figuring Feminine Illness in American Fiction and Culture, 1840–1940* (Chapel Hill: University of North Carolina Press, 1993); David Hevey, *The Creatures That Time Forgot: Photography and Disability Imagery* (New York: Routledge, 1992); Simi Linton, *Claiming Disability: Knowledge and Identity* (New York: New York University Press, 1998); Mitchell and Snyder, eds., *The Body and Physical Difference*; Martin Norden, *The Cinema of Isolation: A History of Physical Disability in the Movies* (New Brunswick: Rutgers University Press, 1996); Susan Wendell, *The Rejected Body: Feminist Philosophical Reflections on the Disabled Body* (New York: Routledge, 1996); David Wills, *Prosthesis* (Stanford: Stanford University Press, 1995).

23. For recent historiographical retrospectives of women's history, see the *Women's Review of Books* 17, 5 (February 2000): 12–30; in particular, Elaine Tyler May, "Redrawing the Map of History," and Linda K. Kerber, "Ripple Effect," discuss the early compensatory impulse in the field.

24. *Women's Review of Books*, 17,5 (February 2000): 12–30. The works that emerged in this phase are too numerous to list; Barbara Welter's classic article "The Cult of True Womanhood," *American Quarterly* 18 (Summer 1966): 151–74, is one of the earliest and best-known examples.

25. Again, the scholarship comprises hundreds of books; classics include, for example, Nancy Cott, *The Bonds of Womanhood: Woman's Sphere in New England, 1780–1835* (New Haven: Yale University Press, 1977); Kathy Peiss, *Cheap Amusements: Working Women and Leisure in Turn-of-the-Century New York* (Philadelphia: Temple University Press, 1986); and in European women's history, Judith Walkowitz, *Prostitution and Victorian Society: Women, Class, and the State* (Cambridge and New York: Cambridge University Press, 1980).

26. Joan W. Scott, "Gender: A Useful Category of Historical Analysis," *American Historical Review* 91 (December 1986): 1053–75. Among important contributions to this explosive phase of U.S. women's history, see, for example, John d'Emilio and Estelle Freedman, *Intimate Matters: A History of Sexuality in America* (New York: Harper & Row, 1988); Jacqueline Jones, *Labor of Love, Labor of Sorrow: Black Women, Work, and the Family from Slavery to the Present* (New York: Basic Books, 1985); Vicki Ruiz, *Cannery Women, Cannery Lives: Mexican Women, Unionization, and the California Food Processing Industry, 1930–1950* (Albuquerque: University of New Mexico Press, 1987).

27. Scott, "Gender"; Mary Beth Norton, "From Parts to Whole," and others in the February 2000 *Women's Review of Books* forum discuss the ongoing struggle to bring gender into "mainstream" history.

28. Adrienne Asch and Michelle Fine, eds., *Women with Disabilities: Essays in Psychology, Culture, and Politics* (Philadelphia: Temple University Press, 1988), introduction; Victor Finkelstein, *Attitudes and Disabled People: Issues for Discussion* (New York: World Rehabilitation Fund, 1980); John Gliedman and William Roth, *The Unexpected Minority: Handicapped Children in America* (New York: Harcourt, Brace, Jovanovich, 1982); Paul Longmore, "The Life of Randolph Bourne and the Need for a History of Disabled People," *Reviews in American History*, 13, 4 (December 1985): 581-87; Paul K. Longmore, "Uncovering the Hidden History of Disabled People," *Reviews in American History* 15, 3 (September 1987): 355-64; Mike Oliver, *The Politics of Disablement* (New York: St. Martin's, 1990); William Roth, "Handicap as a Social Construct," *Society* 20, 3 (March/April 1983): 56-61.

29. Martin S. Pernick, *The Black Stork: Eugenics and the Death of "Defective" Babies in American Medicine and Motion Pictures since 1915* (New York: Oxford University Press, 1996); Harlan Lane, *When the Mind Hears: A History of the Deaf* (New York: Random House, 1985); Harlan Lane, *The Mask of Benevolence: Disabling the Deaf Community* (New York: Knopf, 1992); Van Cleve, ed., *Deaf History Unveiled*; Van Cleve and Crouch, *A Place of Their Own*.

30. For instance: Douglas Baynton, *Forbidden Signs: American Culture and the Campaign against Sign Language* (Chicago: University of Chicago Press, 1996); Harry Best, *Blindness and the Blind in the United States* (New York: Macmillan, 1934); Philip M. Ferguson, *Abandoned to Their Fate: Social Policy and Practice towards Severely Retarded People in America, 1820–1920* (Philadelphia: Temple University Press, 1994); David Gerber, "Anger and Affability: The Rise and Representation of a Repertory of Self-Presentation Skills in a World War II Disabled Veteran," *Journal of Social History*, 27, 2 (Fall 1993), 5-27; Nora Ellen Groce, *Everyone Here Spoke Sign Language: Hereditary Deafness on Martha's Vineyard* (Cambridge: Harvard University Press, 1985); Frances A. Koestler, *The Unseen Minority: A Social History of Blindness in the United States* (New York: David McKay, American Foundation for the Blind, 1975); Matson, *Walking Alone*; Trent, *Inventing the Feeble Mind*; Tyor and Bell, *Caring for the Retarded*; John V. Van Cleve, "Nebraska's Oral Law of 1911 and the Deaf Community," *Nebraska History* 65 (Summer 1984): 195-220; Van Cleve, ed., *Deaf History Unveiled*; Van Cleve and Crouch, *A Place of Their Own*.

31. See, for example, notes 11 and 21 above; and T. E. Bergman Batson, *Angels and Outcasts: An Anthology of Deaf Characters in Literature*, 3rd ed. (Washington, D.C.: Gallaudet University Press, 1965); Douglas Biklen and Lee Bailey, eds., *Rudely Stamp'd: Imaginal Disability and Prejudice* (Washington, D.C.: University Press of America, 1981); Eli M. Bower, ed., *The Handicapped in Literature: A Psychosocial Perspective* (Denver: Love, 1980); Lois Bragg, "From the Mute God to the Lesser God: Disability in Medieval

Celtic and Old Norse Literature," *Disability and Society* 12, 2 (1997): 165–77; S. N. Brody, *The Disease of the Soul: Leprosy in Medieval Literature* (Ithaca: Cornell University Press, 1974); Helen Deutsch, *Resemblance and Disgrace: Alexander Pope and the Deformation of Culture* (Cambridge: Harvard University Press, 1996); Julia Epstein, *Altered Conditions: Disease, Medicine, and Storytelling* (New York: Routledge, 1995); Leslie Fiedler, *Freaks: Myths and Images of the Secret Self* (New York: Simon and Schuster, 1978); Leslie A. Fiedler, "Pity and Fear: Images of the Disabled in Literature and the Popular Arts," *Salmagundi* 57 (Summer 1982): 57–69; Alan Gartner and Tom Joe, eds., *Images of the Disabled/Disabling Images* (New York: Praeger, 1986); Sander L. Gilman, *Disease and Representation: Images of Illness from Madness to AIDS* (Ithaca: Cornell University Press, 1988); Mary Klages, *Woeful Afflictions: Disability and Sentimentality in Victorian America* (Philadelphia: University of Pennsylvania Press, 1999); Georgina Kleege, *Sight Unseen* (New Haven: Yale University Press, 1999); Lauri Klobas, *Disability Drama in Television and Film* (Jefferson, N.C.: Macfarland, 1988); Paul K. Longmore, "Screening Stereotypes: Images of Disabled People in Television and Motion Pictures," *Social Policy* 16, 1 (Summer 1985): 31–37; Felicity Nussbaum and Helen Deutsch, eds., *A Defect: Engendering the Modern Body* (Ann Arbor: University of Michigan Press, 1999); John S. Schuchman, *Hollywood Speaks: Deafness and the Film Entertainment Industry* (Urbana: University of Illinois Press, 1988); Tom Shakespeare, "Cultural Representations of Disabled People: Dustbins for Disavowal," *Disability and Society* 9,3 (1994): 283–99.

Uses and Contests

Part I

1

Disability and the Justification of Inequality in American History

Douglas C. Baynton

Since the social and political revolutions of the eighteenth century, the trend in western political thought has been to refuse to take for granted inequalities between persons or groups. Differential and unequal treatment has continued, of course, but it has been considered incumbent on modern societies to produce a rational explanation for such treatment. In recent decades, historians and other scholars in the humanities have studied intensely and often challenged the ostensibly rational explanations for inequalities based on identity—in particular, gender, race, and ethnicity. Disability, however, one of the most prevalent justifications for inequality, has rarely been the subject of historical inquiry.

Disability has functioned historically to justify inequality for disabled people themselves, but it has also done so for women and minority groups. That is, not only has it been considered justifiable to treat disabled people unequally, but the *concept* of disability has been used to justify discrimination against other groups by attributing disability to them. Disability was a significant factor in the three great citizenship debates of the nineteenth and early twentieth centuries: women's suffrage, African American freedom and civil rights, and the restriction of immigration. When categories of citizenship were questioned, challenged, and disrupted, disability was called on to clarify and define who deserved, and who was deservedly excluded from, citizenship. Opponents of political and social equality for women cited their supposed physical, intellectual, and psychological flaws, deficits, and deviations from the male norm. These flaws—irrationality, excessive emotionality, physical weakness—are in essence mental, emotional, and physical disabilities, although they are rarely discussed or examined as such. Arguments for racial inequality and immigration restrictions invoked supposed tendencies to feeble-mindedness, mental illness, deafness, blindness, and other disabilities in particular races and ethnic groups. Furthermore, disability figured prominently not just in arguments *for* the inequality of women and minorities but also in arguments *against* those inequalities. Such arguments took the form of vigorous denials that the groups in question actually had these disabilities; they were not disabled, the argument went, and therefore were not proper subjects for discrimination. Rarely have oppressed groups denied that disability is an adequate justification for social and political inequality. Thus, while disabled people can be considered one of the minority groups historically assigned inferior status and subjected to discrimination, disability has functioned for all such groups as a sign of and justification for inferiority.

It is this use of disability as a marker of hierarchical relations that historians of disability must demonstrate in order to bring disability into the mainstream of historical study. Over a decade ago, Joan Scott made a similar argument about the difficulty of persuading historians to take gender seriously. Scott noted that despite a substantial number of works on women's history, the topic remained marginal in the discipline as a whole. A typical response to women's history was "Women had a history separate from men's, therefore let feminists do women's history, which need not concern us," or "My understanding of the French Revolution is not changed by knowing that women participated in it." Scott argued that research on the role of women in history was necessary but not sufficient to change the paradigms of the profession. To change the way in which most historians went about their work, feminists had to demonstrate not just that women participated in the making of history but that gender is "a constitutive element of social relationships" and "a primary way of signifying relationships of power."[1]

To demonstrate the ubiquity of gender in social thought, Scott focused on political history, a field in which historians were especially apt to argue that gender was unimportant, and where most historians today would imagine disability to be equally so. She chose as an example Edmund Burke's attack on the French Revolution, noting that it was "built around a contrast between ugly, murderous *sans-culottes* hags ('the furies of hell, in the abused shape of the vilest of women') and the soft femininity of Marie-Antoinette." The contrast Scott highlights calls on not only gender but also notions of beauty, disfigurement, and misshapen bodies that would be amenable to an analysis informed by disability. Even more striking, however, is that in addition to the rhetoric of gender, Burke's argument rested just as fundamentally on a rhetorical contrast between the natural constitution of the body politic and the *monstrous* deformity that the revolution had brought forth. Burke repeatedly referred to "public measures . . . deformed into monsters," "monstrous democratic assemblies," "this monster of a constitution," "unnatural and monstrous activity," and the like (as well as evoking "blind prejudice," actions taken "blindly," "blind followers," and "blind obedience" and alluding to the madness, imbecility, and idiocy of the revolutionary leaders). This rhetoric of monstrosity was by no means peculiar to the conservative cause. Tom Paine, in his response to Burke, also found the monster metaphor an apt and useful one but turned it around: "Exterminate the monster aristocracy," he wrote.[2]

The metaphor of the natural versus the monstrous was a fundamental way of constructing social reality in Burke's time. By the late nineteenth and early twentieth centuries, however, the concept of the natural was to a great extent displaced or subsumed by the concept of normality.[3] Since then, normality has been deployed in all aspects of modern life as a means of measuring, categorizing, and managing populations (and resisting such management). Normality is a complex concept, with an etiology that includes the rise of the social sciences, the science of statistics, and industrialization with its need for interchangeable parts and interchangeable workers. It has been used in a remarkable range of contexts and with a bewildering variety of connotations. The natural and the normal both are ways of establishing the universal, unquestionable good and right. Both are also ways of establishing social hierarchies that justify the denial of legitimacy and certain rights to individuals or groups. Both are constituted in large part by being set in opposition to culturally variable notions of disability—just as the natural was meaningful in relation to the monstrous and the deformed, so are the cultural meanings of the normal produced in tandem with disability.[4]

The concept of normality in its modern sense arose in the mid–nineteenth century in the context of a pervasive belief in progress. It became a culturally powerful idea with the advent of evolutionary theory. The ideal of the natural had been a static concept for what was seen as an essentially unchanging world, dominant at a time when "the book of nature" was represented as the guidebook of God. The natural was good and right because it conformed to the intent or design of Nature or the Creator of nature. Normality, in contrast, was an empirical and dynamic concept for a changing and progressing world, the premise of which was that one could discern in human behavior the direction of human evolution and progress and use that as a guide. The ascendance of normality signaled a shift in the locus of faith from a God-centered to a human-centered world, from a culture that looked within to a core and backward to lost Edenic origins toward one that looked outward to behavior and forward to a perfected future.

Just as the counterpart to the natural was the monstrous, so the opposite of the normal person was the defective. Although normality ostensibly denoted the average, the usual, and the ordinary, in actual usage it functioned as an ideal and excluded only those defined as *below* average. "Is the child normal?" was never a question that expressed fear about whether a child had *above*-average intelligence, motor skills, or beauty. Abnormal signified the *sub*normal.[5] In the context of a pervasive belief that the tendency of the human race was to improve itself constantly, that barring something out of the ordinary humanity moved ever upward away from its animal origins and toward greater perfection, normality was implicitly defined as that which advanced progress (or at least did not impede it). Abnormality, conversely, was that which pulled humanity back toward its past, toward its animal origins.

As an evolutionary concept, normality was intimately connected to the western notion of progress. By the mid–nineteenth century, nonwhite races were routinely connected to people with disabilities, both of whom were depicted as evolutionary laggards or throwbacks. As a consequence, the concept of disability, intertwined with the concept of race, was also caught up in ideas of evolutionary progress. Physical or mental abnormalities were commonly depicted as instances of atavism, reversions to earlier stages of evolutionary development. Down's syndrome, for example, was called Mongolism by the doctor who first identified it in 1866 because he believed the syndrome to be the result of a biological reversion by Caucasians to the Mongol racial type. Teachers of the deaf at the end of the century spoke of making deaf children more like "normal" people and less like savages by forbidding them the use of sign language, and they opposed deaf marriages with a rhetoric of evolutionary progress and decline. Recent work on late-nineteenth-century freak shows has highlighted how disability and race intersected with an ideology of evolutionary hierarchy. James W. Trent argued in a recent article that at the 1904 World's Fair, displays of "defectives" alongside displays of "primitives" signaled similar and interconnected classification schemes for both defective individuals and defective races. Both were placed in hierarchies constructed on the basis of whether they were seen as "improvable" or not—capable of being educated, cured, or civilized. Whether it was individual

Douglas C. Baynton

atavism or a group's lack of evolutionary development, the common element in all was the presence or attribution of disability.[6]

Disability arguments were prominent in justifications of slavery in the early to mid–nineteenth century and of other forms of unequal relations between white and black Americans after slavery's demise. The most common disability argument for slavery was simply that African Americans lacked sufficient intelligence to participate or compete on an equal basis in society with white Americans. This alleged deficit was sometimes attributed to physical causes, as when an article on the "diseases and physical peculiarities of the negro race" in the *New Orleans Medical and Surgical Journal* helpfully explained, "It is this defective hematosis, or atmospherization of the blood, conjoined with a deficiency of cerebral matter in the cranium, and an excess of nervous matter distributed to the organs of sensation and assimilation, that is the true cause of that debasement of mind, which has rendered the people of Africa unable to take care of themselves." Diseases of blacks were commonly attributed to "inferior organisms and constitutional weaknesses," which were claimed to be among "the most pronounced race characteristics of the American negro." While the supposedly higher intelligence of "mulattos" compared to "pure" blacks was offered as evidence for the superiority of whites, those who argued against "miscegenation" claimed to the contrary that the products of "race-mixing" were themselves less intelligent and less healthy than members of either race in "pure" form.[7] A medical doctor, John Van Evrie of New York, avowed that the "disease and disorganization" in the "abnormal," "blotched, deformed" offspring of this "monstrous" act "could no more exist beyond a given period than any other physical degeneration, no more than tumors, cancers, or other abnormal growths or physical disease can become permanent." Some claimed greater "corporeal vigor" for "mixed offspring" but a deterioration in "moral and intellectual endowments," while still others saw greater intelligence but "frailty," "less stamina," and "inherent physical weakness."[8]

A second line of disability argument was that African Americans, because of their inherent physical and mental weaknesses, were prone to become disabled under conditions of freedom and equality. A New York medical journal reported that deafness was three times more common and blindness twice as common among free blacks in the North compared to slaves in the South. John C. Calhoun, senator from South Carolina and one of the most influential spokesmen for the slave states, thought it a powerful argument in defense of slavery that the "number of deaf and dumb, blind, idiots, and insane, of the negroes in the States that have changed the ancient relation between the races" was seven times higher than in the slave states.[9]

While much has been written about the justification of slavery by religious leaders in the South, more needs to be said about similar justifications by medical doctors. Dr. Samuel Cartwright, in 1851, for example, described two types of mental illness to which African Americans were especially subject. The first, Drapetomania, a condition that caused slaves to run away— "as much a disease of the mind as any other species of mental alienation"— was common among slaves whose masters had "made themselves too familiar with them, treating them as equals." The need to submit to a master was built into the very bodies of African Americans, in whom "we see '*genu flexit*' written in the physical structure of his knees, being more flexed or bent, than any other kind of man." The second mental disease peculiar to African Americans, Dysaesthesia Aethiopis—a unique ailment differing "from every other species of mental disease, as it is accompanied with physical signs or lesions of the body"—resulted in a desire to avoid work and generally to cause mischief. It was commonly known to overseers as "rascality." Its cause, similar to that of Drapetomania, was a lack of firm governance, and it was therefore far more common among free blacks than among slaves—indeed, nearly universal among them—although it was a "common occurrence on badly-governed plantations" as well.[10]

Dr. Van Evrie also contributed to this line of thought when he wrote in the 1860s that education of African Americans came "at the expense of the body, shortening the existence" and resulted in bodies "dwarfed or destroyed" by the unnatural exertion. "An 'educated negro,' like a 'free negro,' is a social monstrosity, even more unnatural and repulsive than the latter." He argued further that, since they belonged to a race inferior by nature, *all* blacks were necessarily inferior to (nearly) *all* whites. It occasionally happened that a particular white person might not be superior to all black people because of a condition that "deforms or blights individuals; they may be idiotic, insane, or otherwise incapable." But these unnatural exceptions to the rule were "the result of human vices, crimes, or ignorance, immediate or remote." Only disability might lower a white person in the scale of life to the level of a being of a marked race.[11]

By the turn of the century, medical doctors were still arguing that African Americans were disabled by freedom and therefore in need of greater oversight. J. F. Miller, writing in the *North Carolina Medical Journal*, thought it important to inquire whether "the effect of freedom upon the mental and physical health of the negroes of the South" had been "damaging or otherwise." His conclusion was that there were "more congenital defects" and a dramatic increase in mental illness and tuberculosis, which supposedly had been rare among enslaved African Americans. Freedom, for which the African American's weak mind and constitution were ill suited, had brought to the former slave "a beautiful harvest of mental and physical degeneration and he is now becoming a martyr to an heredity thus established."[12]

While these arguments were often contradictory, incoherent, or simply ludicrous, disability was central to all of them. If freedom for African Americans was undesirable and slavery good, then it was sufficient to note that free blacks were more likely than slaves to be disabled. The decisive argument for miscegenation being morally wrong or socially injurious was that it produced disability. The contention had to be countered, and no argument on other grounds could trump it. Samuel Forry, for example, writing in the *New York Journal of Medicine* in 1844, noted that the supposedly higher rates of insanity among free blacks compared to slaves had been "seized upon by journals devoted to the peculiar institutions of the Southern States, as a powerful argument." Forry retorted, first, that the census did not allow a reliable comparison of deafness, blindness, idiocy, and insanity in free and enslaved blacks and, second, that even were it the case that free blacks in the North suffered more disability than slaves, slavery and freedom might not be the determinants. Instead, perhaps "the whole constitution of the black is adapted to a tropical region," and their mental and physical health was therefore bound to suffer in the northern climate.[13] The argument that a people might be enslaved to protect them from disability he left unchallenged.

Race and disability intersected in the concept of the normal, as both prescription and description. American blacks, for example, were said to flourish in their "normal condition" of slavery, while the "'free' or abnormal negro" inevitably fell into illness, disability, and eventually extinction. The hierarchy of races was itself depicted as a continuum of normality. Just as medical textbook illustrations compared the normal body with the abnormal, so social science textbooks illustrated the normal race and the abnormal ones. Arnold Guyot, in his 1873 textbook *Physical Geography*, under the heading "The White Race the Normal, or Typical, Race," compared the beauty, regularity of features, and "harmony in all the proportions of the figure" of the white race with those who have "gradually deviated" from the normal ideal. Similarly, Dr. John C. Nott, writing in the *American Journal of Medical Sciences* in 1843, invited the reader to "look first upon the Caucasian female with her rose and lily skin, silky hair,

Venus form, and well chiseled features—and then upon the African wench with her black and odorous skin, woolly head and animal features—and compare their intellectual and moral qualities, and their whole anatomical structure." He added for good measure that the American Indian "has many peculiarities which are just as striking." In nineteenth-century freak shows, where disability and race intersected to illustrate familiar narratives of evolutionary progress, disabled adults were displayed as less-evolved creatures from far-off jungles. P. T. Barnum promoted his American Museum exhibit "What Is It?" as the "missing link" between human and animal, a "man-monkey." At least two different men played the role: a white actor with unusually short legs of uneven length and a mentally retarded black man with microcephaly who later became known by the stage name Zip. The presence of disability in both cases, in addition to race in one of them, was in effect the costume that signified the role of "subhuman."[14]

It is not new to point out that images of American blacks have commonly shown them with exaggerated lips, amusingly long or bowed legs, grotesquely big feet, bad posture, missing teeth, crossed or bulging eyes, and otherwise deformed bodies. At least since 1792, when Benjamin Rush explained that the skin color of Africans was due to their suffering from congenital leprosy, black skin itself has been treated as anomalous, a defect and a disfigurement, something akin to an all-body birthmark and often a sign of sin or degeneracy. Advertisements for soap in the nineteenth century often played on this idea of dark skin as defect with, for example, a pink-cheeked child asking an African American child, "Why doesn't your mamma wash you with Fairy Soap?"[15] Another advertisement told a tale of children who were bathed daily, "Because their mother did believe/So white they could be made/So on them with a scrubbing brush/Unmerciful she laid." The mother's efforts were fruitless until she found the right brand of soap: "Sweet and clean her sons became/it's true, as I'm a workman/And both are now completely white, Washed by this soap of Kirkman."[16] Dreydoppel Soap told a similar story of an African American boy ("A mite of queer humanity/As dark as a cloudy night") who scrubbed himself with acids, fasted, took sulfur baths, and "sampled all the medicine that ever was made or brewed" in the attempt to cure his unfortunate skin color. "He built an air-tight sweat box with the/Hope that he would bleach/The sweat poured down in rivers/but the Black stuck like a leech." That is, until he discovered Dreydoppel soap: "One trial was all he needed/Realized was his fondest hope/His face was white as white could be/There's nothing like Dreydoppel Soap."[17]

Daryl Michael Scott has described how both conservatives and liberals have long used an extensive repertory of "damage imagery" to describe African Americans. Conservatives "operated primarily from within a biological framework and argued for the innate inferiority of people of African descent" in order to justify social and political exclusion. Liberals maintained that social conditions were responsible for black inferiority and used damage imagery to argue for inclusion and rehabilitation; but regardless of their intentions, Scott argues, liberal damage imagery "reinforced the belief system that made whites feel superior in the first place." Both the "contempt and pity" of conservatives and liberals—a phrase that equally well describes historically prevalent attitudes toward disabled people—framed Americans of African descent as defective. Scott cites the example of Charles S. Johnson, chair of the social science department and later president of Fisk University, who told students in a 1928 speech that "the sociologists classify Negroes with cripples, persons with recognized physical handicaps." Like Johnson, Scott is critical of the fact that "African Americans were often lumped with the 'defective,' 'delinquent,' and dependent classes." This is obviously a bad place to be "lumped." Scott does not ask, however, why that might be the case.[18] The attribution of disease or disability to racial minorities has a long history. Yet, while many have pointed out the injustice and perniciousness of attributing these qualities to a racial or ethnic group, little has been written about why these attributions are such powerful weapons for inequality, why they were so furiously denied and condemned by their targets, and what this tells us about our attitudes toward disability.

During the long-running debate over women's suffrage in the nineteenth and early twentieth centuries, one of the rhetorical tactics of suffrage opponents was to point to the physical, intellectual, and psychological flaws of women, their frailty, irrationality, and emotional excesses. By the late nineteenth century, these claims were sometimes expressed in terms of evolutionary progress; like racial and ethnic minorities, women were said to be less evolved than white men, their disabilities a result of lesser evolutionary development. Cynthia Eagle Russett has noted that "women and savages, together with idiots, criminals, and pathological monstrosities [those with congenital disabilities] were a constant source of anxiety to male intellectuals in the late nineteenth century."[19] What all shared was an evolutionary inferiority, the result of arrested development or atavism.

Paralleling the arguments made in defense of slavery, two types of disability argument were used in opposition to women's suffrage: that women had disabilities that made them incapable of using the franchise responsibly, and that because of their frailty women would become disabled if exposed to the rigors of political participation. The American anti-suffragist Grace Goodwin, for example, pointed to the "great temperamental disabilities" with which women had to contend: "woman lacks endurance in things mental. . . . She lacks nervous stability. The suffragists who dismay England are nerve-sick women." The second line of argument, which was not incompatible with the first and often accompanied it, went beyond the claim that women's flaws made them incapable of exercising equal political and social rights with men to warn that if women were given those rights, disability would surely follow. This argument is most closely identified with Edward Clarke, author of *Sex in Education; or, A Fair Chance for Girls*. Clarke's argument chiefly concerned education for women, though it was often applied to suffrage as well. Clarke maintained that overuse of the brain among young women was in large part responsible for the "numberless pale, weak, neuralgic, dyspeptic, hysterical, menorraghic, dysmenorrhoeic girls and women" of America. The result of excessive education in this country was "bloodless female faces, that suggest consumption, scrofula, anemia, and neuralgia." An appropriate education designed for their frail constitutions would ensure "a future secure from neuralgia, uterine disease, hysteria, and other derangements of the nervous system."[20]

Similarly, Dr. William Warren Potter, addressing the Medical Society of New York in 1891, suggested that many a mother was made invalid by inappropriate education: "her reproductive organs are dwarfed, deformed, weakened, and diseased, by artificial causes imposed upon her during their development."[21] Dr. A. Lapthorn Smith asserted in *Popular Science Monthly* that educated women were increasingly "sick and suffering before marriage and are physically disabled from performing physiological functions in a normal manner." Antisuffragists likewise warned that female participation in politics invariably led to "nervous prostration" and "hysteria," while Dr. Almroth E. Wright noted the "fact that there is mixed up with the woman's movement much mental disorder." A prominent late nineteenth-century neurophysiologist, Charles L. Dana, estimated that enfranchising women would result in a 25 percent increase in insanity among them and "throw into the electorate a mass of voters of delicate nervous stability . . . which might do injury to itself without promoting the community's good." The answer for Clarke, Potter, and others of like mind was special education suited to women's special needs. As with disabled people today, women's social position was treated as a medical problem that necessitated separate and special care. Those who wrote with acknowledged authority on the "woman question" were doctors. As Clarke wrote, the answer to the "problem of woman's sphere . . . must be obtained from physiology, not from ethics or metaphysics."[22]

While historians have not overlooked the use of disability to deny women's rights, they have given their attention entirely to gender inequality and not at all to the construction and maintenance of cultural hierarchies based on disability. Lois Magner has described how women were said to bear the "onerous functions of the female," which incapacitated them for "active life" and produced a "mental disability that rendered women unfit" for political engagement. Nancy Woloch has noted that a "major antisuffragist point was that women were physically, mentally, and emotionally incapable of duties associated with the vote. Lacking rationality and sound judgment, they suffered from 'logical infirmity of mind.' . . . Unable to withstand the pressure of political life, they would be prone to paroxysms of hysteria." Aileen Kraditor, in her intellectual history of the women's suffrage movement, wrote that antisuffragists "described woman's physical constitution as too delicate to withstand the turbulence of political life. Her alleged weakness, nervousness, and proneness to fainting would certainly be out of place in polling booths and party conventions." On the one hand, this was of course an unfounded stereotype deserving of ridicule, as Kraditor's ironic tone suggests. On the other hand, just as it was left unchallenged at the time, historians today leave unchallenged the notion that weakness, nervousness, or proneness to fainting might legitimately disqualify one for suffrage.[23]

Disability figured not just in arguments *for* the inequality of women and minorities but also in arguments *against* those inequalities. Suffragists rarely challenged the notion that disability justified political inequality and instead disputed the claim that women suffered from these disabilities. Their arguments took three forms: one, women were not disabled and therefore deserved the vote; two, women were being erroneously and slanderously classed with disabled people, with those who were legitimately denied suffrage; and three, women were not naturally or inherently disabled but were *made* disabled by inequality—suffrage would ameliorate or cure these disabilities.

References to the intelligence and abilities of women, countering the imputations of female inferiority, pervaded suffrage rhetoric. Although more common later in the century, this form of argument was already in evidence in 1848 at the Seneca Falls Woman's Rights Convention. Delegates resolved that "the equality of human rights results necessarily from the fact of the identity of the race in capabilities and responsibilities," and further, that "being invested by the Creator with the same capabilities . . . it is demonstrably the right and duty of woman" to participate in public political life. Rebecca M. Sandford avowed, "Our intellect is as capable as man's to assume, and at once to hold, these rights . . . for if we did not believe it, we would not contend for them." Frederick Douglass proclaimed that "the true basis of rights was the capacity of individuals."[24] The converse of their premise that equality in capacity justified political equality, was a warrant too basic to be considered explicitly: differences in capacity, if present, would be justification for political inequality.

A second powerful and recurrent rhetorical device for suffragists was to charge that women were wrongly categorized with those legitimately excluded from political life. A popular theme in both British and American suffrage posters was to depict a thoughtful-looking woman, perhaps wearing the gown of a college graduate, surrounded by slope-browed, wild-eyed, or "degenerate" men identified implicitly or explicitly as "idiots" and "lunatics." The caption might read, "Women and her Political Peers," or, "It's time I got out of this place. Where shall I find the key?" Echoing this theme, suffrage supporter George William Curtis rhetorically asked a New York constitutional convention in 1867 why women should be classed with "idiots, lunatics, persons under guardianship and felons," and at the national Woman Suffrage Convention in 1869, Elizabeth Cady Stanton protested that women were "thrust outside the pale of political consideration with minors, paupers, lunatics, traitors, [and] idiots."[25]

These challenges directly confronted the euphemisms used by the antisuffragists, whose attributions of mental and psychological inferiority to women were couched in less direct language. Antisuffragists were wont to counter that it was "a noble sort of disfranchisement" that women enjoyed, "something wholly different from the disfranchisement of the pauper, the criminal, the insane. . . . These are set aside as persons not human; women are absolved as constituting a higher class. There is a very real distinction between being placed among the beasts, and being placed among the 'ministering angels.'"[26] The suffragist answer to these sentimental claims made clear that the antisuffrage argument was rooted in the attribution of disability.

Suffragists did on occasion take issue with the argument that rights rested on capacity. Lucretia Mott, speaking at Seneca Falls, conceded that "woman's intellect may be feeble, because she had been so long crushed; but

Douglas C. Baynton

is that any reason why she should be deprived of her equal rights? Does one man have fewer rights than another because his intellect is inferior? If not, why should woman?" But she immediately undercut the point by avowing, "Let woman arise and demand her rights, and in a few years we shall see a different mental development." Charlotte Perkins Gilman was the most prominent of those who argued that women's capacities had been stunted over time by restricted activity, which had come to represent a genetic inheritance that could be undone only by access to an unfettered social and political life. Matilda Gage similarly suggested that "obedience to outside authority to which woman has everywhere been trained, has not only dwarfed her capacity, but made her a retarding force in civilization."[27] These arguments were an implicit acknowledgment that capacity was indeed relevant to the question of rights. They are also examples of the third variant on the suffrage disability argument, that women were disabled by exclusion from political equality. This argument answered the antisuffrage accusation that women were inherently and unchangeably disabled with the claim that, given equal rights, they would attain equality in capacity. Like the antisuffrage position, it was a powerful argument precisely because of the cultural power of disability to discredit.

Ethnicity also has been defined by disability. One of the fundamental imperatives in the initial formation of American immigration policy at the end of the nineteenth century was the exclusion of disabled people. Beyond the targeting of disabled people, the concept of disability was instrumental in crafting the image of the undesirable immigrant. The first major federal immigration law, the Act of 1882, prohibited entry to any "lunatic, idiot, or any person unable to take care of himself or herself without becoming a public charge." Those placed in the categories "lunatic" and "idiot" were automatically excluded. The "public charge" provision was intended to encompass people with disabilities more generally and was left to the examining officer's discretion. The criteria for excluding disabled people were steadily tightened as the eugenics movement and popular fears about the decline of the national stock gathered strength. The Act of 1891 replaced the phrase "*unable* to take care of himself or herself without becoming a public charge," with "*likely* to become a public charge." The 1907 law then denied entry to anyone judged "mentally or physically defective, such mental or physical defect being of a nature which *may affect* the ability of such alien to earn a living." These changes considerably lowered the threshold for exclusion and expanded the latitude of immigration officials to deny entry.[28]

The category of persons *automatically* excluded was also steadily expanded. In 1903, people with epilepsy were added and, in addition to those judged insane, "persons who have been insane within five years previous [or] who have had two or more attacks of insanity at any time previously." This was reduced to one "attack" in the 1917 law; the classification of "constitutional psychopathic inferiority" was also added, which inspection regulations described as including "various unstable individuals on the border line between sanity and insanity . . . and persons with abnormal sex instincts."[29] This was the regulation under which, until recently, gays and lesbians were excluded. One of the significant factors in lifting this ban, along with other forms of discrimination against gays and lesbians, was the decision by the American Psychiatric Association in 1973 to remove homosexuality from its list of mental illnesses. That is, once gays and lesbians were declared not to be disabled, discrimination became less justifiable.

Legislation in 1907 added "imbeciles" and "feeble-minded persons" to the list, in addition to "idiots," and regulations for inspectors directed them to exclude persons with "any mental abnormality whatever . . . which justifies the statement that the alien is mentally defective." These changes encompassed a much larger number of people and again granted officials considerably more discretion to judge the fitness of immigrants for American life. Fiorello H. LaGuardia, who worked his way through law school as an interpreter at Ellis Island, later wrote that "over fifty percent of the deportations for alleged mental disease were unjustified," based as they often were on "ignorance on the part of the immigrants or the doctors and the inability of the doctors to understand the particular immigrant's norm, or standard."[30]

The detection of physical disabilities was a major aspect of the immigration inspector's work. The Regulations for the medical inspection of immigrants in 1917 included a long list of diseases and disabilities that could be cause for exclusion, among them arthritis, asthma, bunions, deafness, deformities, flat feet, heart disease, hernia, hysteria, poor eyesight, poor physical development, spinal curvature, vascular disease of the heart, and varicose veins. A visiting physician in 1893, when admission standards were still relatively liberal, described the initial inspection: "If a man has a hand done up, or any physical injury in any way . . . , or if a person has but one leg or one arm, or one eye, or there is any physical or mental defect, if the person seems unsteady and in any way physically incapacitated to earn his livelihood, he is passed to one side to be examined later."[31] An immigration official later recalled a young Italian couple who would have been deported (the man had a "game leg" that required use of a crutch) had not a wealthy philanthropist visiting Ellis Island taken an interest in the couple and intervened, guaranteeing that they would not become a public charge.[32]

In short, the exclusion of disabled people was central to the laws and the work of the immigration service. As the Commissioner General of Immigration reported in 1907, "The exclusion from this country of the morally, mentally, and physically deficient is the principal object to be accomplished by the immigration laws." Once the laws and procedures limiting the entry of disabled people were firmly established and functioning well, attention turned to limiting the entry of undesirable ethnic groups. Discussion on this topic often began by pointing to the general public agreement that the laws excluding disabled people had been a positive, if insufficient, step. In 1896, for example, Francis Walker noted in the *Atlantic Monthly* that the necessity of "straining out" immigrants who were "deaf, dumb, blind, idiotic, insane, pauper, or criminal" was "now conceded by men of all shades of opinion"; indeed there was a widespread "resentment at the attempt of such persons to impose themselves upon us." As one restrictionist wrote, the need to exclude the disabled was "self evident."[33]

For the more controversial business of defining and excluding undesirable ethnic groups, however, restrictionists found the *concept* of disability to be a powerful tool. That is, while people with disabilities constituted a distinct category of persons unwelcome in the United States, the charge that certain ethnic groups were mentally and physically deficient was instrumental in arguing for *their* exclusion. The belief that discriminating on the basis of disability was justifiable in turn helped justify the creation of immigration quotas based on ethnic origin. The 1924 Immigration Act instituted a national quota system that severely limited the numbers of immigrants from southern and eastern Europe, but long before that, disabilities stood in for nationality. Superintendents of institutions, philanthropists, immigration reformers, and politicians had been warning for decades before 1924 that immigrants were disproportionately prone to be mentally defective—up to half the immigrants from southern and eastern Europe were feebleminded, according to expert opinion.[34] Rhetoric about "the slow-witted Slav," the "neurotic condition of our Jewish immigrants," and, in general, the "degenerate and psychopathic types, which are so conspicuous and numerous among the immigrants," was pervasive in the debate over restriction.[35] The laws forbidding entry to the feebleminded were motivated in part by the desire to limit immigration from inferior nations, and conversely, it was assumed that the 1924 act would reduce the number of feebleminded immigrants. The issues of ethnicity and disability were so intertwined in the immigration debate as to be inseparable.

Arguments for immigration restriction often emphasized the inferior appearance of immigrants, and here also ethnicity and disability overlapped and intertwined. Disability scholars have emphasized the uncertain and shifting line between an impairment of appearance and one of function. Martin Pernick, for example, has described the importance of aesthetics in eugenics literature—how fitness was equated with beauty and disability with ugliness. Lennard Davis has maintained that disability presents itself "through two main modalities—function and appearance." Restrictionists often emphasized the impaired appearance of immigrants. An Ellis Island inspector claimed that "no one can stand at Ellis Island and see the physical and mental wrecks who are stopped there . . . without becoming a firm believer in restriction."[36] A proponent of restriction avowed, "To the practised eye, the physiognomy of certain groups unmistakably proclaims inferiority of type." When he observed immigrants, he saw that "in every face there was something wrong . . . . There were so many sugar-loaf heads, moon-faces, slit mouths, lantern-jaws, and goose-bill noses that one might imagine a malicious jinn had amused himself by casting human beings in a set of skew-molds discarded by the Creator." Most new immigrants were physically inadequate in some way: "South Europeans run to low stature. A gang of Italian navvies filing along the street present, by their dwarfishness, a curious contrast to other people. The Portuguese, the Greeks, and the Syrians are, from our point of view, undersized. The Hebrew immigrants are very poor in physique . . . the polar opposite of our pioneer breed."[37]

The initial screening of immigrants was mostly a matter of detecting visible abnormality. Inspectors, who prided themselves on their ability to make a "snapshot diagnosis," had only a few seconds to detect the signs of disability or disease as immigrants streamed past them in single file. Inspection regulations specified that "each individual should be seen first at rest and then in motion," in order to detect "irregularities in movement" and "abnormalities of any description." If possible, inspectors watched immigrants as they carried their luggage up stairs to see if "the exertion would reveal deformities and defective posture."[38] As one inspector wrote, "It is no more difficult to detect poorly built, defective or broken down human beings than to recognize a cheap or defective automobile. . . . The wise man who really wants to find out all he can about an automobile or an immigrant, will want to see both in action, performing as well as at rest."[39]

For most immigrants, a normal appearance meant a quick, uneventful passage through the immigration station. An abnormal appearance, however, meant a chalked letter on the back: "L for lameness, K for hernia, G for goiter, X for mental illness," and so on.[40] Once chalked, a closer inspection was required. The inspection then would be general, not confined to the abnormality that set them apart, which meant that visibly disabled people—as well as those whose ethnic appearance was abnormal to the inspectors—were more likely to be set apart for close examination and therefore were also more likely to have other problems discovered and to be excluded.

Aesthetic and eugenic considerations were at least as important as concerns about the functional limitations of disabled immigrants. For example, on June 30, 1922, Israel Raskin was refused entry to the United States as "physically defective and likely to become a public charge." The diagnosis on the medical certificate was "lack of sexual development which may affect his ability to earn a living." The United States Surgeon General explained that the diagnosis warranted exclusion because "these persons present bad economic risks . . . due to the fact that their abnormality soon becomes known to their associates who make them the butt of coarse jokes to their own despair, and to the impairment of the work in hand." Since this was "recognized pretty generally among employers, it is difficult for these unfortunates to get or retain jobs, their facial and bodily appearance, at least in adult life, furnishing a patent advertisement of their condition."[41]

Medical exclusions on the basis of "poor physique" and "lack of physical development" began to appear around the turn of the century. The immigration service defined it as covering individuals "who have frail frame, flat chest, and are generally deficient in muscular development," or those who are "undersized—markedly of short stature—dwarf."[42] In part, this diagnosis represented a judgment of employability, and in part it was a eugenic judgment. Both concerns were expressed in a letter from the Bureau of Immigration, which explained that "a certificate of this nature implies that the alien concerned is afflicted with a body but illy adapted . . . to the work necessary to earn his bread." The diagnosis further indicated that the immigrant was "undersized, poorly developed [and] physically degenerate, and as such, not only unlikely to become a desirable citizen, but also very likely to transmit his undesirable qualities to his offspring, should he unfortunately for the country in which he is domiciled, have any."[43]

As one medical officer explained it, the "immigrant of poor physique is not able to perform rough labor, and *even if he were able*, employers of labor would not hire him."[44] The belief that an immigrant with a disability was unfit to work was justification for exclusion; but the belief that an immigrant was *likely to encounter discrimination* because of a disability was equally justification for exclusion. The disability that justified exclusion in these cases was largely or entirely a matter of an abnormal appearance that might invite employment discrimination.

The laws excluding disabled immigrants could be used by inspectors to target particular ethnic groups. The Hebrew Sheltering and Immigrant Aid Society in New York expressed concern in 1909 that the "lack of physical development" diagnosis was "constantly increasing" and being applied to Jewish immigrants disproportionately. An investigation by the Jewish Immigrants' Information Bureau in 1910 discovered that an inspector in Galveston was using the diagnosis to discriminate against Jewish immigrants. Nationality and disability might be implicitly linked in anti-immigration rhetoric, as when William Green, president of the American Federation of Labor, argued that quotas were "necessary to the preservation of our national characteristics and to our physical and our mental health."[45] They also were explicitly connected, as when a New York Supreme Court justice worried that the new immigrants were "adding to that appalling number of our inhabitants who handicap us by reason of their mental and physical disabilities."[46]

Historians have scrutinized the attribution of mental and physical inferiority based on race and ethnicity, but only to condemn the slander. With their attention confined to ethnic stereotypes, they have largely ignored what the attribution of disability might also tell us about attitudes toward disabled people. Racial and ethnic prejudice is exposed while prejudice against people with disabilities is passed over as insignificant and understandable. As a prominent advocate of restriction wrote in 1930, "The necessity of the exclusion of the crippled, the blind, those who are likely to become public charges, and, of course, those with a criminal record is self evident."[47] The necessity has been treated as self-evident by historians as well, so much so that even the possibility of discrimination against people with disabilities in immigration law has gone unrecognized. In historical accounts, disability is present but rendered invisible or insignificant. While it is certain that immigration restriction rests in good part on a fear of "strangers in the land," in John Higham's phrase, American immigration restriction at the turn of the century was also clearly fueled by a fear of *defectives* in the land.

Still today, women and other groups who face discrimination on the basis of identity respond angrily to accusations that they might be characterized

Douglas C. Baynton

by physical, mental, or emotional disabilities. Rather than challenging the basic assumptions behind the hierarchy, they instead work to remove themselves from the negatively marked categories—that is, to disassociate themselves from those people who "really are" disabled—knowing that such categorization invites discrimination. For example, a recent proposal in Louisiana to permit pregnant women to use parking spaces reserved for people with mobility impairments was opposed by women's organizations. A lobbyist for the Women's Health Foundation said, "We've spent a long time trying to dispel the myth that pregnancy is a disability, for obvious reasons of discrimination." She added, "I have no problem with it being a courtesy, but not when a legislative mandate provides for pregnancy in the same way as for disabled persons."[48] To be associated with disabled people or with the accommodations accorded disabled people is stigmatizing.

Even disabled people have used this strategy to try to deflect discrimination. Rosemarie Garland Thomson notes that "disabled people also often avoid and stereotype one another in attempting to normalize their own social identities." Deaf people throughout the twentieth century have rejected the label of disability, knowing its dangers; and the tendency of those with less-stigmatized disabilities to distance themselves from those with more highly stigmatized disabilities is a common phenomenon. In 1918, the associate director of what was known as the "Cleveland Cripple Survey" reported that some of those surveyed "were amazed that they should be considered cripples, even though they were without an arm or leg, or perhaps seriously crippled as a result of infantile paralysis. They had never considered themselves handicapped in any way."[49]

This common strategy for attaining equal rights, which seeks to distance one's own group from imputations of disability and therefore tacitly accepts the idea that disability is a legitimate reason for inequality, is perhaps one of the factors responsible for making discrimination against people with disabilities so persistent and the struggle for disability rights so difficult. As Harlan Hahn has noted, "Unlike other disadvantaged groups, citizens with disabilities have not yet fully succeeded in refuting the presumption that their subordinate status can be ascribed to an innate biological inferiority."[50] If Hahn is perhaps too optimistic about the extent to which women and minority groups have managed to do away with such presumptions, nevertheless it is true that such views are no longer an accepted part of public discourse. Yet the same views regarding disability are still espoused widely and openly.

Disability is everywhere in history, once you begin looking for it, but conspicuously absent in the histories we write. When historians do take note of disability, they usually treat it merely as personal tragedy or an insult to be deplored and a label to be denied, rather than as a cultural construct to be questioned and explored. Those of us who specialize in the history of disability, like the early historians of other minority groups, have concentrated on writing histories of disabled people and the institutions and laws associated with disability. This is necessary and exciting work. It is through this work that we are building the case that disability is culturally constructed rather than natural and timeless—that disabled people have a history, and a history worth studying. Disability, however, more than an identity, is a fundamental element in cultural signification and indispensable for *any* historian seeking to make sense of the past. It may well be that all social hierarchies have drawn on culturally constructed and socially sanctioned notions of disability. If this is so, then there is much work to do. It is time to bring disability from the margins to the center of historical inquiry.

NOTES

1. Joan Scott, "Gender: A Useful Category of Historical Analysis," *American Historical Review* 91 (December 1986): 1053–75.

2. Edmund Burke, *Reflections on the Revolution in France* ("Books-on-Line" Internet edition—gopher://gopher.vt.edu:10010/02/55/1): for rhetoric of monstrosity, see 13–14, 63, 118–19, 261, 355, 384, 396, 412; for blindness, see 70, 89, 171, 308, 378; for imbecility and madness, see 165, 173, 217, 346, 394, 419, 444, 448. Tom Paine, *The Rights of Man* ("Books-on-Line" Internet edition), 86; see also 12, 15.

3. Ian Hacking, *The Taming of Chance* (Cambridge and New York: Cambridge University Press, 1990), 160–66. See also Georges Canguilhem, *The Normal and the Pathological* (New York: Zone Books, 1989); Douglas C. Baynton, *Forbidden Signs: American Culture and the Campaign against Sign Language* (Chicago: University of Chicago Press, 1996), chaps. 5–6.

4. Francois Ewald, "Norms Discipline, and the Law," *Representations* 30 (Spring 1990): 146, 149–50, 154; Lennard Davis, *Enforcing Normalcy: Disability, Deafness, and the Body* (London: Verso, 1995); Baynton, *Forbidden Signs*, chaps. 5 and 6.

5. Late nineteenth-century educators began using "normal child" as the counterpart to "deaf child" instead of the "hearing" and "deaf" of previous generations. "Normal" appears to refer to an average, since the "average" person is hearing. Since it does not exclude those with superior hearing, however, it does not denote the average but those *above* a certain standard.

6. Daniel J. Kevles, *In the Name of Eugenics: Genetics and the Uses of Human Heredity* (Berkeley: University of California Press, 1985), 160; Baynton, *Forbidden Signs*, chap. 2; James W. Cook, Jr., "Of Men, Missing Links, and Nondescripts: The Strange Career of P. T. Barnum's 'What Is It?' Exhibition," in Rosemarie Garland Thomson, ed., *Freakery: Cultural Spectacles of the Extraordinary Body* (New York: New York University Press, 1996); James W. Trent, Jr., "Defectives at the World's Fair: Constructing Disability in 1904," *Remedial and Special Education* 19 (July/August 1998): 201–11.

7. Samuel A. Cartwright, "Report on the Diseases and Physical Peculiarities of the Negro Race," *New Orleans Medical and Surgical Journal* 7 (May 1851): 693; George M. Fredrickson, *The Black Image in the White Mind* (New York: Harper and Row, 1971), 250–51; J. C. Nott, "The Mulatto a Hybrid," *American Journal of Medical Sciences* (July 1843), quoted in Samuel Forry, "Vital Statistics Furnished by the Sixth Census of the United States, " *New York Journal of Medicine and the Collateral Sciences* 1 (September 1843): 151–53.

8. John H. Van Evrie, *White Supremacy and Negro Subordination, or Negroes a Subordinate Race* (New York: Van Evrie, Horton, & Co., 1868), 153–55; Forry, "Vital Statistics," 159; Paul B. Barringer, *The American Negro: His Past and Future* (Raleigh: Edwards & Broughton, 1900), 10.

9. Cited in Forry, "Vital Statistics," 162–63. John C. Calhoun, "Mr. Calhoun to Mr. Pakenham," in Richard K. Cralle, ed., *The Works of John C. Calhoun* (New York: D. Appleton, 1888), 5:337.

10. Cartwright, "Report," 707–10. See also Thomas S. Szasz, "The Sane Slave: A Historical Note on the Use of Medical Diagnosis as Justificatory Rhetoric," *American Journal of Psychotherapy* 25 (1971): 228–39.

11. Van Evrie, *White Supremacy*, 121, 181, 221. Van Evrie notes in his preface that the book was completed "about the time of Mr. Lincoln's election" and was therefore originally an argument in favor of the continuation of slavery but presently constituted an argument for its restoration.

12. J. F. Miller, "The Effects of Emancipation upon the Mental and Physical Health of the Negro of the South," *North Carolina Medical Journal* 38 (Nov. 20, 1896): 285–94.

13. Samuel Forry, "On the Relative Proportion of Centenarians, of Deaf and Dumb, of Blind, and of Insane in the Races of European and African Origin," *New York Journal of Medicine and the Collateral Sciences,* 2 (May 1844): 313.

14. Van Evrie, *White Supremacy* 199, chap. 15 *passim*; Arnold Guyot, *Physical Geography* (1873; reprint, New York: American Book Co., 1885), 114–18; Nott, "Mulatto a Hybrid," quoted in Forry, "Vital Statistics," 163–64; Cook, "Of Men, Missing Links, and Nondescripts," 139–57; Robert Bogdan, *Freak Show: Presenting Human Oddities for Amusement and Profit* (Chicago: University of Chicago Press, 1988), 134–42.

15. Winthrop D. Jordan. *White over Black: American Attitudes toward the Negro, 1550–1812* (Chapel Hill: University of North Carolina Press, 1968), 518–25; Rush

explained not only African skin this way but the nose, lips, and hair as well. Smithsonian Institution Archives, Collection 60—Warshaw Collection, "Soap," Box 4, Folder: Fairbanks; dated 1893 or 1898 (illegible).

16. Smithsonian Institution Archives, Collection 60—Warshaw Collection, "Afro-Americana," Box 4, Folder 7, n.d.

17. Smithsonian Institution Archives, Collection 60—Warshaw Collection, "AfroAmericana," Box 4, Folder 4, n.d., ca. 1893.

18. Daryl Michael Scott, *Contempt and Pity: Social Policy and the Image of the Damaged Black Soul, 1880–1996* (Chapel Hill: University of North Carolina Press, 1997) xi–xvii; 12, 208 n. 52.

19. Cynthia Eagle Russett, *Sexual Science: The Victorian Construction of Womanhood* (Cambridge, Mass.: Harvard University Press, 1989), 63. See also Lois N. Magner, "Darwinism and the Woman Question: The Evolving Views of Charlotte Perkins Gilman," in Joanne Karpinski, *Critical Essays on Charlotte Perkins Gilman* (New York: G. K. Hall, 1992), 119–20.

20. Grace Duffield Goodwin, *Anti-Suffrage: Ten Good Reasons* (New York: Duffield and Co., 1913), 91–92 (in Smithsonian Institution Archives, Collection 60—Warshaw Collection, "Women," Box 3). Edward Clarke, *Sex in Education; or, A Fair Chance for Girls* (1873; reprint, New York: Arno Press, 1972), 18, 22, 62.

21. William Warren Potter, "How Should Girls Be Educated? A Public Health Problem for Mothers, Educators, and Physicians," *Transactions of the Medical Society of the State of New York* (1891): 48, quoted in Martha H. Verbrugge, *Able Bodied Womanhood: Personal Health and Social Change in Nineteenth-Century Boston* (Oxford and New York: Oxford University Press, 1988), 121.

22. A. Lapthorn Smith, "Higher Education of Women and Race Suicide," *Popular Science Monthly* (March 1905), reprinted in Louise Michele Newman, ed., *Men's Ideas/Women's Realities: Popular Science, 1870–1915* (New York: Pergamon Press, 1985), 149; Almroth E. Wright quoted in Mara Mayor, "Fears and Fantasies of the Anti-Suffragists," *Connecticut Review* 7 (April 1974): 67; Charles L. Dana quoted in Jane Jerome Camhi, *Women against Women: American Anti-Suffragism, 1880–1920* (New York: Carlson Publishing Co., 1994), 18; Clarke, *Sex in Education*, 12.

23. Magner, "Darwinism," 119–20; Nancy Woloch, *Women and the American Experience, vol. 1: To 1920* (New York: McGraw-Hill, Inc., 1994), 339: Aileen S. Kraditor, *The Ideas of the Woman Suffrage Movement* (New York: W. W. Norton & Co., 1981), 20. See also Anne Digby, "Woman's Biological Straitjacket," in Susan Mendas and Jane Randall, eds., *Sexuality and Subordination: Interdisciplinary Studies of Gender in the Nineteenth Century* (New York: Routledge, 1989), 192–220.

24. *Woman's Rights Conventions: Seneca Falls and Rochester, 1848* (New York: Arno Press, Inc., 1969), 4–6; originally published as *Proceedings of the Woman's Rights Convention, Held at Seneca Falls and Rochester, N.Y., July and August, 1848* (New York: Robert J. Johnston, 1870), 4–6.

25. Lisa Tickner, *The Spectacle of Women: Imagery of the Suffrage Campaign, 1907–14* (Chicago: University of Chicago Press, 1988), illustration IV; Alice Sheppard, *Cartooning for Suffrage* (Albuquerque: University of New Mexico Press, 1994), 30; Elizabeth Cady Stanton, Susan B. Anthony, and Matilda Joslyn Gage, eds., *History of Woman Suffrage* (1881; reprint, New York: Arno Press, 1969), 2:288, quoted in Yvonne Pitts, "'Under This Disability of Nature': Women and Constructions of Disability in the National Suffrage Debates, 1870–1920" (paper presented to the Berkshire Conference on the History of Women, June 1999); Elizabeth Cady Stanton, "Address to the National Woman Convention, Washington, D.C., January 19, 1869," in Mari Jo Buhle and Paul Buhle, eds., *The Concise History of Woman Suffrage* (Urbana: University of Illinois Press, 1978), 256.

26. O. B. Frothingham, "The Real Case of the 'Remonstrants' against Woman Suffrage," *The Arena* 2 (July 1890): 177.

27. *Woman's Rights Conventions*, 11; on Charlotte Perkins Gilman, see Kraditor, *Ideas of the Woman Suffrage Movement*, 97–101; "Preceding Causes, written by Matilda Joslyn Gage, in 1881," in Buhle and Buhle, eds., *Concise History*, 53.

28. *United States Statutes at Large* (Washington, D.C.: Government Printing Office, 1883), 22:214. *United States Statutes at Large* (Washington, D.C.: Government Printing Office, 1891), 26:1084; *United States Statutes at Large* (Washington, D.C.: Government Printing Office, 1907), 34:899. Emphases added.

29. *United States Statutes at Large* (Washington, D.C.: Government Printing Office, 1903), 32:1213; United States Public Health Service, *Regulations Governing the Medical Inspection of Aliens* (Washington, D.C.: Government Printing Office, 1917), 28–29.

30. *Statutes* (1907), 34:899; United States Public Health Service, *Regulations*, 30–31; Fiorello H. LaGuardia, *The Making of an Insurgent: An Autobiography, 1882–1919* (1948; reprint, New York: Capricorn, 1961), 65.

31. United States Public Health Service, *Regulations*, 16–19; U. O .B. Wingate, "Quarenteen Immigration at the Port of New York," *Milwaukee Medical Journal* 1 (1893): 181, quoted in Elizabeth Yew, "Medical Inspection of Immigrants at Ellis Island, 1891–1924," *Bulletin of the New York Academy of Medicine* 56 (June 1980): 494.

32. Philip Cowen, *Memories of an American Jew* (1932; reprint, New York: Arno Press, 1975) 148–49.

33. U.S. Bureau of Immigration, *Annual Report of the Commissioner of Immigration* (Washington, D.C.: Government Printing Office, 1907), 62; Francis A. Walker, "Restriction of Immigration," *Atlantic Monthly* 77 (June 1896): 822; Ellsworth Eliot, Jr., M.D., "Immigration," in Madison Grant and Charles Steward Davison, eds., *The Alien in Our Midst, or Selling our Birthright for a Mess of Industrial Pottage* (New York: Galton Publishing Co., 1930), 101.

34. See James W. Trent Jr., *Inventing the Feeble Mind: A History of Mental Retardation in the United States* (Berkeley: University of California Press, 1994), 166–69.

35. Thomas Wray Grayson, "The Effect of the Modern Immigrant on Our Industrial

Centers," in *Medical Problems of Immigration* (Easton, Penn.: American Academy of Medicine, 1913), 103, 107-9.

36. Martin Pernick, *The Black Stork: Eugenics and the Death of "Defective" Babies in American Medicine and Motion Pictures since 1915* (Oxford and New York: Oxford University Press, 1996), 60-71; Davis, *Enforcing Normalcy*, 11-12. See also Harlan Hahn, "Antidiscrimination Laws and Social Research on Disability: The Minority Group Perspective," *Behavioral Sciences and the Law* 14 (1996): 54; Alfred C. Reed, "Going through Ellis Island," *Popular Science Monthly* 82 (January 1913): 8-9.

37. Edward Alsworth Ross, *The Old World and the New: The Significance of Past and Present Immigration to the American People* (New York: Century Co., 1914), 285-90.

38. Elizabeth Yew, "Medical Inspection of Immigrants at Ellis Island, 1891-1924," *Bulletin of the New York Academy of Medicine* 56 (June 1980): 497-98; United States Public Health Service, *Regulations*, 16-19; Alan M. Kraut, *Silent Travelers: Germs, Genes, and the "Immigrant Menace"* (New York: Basic Books, 1994), 54-57.

39. Victor Safford, *Immigration Problems: Personal Experiences of an Official* (New York: Dodd, Mead, 1925), 244-46.

40. Kraut, *Silent Travelers*, 55.

41. Letter from W. W. Husband, Commissioner General, Bureau of Immigration, to H. S. Cumming, Surgeon General, United States Public Health Service, September 27, 1922; and reply from Cumming to Husband, September 29, 1922; National Archives, RG 90, Entry 10, File 219.

42. Letter from George Stoner, Chief Medical Officer, Public Health and Marine Hospital Service, to Surgeon General of the Public Health and Marine Hospital, Nov. 29, 1912, National Archives, RG 90, Entry 10, File 219.

43. Letter from F. P. Sargent, Commissioner-General of the Bureau of Immigration, to the Commissioner of Immigration on Ellis Island, April 17, 1905, National Archives, RG90, E10, File 219.

44. Allan McLaughlin, "The Problem of Immigration, " *Popular Science Monthly* 66 (April 1905): 532 (emphasis added).

45. Letter from Leon Sanders, President of the Hebrew Sheltering and Immigrant Aid Society, to Surgeon General of the Public Health and Marine Hospital, Nov. 14, 1909, National Archives, RG 90, Entry 10, File 219. Kraut, *Silent Travelers*, 65. William Green, "Immigration Should Be Regulated," in Grant and Davison, *Alien in Our Midst*, 2.

46. Norman S. Dike, "Aliens and Crime," in Grant and Davison, *Alien in Our Midst*, 81.

47. Ellsworth Eliot, Jr., M.D., "Immigration," in Grant and Davison, *Alien in Our Midst*, 101.

48. Heather Salerno, "Mother's Little Dividend: Parking," *Washington Post* (September 16, 1997): A1.

49. Rosemarie Garland Thomson, *Extraordinary Bodies: Figuring Physical Disability in*

American Culture and Literature (New York: Columbia University Press, 1997), 15. Amy Hamburger, "The Cripple and His Place in the Community," *Annals of the American Academy of Political and Social Science* 77 (1918): 39.

50. Harlan Hahn, "Antidiscrimination Laws and Social Research on Disability: The Minority Group Perspective," *Behavioral Sciences and the Law* 14 (1996): 43.

2

"Speech Has an Extraordinary Humanizing Power"

Horace Mann and the Problem of Nineteenth-Century American Deaf Education

R. A. R. Edwards

"The best friends of the sign language," S. G. Davidson commented in 1899, "will not deny that it is immeasurably inferior to English, and it follows that the culture dependent upon it must be proportionately inferior."[1] By 1899, as oral education, with its emphasis on speech and speechreading, won more and more practitioners in schools for the deaf across the country, few voices were raised to challenge Davidson's assessment. Yet the best friends of the sign language in 1830, including many members of the founding generation of deaf educators in the United States, would have been appalled by his ignorance. They would have declared the sign language not only the equal but in some respects the superior of English.[2] Not only this pedagogical reversal but this reversal in linguistic understanding must be explained.

Most historians of deaf education have explained the pedagogical reversal by pointing to generational change. Both Harlan Lane and Douglas Baynton argue that the transformation of deaf education from a manually based system to an orally based system can be explained in this way. Lane concludes, "Incredible as it may seem, it took only a small clique of hearing educators and businessmen, *late in the last century*, to release a tidal wave of oralism that swept over Western Europe, drowning all its signing communities. In America, the submersion of sign language was nearly as complete."[3] And Baynton believes that manualism appealed, for a variety of reasons, to a generation of educators raised in the antebellum period, while oralism made more cultural sense to those who came of age after the Civil War.[4]

And yet the first cohesive arguments for oral education came in 1844 from Horace Mann, a figure the accounts by Lane and Baynton disregard.[5] Lane views Mann as a dupe, first of German teachers of the deaf, whose articulation teaching greatly impressed him on a visit to Germany in 1843, and then of Samuel Gridley Howe, who, according to Lane, convinced Mann to praise oralism in order to help Howe "wrest the education of the deaf from Hartford and place it under his aegis at the Perkins Institute of the Blind."[6] This view ignores the real possibility that Mann may have had his own reasons for taking an interest in the issue of deaf education. Baynton likewise downplays Mann's influence in this regard, arguing that though he was "America's pre-eminent educator," the results of his efforts on behalf of oralism were "negligible."[7] According to Baynton, the 1840s were not the right cultural environment for oralism. Manualists romanticized deafness, seeing deaf people as closer to God and blessed by God with a special gift, sign language, that rescued them from silent ignorance. Mann's scientific oralism could not compete with this evangelical piety.[8]

But when Clarke School for the Deaf, the first oral school in New England, opened in 1867, in competition with the manual American Asylum in Connecticut, the ghost of Horace Mann hovered over the event. Samuel Gridley Howe invoked Mann's memory at the legislative hearings held to decide the issue of the proposed school's funding and methods. On the opening day of committee arguments, January 24, 1867, Howe begged, "If the gentlemen will allow me to go back to 1843, I will state that at that time I went through Germany with Horace Mann, then a member of the Board of Education. We went into schools there and I was astonished at the ease with which we made ourselves understood by the deaf-mute pupils, speaking to them from the lips. . . . Mr. Mann said to me, 'When we get home we must give Massachusetts the benefit of this system'; and up to the day of his death he cherished this idea, and in his last letter to me made mention of this wish."[9] It seems clear that Howe saw the events of 1843 as intimately connected to those of 1867.

Howe was right. The standard periodization of deaf historians needs to be modified. The nineteenth century should not be understood as neatly divided into ante- and postbellum periods. Rather, the century can be understood as building from the American Asylum to Clarke, a path from manualism to oralism, a tortuous journey to be sure but one continuous path nonetheless, marked most strongly by continuity with the past and not by a sharp mid-century break.

In fact, nineteenth-century deaf education can best be understood as an involved conversation about linguistics, as educators struggled to answer the following questions: What is the nature of language? What is the nature of the sign language? How do we, both deaf and hearing, learn language? As the answers to these fundamental questions changed over the course of the century, so too did the pedagogy of deaf education. Framing the century in the light of these questions lets us recover the understanding and perspective of the participants themselves, men who saw the past as deeply connected to the present and who were therefore extraordinarily interested in the history of their profession.[10] It allows us to see manualists and oralists as individuals in contact and conversation over the course of the century, and not as two distinct generational camps. It forces us to investigate the specific linguistic and pedagogical arguments offered by both sides. And finally, this approach recognizes Horace Mann's pivotal role. He is no bit player in this telling of the tale but is rather a crucial figure whose influence reaches to 1867 and beyond.

To trace the evolution of this conversation, one must go back to 1817, the year the American Asylum for the Education and Instruction of Deaf and Dumb Persons opened its doors.[11] The co-founders of the school, Thomas Hopkins Gallaudet, a hearing American and minister, and Laurent Clerc, a Deaf Frenchman and teacher, decided on a manualist course. The new school would use the natural language of signs,[12] methodical signs, the manual alphabet,[13] and written English to instruct their eager pupils. Articulation and speechreading were not part of the curriculum.[14]

Clerc was a Deaf man who did not speak. Educated at the National Institute in Paris, a school that strongly favored the manual method, he left a teaching post there to come to America. Clerc was an impressive figure. His lack of speech did not seem to distress antebellum Americans. On a fundraising and promotional tour for the new American school, he addressed audiences in sign, ably translated by his educational partner Gallaudet. As one listener remarked, "The Rev. Mr. Gallaudet returned to his friends, a qualified instructor upon the French system. He brought with him as an assistant, a most interesting man, Mr. Clerc. This person never heard a sound or uttered a word, being deaf and dumb from his birth. Yet he is so quick and intelligent, that he has become acquainted with both the French and English tongues, which he writes with grammatical accuracy. . . . In him we have an example of the ability of a person, himself deaf and dumb, to give the necessary instruction to others labouring under similar disabilities."[15] Clerc was a powerful symbol of the benefits of the manual system. He was obviously intelligent and he could teach others. He offered Americans a glimpse of the future for their own deaf citizens; they could be useful citizens, intelligent and self-sufficient, if only they too were given the education that Clerc had received and was now willing in turn to offer.

It was Clerc who brought with him the French system of methodical signs, and these need some explanation. An invention of the Abbé de l'Epée,[16] methodical signs were described as the "natural language of signs . . . reduced to one general standard, and methodized, and enlarged . . . so as to accommodate [the language of signs] to the structure and idioms of written language, and thus render it in itself a perspicuous, complete, and copious medium of thought."[17] Methodical signs were meant to present French gesturally, in the belief that such a visual presentation would be more effective for deaf students accustomed to receiving information through their eyes. Clerc and Gallaudet adopted this system in order to sign English methodically.

But methodical signs did more than "accommodate [signs] to the structure and idioms of written language." As Harlan Lane describes them, methodical signs also indicated the word's part of speech and case; essentially, the system diagrammed sentences visually. In this way, "even the simplest sentence took on enormous complexity. One example: a line from Racine, 'To the smallest of the birds, He gives their crumbs,' required forty-eight signs from Epée's pupils. 'Gives' alone required five signs: those for verb, present tense, third person, singular, and 'give.'"[18] This kind of signing was considered best for teaching English. Deaf students were not expected to sign this way in daily conversations.[19]

For daily life, and indeed, for all other academic subjects, the natural language of signs was used. It is educators' understanding of the natural language of signs that is most important to recover here. Did early educators believe they were using a language, just like English? And what did this language look like? Did early educators recognize it as having a syntax and grammar all its own? Where did it come from? Antebellum school reports and professional journals again provide the clues.

According to the American Asylum, the first and most important tool in teaching the deaf was the natural language of signs. It was the approach "on which all the rest are founded and without which every attempt to teach the deaf and dumb would be utterly vain and fruitless."[20] This natural language, unlike the methodical signs, was "singularly adapted to their necessities" and was "significant and copious in its various expressions.[21] Fledgling hearing teachers of the deaf needed to learn this language "by a long and intimate acquaintance" with their deaf students.[22] Newcomers to the field were advised to watch the deaf "to learn all their various modes of expressing their ideas by the natural signs, which they themselves have invented."[23] This advice to new teachers is astonishing for several reasons. First, all teachers were expected to know this natural language of signs well. Knowing the methodical signs was simply not enough. This may not seem like the most astonishing advice, but by late-twentieth-century standards it is nothing short of radical. Most teachers working in the field today do not know the natural language of signs in which their predecessors were expected to be fluent. Rather than use American Sign Language (ASL), most teachers today sign a form of manually coded English, the very thing nineteenth-century educators believed was not enough.[24] Second, this natural language of signs was understood to be of deaf origin; therefore, deaf people were considered the best teachers. Third, this language offered "various modes of expressing their ideas," suggesting a use of idioms and constructions different from those used in English.

As the nineteenth century progressed, hearing educators offered more sophisticated linguistic descriptions of this natural language of signs. As early as 1822 it was described in this way: "Signs and gestures, combined with the endless varieties of the expressions of the eye and countenance, is the native and favourite language of the deaf and dumb."[25] This remarkable characterization acknowledges an important piece of linguistic truth about ASL, namely, that it is not all on the hands. Antebellum educators recognized that expressions of the eye and face were crucial aspects of ASL. This understanding, expressed so readily in 1822, would be dismissed by educators by the end of the century and lost altogether until William Stokoe's study of ASL sparked new investigations of the language in the 1970s.[26] Yet, in the nineteenth century, so well was this principle understood that by 1848, teacher Charles Turner could declare that expression was "an indispensable concomitant to the entire sign language. Should the instructor wish to communicate any idea, the pupil observes his motions, and at the same time watches with close scrutiny every change of expression."[27] Turner continued:

Again, expression not only necessarily accompanies certain signs, but moreover with the same sign a change of expression may essentially modify its signification. . . . Degrees of comparison . . . are appropriately illustrated by grimaces; slight or more strongly marked in proportion to the required quantity. Thus, for example, let the adjective *large* be compared. The process is as follows: Positive, *large*. The sign, accompanied by a slight swelling of the cheeks and a dilation of the eyes. Comparative, *larger*. Cheeks and eyes still further distended. Superlative, *largest*. Cheeks fully inflated and eyes ready to start from their sockets.[28]

Turner clearly proved his point. The natural language of signs indeed possessed "various modes" of expressing concepts similarly found in English.

Antebellum educators also understood that the natural language of signs had a syntax different from English. In the first issue of the *American Annals of the Deaf and Dumb*, the first professional journal of the field, instructor Lucius Woodruff described the language this way:

> Again [the teacher] expresses by signs the phrase *a black hat*, in the inverted or natural order of ideas, by which the object itself as most important is placed before its quality. . . . For example, the shape and size of the hat are portrayed to the eye accompanied with an action significant of its use; and then in addition the finger is laid on the eyebrow, which is the symbol of *black* as a color. This, literally translated in its own order . . . is obviously *hat black*, and without instruction to the contrary the pupil would thus write it. In order to prevent this, the signs are then repeated in the proper order of speech. First the article *A* is given on the hand; next the sign for *black* . . . and lastly the sign for *hat*.[29]

Woodruff went on to indicate that sentences in the natural language of signs followed their own structure. The English sentence "I see a large dog" would be rendered in signs "Dog large I see."[30] As another observer put it, "The general principles which regulate the order [of the sign language] are that those most nearly related be in closest proximity, and that the subject be followed by the signs which qualify it, and then by those which predicate something of it. The predicate may be accompanied with an air of a sign of affirmation or of negation or of uncertainty. . . . The sign language may be considered as nearly in the condition of certain spoken languages which have no verb *to be*."[31] Again, this description reveals a sophisticated understanding of the sign language as a language with its own grammar and syntax. These educators obviously understood that one could utter an ungrammatical sentence in sign; the language had rules of its own. In this way, the natural language of signs explicitly resembled all other languages. Early-nineteenth-century educators recognized that they were involved in bilingual education. They instructed students in the use and mastery of two languages, by requiring them to translate back and forth between them.[32] The natural language of signs was crucial in this work. As one commentator explained, "[The] use of signs . . . in their improved condition, accustoms the pupil to the free and familiar use of a real language . . . and thus . . . forms an excellent preparation for the ready apprehension of a language of words."[33]

Still, educators knew that this would be a slow process. "[This] power of thinking in an order of ideas corresponding to the order of words is to be acquired only by slow degrees—by beginning with short and simple sentences and allowing sufficient time for these to become familiar before proceeding to more complicated modes of expression. In short, in this, as in so many cases, we make the greatest real progress by not hurrying too impatiently at the outset."[34] The New York Institution warned that impatience could lead to the unfair treatment of students. If one wanted to test their knowledge of a subject but asked the questions in English, the test "becomes a double one, involving at the same time a test of their knowledge of the subject at hand and a critical exercise in the use of language."[35] Such an approach could cause students to be "arrested by anxiety" and could "materially . . . embarrass their freedom in expressing their thoughts."[36] It was akin to "examining a class of English pupils in geography through the medium of the French or Latin language, which they had partially acquired."[37] Deaf students could gain much knowledge in "their own language of signs" while their English skills were still limited to fairly simple sentence structures[38]

These references to the language as "their own language of signs" and "the use of signs . . . in their improved condition" need further attention. Educators understood that their students arrived at school with what we in the twenty-first century would call "home signs"; that is, those signs that deaf children in hearing homes create in order to communicate, at least in a rudimentary way, with their families.[39] Nineteenth-century educators generally called them "natural signs," meaning the gestures that nature prompted deaf children to make to communicate.[40] Once a deaf student arrived at school, he found himself, as Thomas Hopkins Gallaudet put it, "among his countrymen [for] they use his native language."[41] At school, he met "many who, in like manner, have constituted their individual languages, but who by common consent, abandon them for the more copious dialect which results from the combination of the whole."[42] The newcomer "makes rapid progress in this natural language of signs, enlarged as it is by culture into greater copiousness, and marked by more precision and accuracy than in those detached families throughout the country in which isolated deaf-mutes exist."[43] Basically, nineteenth-century educators outlined a process of creolization. The natural language of signs, or ASL, emerged from the linguistic crucible of the first residential schools for the deaf that gathered, for the first time, large numbers of deaf Americans together in one place.[44] The result was a language created by and for the deaf, a "visual language of natural signs, manifested by the countenance, and the attitudes, movements, and gestures of the body."[45]

Nineteenth-century educators even ventured to suggest a mechanism that guided the creolization process. One author called it "reduction":

> However accurate originally may be its imitations, however striking its analogies, it invariably undergoes, in the hands of the dumb, a species of abbreviations. . . . By the institution of these abbreviation signs, usually denominated signs of reduction, the language of action becomes singularly elliptical, as well as figurative.[46]

This process of abstraction, of moving signs away from their pantomimic origins, educators perceived, would continue over the course of generations.[47] "That the language of action is capable of being reduced to system and advanced to the perfection of spoken language," this author continued, "is a truth self-evident, at least to those who have been accustomed to its use."[48] Indeed, it was not inconceivable that deaf people, over time, "would add to this a corresponding system of ideographic writing."[49]

Manualists stressed that the process of reduction upon the natural language of signs was not related in any way to the process of methodizing signs, as de l'Epée had done. The sign language was "not reduced . . . to conformity with a language that must be understood before the conformity can be comprehended."[50] Rather, this was a natural process of evolution. The passing of time and the efforts of deaf signers slowly reshaped and cultivated the language. Manualists understood the importance of the residential schools for the deaf in this process, as they were the places where deaf people in large numbers used the language daily. In fact, manualists saw their linguistic role here as nearly as important as their educational role. The founders of the American Asylum declared that they hoped their educational method would spread across the country, for "it is desirable that a uniform system should prevail, that the Deaf and Dumb, who form in some measure a distinct community, should have a common language."[51] This is a truly remarkable statement. We have long known that the Deaf consider themselves a distinct community; it is an understanding that underlies all of Deaf culture. We have not believed that hearing people thought about the deaf in this same way, yet here we see that understanding clearly articulated, and barely eleven years after the opening of the American Asylum.

Given the sophisticated linguistic understanding of the natural language of signs that developed during the antebellum period, a corresponding reconsideration of methodical signs comes as no surprise. These, after all, were recognized as adjuncts to English. Educators never confused using methodical signs with the "free and familiar use of a real language." Accordingly, in 1833, the New York Institution took the bold step of dropping them from use entirely. The natural language of signs and the manual alphabet would henceforth be the only signed systems in use in their school.[52] Both would be used to teach English—which would appear in the classroom now only in written form—and all other academic subjects.

As Laurent Clerc, one of the founding fathers of American deaf education, had brought the methodical signs to the United States, they had quite a pedigree.[53] The New York Institution therefore carefully explained its reasons for dropping them. The methodical signs were an invention of hearing educators and had to be formally taught to the students. While meant to introduce students to English visually, educators now perceived that, "however closely they may imitate the grammatical forms of written languages, they present these forms in a garb no more intelligible to the learner than the alphabetic characters themselves."[54] They really succeeded only in "imposing the task of learning *two* languages instead of one."[55] By using methodical signs, instructors forced deaf students to learn an unfamiliar aural language by using an equally unfamiliar signed version of that language. Why not simply teach the students English with the aid of familiar natural signs?

New York officials held the same linguistic understanding of the natural language of signs as their colleagues. Therefore, they argued that bilingual education could succeed because "this language, like every other, so far as the dictionary of signs extends, admits of direct translation."[56] The methodical signs were a wholly unnecessary step. It was perfectly possible to translate from one real language to another without them. In fact, the New York Institution declared, to say one used the methodical signs to translate the English for the deaf students was "a perversion of the term, if translation be understood in its widest and most important meaning. . . . To translate really is to enunciate the complete sense contained under a given combination of signs, by another combination made up of signs entirely different. When a school boy, by help of his dictionary, renders for each word of a Latin sentence a corresponding English word, without regard to the signification of the author, we do not think of dignifying his performance with the title of translation."[57] In the same way, methodical signs could not be understood to translate anything. Rather than wasting time with them, deaf students should be asked to translate from the natural language of signs to English and back again, in order to gain mastery over both languages.

Methodical signs added nothing to this project of language learning. The whole system of methodical signs had "become unwieldy in its material, and burdensome in its use, retarding the labor of the instructor and seriously impeding the progress of the pupil."[58] The instructors would now rely exclusively on the "colloquial signs."[59] The addition of the description "colloquial" is significant. No longer was the language simply "natural"; the signs were also "colloquial," suggesting that only such natural signs ever found their way into common parlance. In contrast, the deaf community consistently rejected methodical signs for colloquial use. An important charge leveled against them by the New York Institution was that they were "never used in the daily intercourse of the deaf and dumb."[60] They were not merely methodical; now educators called them "artificial."[61] And they no longer wanted their students to use any such artificial signs.

A year later, the school reported its satisfaction with the decision:

> And the board feel happy in being able to state that the results of the instruction communicated since the change took place, have been such as abundantly to satisfy their highest expectations. They are convinced that the employment of the signs used by the deaf and dumb themselves, as a means of explaining and dictating words and sentences is as much superior, in fact, to the use of artificial signs invented by the teacher, as it is more plausible and philosophical in theory.[62]

As the New York Institution's experiment proceeded, other residential schools slowly followed suit. John Burnet, a deaf teacher at the New York Institution, confidently stated that "where their use was once universal, or nearly so, [methodical signs] have been disused wholly in some schools [and] partially in others.[63]

Burnet expressed satisfaction that classrooms at his school no longer saw signs "devised by the teacher to render the language of signs parallel to that of speech."[64] He was fortunate to have entered the profession at a time when deaf teachers were accepted and respected.[65] Their views as native users of the sign language were especially appreciated. Burnet strongly believed that methodical signs were inappropriate for classroom use. He thought it unlikely that the methodical signs would ever be accepted by deaf signers, saying, "[S]ince the best masters of methodic signs have never been able to bring them into colloquial use among their pupils, there must be some principle of repugnance, some antagonism in the mental habits of the deaf and dumb and in the genius of their native language, which opposes this attempt to make a language of one set of elements conform in syntax to a language of a totally diverse set of elements."[66] By his lights, educators, both hearing and deaf, would have to embrace the natural language of signs for residential schools to succeed in their mission to educate the deaf. He therefore offered this advice to his hearing colleagues: "Endeavor, as far as in you lies, to forget words and think only of things; become for the time dumb if you would converse with the dumb."[67]

It would seem that by 1844 and Horace Mann's arrival into the field, manualist educators had outlined both a sophisticated linguistics and a successful pedagogy. Why should Mann, the most prominent educator of his day and a man who had no experience in deaf education, have objected so strongly to this manualist system? Why, in 1844, did he choose to involve himself in this issue? What did he hope to accomplish by using his influence to address the issue of deaf education in his *Seventh Annual Report of the Board of Education* in Massachusetts? And finally, why would he prefer the oral method to the manual?

Jonathan Messerli, in his biography of Horace Mann, offers two clues to understanding Mann's actions in 1844. First, as Messerli views it, Mann intended for the *Seventh Annual Report* to alert Americans to the fact that they were falling behind the Prussians in education. A tour of Prussian schools, undertaken during his honeymoon, inspired Mann's report. In it, he everywhere praised the Prussian system as a model of practicality and efficiency, run by professionally trained teachers and following a systematic curriculum. While not supportive of the political ends that the Prussian system was designed to support, Mann argued that an American system modeled along Prussian lines could use those means toward very different ends, namely, the development of good republican citizens.[68] When Mann complained that American schools lagged behind their Prussian counterparts, he clearly had both hearing and deaf schools in mind; after all, he toured both. And Prussian schools for the deaf followed a strict oral method, which Mann declared to be "decidedly superior" to the system used in American schools.[69]

Second, Messerli suggests that Mann thought of children not as individuals but rather as a mass, as a whole generation in need of education. "There was in this man's mind," Messerli comments, "both the power and compulsion towards an invincible abstractness."[70] It was as the American future in miniature that children needed to be understood and accordingly educated. As such, Mann's educational thinking was directed toward a common school, a program for all American children. As Messerli puts it, this was "a vision of an entire nation going to school" and thereby gaining for itself a common set of values and mores.[71] By acquiring this common culture together in the common school, all republican citizens, rich and poor, deaf and hearing, would be properly equipped to work together to eliminate poverty, crime, ignorance, and disease from their society. Education was the cure for all that ailed America.[72] Deaf people, it appeared, could not be left out of this vision. It was simply not enough for Mann that the deaf were learning to read and write English in their own residential schools. By being educated in separate schools with a different language, deaf people would be left out of the common culture that his common schools promised to create.

Manualists tried to respond, arguing that they, too, strove to bring deaf people into communion with the wider, generally hearing society. They believed that literacy was the key to this inclusion. Manualists knew that fluency in written English was crucial for the deaf, for "this is the only avenue to the various departments of knowledge which books contain, and which must, forever, be inaccessible to the deaf and dumb until they become familiar with the powers and use of letters in their various forms and combinations. This also is necessary even for the purposes of their common intercourse with mankind, most of whom know nothing of the manner in which thoughts can so easily be expressed by signs and gestures."[73] Why was reading and writing English not enough for Mann? Why did the deaf need to *speak* English, above all?

Looking at Mann's ideas about the nature of language, as outlined in his *Second Annual Report*, the reasons for his strong support for oralism become clearer. Mann considered language training an essential part of a child's education because "language is not merely a necessary instrument of civilization, past or prospective, but it is an indispensable condition of our existence as rational beings." As rational beings, Mann argued, we would find that "for all social purposes, thought and expression are dependent each upon the other."[74]

Mann elaborated on this point:

> An unscientific language . . . will keep a people unscientific forever. So the knowledge of a people on any subject cannot far exceed the compass of the language which they fully comprehend . . . language reacts upon the mind that uses it. It is like the garment in which some nations clothe themselves, which shape the very limbs that draw them on. Men are generally very willing to modify or change their opinions and views while they exist in thought merely, but when once formally expressed, the language chosen often becomes the mould of the opinion. The opinion fills the mould but cannot break it and assume a new form. Thus errors of thought and of life originate in impotence of language.[75]

Following this line of reasoning, one can begin to see why Mann would attack the American system of manualist education. The use of the natural language of signs would clearly pose a serious problem for him. The sign language would "react upon the mind that uses it," forming an unbreakable "mould of opinion" and literally "shaping the very limbs that draw [it] on." By using a different language, deaf people would be all too likely to think in that language. Therefore, despite their fluency in written English, they would not truly be living in the same culture as hearing people. The sign language, and not English, would be the garments their minds would wear.

The *Seventh Annual Report* provides still more clues as to why an oral language is to be preferred to a signed one. Mann argued that very few hearing people "have the time, means, or inclination to hold written communication" with their deaf neighbors. But, if the deaf could speak and read lips, hearing people would "converse with them willingly."[76] Mann acknowledged that some deaf people would have to abandon speaking, "on account of being unintelligible," but stressed that if they mastered lipreading, they could at least follow the conversation of hearing people well enough to participate in society.[77] While proponents of the manual method believed widespread literacy was the way to establish social equality between the deaf and the hearing, Mann completely disagreed. "The power of uttering articulate sounds," he wrote, "of speaking as others speak, alone restores [the deaf person] to society."[78]

From Mann's perspective, the manualist faith in a common written language was misplaced; written language was simply not good enough. Mann's own philosophy of language led him to believe that all Americans had to share a common mode of expression. The majority of people spoke English. If deaf people were ever truly to become the equals of hearing people, fully restored to society, they, too, would have to speak. In the social vision of the manualists, both groups accommodated to each other; manualists urged hearing people to learn at least the manual alphabet, while deaf people worked to become fluent in English. In the social vision of the oralists, deaf people would have to do all the accommodating.

Mann was not content merely to make a functionalist argument about the power of speech to restore the deaf to society. He also made a rather remarkable claim. Speech, he wrote, "has an extraordinary humanizing power, the remark having often been made, and with truth, that all the deaf and dumb which have learned to speak have a far more human expression of the eye and countenance than those who have only been taught to write."[79] Speech made deaf people more human in a way that writing, and, one can imagine, signing, did not.

Here Mann's beliefs about language become especially relevant. Recall that he believed that language was part of our existence as "rational beings," and "since thought and expression are dependent each upon the other," the kind of language we use makes us the people we are, as language "moulds our opinions." People who spoke English thought in English. Their thought and expression were inextricably linked together. This union would presumably "react upon the mind" forcefully, and the result would be a more rational and human being. Deaf people, if taught English by the sign language, would forever experience a bifurcation of thought and expression. Teaching the deaf English alone, and especially in its oral form, would essentially make them more human.

Mann died in 1859, so he did not live to see oralism finally triumph over manualism in schools for the deaf.[80] Yet his ideas provided the essential framework for all oralist arguments that would follow. His belief about the humanizing power of speech became a cliché in oralist circles; it would only gain strength as oralists added Darwinian ideas to their study of languages, and as gestures became associated with the behavior of monkeys. As Douglas Baynton puts it, "The value of speech was, for the oralists, akin to the value of being human. To be human was to speak. To sign was to step downward in the scale of being."[81] For oralists, Darwinian linguistics simply offered scientific confirmation of Horace Mann's insight.[82]

Similarly, Mann's belief that speech alone could restore the deaf to society became a favored oralist argument. In 1866, Samuel Gridley Howe argued,

"Speech is essential for human development. Without it full social communion is impossible, since there can be no effectual substitute for it."[83] Other oralists of Howe's generation, such as Frank B. Sanborn and Gardiner G. Hubbard, agreed.[84] By century's end, oralists would so take such arguments for granted that Alexander Graham Bell could state simply in 1884 that to "ask the value of speech is like asking the value of life."[85] Once again, oralists walked the path Horace Mann first laid out.

But, given the strong manualist presence of the antebellum period, why should Mann's ideas have had such an impact? Where were the manualists to counter him? They did, at first. Several articles appeared in the wake of Mann's *Seventh Annual Report*, challenging his conclusions and recommendations.[86] But cracks began to appear in the manualist camp in the 1850s. The *American Annals* published numerous articles about the place of methodical signs in deaf education throughout the decade. Since we already know that methodical signs had been increasingly abandoned after 1833, it seems curious that manualists would belatedly decide to take another look at them. Collins Stone, an instructor at the American Asylum, first published an article on methodical signs in the *Annals*. He recommended their complete abandonment, calling them misleading. Methodical signs "represent the word merely as a certain combination of letters, and not the *idea* which the word conveys."[87] Stone complained that this made them useless in the classroom. He provided the following example:

> Methodical signs are . . . made for the words in the order in which they stand, and the pupil is required to write the sentence, by substituting the word for the sign. What has he gained by the . . . process? It has obviously been to him simply one of translation—not *of course* of ideas, which he comprehends, into words which also have a meaning to him, but it may have been, as far as methodical signs are concerned, a mere substitution of words for signs; and all he knows about either may be that one represents the other. This association may be remembered, and the sentence written with entire accuracy, while the pupil knows as little of its meaning as he does of a Latin or Spanish sentence. . . . The dictation has accomplished a certain result: it has shown the position which the given word, known or unknown as the case may be, holds in the given sentence. It has done no more than this, as in every other sentence the pupil can form, the word may have a different meaning, and require a different place.[88]

Stone also pointed out that English words can have more than one meaning, yet the methodical sign system assigned only one sign per word. Such a system, he argued, left its deaf students at a loss to understand, let alone explain, the meaning of and difference between the phrases "bear in mind," "bear pain," and "bear witness."[89] Stone argued that deaf students should engage in real acts of translation, from the sign language to English, repeatedly, in order truly to master English.

Other educators agreed. "How long," *Annals* editor Luzerne Rae demanded to know, "shall we continue to wrap ourselves in the cast-off garments of European schools!"[90] But not everyone agreed. Educators at the Third Convention of American Instructors of the Deaf and Dumb in 1851 debated the issue. James Brown, the superintendent of the Louisiana Institution, said that he believed deaf people used the sign language too frequently among themselves. "The great thing is to communicate the English language as it is written," he explained. "The best way is not to employ a jargon under the title of a natural language. [I] would not say, City New York, tomorrow, I go,' when meaning to express the idea, 'I shall go to New York tomorrow.'"[91] William Turner from the American Asylum announced himself "surprised to hear the gentleman from Louisiana denounce the language of signs as a 'jargon.'"[92] Indeed, he should have been surprised. Such a linguistic judgment of the sign language would have been unthinkable twenty years earlier. Turner could not have been comforted when Brown hastened to respond that by "jargon" he meant the signs the deaf used themselves and not the methodical signs, which he much preferred.[93]

Brown would find he had supporters. J. A. Jacobs offered his plan for deaf education, calling for "the disuse of colloquial signs" and urging recognition of what he called "the necessity of general signs following the order of the words."[94] Jacobs charged that even residential school graduates tended to "*think in signs*."[95] He was sad to hear it, saying, "[I]t seems to me important to call attention to the fact that as a general thing educated deaf mutes continue to think in signs . . . ; hence the utility and necessity of confining ourselves to the employment of signs following the order of the words, or methodical signs . . . we could not rely upon our pupils thinking in the order of written language, when we used . . . colloquial signs in communicating."[96] Others tried to argue the case for the sign language in the pages of the *Annals*, including Harvey Prindle Peet and John Burnet, but it was clear a new song was being sung.[97] And Horace Mann was calling the tune. He was the first to raise the issue of what language the manually educated deaf would think in. Now, even manualists expressed their own concerns. But these were not the same manualists as Gallaudet and Clerc. These men were actively opposed to oralism and did not think articulation would work. None of these contributors to the *Annals* wrote in favor of the oralist system. But they rejected colloquial signs and favored methodical signs, by which they now meant not so much the whole system as de l'Epée had devised it but a more streamlined style of signs in the order of words. They wanted to ensure that deaf people would think in English, so they wanted to sign to them exclusively in English. These were manualists of a brand-new type, more recently arrived in the profession and clearly influenced by the writings of Horace Mann.

The new manualists were also influenced by something else: the emergence of Deaf culture.[98] By the 1850s, it was clear that deafness was more than a physical condition for the students. Even Luzerne Rae, who rejected methodical signs as "cumbrous and complicated, [serving] no useful purpose whatever," questioned the way the students signed, saying, "I would not have [signs] employed as they now too often are, in such a manner as to reveal, most painfully the monkey element in man. Those contortions of the countenance and of the body in which so many of our pupils indulge, should be prevented in every possible manner, as half ludicrous and half disgusting."[99] Rae was a manualist, but he wanted the students to sign the colloquial signs in a hearing way. He rejected the facial expressions and grimaces that Charles Turner had seen, correctly, as part of the sign language's unique grammar, comparing these expressions to the behavior of monkeys well before Darwin's ideas reached these shores. It was not the descent of man that disturbed Rae but the rise of Deafness.

Oralists commented on this Deafness as well. Samuel Gridley Howe argued, "Certain effects grow out of these infirmities which are undesirable; and the main object in the education of these children, taken as a class, should be to counteract the effect of this infirmity; to prevent it having any influence on the character; to make them just as much as possible like other children."[100] Howe was never more specific than this; he never defined what it was he meant by "certain effects," but clearly something beyond the physical deafness of these children disturbed him. Their deafness was influencing their characters in ways he found undesirable. Like other oralists, he wanted to make the deaf "as much as possible like other children," in other words, as much as possible like hearing children. If they could not physically be made to hear, they could at least be made to behave in culturally appropriate hearing ways. Oralists aimed to eliminate not deafness but Deafness.

A writer who called himself simply "An Extremist" in 1878 would offer more details. The deaf, he complained, exhibited a "spirit of clannishness . . . talking in signs, attending deaf-mute conventions, reading deaf-mute papers, marrying deaf-mutes. Surely this can only be utter perversity or original sin."[101] Even in these unflattering terms, it is obvious that the deaf had formed their own Deaf community, complete with organizations, newspapers, and, of course, a language.

Unfortunately, by the 1870s, even those who called themselves manualists shared this frustration at the existence of the Deaf community. Edward Miner Gallaudet, Thomas's son and a deaf educator in his own right, condemned deaf associations, newspapers, and conventions in the pages of the *Annals* in 1873. He warned the deaf that it was "injurious" to their best interests to consider themselves as "members . . . of a community with its [own] leaders and rulers."[102] If even the president of Gallaudet College spoke against the Deaf community, no wonder an extremist felt free to call the behavior of the Deaf a form of "original sin."

In the world Horace Mann helped to shape, oralists and manualists had come to share certain assumptions. Both sides shared certain cultural beliefs. Both sides viewed Deafness as undesirable. Each offered different ways to prevent it. Oralists suggested banning the sign language completely, while manualists called once again for signs to follow the order of words. Attacked from two fronts, manualists who still believed in the colloquial signs and denied the possibility of "mak[ing] hearing and speaking persons of these deaf mutes,"[103] men like William Turner and Collins Stone, found themselves hopelessly outnumbered. Horace Mann had raised cultural concerns that would increasingly be shared by more people as the century wore on.[104] Oralism would only gain strength and, ultimately, Deaf people would be the losers.

NOTES

1. S. G. Davidson, "The Relation of Language to Mental Development and of Speech to Language Teaching," *Association Review* 1 (1899): 131–32.

2. As one anonymous commentator put it, "The language of signs has peculiar advantages. Not only is it picturesque and expressive, but it can indicate shades and niceties of meaning beyond the power of words" ("Education of the Deaf and Dumb," *American Whig Review* 3 [1846]: 510). See also the *Third Report of the Directors of the Connecticut Asylum for the Education and Instruction of Deaf and Dumb Persons, Exhibited to the Asylum, May 15, 1819* (Hartford: Hudson and Co., 1819), 5–6; the *Sixth Report of*

the Directors of the American Asylum at Hartford for the Education and Instruction of the Deaf and Dumb, Exhibited to the Asylum, May 11, 1822 (Hartford: Hudson and Co., 1822), 4; the *Fifteenth Report of the Directors of the American Asylum at Hartford for the Education and Instruction of the Deaf and Dumb, Exhibited to the Asylum, May 14, 1831* (Hartford: Hudson and Skinner, 1831), 16. All of the reports of the early years of the American Asylum testify repeatedly to this understanding of the sign language.

3. Harlan Lane, *When the Mind Hears: A History of the Deaf* (New York: Random House, 1984), 376; emphasis mine.

4. See Douglas C. Baynton, *Forbidden Signs: American Culture and the Campaign against Sign Language* (Chicago: University of Chicago Press, 1996), 1–10.

5. Another major work of deaf history, John Vickrey Van Cleve and Barry A. Crouch's *A Place of Their Own: Creating the Deaf Community in America* (Washington, D.C.: Gallaudet University Press, 1989), is written with a strong narrative style and offers less of an interpretive framework than Lane's or Baynton's account. Nonetheless, Van Cleve and Crouch, too, dismiss Mann in a sentence, writing simply that "Mann's claims for the effectiveness of oral methods were exaggerated; thus, Mann was ignored" (112).

6. Lane, *When the Mind Hears*, 295; see 295–302 for this interpretation.

7. Baynton, *Forbidden Signs*, 8.

8. See ibid., esp. chap. 5.

9. Samuel Gridley Howe, as quoted in the first hearing of the committee in the appendix of the *Report of the Joint Special Committee of the Legislature of 1867 on the Education of Deaf-Mutes with an Appendix Containing the Evidence, Arguments, Letters, etc., Submitted to the Committee* (Boston: Wright & Potter, 1867), 11.

10. The early issues of the *American Annals of the Deaf*, the profession's first journal, which began publication in 1847, contained articles on the history of deaf education both at home and abroad. Articles included "Memoir on the Origin and Early History of the Art of Instructing the Deaf and Dumb," "Analysis of Bonet's Treatise on the Art of Teaching the Dumb to Speak," "Historical Sketch of the Instruction of the Deaf and Dumb before the Time of De L'Epée," and "History of the American Asylum I and II."

11. For more on the founding of the American Asylum, see Phyllis Valentine's unpublished dissertation, "American Asylum for the Deaf: A First Experiment in Education, 1817–1880" (University of Connecticut, 1993).

12. What nineteenth-century educators called "the natural language of signs" or "the sign language" in the twentieth century would be recognized as American Sign Language, or ASL. I have tried to respect their usage throughout.

13. The manual alphabet was, and is, a system of twenty-six different handshapes, each corresponding to an individual letter of the English alphabet. It should be noted that educators believed that this alphabet offered a way for deaf people to communicate precisely using English words with the same speed as written language. Educators encouraged hearing people to learn it so the deaf would more easily be able to

communicate in society. While not many hearing people would learn to sign, even "A person of common understanding can very soon learn this alphabet, and it affords to all who will bestow the trifling pains which are necessary to acquire it, a ready, easy, sure, and expeditious mode of conversing on all subjects with the deaf and dumb" (*Third Report of the Directors of the Connecticut Asylum,* 7). Manual alphabets vary from country to country. The American alphabet is the same as the French, which is derived from the Spanish, but both are entirely different from the British manual alphabet. The British alphabet is two-handed whereas the others are all one-handed systems.

14. *Third Report of the Directors of the Connecticut Asylum,* 5–8.

15. Samuel L. Mitchell, *A Discourse Pronounced by Request of the Society for Instructing the Deaf and Dumb, at the City Hall in the City of New York, on the 24th Day of March, 1818* (New York: E. Conrad, 1818), 29.

16. Charles-Michel de l'Epée outlined his system in two books, *Institution des sourds et mutes par la voie des signes méthodiques* (Paris: Nyon, 1776) and *La Véritable Manière d'instruire les sourds et muets, confirmée par une longue expérience* (Paris: Nyon, 1784). The latter was translated and published in an English edition by Francis Green in 1802. See Harlan Lane, ed., *The Deaf Experience: Classics in Language and Education* (Cambridge: Harvard University Press, 1984), for an accessible selection of de L'Epée's writings.

17. *Third Report of the Directors of the Connecticut Asylum,* 6.

18. Lane, *When the Mind Hears,* 62.

19. *Fifteenth Annual Report of the Directors of the New York Institution for the Instruction of the Deaf and Dumb for the Year 1833* (n.p., 1834), 24–26; *Twenty-seventh Annual Report of the New York Institution* (n.p., 1845), 35–36.

20. *Third Report of the Directors of the Connecticut Asylum,* 5.

21. Ibid., 5–6.

22. *Fifth Report of the Directors of the American Asylum at Hartford for the Education and Instruction of the Deaf and Dumb, Exhibited to the Asylum, May 12, 1821* (Hartford: Hudson and Co., 1821), 4.

23. Ibid.

24. In fact, teachers today frequently cannot understand the ASL of their students. Leah Hager Cohen relates the story of a deaf student asking if Halloween was a religious holiday. He signed the question correctly in ASL. The teacher, Marcy Rosenbaum, however, did not know the sign RELIGIOUS and shook her head in confusion. He tried to fingerspell for her but was not sure of the correct English and offered R-E-G-I-L-A-R-Y. Cohen concludes, "He shakes his head, dimples set in resignation. Marcy crinkles her eyes in an apologetic smile. The question goes unanswered" (*Train Go Sorry: Inside a Deaf World* [New York: Vintage Books, 1994], 29). Antebellum educators did not want their deaf students to have to master English before they could learn anything else. They would be appalled both at this educational approach and at what they would perceive as unqualified teachers in deaf classrooms.

25. *Sixth Report of the Directors of the American Asylum,* 4.

26. See Baynton, *Forbidden Signs,* esp. chap. 2, "Savages and Deaf Mutes: Species and Race." Oralists, he argues, influenced by Darwinian thought, would come to see the use of facial expression not as carrying critical linguistic information but rather as "a mere vestige of our animal past." By the 1890s, Deaf students were advised not to "grimace" so much, "lest they be accused of 'making a monkey' of themselves" (54). Stokoe's breakthrough study, written with his collaborators Carl Croneberg and Dorothy Casterline, was *A Dictionary of American Sign Language* (Washington, D.C.: Gallaudet College Press, 1965).

27. Charles Turner, "Expression," *American Annals of the Deaf and Dumb* 1 (January 1848): 78.

28. Ibid.

29. Lucius H. Woodruff, "Primary Instruction of the Deaf and Dumb," *American Annals of the Deaf and Dumb* 1 (October 1847): 51–52.

30. Ibid., 52–53.

31. Anonymous, "Education of the Deaf and Dumb," *American Whig Review,* 508.

32. See *Fourteenth Report of the Directors of the American Asylum at Hartford for the Education and Instruction of the Deaf and Dumb, Exhibited to the Asylum, May 8, 1830* (Hartford: Hudson and Skinner, 1830), for more on this process.

33. Ibid., 514. Again, there are still those today who challenge the idea that using ASL is the "free and familiar use of a real language." See Tom Bertling, *A Child Sacrificed to the Deaf Culture* (Wilsonville, Ore.: Kodiak Media Group, 1994). Or consider the fact that deaf education today is not bilingual; most schools use some form of signed English. We have lost this nineteenth-century faith in the power of bilingual education for the deaf and the role of ASL as a language of instruction. Worse, so ignorant are we of this history that today many deaf educators will tell you that bilingual, ASL-based instruction is an "untested experiment" or a "brand new idea."

34. *Thirty-first Annual Report of the New York Institution* (n.p., 1849), 25–26.

35. Ibid., 41–42.

36. Ibid.

37. Ibid., 41.

38. Ibid., 26.

39. For more on home signs, see Harlan Lane, Ben Bahan, and Robert Hoffmeister, *A Journey into the DEAF-WORLD* (San Diego: Dawn Sign Press, 1996), esp. chap. 3.

40. See Thomas Hopkins Gallaudet, "On the Natural Language of Signs; and Its Value and Uses in the Instruction of the Deaf and Dumb—II," *American Annals of the Deaf and Dumb* 1 (January 1848): 93.

41. Thomas Hopkins Gallaudet, "On the Natural Language of Signs; and Its Value and Uses in the Instruction of the Deaf and Dumb—I," *American Annals of the Deaf* 1 (October 1847): 58.

42. *Fifteenth Annual Report of the Directors of the New York Institution,* 24.

43. Gallaudet, "Natural Language—I," 57–58.

44. The perceptions of the early educators support modern accounts by linguists of the origins of ASL. ASL is in essence a language born of the contact of several sign systems. Nineteenth-century educators focused on home signs, but others were present as well. Clerc brought with him to America French Sign Language (Langue des Signes Française, or LSF), which he taught to other instructors. Still today, ASL and LSF are closely related; they contain about 58 percent cognates. And some deaf children arrived at the school with their own sign language, Martha's Vineyard Sign Language. In the nineteenth century, Martha's Vineyard had a high rate of deafness: 1 out of every 155 people, compared to the mainland rate of 1 out of every 5,728. Due to uneven settlement patterns, parts of the island were more deaf than others. About 25 percent of the island town of Chilmark, for instance, was deaf. As a result, both deaf and hearing people on the island knew sign language. When the American Asylum opened, deaf children from the island attended, bringing this sign language with them. For more on the historical development of ASL, see Lane, Bahan, and Hoffmeister, *Journey into the DEAF-WORLD*, chap. 3; Charlotte Baker and Carol Padden, *American Sign Language: A Look at Its History, Structure, and Community* (Silver Spring, Md.: T.J. Publishers, 1978); Nancy Frishberg, "Arbitrariness and Iconicity: Historical Change in American Sign Language," *Language* 51 (1975): 690–719. For more on Martha's Vineyard, see Nora Ellen Groce's *Everyone Here Spoke Sign Language: Hereditary Deafness on Martha's Vineyard* (Cambridge: Harvard University Press, 1985).

45. Gallaudet, "Natural Language—II," 82.

46. Anonymous, "Education of the Deaf and Dumb," *North American Review* (April 1834): 318.

47. This nineteenth-century insight has proven correct. Historical studies of ASL have revealed that signs grow less pantomimic and iconic over time. See Frishberg, "Arbitrariness and Iconicity," 690–719. See also James Woodward, "Historical Bases of American Sign Language," in Patricia Siple, ed., *Understanding Language through Sign Language Research* (New York: Academic Press, 1978). For modern research on the process of reduction, see a recent interview with the linguist Ted Supalla, who argues that ASL users contract signs over time, much as English users developed "don't" for "do not," in "Signs of New Languages," *Rochester Review* (Winter 1999/2000): 32–35.

48. Anonymous, "Education," *North American Review*, 332.

49. Ibid.

50. Ibid., 334.

51. *Twelfth Annual Report of the Directors of the American Asylum at Hartford for the Education and Instruction of the Deaf and Dumb, as Exhibited to the Asylum, May 10, 1828* (Hartford: Hudson and Skinner, 1828), 20.

52. See *Fifteenth Annual Report of the Directors of the New York Institution.*

53. Clerc was still working in the field in 1833; the New York Institution clearly had to tread carefully.

54. *Fifteenth Annual Report of the Directors of the New York Institution*, 26.

55. *Sixteenth Annual Report of the Directors of the New York Institution for the Instruction of the Deaf and Dumb, for the Year 1834* (n.p., 1834), 7.

56. *Fifteenth Annual Report of the Directors of the New York Institution*, 24.

57. Ibid., 26-27.

58. Ibid., 27.

59. *Sixteenth Annual Report of the Directors of the New York Institution*, 7.

60. Ibid., 7. John Burnet, a deaf instructor at the New York Institution, would years later argue a "principle of repugnance, some antagonism in the mental habits of the deaf and dumb and in the genius of their native language," that kept methodical signs from spreading into colloquial use ("The Necessity of Methodical Signs Considered," *American Annals of the Deaf and Dumb* 7 [October 1854]: 5). Modern studies of manually coded English systems, twentieth-century methodical signs, have borne out Burnet's hunch. See Lane, Bahan, and Hoffmeister, *Journey into the DEAF-WORLD*, esp. chaps. 8 and 9.

61. *Sixteenth Annual Report of the Directors of the New York Institution*, 7.

62. Ibid., 7-8.

63. Burnet, "Necessity of Methodical Signs Considered," 1. It is difficult to pinpoint which schools abandoned methodical signs and when. In *When the Mind Hears*, Lane claims that they disappeared entirely in the 1830s (63). In *Forbidden Signs*, Baynton suggests that they were still in use in the 1850s, though he admits that "the precise extent to which they continued to be used is less clear" (204). It would seem clear enough that after the New York Institution's decision, methodical signs slowly fell out of favor and were increasingly abandoned.

64. John Burnet, *Tales of the Deaf and Dumb, with Miscellaneous Poems* (Newark: B. Olds, 1835), 86.

65. In the mid–nineteenth century, nearly half of all teachers of the deaf were deaf themselves (Lane, *When the Mind Hears*, 369). By the turn of the century, that percentage had fallen to 17 percent and would continue to fall (Baynton, *Forbidden Signs*, 60).

66. Burnet, "Necessity of Methodical Signs Considered," 5.

67. Ibid., 17.

68. Jonathan Messerli, *Horace Mann: A Biography* (New York: Alfred A. Knopf, 1972), 407.

69. Horace Mann, "Seventh Annual Report of the Secretary of the Board of Education," *Common School Journal* 6 (March 1, 1844): 75.

70. Messerli, *Horace Mann*, 342.

71. Ibid., 445.

72. See Christopher Lasch's essay "The Common Schools: Horace Mann and the Assault on Imagination," in his book *The Revolt of the Elites and the Betrayal of Democracy* (New York: W. W. Norton and Co., 1995).

73. *Second Annual Report of the Directors of the Connecticut Asylum for the Education and*

Instruction of Deaf and Dumb Persons, Exhibited to the Asylum, May 16, 1818 (Hartford: Hudson and Co., 1818), 5.

74. Horace Mann, *Second Annual Report of the Board of Education Together with the Second Annual Report of the Secretary of the Board* (Boston: Dutton and Wentworth, 1839), 40.

75. Ibid., 43.

76. Horace Mann, *Seventh Annual Report of the Board of Education Together with the Seventh Annual Report of the Secretary of the Board* (Boston: Dutton and Wentworth, 1844), 33.

77. Ibid.

78. Ibid., 52–53.

79. Ibid., 33.

80. By the turn of the century, nearly half of all deaf children were taught without the use of the sign language. By the end of World War I, nearly 80 percent were taught in a pure oral environment, a percentage that would hold steady until the 1970s. See Baynton, *Forbidden Signs*, 5.

81. Baynton, *Forbidden Signs*, 55. See his chapter 2 for more details on the impact of Darwinian theory on oralist educators.

82. Well before late-nineteenth-century oralists began to couch their arguments in explicitly Darwinian terms, as in Joseph Jastrow's piece "The Evolution of Language," which appeared in *Science* in June of 1886 (cited in Baynton's *Forbidden Signs*), 177, n13. Samuel Gridley Howe argued that "pantomime" was a "rudimentary and lower part of language," whereas speech was "the higher and finer part" (*Second Annual Report of the Board of State Charities; to Which Are Added the Reports of the Secretary and the General Agent of the Board, January 1866* (Boston: Wright & Potter, 1866), 53. Howe, as we already know, was a friend of Mann's and intimately familiar with his thinking.

83. Howe, *Second Annual Report of the Board of State Charities*, 53.

84. Both men had been involved with Howe in the effort to open the Clarke School for the Deaf.

85. Alexander Graham Bell, as quoted in *Proceedings of the Fifth National Conference of Principals and Superintendents of Institutions for Deaf-Mutes* (St. Paul: n.p., 1884), 178.

86. Two major responses were published in the months immediately after Mann's report appeared. One was the New York Institution's *Twenty-sixth Annual Report of the New York Institution for the Instruction of the Deaf and Dumb for the Year 1844* (n.p., 1845), and the other was a piece attributed to Harvey Prindle Peet, "Seventh Annual Report of the Secretary of the Massachusetts Board of Education," *North American Review* 59 (October 1844): 329–52. The *Review* had a long-standing interest in deaf education. It published two other major articles, both in favor of the manual method, in 1818 and 1834.

87. Collins Stone, "On the Use of Methodical Signs," *American Annals of the Deaf and Dumb* 4 (April 1852): 188–89.

88. Ibid., 190.

89. Ibid., 191. This was still an issue in the twentieth century, when educators in

the 1970s tried to invent similar systems to code English manually. See Lane, Bahan, and Hoffmeister, *A Journey into the DEAF-WORLD*, 267–78.

90. Luzerne Rae, "On the Proper Use of Signs in the Instruction of the Deaf and Dumb," *American Annals of the Deaf and Dumb* 5 (October 1852): 31.

91. James Brown, as quoted in "Proceedings of the Third Convention of American Instructors of the Deaf and Dumb," *American Annals of the Deaf and Dumb* 6 (October 1853): 12–13.

92. William Turner, quoted in "Proceedings," 20.

93. Brown, quoted in "Proceedings," 20.

94. J. A. Jacobs, "On the Disuse of Colloquial Signs in the Instruction of the Deaf and Dumb, and the Necessity of General Signs Following the Order of Words," *American Annals of the Deaf and Dumb* 7 (January 1855), 69.

95. Ibid., 74.

96. Ibid., 75.

97. See Harvey Prindle Peet, "Words Not Representatives of Signs but of Ideas," *American Annals of the Deaf and Dumb* 11 (January 1859): 1–8; John Burnet, "Colloquial Signs versus Methodical Signs," *American Annals of the Deaf and Dumb* 7 (1855): 133–57.

98. I follow here the well-established convention of using "deaf" to refer to physical deafness and "Deaf" to indicate cultural Deafness. Unfortunately, given space constraints, I am unable here to explore nineteenth-century Deaf culture from a Deaf point of view. See my dissertation, "Words Made Flesh: Nineteenth-Century Deaf Education and the Growth of Deaf Culture" (University of Rochester, 1997), particularly chaps. 5 and 6, for more.

99. Rae, "On the Proper Use of Signs," 29, 23–24.

100. Howe, as quoted in the second hearing of the committee in the appendix of the *Report of the Joint Special Committee*, 32.

101. An Extremist, "Perversity of Mutism," *American Annals of the Deaf and Dumb* 18 (October 1878): 262.

102. Edward Miner Gallaudet, "The American System of Deaf-Mute Instruction—Its Incidental Defects and Their Remedies," *American Annals of the Deaf and Dumb* 13 (September 1868): 168.

103. William Turner, as quoted in the third hearing of the committee in the appendix to the *Report of the Joint Special Committee*, 98.

104. See Baynton, *Forbidden Signs*, esp. chap. 1, for more on oralism's increasing appeal.

3

This Unnatural and Fratricidal Strife

A Family's Negotiation of the Civil War, Deafness, and Independence

Hannah Joyner

Elite families in the antebellum South held a picture of southern identity predicated on both mastery and dependency.[1] A small number of privileged white men were masters. Dependents included African Americans, poor whites, women, and, although not previously discussed by historians of the antebellum period, many people with disabilities. The paradigm of mastery and dependency was thoroughly acted out on the stage of daily life, as is evident in the case of slavery. Although Deaf people in the North also faced discrimination by hearing society, the cultural rhetoric of paternalism and dependency in the South codified a rigid system of oppression and hierarchy that left little room for self-determination for Deaf southerners.

In this essay we see how one elite Deaf man struggled with his own definition of self. Even though he was a man born to the slaveholding class, because of his deafness his family did not bestow on him a birthright of mastery. Instead, they viewed him as a dependent to be protected. What follows is the story of how David Tillinghast recognized his own competency, struggled against the role of dependency, and fought to gain his family's acceptance of his independence. As long as the girdings of slavery held the system of mastery intact, it seemed impossible for David to be recognized by his family as both self-reliant and southern. The upheaval of the Civil War, which fractured the system of mastery, enabled David to force his society to accept his position as an independent Deaf man.[2]

Because of the disruptions and uncertainties of education at southern schools for the Deaf at the outbreak of the Civil War, many southerners who could afford it considered sending their Deaf children to northern institutions, especially those in New York, Philadelphia, and Connecticut. Although many parents had qualms about sending their young children away from home—and especially to schools across enemy lines—during such a crisis, it was often the children's only chance for education during the war years. But elite white southern families who sent their children to northern institutions risked having their Deaf children question the meaning of their southern identities.

Many white southerners were concerned that young Deaf southerners could be duped into believing abolitionist northern rhetoric. Deaf individuals often did not have well-developed bonds with their families. Unlike their hearing counterparts, they had not necessarily absorbed a strong pro-slavery southern identity at their families' hearths. Instead, Deaf children had grown up at state institutions, learning American Sign Language, a language separate from that used by their hearing neighbors and kin. Deaf people were set apart from the hearing South. Because a Deaf person was an "utter stranger to the language in use all around him," the individual was made "an exile in his own land."[3] When loyalty to the white South rose to the height of virtue in the late antebellum period, Deaf educators and Deaf individuals could become tainted with the threat of treason.

In January 1860, the Tillinghast family of North Carolina began to articulate their concerns that young David, already a student at the New York school for the Deaf,[4] would be influenced more by the ideology of his northern teachers and friends than by the perspectives of white southerners. David's hearing sister Sarah Ann wrote to him, "I fear that they will make an abolitionist of you way off so far from your home."[5] The Tillinghasts feared that David's exposure to northern values and perspectives, and perhaps more specifically to the values of his teachers, many of whom were reformers intimately connected to the abolitionist movement, would distance him from his home and his family.

In mid-May of 1861, Sarah Ann wrote a long letter to David telling him she feared for his safety as well as his values. The family had recently sent several letters to David but had not received one reply. "We have been anxiously expecting a letter from you for some time," wrote his sister. Although the Tillinghasts thought the young man was in "no particular danger" and "safe from molestation," they could not "help feeling anxious" because of David's "southern birth." Sarah Ann feared, she wrote, the uncontrolled "mob law of New York," which might do anything to her Deaf brother. After expressing her fears, she again exhorted David to send word: "You must write to us very soon now that letters can come through." Sarah Ann knew that he was not fond of sitting down to his correspondence, but she felt an exchange of letters was more important than ever before. The family wanted to be reassured of both David's safety and his continuing commitment to the South.[6]

Sarah Ann continued her May 1861 letter by sharing the family's Confederate perspective on the mounting tensions between the North and the South. She feared that David's exposure to northern newspapers such as the *New York Herald* and the *Boston Courier* might lead David astray. He believed, she feared, that northerners were acting out of goodness and justice. She assured him it was otherwise: "Have the men of the North become transformed into *devils*; have they lost all sense of decency and *honor?*"[7]

Near the end of the long and angry letter to David, Sarah Ann addressed her brother's unacceptable political views. Although surrounding states had already seceded, North Carolina had not yet severed ties with the United States. "We were quite shocked at your idea of NC standing neutral in the great question," wrote Sarah Ann. "Did you think that we would stand and see our brave brothers north and south V[irginia] and S[outh] C[arolina] suffer in the cause and not fly to their help?" she continued. "Never, never. We will fight with them, bleed with them, die with them ere we submit to a tyrant." Sarah Ann feared that David's northern friends would continue to urge their political views on her brother but hoped that her own viewpoint could be at least as persuasive. She encouraged him to show her letter around the school: "you have my free permission to show this hastily written letter to *any* of *your Republican friends*." Sarah Ann apologized for its careless quality but assured David it was "not hasty as to sentiment but only in execution."[8]

David wrote a careful, controlled letter in response to Sarah Ann's outpouring. He chose not to respond to the majority of her claims. He did write assurances to his family: "You were right in supposing I was safe from any molestation on account of being from the South." He told Sarah Ann that even if he were a secessionist he would be "safe from physical abuse," since his peers never injured anyone regardless of their politics. Three students at the New York school were southerners, and David assured his sister that all of them would be "taken good care of as long as war prevents them from going home." It was "impossible for any one here to molest me unless," David teasingly added, quoting her words, "he should be 'transformed into a devil.'"[9]

David's hearing brother John agreed with Sarah Ann. "I regret to see that your mind is biased so much by your surrounding association," he stated, "tho'

I confess I am little surprised." David's long association with northern reform-ers and abolitionists had prepared some in the family for his resistance to white southern ways. John tried to reason with him: "We of the South consider that the US gov't which was framed for our protection, is now to be used to oppress us and make war on us and our institutions." John continued, "We therefore, as did our fathers of the Revolution under like circumstances, have resolved to withdraw and frame a government for ourselves."[10]

After receiving intense letters from several of his family members, David sus-pected his siblings would hesitate to allow him to remain at the New York school for the duration of the war, especially after he realized how much "spirit . . . animates the South." Nevertheless, he asked his sister her opinion on whether he could "continue as a pupil here next session." He suggested that even after graduation, he would like to remain in the North: "I think I can con-trive to get a situation at the North and stay in it till the war is over."[11]

John soon wrote David that the family hoped he would stay in New York until the academic session ended. He hoped by then that the situation be-tween the Union and the Confederacy would "take a decided change, for bet-ter or worse," and that the Tillinghasts could then decide on the best course for David. The family was committed that he should complete his education "if it can be done." They believed that at the school he was "perfectly safe," despite the poor influences on his character.[12] Brother William reiterated the family's belief in his safety: "I have no fear whatever for your personal safety while you are at the Institution." He did, however, fear that David's return home was impossible for a while: "I should be afraid to have you attempt to come home now while Maryland is filled with troops—many of whom would like nothing better than to maltreat a Carolinian." But the Tillinghasts could not condone David's idea of staying in the North after his graduation. His sister Eliza wrote, "I reckon that Ma and brother William will want you to come home as soon as the session is out. . . . I think when we get you at home we will soon make a good *Southern rights* man of you."[13]

By December, the family had determined to bring David home as soon as possible. They continued to believe that he was safe at the school for the Deaf: "Knowing the kind feelings of the teachers in the Institution toward you, . . . [we] have felt anxious for you only as regards your health and com-fort." Nevertheless, the tumult of war experiences convinced the Tillinghasts that David should be home with them. William arranged for his brother to travel back to North Carolina under the flag of truce. The young man would be able to travel, suggested William, as long as he carried a passport that would "shew that you are a mute." If he did not carry such proof of his deafness, William warned David, he "might be suspected and meet with difficulty" while on his journey.[14] Being Deaf meant David could not, according to hearing Americans, participate in the war effort in any substantial way.

David did not come home in 1861, although no letters exist to explain why. After his graduation in June 1862, his family continued to pressure him to return to North Carolina. He applied for a passport, but his request was denied and he "was told that passes were not granted," as he wrote his brother William. David decided he wanted to stay in New York for a least another year. Although he might "visit . . . next winter," he had determined to "not go home till next year." He confessed that he could have returned home "several times" but was always "kept back" for reasons he did not explain in his letter.[15]

In fact, David had just accepted a three-year appointment as an instructor at the New York Institution. He tried to explain the decision to his family: "I think I had better stay where I can be useful and have employment." At the school he felt appreciated and needed: "Providence seems to me to keep me here that I may do some good to the deaf mutes." At home, he would not have that opportunity. David dreaded the idea of returning to North Carolina. Although he might help support himself and even assist his family there, as his Deaf brother Thomas was doing, he would be constantly reminded that society did not consider Deaf men equal to hearing men. He and Thomas would be kept at home with his sisters—and barred from serving in the Confederate military with their hearing brothers. By staying in New York at the school for the Deaf, David could live as a respected member of his society. He tried to explain to his family the kind of respect he garnered at the institution by telling them of his graduation: "I graduated here under circumstances that would be flattering to your pride if you had seen them. I received a gold medal for excellence in all my studies and exemplary conduct during my whole connection with the school. I was the only person that had such an honor."[16] David did not want to trade that acknowledgment of his talents for the life of a subordinate.

The Tillinghast family members were not willing to acknowledge David's desire to stay in New York. They continued to refer to his decision to stay as a "compelled separation from home and kindred." But brother John did congratulate David that he was in a "situation to gain a comfortable support." John reluctantly admitted that "perhaps it is all for the best" that David had not come home. Perhaps he understood why David wanted to stay, or perhaps

John was thinking only of the privations the family faced as the hostilities between North and South continued.[17] Despite the positive elements John saw in David's situation, the family continued to press David to be loyal to the Confederacy and to encourage him to come home to North Carolina.

As the months passed, the Tillinghasts began to realize that David deliberately missed opportunities to come home. After the receipt of yet another letter from him apologizing for not fulfilling the family's wishes, brother William finally confronted him.[18] Apparently David decided not to respond, since William later wrote that "we . . . never heard from you."[19] He was frustrated with his brother and felt the young man was not trying hard enough to return to the family circle. "We cannot imagine why you should have been refused passports, "wrote William, "when so many people are constantly crossing."[20] He could not understand why the Union authorities had stopped the Deaf young man. His crossing could be no threat, said William: "As you cannot be a soldier and are not a mechanic I can see no reason on earth why you should not come home."[21] The family continued to believe their brother might not be at fault; the Tillinghasts felt David was being brainwashed and tricked by his northern acquaintances. Said William, "We *do* believe that those with whom you are living used every influence and method to prevent your coming," especially since "other people can come whenever they get ready." With great hope, the family wrote David that they would continue to "trust that you have no part or lot in *their* object." William wrote, "They want to *use you* (Yankee like) and prevent your coming to those to whom you naturally would yearn to be with."[22] He was sure that if the principal of the New York Institution had "chosen to interest himself in the matter," David would already be home in North Carolina with the family.[23]

Despite the family's hopes, they were beginning to fear the decision was David's alone. His brother William wrote, "We fear you have not been so anxious to come as we hoped for."[24] Sister Robina echoed William's suspicions: "I hear of truce boats very often; persons are constantly coming, if you would only come we would be so happy."[25] Sarah Ann reiterated Robina's thoughts: "People are constantly coming and going—and we can't see why it is that you can't come too."[26]

In the autumn of 1862, David's mother died. The family was "almost thankful" that she was now in "a better country," no longer suffering "the sorrow and anguish" of the "horrid war" that disrupted her earthly country. John wrote David that because he was "detained" in New York, David was "cut off from the opportunity of meeting our dear mother once more."[27] Guilt, however, did not induce David to come south after his mother's death.

The Tillinghasts then tried to persuade David that his Deaf brother Thomas, living at home in North Carolina, needed his companionship. William told him that Thomas had a great deal of work and professional responsibility in his envelope business but that he was lonely, with no Deaf companions nearby. "Thomas would be delighted to have you with him," wrote William. "It would be such a comfort to him to have you here."[28] Unlike some of the hearing Tillinghast family members, David signed fluently and understood the experiences and perspectives of a Deaf person. The two Deaf brothers had always been close, and the family sought to exploit that closeness and identification to bring David back to North Carolina.[29] The first attempt did not work. Soon, sister Robina intensified the family effort: "Brother Tom is very poorly. He has had several attacks of asthma this winter," she wrote, "one quite lately from which he has not recovered. He looks pale and thin." She begged, "I wish you were here on his account. . . . It would be such a comfort to him to have you with him."[30] A few months later, William supported Robina's claims. "Thomas has had several attacks of asthma within the last year," he wrote. "He often wishes you were here." William added that David could earn much more working with Thomas in the envelope business than he could teaching at the institution.[31] David was not convinced. By the middle of 1863, Sarah Ann was more plaintive in her request: "Tom wants you," she wrote. "He needs your company."[32]

The family continued to worry about David's political commitments in addition to his geographical location. At first they denied they felt such concerns: "We trust that from your long residence among them [northerners] will not come one shred of sympathy for any of the accursed notions."[33] The family's denials merely proved to David that they did worry. Perhaps the most disturbing to the Tillinghasts of David's attitudes were his pro-abolitionist statements. In letters to the young man, the family vehemently defended the system of slavery and viciously attacked the motives of northern abolitionists and emancipators. William argued that the Emancipation Proclamation was "surely the most ridiculous production of modern times," since Lincoln had no authority in the Confederacy. Further, he argued, freedom would ruin the lives of the slaves themselves. Hundreds of African Americans had left "homes of plenty" and exchanged their lives as slaves for "a life of penury." This exchange had been "entailed upon them" by Union soldiers who encouraged them to leave plantation life. "Poor misguided wretches," William lamented, "who in their ignorance think freedom and Yankeedom better than their homes and friends and plenty to eat and wear, plenty of wood and everything necessary to their comfort!" Slaves, he claimed, worked "not half so hard" as free Blacks, whom he labeled "the most *debased* and degraded of our population." William confronted David, "You know yourself that a free negro is not considered nearly as respectable" as the slave of an elite white family.[34]

Early in the war, the Tillinghast family began to experience economic shortages and the disadvantages of the Union blockade of the Confederacy. "We now find that many things which were once thought indispensable were mere luxuries and that we can not only do without them," wrote William, "but are really better without them." Without the trade from Europe, the elite of the South were reduced from imported high fashion to clothes they could make themselves. William said, "I think our Girls look prettier in their Homespun dresses than they ever did before."[35] As soon as William told his brother about the deaths and the many shortages, he realized that in order to encourage David to return home, he needed to reassure the young man that the Confederacy was not truly suffering and not giving up hope. "I understand the Northern people think we are almost in a state of starvation here," noted William. "They are mistaken."[36]

Sarah Ann reaffirmed to David, "Don't let them persuade you that you will starve here. People look as fat and well as ever and every thing goes on very smoothly in spite of the falsehood that the Yankee papers are constantly publishing to inflame the minds of the populace against the South."[37] The South would not starve, she assured him, as long as the rich southern soil continued to give to them: "As to our starving there's no danger of that I assure you—we have out of our garden peas, beans, lettuce, turnips, onions, cabbage, and will soon have plenty of potatoes and root vegetables; we try our potatoes today for the first time." She summarized that "our garden is very fine indeed."[38]

Southerners continued to have faith in the Confederacy's military prowess: "*As a people* we are now *confident* of the success of our cause," wrote William. "Our troops are now all veterans and they have beaten the Yankees so often that they feel perfect confidence in their ability to do so whenever they have any thing approaching to equal terms."[39] Sarah Ann suggested reasons the Union would fail: "The fact is their *cause* is a bad one, and they *can't fight well* when their *cause* is not one that calls forth every spark of bravery and patriotism existing in their natures." Nevertheless, the Union bragged about their successes. "Great goodness! How the Yankee papers can *lie,*" wrote David's sister. "I think from their abominable lying about everything that they must have given up all hope of conquering us. The very idea of the cowardly wretches conquering us is ridiculous."[40]

Immediately after writing David a vitriolic account of Yankee aggression and degradation, Sarah Ann yet again told him that she and the family continued to "hope and hope that you will manage to come home this summer. . . . Please do try to come this summer." In addition to missing her brother, Sarah Ann felt the family's honor was tainted by David's absence and the infrequency of his letters home: "We are tired of telling people how long it is since we heard from you."[41] All were bothered by not only his absence but his associations. Even Tom's Deaf friend Hart Chamberlayne asked, "What has become of your brother David? Is he still in Lincolndom?"[42]

In early June 1863, the Tillinghasts received a long-awaited letter from David. "*Everybody* was pleased to hear from you," wrote Sarah Ann.[43] David's Deaf brother Tom agreed: "I was very much relieved by hearing that you were still safe and well. It has been about *8 months* since we heard from you. You can imagine how anxious we were to hear from you." It is unclear if David had not written or if his letters had not been delivered because of the pandemonium of war. Tom told David, "You spoke of having written two letters to us. If they were not the same letters we read last summer, we have never got them."[44]

After upbraiding their brother for not having written more regularly, the Tillinghasts rejoiced that he was finally planning to come home. Everyone in the community, wrote Sarah, was excited to know that her brother would return to them.[45] Tom echoed the family's deep desire to see David again: "Be sure to come home as soon as possible. We cannot endure the idea of you staying away from home any longer."[46] Brother William, however, was still convinced that somehow David would manage not to come home after all. "I think if you will try in the *right way* you can get a passport to come home," wrote an impatient William. He gave David explicit instructions: "Write to the sec'y of war. Tell him you are a deaf mute," counseled William. "Tell him that you have no trade i.e. you are not a mechanic who can make munitions of war or anything of the kind, and that being a mute you are not capable of being a soldier." He hoped to convince the officer that David could not be a threat because his Deaf status rendered him less than a man. Finally, William urged David to further manipulate the officer's sense of pity: "Tell him that you have lost both your Father and Mother." William was certain that this portrayal of the situation, complete with a certification by the New

York institution's superintendent that the statements were true, would leave no room for rejection by the secretary of war: "I can see no reason why you should not be permitted to come home."[47] David must have felt uneasy about William's portrayal of his dependent status.

Sarah Ann began to prepare David for his return. She suggested that he bring "plenty of clothes, shirts, coats, pants etc." because all were unavailable in the Confederacy—unless they were smuggled goods, transported illegally across the northern blockade at "an immense risk" and therefore at "enormous prices." Because of this shortage, the Tillinghasts all wore clothes made from homespun, of which Sarah enclosed a sample. Wearing homespun clothes was a point of Confederate pride, showing that southerners were not dependent on "Yankee goods and notions."[48] The Tillinghasts were "living in comfort," and despite being deprived of many things, they "seldom miss[ed] them," according to William. "So much for having a resolute purpose. We are willing to *suffer* if need be" for the sake of the Confederacy.[49]

Inflation had hit the South hard. As Tom confirmed, "I must tell you that every thing here is very high." He added, "I hope you will come home safely. . . . I trust God will protect you from all danger and attend to your safety in coming home."[50] Like his family members, Tom wrote his brother that he was sick of the war: "O! I wish to Heaven that we had no war. It is a great calamity that has inflicted upon this country but I trust to God whose almighty hand will alone stay the progress of the war."[51]

Unlike his hearing sisters and brothers, however, Tom asked David about his work experiences and shared his own. He wrote David that he was "glad to hear that you have been doing well in teaching," and he hoped that after the public examination of his pupils, David would "receive much credit for it." His own work making envelopes, begun in July 1862, kept Tom "busy" and "doing very well." He claimed he was "very fortunate to have been engaged in such business for it is very profitable." Despite his claims to love his work, Tom added at the end of his letter that he was considering "going to the mountains" in order to "refresh" himself, as he was "considerably broken down by being engaged in making the envelopes." He then tantalized his brother with a promise: "When you come home, I will tell you about my other business."[52] Tom continued his letter with family news. The boys' younger brother Walter was still "rather small for his age" and "still retains the looks of a baby." The boy had "improved much in the art of talking to me in the finger language," said Tom, "though not very rapid[ly]."[53]

In 1863, David wrote his family about his work experiences at the New

York school. Although the institution helped create his belief in himself as an independent man, examples of institutional discrimination against the Deaf are all too clear. The year before, David had taught a class of fourth-year students, working "hard to get knowledge into about twenty heads,"[54] and now he had followed his pupils to the fifth grade. He noted his exceptional position: "It is flattering to my vanity to confide such a class to my care," wrote David, "considering that it has been regarded many years unsafe and unwise to trust a class more than thrice years old with a deaf mute teacher." He continued, "I shall try to justify the confidence evinced by the principal in my abilities as a teacher." Although he was flattered that the institution recognized his abilities enough to place him in charge of such an advanced grade, the school's traditional policy of not hiring Deaf teachers for such jobs rankled David.[55]

He was also frustrated with the pay scale at the institution: "I confess that I am not satisfied with the compensation for my services," he wrote his brother. "Several teachers who evidently do considerably less good than I do receive a larger salary than me." One new teacher, "a speaking young man," who taught an elementary class, was paid over one hundred dollars per year more than David. David was irked by such an imbalance: "There is a great disparity between the salaries of deaf mute teachers and those of teachers who hear." The institution suggested that the reason for the different pay scales was the ease of recruiting young Deaf teachers and the difficulty obtaining "speaking teachers of education without the inducement of good remuneration." David did not find the "alleged reason" at all convincing.[56] Instead, he found it to be straightforward discrimination. His irritation mounted: "They here pay speaking teachers about thrice more than deaf mutes," he told Robina. He continued fiercely, "I do not intend to sit down tamely under such injustice."[57]

At the same time that David was contemplating such matters, he received a letter from a former classmate who chafed against one of the paternalistic restrictions of the institution: "The members of the H[igh] C[lass] were to my recollection, not allowed to take a sail [boat] or play with a football, for the reason of the rules of Dr. Peet," who was the chief officer of the institution. Harvey Peet feared for the students' safety, David's friend said. The young man wrote, "I think the restrictions were not right. . . . The members of the HC should have the privilege of enjoying the sailing in the river and kicking the football." David was beginning to feel that teaching required more dedication than he sometimes had. "Teaching the deaf mutes is not always pleasant," he explained. "One of the requisites in a teacher of the Deaf and Dumb is an ample stock of patience."[58]

In July 1863, the Tillinghasts again tried to persuade David to return to his southern home. His brother John, at William's request, wrote to the United States secretary of war on David's behalf, requesting that the young man be given a pass to come home and that the pass be delivered to David in New York. He told David that when he reached the border of the Confederacy he should hand over the pass and request passage aboard a flag-of-truce boat.[59] Yet, despite all the efforts of the family, David did not come home in 1863. William told him in August that he had not written recently because he assumed the young man would be traveling home by the time the letter arrived in New York. When David did not arrive in North Carolina, William understood that yet again David's trip was postponed.[60]

What David had failed to do was get certification of his deafness by the head of the New York school for the Deaf to accompany the letter to the secretary of war. William was sure that if the institutional superintendent would assist him in his plans, there would be "no difficulty" in coming home.[61] But David seemed unwilling to go to Dr. Peet. He would not have embraced the idea of showing his employer and mentor, who he felt discriminated against him, that his family considered him somehow less than a man—mute, unskilled, unable to become a soldier, orphaned. David would not have accepted that his deafness, which he considered a core part of his identity and in no way pitiable, could be used in such a negative way. He rejected his family's view of him as a dependent. His pride and perhaps even his southern honor made him refuse to be cast as helpless and powerless. David implied that the secretary of war had refused him and told his family that he would not return home at least until the Civil War ended.[62]

Despite his decision, David confessed that he missed his family and his home. He wrote his brother, "It has sometimes saddened me to think that I was absent from home at times when I might be very happy there."[63] His brother suggested that David might make a living at home, teaching at a southern institution, and reminded him that there were many Deaf children in the South whom he could instruct. David replied, "I have thought of it and wished to be in the N[orth] C[arolina] Institution at Raleigh." He confessed to his family: "Long before the war and when I was at school I had a dream of what I should do when I left school—It was to establish a small school for deaf and dumb sons of rich parents in the south." His plans fell through in the early 1860s when, "alas, war came" to his home region. "I am here far from the place where my imagination located my school," he ended his letter.[64] Coming home was in David's plans, if he could have fulfilling and respected employment. But as long as southern institutions were floundering in the turmoil of war, no opportunities emerged for David to return on his own terms.

Between his frustration with his employment at the New York school for the Deaf and his unwillingness to go home to the South, David began to consider other job opportunities. He "decided on a course" for his new life: during the institution's summer vacation, he would move upstate to work on a farm. "If I should find it suits my taste and capacity to learn the business of farming," David wrote home, "I shall give up teaching." Farming could pay more than teaching at the school for the Deaf, he believed. David knew that if he could "perfect his knowledge of farming," he could borrow money from "some rich friends" and buy a farm of his own, possibly in New York. After he was installed on his own land, he wrote, he would work to pay back the money he had borrowed to buy farmland.[65]

When William received news of David's plan, he wrote him that he "did not approve" of his brother's "scheme." William warned his brother: "You would be considered a laborer and required to *work hard while well* and be expected to care for yourself or be taken care of by your friends if taken sick." He continued that he would "not be likely to find *friends* who would be kind to you and take care of you in case of sickness." William understood that a job on a rural farm would almost certainly isolate David from the Deaf community. But he also felt that David needed the paternalistic care of the hearing administrators of the Deaf institution, despite David's age. "I think your farming plan Utopian," he concluded.[66] Perhaps the hearing members of the Tillinghast family were upset by David's plans to establish a small farm because such a position would remove him both from the family's protection and from their social class. If he owned a plot that he farmed himself, he would be abandoning his family's elite status to become a simple yeoman. His family may well have been disturbed that the young man would trade his standing in the community for his personal independence. William strongly encouraged David to remain at the institution rather than move to a country farm. "You have abundance for all your personal wants and a pleasant position," counseled William. "That, under the present times, is a great boon." He seemed peeved that his Deaf brother complained about the unfairness of his situation. Perhaps thinking of his own difficult situation in the war-torn Confederacy, William continued, "When you learn to know life and *this world* better you will find that [unfairness] is as much as it gives any of us."[67]

David understood his family's desire to see him: "I sympathize with you in your wish that I should go home next summer," he told his sister Robina.[68] In June 1864, David apparently agreed to come for a short visit. Family members asked David to bring with him goods hard to procure in the Confederacy. Tom and Eliza requested such goods as linen tape, a comb, and black shoestrings.[69] As they had before, the Tillinghasts warned him of the changes that had occurred in the South and to his family during his absence. They no longer had access to much meat, so they hoped their brother was "fond of vegetables," as these were the family's "principal food." Tom was the family gardener, and he grew the majority of what the family ate. He had, according to William, "some delicious muskmelons to regale you with." But, William warned David, he would have to "bid goodbye to beef-mutton and butter." The Tillinghasts had milk and bread, said William, "and sorghum syrup," which he claimed was "much better than West India Molasses."[70] The losses the family faced were not primarily culinary, however. William cautioned David that he would see "many sad changes" and "miss many once-familiar faces." Even though the Tillinghast home would look so changed to David, William told him, "I trust you will find it still a happy one and feel that it is really *home*." He was not only thinking about the family land and house; William was concerned that David did not believe the South was his homeland.[71] Once again, when the time came, David did not visit his family in North Carolina.[72]

One month before Robert E. Lee's surrender to Union forces at Appomattox, General William Tecumseh Sherman moved through North Carolina and occupied the Tillinghast's hometown. Sarah Ann felt violated and tried to express her fury to David in a letter written the day after the Union army's invasion of their house. After ransacking neighbors' houses and "impressing" all the alcoholic spirits they found there, Sherman's "foraging parties" were wild by the time they reached the Tillinghast's home. The girls were afraid of the drunk soldiers and locked themselves in their room. But when the men threatened to "break the door down," the girls agreed to open it. One of the soldiers opened Sarah's writing desk and began to read one of her letters. The drunk men took control of the family's food supplies, leaving them "entirely dependent" on the "enemies' commissariat." Sarah Ann begged to retain the family cow so that she could prevent the youngest Tillinghasts from starving. The experience of defeat left her feeling broken and vulnerable. The whole family had "excitement and trouble in our hearts." As Sarah stated, "We tried to treat [the soldiers] politely, but were we to live a million years the 11th of March will be one of the darkest spots in our memories."[73] The Tillinghasts were personally vanquished by Sherman's army. With the ruins of their country all around them, the family was, as Sarah wrote, "dependent upon the *charity* of our enemy." Their provisions for the year were raided by the Union soldiers and they had no money—except "a little Confederate, which is no more than waste paper now."[74]

Despite their defeat, the Tillinghasts remained defiant. In her letter detailing Sherman's invasion of the family home, Sarah Ann continued to refer to southern whites as "the just."[75] That emotion, however, was only the beginning of the anger expressed by her and her sisters. "I tell you as *upon oath*, 'the truth, the whole truth, and nothing but the truth,'" insisted Sarah in a letter to David six weeks after Sherman's army had visited their home: "The South is *not whipped*—it is overwhelmed, and by *brute* force." The Union army had fought unjustly: "Had the Yankees carried on the war by the rules of warfare, we would have been successful. Our men have *never* been whipped on a *fair field*." The Union army had traveled throughout the Confederacy, tearing down mills and burning farm equipment, explained Sarah Ann. This destruction was "*mean*" and "*low*." She concluded, "We are not *humiliated* that our army . . . had to surrender." She admitted that the Confederate army had been "completely overwhelmed by an immense army of well-fed, well-equipped men" but reminded David that they had been nobly "resisting, to the bitter end, the aggressions of the tyrant." She continued, "*No*, we are as *proudly defiant* as ever. We can *hate* them and we will hate them forever. We had *a right* to be governed as we pleased. We only asked to be left alone." The Union, led by "that scab upon humanity, Lincoln," lied constantly about the white South, claimed Sarah Ann. She concluded, "Such a pack of falsehoods are enough to make Satan grin with delight."[76]

Sarah Ann recognized that David might be stunned by her violent rhetoric: "You think I am *needlessly bitter*," she defended herself, "but, oh my brother, if you knew what we have suffered in the cause of our Precious Country you would not wonder." She continued, "Our beautiful 'sunny land' is ruined. We have lost everything but our homes, and poor North Carolina . . . has almost lost that." She struggled with the connection between the state's great loss and her own identity: "Were it not for the noble blood that has been so freely shed on every battle field I would be ashamed that I was born a North Carolinian." Family and friends had been killed, along with many more countrymen. She could see that a "river of blood" would "flow forever" between the South and its foe. The dead had been "laid upon the altar of our country. *Our country!*" She mourned its death. Sarah vowed never to forgive the North's hateful actions: "Until they cut a canal to the waters of oblivion and deluge our land with Forgetfulness, we can never consider a Yankee anything but an oppressor and an enemy." She continued, "I hate the nation from the bottom of my soul, even as I hate Satan, and all things low, mean, and hateful." Sarah promised David that "the sun [would] rise yet upon the retribution of Heaven upon the Yankee nation." She understood that God was then punishing the South yet also swore that "as there is justice in Heaven, the Yankees will get theirs in due time."[77]

Sarah Ann, in order to prove to David that her anger was "not personal," told her brother the story of "poor crippled Jim." The man who had "not walked a step in years" could not follow the Union soldiers off the Tillinghast plantation as did most of the other slaves. Before "Sherman's robbers" left, they stripped Jim of his socks and shoes and removed a small knife from his pants pocket. Seeing how the Yankees treated a disabled slave whom she deemed pitiable verified in Sarah's mind how truly evil the Union soldiers were. Still, she wrote, white southerners could not give up hope for a new nation: "Were it not for hope in the future," wrote Sarah, "I would rather that the last brother I have in the world was in his grave. I would far prefer seeing the last one buried than be sure that they were to live victims of Yankee tyranny and taxed to the utmost to pay the debt contracted by Yankeedom." Yankees, she tried to convince David, were the kind of people who "murder their kindred" and "insult their sisters."[78]

Sarah ended her letter to David with a plea: "Come to us as soon as you can, and come with a heart full of love to your country," she begged, "your country that your mother's last efforts, last thoughts, and last prayers were for—your country that your father loved, honored, and hoped for." She reminded her brother, "Your country! that your kindred have laid down so many lives for, that your sisters have worked and prayed for." She was tired of David's opposition to the Confederacy and felt certain that when he was home with the family he would begin to feel as they did.[79]

In early June 1865, David's sister Eliza echoed Sarah's defense of the Confederacy and attack on the North. The family had recently received a letter from David and were yet again horrified, but "not at all surprised," by his abolitionist politics: "we all expected that your opinions would be just what they are," she wrote to him. David, they feared, empathized with the argument that all people, including African Americans, deserved self-determination. "I am very sorry that we should differ so widely," lamented Eliza. Nevertheless, she knew that he had received a very different education from her own and had not lived among slaves and slave owners for many years. The North Carolina Tillinghasts "had daily intercourse with the negroes," said Eliza. Therefore, she argued, they had "the best opportunity of knowing the falseness of the abolition theory." The Tillinghasts had by that point been abandoned by all but one of their former slaves: "Granny . . . will not desert us as long as she lives," claimed Eliza, because the Tillinghast family had "always treated her with more kindness" than her own children had. "If she had not been a slave, she would probably die in neglect and want," Eliza wrote, "but we will take care of her as long as she lives, and divide our last crumb with her." Eliza claimed that Granny was "now and always . . . as free as any laboring woman could be." In Eliza's mind, Granny loved all of the Tillinghasts "more than she [did] her own children."[80]

Eliza explained the desertion of all the other Tillinghast slaves by arguing that they had been duped by seductive promises by disingenuous Union soldiers. She herself felt that "the abolition of slavery has been the most inhuman" Yankee atrocity committed during the Civil War. Although she knew that David would disagree with her, she tried to convince him that if he knew the truth, he would see things from her perspective. "You have been kept in ignorance of many things by the falsehoods Northern papers are filled with," she wrote. If only he could "see the horrors that are enacted among the *freed* negroes," she told him, "you would think the negroes were better off in slavery." As slaves, argued Eliza, African Americans were well fed and "cared for and nursed by their mistresses." Without masters, she said, the ex-slaves were "dying by the thousands with no one to look after them. I *know* this to be true."[81]

Eliza gave David accounts of several former slaves, "crazy like the rest with the idea of freedom," who had lost their families and had no employment. Eventually, all of them had been forced to return to their masters and had begged to be taken in by them again. She had heard unbearable accounts of "suffering and cruelty" by Union soldiers to the ex-slaves and claimed that even "the most inhuman masters in the South (and such I think were rare) never practiced such punishments as are inflicted on refractory negroes by the US officers." Even if the soldiers had treated them with respect, there was too little food and not nearly enough opportunity for employment for able-bodied and hard-working African Americans. "God only knows what is to become of the poor wretches, the old, infirm, and helpless, who have been deprived of their protectors," she continued. Under the system of slavery, she claimed, "the young, old, and helpless," as well as the sick, were cared for. Under the capitalist system practiced in the North and in England, she added, such dependents had nothing.[82]

Eliza believed that slavery was a morally just institution, allowed by both the Old and New Testaments and "instituted by God." As she reminded her rebellious brother, "I have been taught opinions by my intelligent and Christian parents with the Bible in my hands." In contrast, she argued, David had come to his own beliefs about slavery with only the evidence of "lying newspapers and by friends who, however good and sincere, know nothing of the institution of slavery." The reporters did not understand the abolition of slavery to be, according to Eliza, "a curse to the negro more than to the master" or understand that liberation would eventually lead to the "extermination of the negro." White southerners did not believe that abolitionists were truly sympathetic with slaves. They were motivated by "hatred and jealousy of the masters," argued Eliza, "not love for the slave."[83]

By the end of the Civil War, the Yankees had "enslaved their Southern [white] brethren" even as they had tried to "free (?) and annihilate the negroes," wrote Eliza. But the Confederacy was not trying to preserve slavery, she claimed: they had "fought not for slavery but for freedom, for our rights as states, for republican governments." The Union would not grant this "freedom" to the white South; federal troops had put down the Confederate protest violently. Because of the repression of southern independence, argued Eliza, the country had become "nothing more than a great military despotism."[84]

Eliza knew that despite her arguments and anger, David was committed to his abolitionist beliefs. "I am aware that nothing I can say will overturn the opinions which you have been forming for years," she wrote to him, "but I hope when you come home and see for yourself, you will in time change your mind." Only residence among them, and isolation from his reformist community in New York, would make David a "true southerner" again. She missed her brother: her heart had been yearning for him more than five years. David's family had grown older, but it was not only the years that had aged them. They were "sadly changed" and "altered" by the "sorrow and care" that turned them "from happy careless children" to adults who had "felt the realities of life." The Civil War had been a punishment, Eliza began to think, for the antebellum South's "boastfulness and self-confidence." She knew the privileged life the Tillinghasts had experienced before the war had now ended: "I never expect to be as happy again as I was in my childhood," she wrote. She anticipated "struggling with poverty to the end of my days."

Eliza continued, "But this world is not made for happiness, and I can be contented, knowing that it is through much tribulation that we must enter into the kingdom of heaven."[85]

William sympathized with his sisters' feelings about David's abolitionist leanings: "The injustice which has caused such shedding of blood, and the vandal-like barbarity with which the war was waged by northern troops," he said, "has caused a hatred towards the 'Yankees' wide and deep." He warned that the hatred would "*last* until the children now living and to be born of all the women now old enough to remember this war shall have died." He knew that "whatever government we may live under, henceforth the northern and southern people will be distinct peoples." Nevertheless, William felt responsible for the solidarity of the family—and specifically responsible for his Deaf brothers. He knew he could not allow David to be estranged from the rest of the family yet feared that David's opinions would cause just such a division. He advised his brother to stay silent about his beliefs. "When you write again," said William, "say nothing about political beliefs. It can do no good to talk about things which are now settled and fixed facts." William recognized that his sisters did not have the cool head that he himself did: "The girls feel so deeply that it only hurts their feelings," William told David, "and in some measure *alienates* their affections." He concluded, "You may see it is best to let the matter drop." Once again he begged his brother to return to them, at least for a visit, and tried to put a brave face on the destruction of their homeland.[86]

David responded that he would come for a visit as soon as the school session was out: "Only three weeks are between me and you." He intended to fill his trunk with all the goods impossible to get in the South and looked forward to his homecoming as provider.[87] Sarah Ann urged David to bring whatever he could to help his brother and sisters: "If you have any money bring it or lay it our way in any way that you think will benefit us most."[88] The hearing Tillinghasts had always imagined David as a dependent member, but now he could be a support to the family. Now David would prove he was far from dependent. Although William tried to assure David he need not bring home all his money for the family, he made long lists of goods the family required that they could not obtain in the devastated southern states.[89]

After five years away from his brothers and sisters, David finally came home. He came home a self-reliant man on whom his family must depend. He visited them for the summer of 1865. When North Carolina's financial situation precluded him from finding high-paying employment in the region, David returned to his teaching job in New York and regularly sent money to Tom for his Deaf brother to distribute to the family.[90] David and Thomas began a vineyard in North Carolina, eventually employing their hearing brother Willard to communicate with illiterate clients who could not pass notes with the Deaf brothers. The profits of the vineyard, Thomas hoped, would allow the two Deaf brothers to "lighten the weight" on eldest brother William and "relieve" the family "from their pecuniary difficulties."[91]

David Tillinghast returned to the South on his own terms, as a proud and independent man commanding the respect of his family. In 1868 he moved back to North Carolina as a teacher at the North Carolina school for the Deaf, bringing with him a Deaf wife whom he had met at the New York school. In 1874, Thomas joined David as a teacher at the North Carolina school. David procured employment there for at least two of their hearing siblings. In the generations that followed, many members of the Tillinghast clan, both hearing and Deaf, became teachers in Deaf schools throughout the country and the world.[92]

David's goal was not the destruction of his family's position within the Old South hierarchy, nor was it the destruction of the hierarchy itself.[93] His goal was personal: he wanted respect and a self-supporting life. To achieve such a goal required a rupture in his family's definition of a southerner. The Civil War cracked the wall of the Old South's ideology of mastery and dominance. Such fissures allowed (to differing degrees) groups of dependents—former slaves, women, and poor whites—to create new spaces for themselves as independent southerners. The story of David Tillinghast demonstrates that the Civil War also created opportunities for some people with disabilities.

NOTES

1. The title for this chapter is quoted in part from the *Biennial Report of the Kentucky Institute for the Education of the Deaf and Dumb* (Frankfort Ky.: J. B. Major, State Printer, 1861), 9.

2. The literature on southern mastery and the culture of honor undergirds the argument of this essay. See, especially, Drew Gilpen Faust, *James Henry Hammond and the Old South: A Design for Mastery* (Baton Rouge: Louisiana State University Press, 1982); Stephanie McCurry, *Masters of Small Worlds: Yeoman Households, Gender Relations, and the Political Culture of the Antebellum South Carolina Low Country* (New York: Oxford University Press, 1995); Peter Bardaglio, *Reconstructing the Household: Families, Sex, and Law in the Nineteenth-Century South* (Chapel Hill: University of North Carolina Press,

Hannah Joyner

1995); Bertram Wyatt-Brown, *Southern Honor: Ethics and Behavior in the Old South* (New York: Oxford University Press, 1981); Kenneth S. Greenberg, *Honor and Slavery: Lies, Duels, Noses, Masks, Dressing as a Woman, Gifts, Strangers, Humanitarianism, Death, Slave Rebellions, the Proslavery Argument, Baseball, Hunting, and Gambling in the Old South* (Princeton, NJ: Princeton University Press, 1996); and Edward Ayers, *Vengeance and Justice: Crime and Punishment in the Nineteenth-Century Antebellum South* (New York: Oxford University Press, 1983).

3. *Annual Report of the Virginia Institution for the Education of the Deaf and Dumb and of the Blind* (Richmond: B. F. Walker, Superintendent Public Printing, 1870), 9. For a full discussion of Deaf Americans as "foreigners in their own land," see Douglas C. Baynton, *Forbidden Signs: American Culture and the Campaign against Sign Language* (Chicago: University of Chicago Press, 1996), 15–35.

4. Why the Tillinghasts did not consider enrolling David in the North Carolina school for the Deaf is unclear. Beginning his education before the building of the North Carolina school, Tom Tillinghast graduated from the Virginia Institution for the Deaf. The family then decided to send both boys to the New York school. Tom finished his additional education and came home before the war. Perhaps the Tillinghasts decided to keep David at the New York Institution because of their fears about the future prospects of the North Carolina school.

5. Sarah Tillinghast to David Tillinghast, 21 January 1860, Tillinghast Family Papers, William R. Perkins Library, Duke University, Durham, North Carolina. Hereafter the collection is cited as "Tillinghast Papers."

6. Sarah Tillinghast to David Tillinghast, 6 May 1861, Tillinghast Papers.

7. Ibid.

8. Ibid.

9. David Tillinghast to Sarah Tillinghast, 13 May 1861, Tillinghast Papers.

10. John Tillinghast to David Tillinghast, 14 May 1861, Tillinghast Papers.

11. David Tillinghast to Sarah Tillinghast, 13 May 1861.

12. John Tillinghast to David Tillinghast, 14 May 1861.

13. William Tillinghast to David Tillinghast, with addendum by Eliza Tillinghast to David Tillinghast, 20 May 1861, Tillinghast Papers.

14. William Tillinghast to David Tillinghast, 21 December 1861, Tillinghast Papers.

15. David Tillinghast to William Tillinghast, 18 July 1862, Tillinghast Papers.

16. Ibid.

17. John Tillinghast to David Tillinghast, 9 November 1862, Tillinghast Papers.

18. Unfortunately, this letter is not in the archives. It is referred to in the next letter.

19. William Tillinghast to David Tillinghast, 13 January 1863, and undated older letter, Tillinghast Papers. Although David appears not to have written, it is important to remember that the only reason historians have his siblings' letters to him is that David saved them all.

20. William Tillinghast to David Tillinghast, 13 January 1863, and undated older letter.

21. William Tillinghast to David Tillinghast, 14 April 1863, Tillinghast Papers.

22. William Tillinghast to David Tillinghast, 13 January 1863, and undated older letter.

23. William Tillinghast to David Tillinghast, 14 April 1863.

24. William Tillinghast to David Tillinghast, 13 January 1863, and undated older letter.

25. Robina Tillinghast to David Tillinghast, 27 January 1863.

26. Sarah Tillinghast to David Tillinghast, 20 April 1863.

27. John Tillinghast to David Tillinghast, 9 November 1862.

28. William Tillinghast to David Tillinghast, 13 January 1863, and undated older letter.

29. On the backs of many family letters are back-and-forth notes showing that many hearing family members communicated with Deaf members via writing.

30. Robina Tillinghast to David Tillinghast, 27 January 1863.

31. William Tillinghast to David Tillinghast, 14 April 1863.

32. Sarah Tillinghast to David Tillinghast, 20 April 1863.

33. William Tillinghast to David Tillinghast, 13 January 1863, and undated older letter, Tillinghast Papers.

34. Ibid.

35. William Tillinghast to David Tillinghast, 14 April 1863.

36. Ibid.

37. Sarah Tillinghast to David Tillinghast, 20 April 1863.

38. Sarah Tillinghast to David Tillinghast, 6 June 1863, Tillinghast Papers.

39. William Tillinghast to David Tillinghast, 14 April 1863.

40. Sarah Tillinghast to David Tillinghast, 6 June 1863.

41. Sarah Tillinghast to David Tillinghast, 20 April 1863.

42. Hartwell M. Chamberlayne to Thomas Tillinghast, 21 November 1863, Tillinghast Papers.

43. Sarah Tillinghast to David Tillinghast, 6 June 1863.

44. Thomas Tillinghast to David Tillinghast, 6 June 1863, Tillinghast Papers.

45. Sarah Tillinghast to David Tillinghast, 6 June 1863.

46. Thomas Tillinghast to David Tillinghast, 6 June 1863.

47. Note from Thomas Tillinghast to David Tillinghast, appended to William Tillinghast to David Tillinghast, 8 June 1863, Tillinghast Papers. A few months later William reinforced his beliefs about the dependence of his Deaf brothers by telling David that Thomas was unable to live alone "as he is subject to asthma and mute too." William Tillinghast to David Tillinghast, 13 October 1863, Tillinghast Papers.

48. Sarah Tillinghast to David Tillinghast, 6 June 1863.

49. William Tillinghast to David Tillinghast, 22 January 1864, Tillinghast Papers.

50. Thomas Tillinghast to David Tillinghast, 6 June 1863.

51. Thomas Tillinghast to David Tillinghast, 6 June 1863.

52. Ibid.

53. Ibid.

54. David Tillinghast to brother, 26 August 1863, Tillinghast Papers.

55. David Tillinghast to brother, 15 October 1863, Tillinghast Papers. "Thrice years old" refers to the years the class had spent in school, not to the age of pupils. In other words, the students had attended school for three years.

56. Ibid.

57. David Tillinghast to Robina Tillinghast, 7 March 1864, Tillinghast Papers.

58. David Tillinghast to brother, 15 October 1863, Tillinghast Papers; John Witzchief to David Tillinghast, 21 September 1863, Tillinghast Papers.

59. John Tillinghast to David Tillinghast, 15 July 1863, Tillinghast Papers.

60. William Tillinghast to David Tillinghast, 8 August 1863, Tillinghast Papers.

61. Ibid.

62. David Tillinghast to brother, 26 August 1863.

63. David Tillinghast to brother, 15 October 1863.

64. Ibid.

65. David Tillinghast to Robina Tillinghast, 7 March 1864.

66. William Tillinghast to David Tillinghast, 21 March 1864, Tillinghast Papers.

67. Ibid.

68. David Tillinghast to Robina Tillinghast, 7 March 1864.

69. William Tillinghast to David Tillinghast, 18 June 1864, Tillinghast Papers.

70. Ibid.

71. Ibid.

72. Although there is a period of several months with no letters that may suggest the family members were all together, a letter written almost one year later indicates that David had not yet been home at all during the war. In it, Sarah begged her brother to visit them, stating that she would embrace "this first opportunity" to see him. Sarah Tillinghast to David Tillinghast, 12 March 1865, Tillinghast Papers.

73. Sarah Tillinghast to David Tillinghast, 12 March 1865.

74. Ibid.

75. Ibid.

76. Sarah Tillinghast to David Tillinghast, 3 May 1865, Tillinghast Papers.

77. Ibid.

78. Ibid.

79. Ibid.

80. Eliza Tillinghast to David Tillinghast, 8 June 1865, Tillinghast Papers.

81. Ibid.

82. Ibid.

83. Ibid.

84. Ibid.

85. Ibid.

86. William Tillinghast to David Tillinghast, undated [1865], Tillinghast Papers.

87. David Tillinghast to William Tillinghast, 5 June 1865, Tillinghast Papers.

88. Sarah Tillinghast to David Tillinghast, 12 March 1865.

89. William Tillinghast to David Tillinghast, undated [1865].

90. See, for example, David Tillinghast to Thomas Tillinghast, 16 December 1865; David Tillinghast to Thomas Tillinghast, 2 February 1866; David Tillinghast to Thomas Tillinghast, 26 March 1866; David Tillinghast to Thomas Tillinghast, 1 May 1866; David Tillinghast to Thomas Tillinghast, 6 June 1866; David Tillinghast to Thomas Tillinghast, 18 June 1867, all in the Tillinghast Papers.

91. Thomas Tillinghast to William Tillinghast, 27 September 1867, Tillinghast Papers. More about the hiring of the men's hearing brother Willard can be found in David Tillinghast to Thomas Tillinghast, 15 October 1867, Tillinghast Papers.

92. John Vickrey Van Cleve and Barry A. Crouch, *A Place of Their Own: Creating the Deaf Community in America* (Washington, DC: Gallaudet University Press, 1989), 57–59.

93. It is clear, for example, that David did not reject his family's racial views. As one of his siblings stated, "I was very glad you showed your Southern raising by taking the side you did about the darkies doing menial work. I believe that God in his wisdom put the negroes in the south to do the menial work because the climate is such that it kills white women or worse than kills them." Sibling to [David Tillinghast], 5 May 1866, Tillinghast Papers.

4

"Trying to Idle"
Work and Disability in *The Diary of Alice James*

Natalie A. Dykstra

Alice James, the brilliant youngest sister of William and Henry James, contended with lifelong chronic illness subsequent to an emotional and physical breakdown at age nineteen. By the time she was thirty-six, she could no longer walk, and she remained bedridden until her death from breast cancer in March 1892, at age forty-four. Late in her life, Alice began a diary that she kept from late spring 1889 until shortly before her death in 1892.[1] In the privacy of its pages, she included shrewd social observation, transcribed letters, and descriptions of her relations with her much-treasured brothers, her nurses, and her companion Katherine Loring. She also recorded her keenly felt awareness of the circumscription of her life. She was not engaged in arenas of public success, as were William and Henry, nor did she fulfill the more private roles of wife and mother.[2] With her typical witty despair, Alice characterized herself at one point as "an appendage to five cushions and three shawls" (81).

At other times, however, Alice refuted such conflations, insisting on a distance between what disabled her and what she understood to be her real life. Her entry on March 23, 1891, implies that her physical deprivation has afforded her a spiritual advance:

> If the aim of life is the accretion of fat, the consumption of food unattended by digestive disorganization, there is no doubt that I am a failure. ... [B]ut every fibre protests against being taken simply as a sick carcass ... for what power has dissolving flesh and aching bones to undermine a satisfaction made of imperishable things. (183)

In this way, she claimed a remarkable fullness of experience for herself within the putative confinements of chronic illness.

Indeed, Alice's resistance to being seen simply within the frame of her physical life was so central to the project of her diary that she probably would have felt chagrined at her inclusion in this collection on the history of disability. My focus on her disability, however, is not an attempt to recontain her experience in the very parameters she sought to defy. Rather, my aim is to support the complexity she suggests by exploring how she enlisted her ill body to be herself. Illness—and in her instance, disabling illness—was labor central to her project of building a self both legible and faithful to her own desires. Alice reconfigured illness as a kind of women's work in the context of her family and larger cultural preoccupations with domesticity, work, and the requirements of an industrializing economy. In this way, she defended against being dismissed as useless within a familial and cultural paradigm that prized individual productivity.

Certainly, Alice's story of debility testifies to how a particular Jamesian family pride and her own talents and idiosyncrasies colluded to keep her in bed. Like their sister, oldest brothers William and Henry James were both diagnosed with neurotic and physical ailments of various sorts, but unlike Alice, the brothers largely recovered, overcoming their illnesses when they found satisfying work. In other words, their illnesses never accumulated into the type of sustained disability that so becalmed Alice's progress to adulthood. Release and resolution were not available to her in the same ways as they were to her brothers. Moreover, to risk failure as a proper woman imperiled her strongly held identity of being a "James."[3] Her circumstances were thus very specific: she was the doted-on daughter of a wealthy, well-known family with its own set of requirements and codes that no doubt played a powerful role in her incapacity. She is not, then, "a representative figure in any obvious sense."[4]

Yet Alice's strategy for managing intolerable conflict through nonsomatic and chronic illness and her consequent defiance of the public arena were entirely consonant with her time and place. Finding no tenable outlet for her considerable abilities, she turned toward herself and the material most culturally available to her—her body. With her body, she created a meticulously feminine identity that met cultural demands and kept with family tradition, even as she insisted on her own, albeit elusive individuality. And so, if she resides within the dramatic and intensely private borders of the sickroom, it is a room, one might say, that culture built. The space of the sickroom—with its required attributes of shaded windows, hushed tones, and soft voices—was only the most inert and exaggerated example of the domains described and required by the discourse of true womanhood aimed at white, middle-class women.

At the same time, to understand Alice as only a passive recipient and product of cultural and familial dictates is to miss the point. She herself actively constructed the space of the sickroom as a means to establish a measure of personal value and freedom with her work of being ill. The diary is thus a kind of ledger wherein she could represent herself as disabled even as she undermined this interpretation. She does not confess so much as protest. In this way, her story powerfully confirms how, as Rosemarie Garland Thomson avers, "the actual experience of disability is more complex and more dynamic than representation usually suggests."[5]

But why is this? Why does representation so often fail or refuse to account for the manifold complexity of how people experience disabilities? David T. Mitchell and Sharon L. Snyder contend that disability promises an unmistakable and noncontingent correspondence between biology and the self. Within this paradigm, the physical world purportedly "provides the material evidence of an inner life (corrupt or virtuous) that is secured by the mark of visible difference."[6] The mark of physical difference secures interpretive certainty. And yet, a disabled body is not any more a static figure of meaning than any other body. As Garland Thomson reminds her readers, all of us are vulnerable to the possibility of disability at some time during our lives because of age, accident, or disease. Because of this, the figure of the disabled body is even more fluid than other categories of identity, such as race and gender, which are presumably more fixed and stable.[7]

It is precisely this fluidity and contingency of value and meaning that Alice's story insists on and so memorably dramatizes. Indeed, Alice destabilizes easy and sure categories of ability and disability, isolation and connection, body and mind, by denoting both terms of the opposition simultaneously so that—if only for a moment—she makes the borders between such designations dissolve. In these narrative suspensions or clearings, she disallows her readers from determining once and for all that she is only or simply disabled. This disavowal of narrative certainty, in turn, enables her better to contend with and momentarily elude definitions that otherwise overdetermine what meanings might be ascribed to the self, whether those discourses refer to her experience of being a

"James," being a woman, or being disabled. This release from certainty, however temporary, was fundamental to Alice's work in the world.

Alice sailed to Europe in 1884 with her friend Katherine Loring, and though she had not intended to stay permanently, "[c]ircumstances dictated otherwise."[8] She began her diary on May 31, 1889, while renting two large rooms at Leamington Spa, an English health resort northwest of London. By then she had already endured more than two decades of ill health. As a child she was bright, eager, but also withdrawn and to the periphery of action.[9] The youngest in a family of four sons, she was made aware of her difference from her siblings and, with it, the range of possibilities attending her future. Henry Sr., whom Alice adored, recognized his only daughter's intelligence and seems to have enjoyed it, addressing her at one point as "heiress of the paternal wit and of the maternal worth."[10] But recognizing himself in her promise did not signal much more than paternal appreciation. Thus her education consisted of instruction and guidance somewhat more conservative than typical of her generation of young women: sewing, music, dance, and French.[11]

For her oldest brother, William, Alice was the "cherry lipped apricot nosed double chinned little Bal" to whom he wrote flirtatious and affectionate letters. In an 1862 letter, when Alice was fourteen and William was twenty, the older brother appreciates her for her ornamental presence and her ability to inspire him. And yet, even as he approximates intimacy, he makes her anonymous by referring to her in the third person: "Her transparent eyes, soft step, and gentle hands . . . never seemed to me more desirable or lovable than now."[12] Though undoubtedly flattering, William's attention was commensurate more with his desires of what a woman should be than with Alice herself. It was a message that no doubt helped teach her what the mantle of young womanhood might entail.[13]

By her late adolescence, Alice felt hemmed in and bored by her world. Remembering her youth, she wrote in February 1890:

> Owing to muscular circumstances my youth was not of the most ardent, but I had to peg away pretty hard between 12 and 24, "killing myself," as some one calls it—absorbing into the bone that the better part is to clothe oneself in neutral tints . . . and possess one's soul in silence. (95)

The limits that confined her were crushing, but they were limits Alice would take up as her own, eventually externalizing them in the walls of the sickroom.

During the winter of 1867–68, Alice, then nineteen, was sent by her family to New York City for treatments with Dr. Charles Fayette Taylor, a leading orthopedic surgeon and author of *Theory and Practice of the Movement Cure* (1861). Dr. Taylor had developed an exercise program for women with nervous disorders, also known as motorpathy, where patients would stretch and exercise muscles as well as receive massage in order to redirect energy back into the body.[14] By the spring of 1868, after several cycles through various declines and recoveries, her mother, Mary James, acknowledged that the family's attentions were drawn around Alice: "All our time and thoughts are given over to dear Alice who is not better, her nervous turns are very frequent and brought on by the slightest exertions." Mary reported that Alice has had "genuine hysteria," conceding it "the most distressing form of illness, and the most difficult to reach, because so little is known about it."[15]

Certainly, Alice exhibited symptoms in confusing and variable combinations: stomach pains, fainting spells, partially paralyzed legs, and, most persistently, nervous exhaustion. Throughout her life she would be diagnosed with a virtual compendium of nineteenth-century disorders, including: "neurasthenia, hysteria, rheumatic gout, cardiac complication, spinal neurosis, and spiritual crisis."[16] No organic basis for her disablements was ever identified. Whatever their specific etiology, Alice and her family linked her early breakdowns to attempts at study and intellectual pursuit. Alice held to this interpretation twenty years later when, in the diary, she described that period of her life as a series of abandonments:

When the fancy took me of a morning at school to *study* my lessons . . . the most impossible sensations of upheaval, violent revolt in my head overtook me so that I had to "abandon" my brain, as it were. (149)

The same entry of October 26, 1890, began as a response to William's essay "The Hidden Self," published in *Scribner's* the previous March. In it Alice agrees with his conclusion that hysterical patients experience a contraction of consciousness through a series of abandonments. Moreover, the divisions that seem to contend for supremacy are distinctly gendered arenas that were, in Alice's youth, taken up or inhabited by her father and mother, respectively.

In describing these effects in herself, she reveals one of the animating sources of a rage she had felt unsafe to express outright—her father:

I used to sit immovable reading in the library with waves of violent inclination suddenly invading my muscles taking some one of their myriad forms such as throwing myself out of the window, or *knocking off the head of the be-nignant pater as he sat with his silver locks, writing at his table.* (149; my emphasis)

Her father is pictured "writing at his table," exactly that activity which so defeated Alice in her youth. He was what Alice was not: a definer of worlds through language.

The feminine sphere to which Alice felt consigned was fully occupied by her mother, Mary Walsh James. The portrait of Mary is remarkably consistent throughout the many accounts of her more famous husband and progeny. She was the very emblem and paragon of domestic virtue: self-sacrificing, warm, compliant, encouraging.[17] When remembering Mary's death, Alice recounted in her diary what she learned from her mother:

[S]he has dwelt in my mind a beautiful illumined memory, the essence of divine maternity from which I was to learn great things, give all, but ask nothing. (221)

Mary had modeled to Alice a maternity that transcended the desires of the body—"ask nothing"—by means of ignorance so that the spiritual, the "divine," might be most visible, most remembered. Mary was remembered by Alice also in relation to language, as was her father; but Mary's words were of an "unconscious essence." After coming on a cache of her old letters, Alice was swept away, as if in a "postscript of the past," recalling "Mother's words breathing her extraordinary selfless devotion as if she simply embodied the unconscious essence of wife and motherhood" (78, 79).

But therein lay Alice's conundrum. Her mother embodied the unconsciousness required by domesticity, exactly what Alice would not and could not be. Alice's response was to embody the opposite—an insistent and all-pervasive body that bolted her in place even as she distanced herself from it:

How sick one gets of being "good," how much I should respect myself if I could burst out and make every one wretched for 24 hours; embody selfishness, as they say [two words erased] does. (64)

Moreover, the division of particular parts of herself had begun, with each term, whether mind/body, will/feelings, public/private, contending for supremacy and authority of the whole.[18]

By early 1869, Alice was recovering again, busying herself with traditional feminine activities and traveling with various family members to their country retreat in Pomfret, Connecticut. But her main task in that year and in the years to follow was maintaining her health. In a letter to Henry, Mary James indicated as much, forecasting what would be the work of Alice's life: "Alice is busy trying to idle, and it is always very hard depressing work, this to her, but I think it will tell in the end."[19]

In the spring of 1878, Alice, who would turn thirty on August 7, lived in Cambridge with her parents, who were then in their late sixties. That April, she took to her bed. Henry Sr. wrote to Robertson, the youngest son: "Alice is half the time, indeed much more than half, on the verge of insanity and suicide."[20] All this was intensified by her changing relationship with William, who announced his betrothal to Alice Howe Gibbens. Alice registered her fear of abandonment and what she felt as betrayal with a language she knew would secure her attention and care: an ill body.

The siege of the summer continued into the following fall and spring. Early in 1879, Alice found again a limited equilibrium, but it was the beginning of a more consistent decline. Mary James's early diagnosis of hysteria was apt, but the newer disease category of neurasthenia, which at one point had been ascribed to Alice, more accurately describes the later manifestations of her illness. Alice no longer "acted out" but instead imploded with a dizzying variety of ailments that matched much of the symptomology of neurasthenia. First considered a deficiency of the nervous system by Dr. George Beard in 1869, neurasthenia included complaints as various as ringing in the ear, listlessness, atonic voice, fainting, food refusal, irritability, sick headaches, fears of contamination, and hopelessness.[21] Treatment and remedy were at best uncertain. Women especially were encouraged to take some form of Dr. S. Weir Mitchell's Rest Cure, where the patient would be isolated from her family; served by a nurse, a doctor, or both; force-fed several times a day and administered daily enemas; and forbidden to write, read, or talk with friends.[22]

Alice was not administered the fullest version of the Rest Cure, but by the time of her overseas voyage with Katherine Loring in 1884, at age thirty-six, she was mostly bedridden. As her days pivoted around the vicissitudes of her increasing disability, her goal became not health so much as moral triumph over ill health. The only undisputed diagnosis of her life would come in the spring of 1891. Exactly two years after she had begun the diary, doctors told her she had breast cancer. Finally, an enemy she could name had invaded her disobedient body:

To him who waits, all things come! My aspirations may have been eccentric, but I cannot complain now, that they have not been brilliantly fulfilled. (206)

Her expression of relief, though her reaction is also self-mocking and sarcastic, indicates how baffled she herself had been by her long debility.

Though Alice's biographers differ in the details regarding her illnesses, all agree that the hallmark effect of her ailments was an enduring and profound immobility. A photograph of her taken in 1889 in one of the rooms at Leamington Spa, where she began her diary, supports this conclusion. Alice is settled on a daybed positioned near a large window, clasping something in her hands, though the detail is not clear enough to determine exactly what. She is sitting upright against several pillows, draped in blankets. Her companion, Katherine Loring, looks toward the viewer, holding in her hands an open book. Alice's room succeeds in presenting a vision of feminine domesticity: long floral drapes with a gauzy inner curtain hang at the window; a lace-patterned cloth covers the table at the center of the room, decorated by a vase and several books; a fireplace mantel is adorned with an elaborately framed mirror, against which lean framed pictures as well as a vase of dried flowers.[23]

Within this space, Alice appears as immobile as the furniture; indeed, her immovable body is itself a central furnishing to the room. She herself notes this conflation of her physical being with immovable objects. But immobility is not a tangential effect. Instead, it is central to the point of her illnesses. The photograph is but one representation that helps shape and inform the experience itself.

Indeed, Alice represents her immobility in assorted guises, so that it takes on different, often contradictory qualities at various times throughout her narrative. Sometimes, as is presented in the photograph, inertia is a kind of refuge or pleasant stillness.[24] At other moments, Alice converts her refuge to an arena of adventure and a battlefield on which her labors win. She contends that

> [t]he paralytic on his couch can have if he wants them wider experiences than Stanley slaughtering savages . . . ; and the peaceful cotton-spinner win victories beside which those of the reverberating general are dust and ashes. (146)

First paralleling her own activity to that of the far-flung imperial adventures of heroic men, Alice portrays her inert position as an opportunity for wider experiences that are usually linked with the public and masculine world of

Natalie A. Dykstra

Figure 4.1. Alice James and Katherine Loring at Royal Leamington Spa, 1889–1890. By permission of the Houghton Library, Harvard University.

activity. She then compares her position to that of a cotton spinner, work more common to earlier generations of women, claiming that such unrecognized labor would outdo the well-known and public accomplishments of a general. By such inversions of position and value, she attempts to accumulate for herself some special reward for which she has paid such a high price.

Alice is at her most emphatic when she employs the metaphors of nature to describe her sense of isolation. She represents the darkness that envelops her with the language of wild, unseen or unseeable places: "From just behind the eyes my head feels like a dense jungle into which no ray of light has ever penetrated" (150). Sixteen months later she admits defeat, again using vivid metaphors of nature to secure her meaning:

> The fact is, I have been dead so long . . . since that hideous summer of '78 when I went down to the deep sea, its dark waters closed over me and I knew neither hope nor peace. (230)

The constructed limits of Alice's experiences—whether through cultural, familial, or personal factors—are exemplified literally in the walls of the sickroom that enclose her. She articulates such boundaries as if they are natural, however, and if natural, then also destined or fated, beyond the address of individual effort.

Alice was not alone in her fatalism. She had been disabled by illness in a historical moment when illnesses such as hers were a spectral presence in the journals, fiction, art, and advice manuals of postbellum America. In 1894, Dr. Mercy N. Baker published an article in the *American Woman's Journal* where she contended that "[t]he most non-observant must have seen that maladies referable to the nervous system are largely on the increase." Dr. Baker tried to account for this increase, noting that, since the Civil War, life had been regimented according to a military and technological model that "takes no cognition of individual constitution." Such an elision of the individual had disabling effects.[25]

Though men and women were equally susceptible to nervous symptoms, the meaning of those symptoms differed according to gender.[26] Complaints by men were most often considered contrary to a man's authentic character and thus a problem of work in a mentally and physically exhausting marketplace.[27] Work in an industrializing economy was counterpoised against a strong, intact body, imagined not as ensuring but as threatening the wholeness of the individual. The nervous ailments that plagued William and Henry James were thought to be connected to their efforts to define and establish what their work might be. For example, William suffered from neurasthenic complications throughout the 1860s when he wavered between a career in painting, research science—as his father wished—and college teaching. William was relieved of the worst of his symptoms, however, with his appointment to teach physiology at Harvard in the summer of 1872, as if the work itself held restorative powers.[28]

The hallmark symptoms of neurasthenia—exhaustion, inertia, and hopelessness—in women, however, were linked to a susceptible feminine biology and thus became a problem not of society or civilization but of women's bodies. The medical community deemed women susceptible to nervous exhaustion expressly because their unpredictable uteruses rendered their bodies especially vulnerable to disability.[29] A woman was particularly at risk for neurasthenic symptoms when she overtaxed a fragile nervous system with intellectual pursuit.[30] Alice demonstrates that she was influenced by this perspective when she ascribes her breakdown in 1868-69 to an overexertion in her school studies.

In this way, women came to be equated with illness itself. The conflation is obvious in the comments of Dr. S. Weir Mitchell, a leading physician of the time and originator of the Rest Cure, when he declaims that "[h]e who does not know a sick woman, does not know women."[31] As early as 1854, Catharine Beecher suspected that so many women, particularly "married ladies," were sick because the society was making them sick, noting that nervous illnesses differed only in degree from the requirements of proper feminine behavior.[32] Charlotte Perkins Gilman, in *Women and Economics*, argued that it was a middle-class woman's confinement in the domestic sphere as wife and mother and her consequent exclusion from work in the marketplace that made her especially susceptible to debility:

> [T]he consuming female, debarred from any free production, unable to estimate the labor involved in the making of what she so lightly destroys . . . creates a market for sensuous decoration and personal ornament, for all that is luxurious and enervating.[33]

Passive, weak, and withdrawn from the arena of action and production, the figure of the nervous woman was, in Carroll Smith-Rosenberg's formulation, both an "indictment" of white middle-class culture and its direct consequence.[34]

Nineteenth-century gender ideology for white middle-class women constructed their bodies at cross-purposes, yielding a contradictory figure both substantial and insubstantial, active and inactive, able and unable. From one direction, domesticity elided the materiality of women's bodies in the ethereal language of spiritual virtue. A woman was the "angel in the house," a disembodied specter of religious feeling and maternal care. On the other side, women were identified directly with the body, considered identical to it, and feared as a carnal embodiment of the forbidden, the sexual. Thus a woman's biology caused her exhaustion, but it also guaranteed her virtue. In this way, the physical markings of illness—paleness, physical weakness—were evidence of female inferiority and a mark of beauty, both of which proved a "proper" feminine identity.

The site of such neurasthenic activity was, of course, the body, the very material that poses as "natural," as a given escaping the borders of culture. Such a disguise, with its naturalizing reference to physical symptoms, was difficult to unmask. Alice experienced the limits placed on her because of the status of her body—female, susceptible to sickness, and within the home—as though the limits, because they referred to the supposed facts of the body, were themselves "natural." And yet, illness is always already a culturally saturated event. Judith Butler argues that the practices or performances of daily life do not depend on a preceding body with which to work, but these same performances produce that which is intelligible about the body in the first instance.[35] For Alice, cultural discourses about the body gave her a way to make sense of her experience and represent it. Thus, culture haunts the body, tracks it down, makes it matter. And what matters or what is understandable about the body is always decided by means of the specific cultural practices.

And in fact, if neurasthenia was a way of "doing gender," to borrow Candace West and Donald Zimmerman's formulation, "taking to bed" was a way of "doing class" as well.[36] Chronic illness could be an elaborated form of leisure, thereby capable of establishing—or at least maintaining—one's class standing. After all, to be so leisurely as never to leave one's bed was possible *only if* a woman or her family could afford it. In this context, Abba Goold Woolson, a Boston poet and teacher, asserted in 1873 that illness had become a kind of feminine pursuit: "[W]ith us, to be ladylike is to be lifeless, inane and dawdling. . . . [O]ur fine ladies aspire to be called invalids."[37] Likewise, according to Bram Dijkstra, pictorial images of frail and inert women became fervently sought by the art-buying public because "[t]he cult of feminine invalidism . . . was inextricably associated with suggestions of wealth and success."[38]

Thus, Alice James found it possible to take up the mantle of debility because of her gender and because of her family's wealth. Her biographer Jean Strouse contends that "[t]he intelligence and energy Alice might have used in some productive way went into the intricate work of being sick."[39] But Strouse imagines work only as a metaphor to get at what Alice is doing; in other words, she does not understand illness literally as work. She does not see it as productive. Mary Cappello begins her essay "Alice James: 'Neither Dead nor Recovered'" by arguing that to see illness as a way to define the feminine self only replicates an equation from the nineteenth century she so deplores:

I might just as easily say that the moment Alice James gets ill is the moment she stops trying to define herself, and perhaps this is because I want to reject the notion produced by nineteenth century culture, enacted by

Natalie A. Dykstra

hysteria and represented and reproduced in some twentieth century American women's poetry that illness is a means of self-definition.[40]

And yet, to deplore illness as a means to define the self because it is self-defeating and self-limiting is different from contending, therefore, that Alice is *not* using illness as a means to do so. In other words, to want to reject the conflation between feminine identity and illness does not change the fact that women achieved the former by means of the latter, and that they saw such production as their work.

For Alice, illness functioned as productive work that helped establish a valuable self both recognizably her own and recognizably feminine. That this may not have been the most liberated or commendable way for Alice to accomplish such a goal, that she is not in this sense a role model, is beside the point. Instead, considering disability as her work makes sense given how the connections between work and value were being reconfigured by an industrializing economy. Rosemarie Garland Thomson posits the disabled figure as at the center of changes in labor during the nineteenth century:

> Nowhere is the disabled figure more troubling to American ideology and history than in relation to the concept of work: the system of production and distribution of economic resources in which the abstract principle of self-government, self-determination, autonomy, and progress are manifest most completely. . . . As modernization proceeded, the disabled figure shouldered in new ways society's anxiety about its inability to retain the status and old meanings of labor in the face of industrialization and increasing economic and social chaos.[41]

The sickroom was a nineteenth-century space that sheltered the self, because work, so reconfigured by industrializing change, posed a threat to the self even as it promised to establish and maintain the status of that self.

Alice's illnesses positioned her directly within these tensions. She assembled an identity that was comprehensible insofar as a sick woman came into clear focus within the matrixes of gender and class. The figure of the sick woman was both common and legible. At the same time, the sickroom did not provide a retreat from work, a counterposition from which to rescue and recuperate the self. Instead, the sickroom provided her the work space within which to do the tasks of being female.

Alice records her work of being ill in her diary with remarkably vigorous language. She indicates with irony that being sick takes a kind of energy. She opens her entry on July 18, 1890, declaiming: "How well one has to be, to be ill!" At one point, she compares her illness to a "delicate embroidery," a fancywork popular among women in the middle classes. She also compares the paralytic on the couch to a cotton spinner, evoking work of an earlier generation of women. In yet another entry, her illnesses are a kind of agricultural pursuit. Picturing herself doing productive work in the world, she recounts coming down with a fever and declares: "I collapsed for a few days and *cultivated* as much 'prostration' as possible" (my emphasis). This is Alice "trying to idle," as her mother had forecast years before. Within this paradigm, death is understood as the ultimate production. In mid-June 1891, after her diagnosis of breast cancer, Alice recounts her brothers' achievements, noting the publication of Henry's *The Americans* and William's *Psychology* exclaiming that it is "not a bad show for one family," adding "especially if I get myself dead, the hardest job of all" (211).

It was a Jamesian habit to refer to the market system as a way to articulate one's meaning. R. W. B. Lewis notes in his biography of the family that money "in actuality and in metaphor" gripped the "Jamesian imagination."[42] Alice's great-grandfather William James had made his fortune in Albany, New York, in finance and real estate and at one point owned the small but promising hamlet of Syracuse. By the mid-1830s, his fortune was second only to John Jacob Astor of New York. Henry Sr.'s legacy set him free from financial worry, and his children enjoyed a prolonged period of leisure before assuming the obligations of work. The family's response to being unhinged from the rigors of the marketplace, according to Lewis, was

> to displace the language and the motifs of the money world into other realms of discourse: into theology, philosophy, psychology, literature; and to entangle them with other urgencies of experience.[43]

Clearly, illness was another "realm of discourse" onto which the James family projected monetary metaphors.

And yet, there is something literal about how the family understood illness to function in the family economy. What is most interesting is that the siblings thought health and intelligence were a kind of limited fund to which not all members of the family had equal or simultaneous access. Alice said as much when writing William in 1867, a day before turning nineteen.

Natalie A. Dykstra

She referred to herself in the stage voice of the third person: "You must remember that this mental baseness is not her own fault, and that as she is your sister her having so little mind may account for you having so much."[44] So, too, good health was like money in the bank—a resource that had a specific limit and was circulated throughout the family. In 1869, contending with ill health, Henry Jr. wrote back to his family from Europe:

> I have invented for my comfort a theory that this [degeneration] of mine is the result of Alice and Willy getting better and locating some of their diseases on me.[45]

Illness was thus measured on a debt/payment scale, whereby one member would pay the debt with debility of another's health and good fortune. And if illness could pay for a debt in the family economy of health, then illness also had to be productive of something of value to be used in such an exchange. For the two oldest James brothers, illness could produce a penance for too great a fortune both in intellect and material wealth. Ill health also provided a respite from the pressures to find and develop what their father most encouraged—their true selves. But for Alice, illness was not a respite from a search for work to do, as it had been for William and Henry. It was the work itself.

Alice's immobilizing disability also has a compelling logic when put in relation to the bustle and circulation required by commerce in an industrializing economy. Gillian Brown argues that the space of the domestic had been designated as a counterforce to the values and terms of the market. Immobility in this sphere could shore up the instability that threatened to breach the borders of the home and its requisite status as haven, ostensibly separate from the productive and consumptive forces of the market. The opposition between the domestic and the market, however, had the ironic effect of suturing them into a mutually constitutive relation. Brown uses Tocqueville's observations of the American scene in 1835 to make the same point:

> The democratic opportunity and competition for economic advancement, the very mobility of American society, Tocqueville worried in 1835, were apt to render the individual "stationary."[46]

And yet, the relation of immobility to the market is more complicated than protest against or corrective response to too much activity. Brown misses that immobility—lying in the sickroom—was itself a specific form of women's work. Such immobility was positioned as an ideal feminine vocation, for it was in keeping with not only dictates of gender but also a long-standing requirement for women's work: its invisibility. According to Jeanne Boydston, the housewife of nineteenth-century America was "something of a contradiction in terms: the worker whose very claim to importance depends in part on the unseen nature of her labor."[47] Immobility, then, was work of the body that obscured what it produced even as it offered one way of securing a valuable self.

Thus, chronic illness, with its capacity to disable, became one way to build a feminine self and secure value that promised a proper bypass of the marketplace, the very domain where social and economic value was produced under capitalism and in which so many women had been denied a directly productive role. Indeed, women's roles were designated by the marketplace as primarily consuming, a stipulation Alice literalizes with her immobility in the sickroom. Surely, the anonymous narrator in *The Autobiography of the Neurasthene* overstates the case when claiming that "[i]t is a recognized fact that the work of the world is largely done by neurasthenes."[48] Yet, for Alice, illness could display her proficiency and skill at following the rules of femininity even as she undermined many of these expectations. In May 1891 she declared:

> It is decidedly indecent to catalogue oneself in this way, but I put it down in a scientific spirit, to show that though I have no *productive worth*, I have a certain *value* as an indestructible quantity. (207; my emphasis)

This display of feminine value is not coincidently articulated in economic terms; that is, Alice itemized her somatic and psychosomatic ailments using the lingua franca of value production in the nineteenth century: the nouns and verbs of capitalism and industry. In doing so, Alice substantiated a claim that was in keeping with the domestic economy of both her family and the larger culture: her immobile and disabled body was, in fact, a body at work.

The sickroom was both the literal space Alice occupied and the literary space from which she wrote. From its outset, Alice positioned her diary as a practical device that might help her manage the isolation that was her most consistent accompaniment:

Natalie A. Dykstra

I think that if I get into the habit of writing a bit about what happens, or rather doesn't happen, I may lose a little of the sense of loneliness and desolation which abides with me. (25)

But as Alice proceeded, the diary became far more than a mere remedy. It offered her an arena she could control and within which she could define the world and her place in it. Alice's diary is a narrative of disability, a testimony that provides a context for and cohesion to what life was like in the sickroom. As the sickroom was a room for Alice both in her family and in her culture, so her diary was a way for her to make a literary room for herself as well as a way to connect with the world. She accomplished these ends by linking what she was doing in the sickroom to larger notions of work. Her diary, in other words, was a work log wherein she could be both true to herself and legible to others, where she could feel herself autonomous, insofar as she wrote and represented herself as she wished, yet also where she could feel fully situated in the world.

Two years subsequent to her death, four copies of Alice's diary were published privately by Katherine Loring and distributed to William, Henry, and Robertson (Wilkie had died in 1883), Katherine keeping one copy for herself. After reading the diary, Henry recorded his reactions to it in a long letter to William, concluding that "[the diary] is heroic in its individuality, its independence—its face-to-face with the universe for and by herself."[49] Alice, in Henry's reading, was a person who had reckoned with her life on her own terms, and this he greatly admired. Not surprisingly, however, he acknowledged what she had achieved using language more typically reserved for adventuring men, because descriptive language of softness and repose associated with nineteenth-century women could not signal his experience of the diary. Alice had, in effect, defeated the ability of feminine discourse to define and describe her.[50]

Henry James's reaction is instructive, for Alice's diary often has the effect of seeming to defy the very borders that the narrative establishes. In other words, just as Alice, as an acquaintance noted, would sometimes go "away from her face in weariness and pain," she sometimes turned away from the very portrait she was writing (69). To argue that such an effect is but happenstance or endemic to autobiographical prose misses the point and power of her diary. Alice wanted to represent her experiences by writing them down; at the same time, she needed to defy or complicate any easy interpretation of her life. Such elusiveness—about herself, about her disability—was exactly her intent and was central to how she represented herself.

Her hate-filled pique at George Eliot is but a single case in point. On June 28, 1889, Alice wrote:

> Read the third volume of George Eliot's Letters and Journals at last. . . . What an abject coward she seems to have been about physical pain, as if it weren't degrading enough to have head-aches, without jotting them down in a row to stare at one for all time, thereby defeating the beneficent law which provides that physical pain is forgotten. (40–41)

This tirade could be read as Alice's envy for Eliot's writing career. But what seems unaccountable is that Alice should attack Eliot's description of illness within the pages of her own elaborate description of life in the sickroom.

Why does she do this? If Alice gains recognition for her work, such recognition risks that her individuality will be subsumed by the defining cultural stereotype of the sick or disabled woman. Alice excoriates Eliot precisely because she does not want herself to be seen as *only sick*—a risk not as pressing for Eliot, given her public writing career. Moreover, Alice understands her disability not as a necessary impediment to a full life but as a possible path that may lead to self-discovery, insight, even delight. According to this older moral worldview, which industrialization was dismantling, the body is an impediment to true virtue. Disability purportedly disrupts one's fierce attachment to the pleasures of the body and so may be imagined as training and preparation for spiritual awareness and release. In other words, a disabled body gives an advantage in letting go of the flesh and carnality in favor of the spirit and purity. One is already almost there. This spiritual work was an ideal vocation for a true woman, and it trumped or superceded in value any worldly reward of the market.

In a long paragraph concluding her entry of March 23, 1891, and with which this essay began, Alice admits that, if measured according to the supposedly objective indices of value—those of accumulation and consumption—she is a failure. At the same time, she challenges the terms of such a measure by insisting that her experience does have value:

> If the aim of life is the accretion of fat, the consumption of food unattended by digestive disorganization, and succession of pleasurable sensations, there is no doubt that I am a failure . . . but every fibre protests against being taken

simply as a sick carcass, as foolish friends so flatteringly insist, for what power has dissolving flesh and aching bones to undermine a satisfaction made of imperishable things. This winter has been rich beyond compare, the heart all aglow with the affectionate demonstrations of friend and brother, the mind deeply stirred by most varied and interesting events, public and private, the spirit broadened and strengthened, let me hope, by a clearer perception of the significance of experience. (183)

Thus she could not tolerate Eliot's deflation of physical suffering to mere complaint and nuisance. Illness was something Alice could identify with and do. It was her work. At the same time, illness was something she alienated herself from in order to transcend it. Either way, illness was not something Alice could allow herself to complain of.

Alice James offers a vision of the self that seems at the outset so adumbrated by disabling illness as to be wholly defined by it. In December 1891 she wrote to William, acknowledging that "[m]y pains are too much a part of my substance to have any modifications before the spirit & the flesh fall asunder."[51] And yet, her diary articulates an alternative or contrary relation to her "pains." Indeed, it is a text wherein Alice attempted—in Richard Rorty's terms—"to make a self for [her]self by re-describing that impress in terms which are, if only marginally, [her] own."[52] In other words, Alice worked it out with what she had in such a way as to accrue to herself attention in her relationships and a measure of personal value. The price paid was high: a severely circumscribed life that amplified gender stereotypes and recontained what otherwise might have been active protest and critique. But Alice knew this, too, observing: "in emancipating ourselves we forge our chains" (38).

Alice James is neither easy company nor easy to forget. Her endurance of the complications and conundrums of chronic illness was exemplary insofar as she troubled the very terms that defined and constricted her. She wrote:

What a beautiful rhythm this makes in my soul as I cradle myself for a moment in the hope that those with *resignation in passivity* may, equally with those with *resignation in effort*, not surpass Homer, but better still, have some spiritual significance. (56)

Alice's tenacity in reimagining a world for herself in which she stands significant is so powerful because by such remaking she created for herself an identity that was more than or nonidentical to what she suffered. Moreover, though her language is at times maddening, she also mined its contradictory and evocative depths, enabling her to reach toward that which so often eluded her—a clearing, an open space where she mattered. In this, she felt she had attained so much more than other women:

> When will women begin to have the first glimmer that above all other loyalties is the loyalty to Truth, i.e., to yourself, that husband, children, friends and country are as nothing to that. (60)

For Alice, illness was work she could do that would ensure this loyalty to herself, and her diary was a place in which to dramatize and enact such a commitment.

NOTES

1. Two years later the manuscript was published privately by her family. Dodd, Mead & Company first published the diary in 1934, then published the definitive edition, edited by Leon Edel and retitled *The Diary of Alice James*, in 1964. In 1999, Northeastern University Press reissued the *Diary*, keeping the editing and pagination of the 1964 Edel edition.

2. In November 1889, Alice admitted that "my soul will never stretch itself to allowing that it is anything else than a cruel and unnatural fate for a woman to live alone." Yet she did not, in fact, live alone at this point. Katherine Loring came for extended stays, and each day Alice was accompanied by a nurse. But she was not living either with her family of origin or with a husband and/or children. This is what she found "unnatural." Alice James, *The Diary of Alice James*, ed. Leon Edel (New York: Dodd, Mead & Company, 1964), 57. All subsequent citations of the *Diary* will be designated by the page number in the text. For a discussion of the relationship between Alice and Katherine, see Jean Strouse, *Alice James: The Life of the Brilliant but Neglected Younger Sister of William and Henry James* (Boston: Houghton Mifflin Company, 1980), 244–252. See also R. W. B. Lewis, *The Jameses: A Family Narrative* (New York: Farrar, Straus, & Giroux, 1991), 380–381.

3. Strouse, *Alice James*, 292.

4. Ibid., xiv.

5. Rosemarie Garland Thomson, *Extraordinary Bodies: Figuring Physical Disability in American Culture and Literature* (New York: Columbia University Press, 1997), 12.

6. David T. Mitchell and Sharon L. Snyder, "Introduction: Disability Studies and the Double Bind of Representation," in *The Body and Physical Difference: Discourses of Disability* (Ann Arbor: University of Michigan Press, 1997), 3.

Natalie A. Dykstra

7. Garland Thomson, *Extraordinary Bodies*, 13–14.

8. Leon Edel, "Portrait of Alice James," in *The Diary of Alice James*, ed. Edel, 11.

9. Ruth Bernard Yeazell is also right when noting that "the Alice we know best is Alice sick and Alice dying." See Ruth Bernard Yeazell, ed., *The Death and Letters of Alice James* (Boston: Exact Change, 1981), 7.

10. Strouse, *Alice James*, 45.

11. Alice's education was somewhat backward for the times, when women were getting access to more sophisticated pedagogy and curriculum. As early as the 1830s, Elizabeth Cady (Stanton) was studying algebra, Greek, logic, botany, geometry, and modern history. See *In Her Own Right: The Life of Elizabeth Cady Stanton* (New York: Oxford University Press, 1984), 17. For Alice's father's articulation of a woman's proper place, see Henry James, Sr., "Woman and the 'Woman's Movement,'" *Putnam's Monthly* 1 (March 1853): 279–288.

12. William James to Alice James, October 19, 1862; as quoted by Strouse in *Alice James*, 78.

13. Strouse, *Alice James*, 52–59.

14. Charles Fayette Taylor, *Theory and Practice of the Movement Cure* (Philadelphia: Lindsay & Blakiston, 1861), 255–291. Strouse states that Dr. Taylor's treatment program was farsighted insofar as it recognized the health dangers of women's inactivity as required by upper- and middle-class propriety. At the same time, however, his treatment program reminded women that nervous fatigue was a kind of emotional indulgence that would be best remedied by adhering to the precepts of domesticity. See Strouse, *Alice James*, 106–110. Alfred Habegger mentions Dr. Taylor's "withering contempt" for higher education for women, noting that his treatment of Alice in the winter of 1866–67 must have included a dose of "ideological restraint." Habegger, *The Father: A Life of Henry James, Sr.* (New York: Farrar, Straus, and Giroux, 1994), 447.

15. Yeazell, *Death and Letters*, 12.

16. Strouse, *Alice James*, ix–x.

17. Linda Simon, *Genuine Reality: A Life of William James* (San Diego: Harcourt Brace Jovanovich, 1998), 16.

18. See Kristin Boudreau, "'A Barnum Monstrosity': Alice James and the Spectacle of Sympathy," *American Literature* 65, 1 (March 1993): 62, 60.

19. Mary James to Henry James, July 24, 1869; as quoted in Strouse, *Alice James*, 140.

20. Henry James, Sr., to Robertson James, September 14, 1878; as quoted in Strouse, *Alice James*, 185.

21. Barbara Sicherman, "The Uses of a Diagnosis: Doctors, Patients, and Neurasthenia," *Journal of the History of Medicine and Allied Sciences* 32, 2 (January 1977): 33–54.

22. Ellen L. Bassuk, "The Rest Cure: Repetition or Resolution of Victorian Women's Conflicts?" in *The Female Body in Western Culture: Contemporary Perspectives*, ed. Susan Rubin Suleiman (Cambridge: Harvard University Press, 1986), 141–142. See Nancy Theroit convincingly argues that the Rest Cure was first developed for

"male neurotics, not to 'punish' women patients." See Nancy Theroit, "Women's Voices in Nineteenth-Century Medical Discourse: A Step toward Deconstructing Science," *Signs* 19, 1 (Autumn 1993): 8.

23. The decor of the room follows the prescription given by domestic advice writers throughout the nineteenth century. See, for instance, Julia McNair Wright, *The Complete Home* (Philadelphia: J. C. McCurdy & Co., 1879), 139.

24. This characterization is in keeping with how the sickroom is portrayed in much Victorian fiction. See Miriam Bailim, *The Sickroom in Victorian Fiction: The Art of Being Ill* (Cambridge: Cambridge University Press, 1994), 6.

25. Dr. Baker focuses on the displacement of the individual as the signal culprit of illness. See Mercy N. Baker, M.D., "Human Wear and Tear," *American Woman's Journal* 8, 5 (July–August 1894): 405–406. See also Peter Gay, *The Bourgeois Experience: Victoria to Freud*, vol. 3: *The Cultivation of Hatred* (New York: W. W. Norton, 1993), 507; J. Jackson Lears, *No Place of Grace: Antimodernism and the Transformation of American Culture, 1880-1920* (New York: Pantheon Books, 1981), 51.

26. F. G. Gosling states that Dr. Beard himself "believed there were more female neurasthenics" (*Before Freud: Neurasthenia and the American Medical Community, 1870–1910* (Urbana: University of Illinois Press, 1987), 98). For an analysis of how "narratives of illness" comply with gender requirements, see Sheila M. Rothman's study of tuberculosis, *Living in the Shadow of Death: Tuberculosis and the Social Experience of Illness in American History* (New York: Basic Books, 1994).

27. Anthony Rotundo, however, contends that male neurasthenia occurred often during episodes of vocational crisis (*American Manhood* [New York: Basic Books, 1993], 185–193). See Gail Bederman, *Manliness and Civilization: A Cultural History of Gender and Race in the United States, 1880–1917* (Chicago: University of Chicago Press, 1995), 84–94, for a discussion of the "neurasthenic paradox."

28. William, however, wrote as late as 1895 that "I am a victim of neurasthenia, and a sense of the hollowness and unreality that goes with it" (as quoted in George Cotkin, *William James, Public Philosopher* [Baltimore: Johns Hopkins University Press, 1990], 77).

29. Ann Douglas Wood, "The 'Fashionable Diseases': Women's Complaints and Their Treatment in Nineteenth-Century America," in Judith Walzer Leavitt, ed., *Women and Health in America* (Madison: University of Wisconsin Press, 1984), 222-245.

30. Janet Oppenheim, *"Shattered Nerves": Doctors, Patients, and Depression in Victorian England* (New York: Oxford University Press, 1991), 194. For a discussion about how higher education was thought to threaten women's health, see also Carroll Smith-Rosenberg, *Disorderly Conduct: Visions of Gender in Victorian America* (New York: Alfred A. Knopf, 1985), 258–259.

31. S. Wier Mitchell, as quoted in Tom Lutz, *American Nervousness, 1903: An Anecdotal History* (Ithaca: Cornell University Press, 1991), 32. See also Barbara Ehrenreich and Deirdre English, *Complaints and Disorders: The Sexual Politics of Sickness* (Old Westbury, N.Y.: Feminist Press, 1973), 22.

Natalie A. Dykstra

32. Catharine Beecher, *Letters to the People on Health and Happiness* (New York: Harper & Bros., 1855), 129; Kathryn Kish Sklar, *Catherine Beecher: A Study in American Domesticity* (New Haven: Yale University Press, 1973), 204-205.

33. Charlotte Perkins Gilman, *Women and Economics* (Boston: Small, Maynard & Co., 1898), 120.

34. Smith-Rosenberg, *Disorderly Conduct*, 215. See also Diane Price Herndl, *Invalid Women: Figuring Feminine Illness in American Fiction and Culture, 1840-1940* (Chapel Hill: University of North Carolina Press, 1993), 7.

35. Judith Butler, introduction to *Bodies That Matter: On the Discursive Limits of "Sex"* (New York: Routledge, 1993).

36. Candace West and Donald Zimmerman, "Doing Gender," *Gender and Society* 1, 2 (June 1987): 125-151. See also Sicherman, "Uses of a Diagnosis," 41-42, for her discussion of why neurasthenia was a more coveted diagnosis among the upper classes.

37. Abba Goold Woolson, *Women in American Society* (Boston: Roberts Brothers, 1873), 192-193.

38. Bram Dijkstra, *Idols of Perversity: Fantasies of Feminine Evil in Fin-de-Siècle Culture* (New York: Oxford University Press, 1986), 28.

39. Strouse, *Alice James*, 291. Kristin Boudreau uses a similar formulation, asserting that Alice took up a "career intent upon its own demise." Boudreau recuses interest in what this might imply, stating that "I do not wish to ask . . . *why* she embraced such a ghastly 'career'" ("'A Barnum Monstrosity,'" 53).

40. Mary Cappello, "Alice James: 'Neither Dead nor Recovered,'" *American Imago* 45, 2 (Summer 1988): 129.

41. Thomson, *Extraordinary Bodies*, 46-47.

42. Lewis, *The Jameses*, 30. See also George Cotkin, "William James and the Cash-Value Metaphor," in *William James, Public Philosopher*, 37-47.

43. Lewis, *The Jameses*, 13.

44. Alice James to William James, August 7, 1867; as quoted in Strouse, *Alice James*, 115-116.

45. Henry James, Jr., to Henry James, Sr., October 26, 1869, as quoted in Strouse, *Alice James*, 111-112.

46. Gillian Brown, *Domestic Individualism: Imagining Self in Nineteenth-Century America* (Berkley: University of California Press, 1990), 173.

47. Jeanne Boydston, *Home and Work: Housework, Wages, and the Ideology of Labor in the Early Republic* (New York: Oxford University Press, 1990), 11.

48. Margaret A. Cleaves, *The Autobiography of a Neurasthene* (Boston: Gorham Press, 1910), 17.

49. Strouse, *Alice James*, 321.

50. Ralph Barton Perry finds that it is "impossible to apply any adjective to this clear-seeing, self-knowing individual without feeling that she has already thought and passed beyond it" (in *Saturday Review of Literature* 10, 48 [June 16, 1934]: 750).

51. Alice James to William James, December 2, 1891; as quoted in Yeazell, *Death and Letters*, 200.

52. Richard Rorty, *Contingency, Irony, and Solidarity* (Cambridge: Cambridge University Press, 1989), 43.

Redefinitions and Resistance

5

A Pupil and a Patient
Hospital-Schools in Progressive America

Brad Byrom

Around the turn of the twentieth century, a new definition of disability emerged in the United States. As Americans moved from a nineteenth-century system of beliefs rooted in Protestant ideology to a modern culture embedded in secular ideologies, a new understanding of disability evolved. Beginning around 1890, with the creation of the first institutions most aptly referred to as "hospital-schools" and the opening of the first programs for the vocational training of "cripples," an approach to the problem of disability emerged that became known as *rehabilitation*.[1]

In examining the words and deeds of those involved in the movement, it is apparent that the years between 1890 and 1920 constitute a distinctive period in disability history. The movement acted as a bridge spanning the gap between nineteenth-century supernatural and post-1920 medical explanations of disability. The reformers who led this movement identified what they called "crippledom" as a serious social and economic problem. The term *cripple* referred to individuals with mobility impairments, such as amputees and paraplegics. But more than a physical description, in common usage the term also indicated economic dependency. In relying on charity, reformers believed, cripples became immoral characters who siphoned off the lifeblood of the economy. The elimination of dependency among cripples became the focus of the rehabilitation movement.

In attempting to solve the riddle of dependency, reformers struck an uneasy balance between social approaches to disability that sought to reform cultural attitudes and individual or medical approaches intended to correct flaws in disabled people. This balance is evident not only in the discourse that surrounded the rehabilitation movement but in the structure and purpose of the institutions created. Some reformers, whom I describe as "social rehabilitationists," emphasized the need for social and cultural change and saw little need to change the disabled person through surgery, physical therapy, or other such methods. "Medical rehabilitationists," by contrast, viewed the individual as the central problem of disability and focused their efforts on orthopedic surgery, moral education, and other solutions centering on repair of the individual.[2] Yet it is also important to realize that neither group outwardly rejected the tenets of the other. In fact, most rehabilitationists reflected a bit of each perspective in their writings. Thus, it is best to see the differences between the two groups as points along a continuum, separated by degrees of emphasis, rather than as diametrically opposed positions.

The approach taken by medical rehabilitationists forms the core of what is defined by scholars in the field of disability studies as the "medical model." Those who employ this model define disability in the language of medicine, which lends scientific credibility to the notion that physical and mental abnormalities are at the root of all problems encountered by disabled individuals. Medical rehabilitationists absolved society of any complicity in the exclusion of disabled people from such social functions as employment, marriage, and even access to public institutions such as schools or government buildings. On this point social rehabilitationists clearly differed. Yet, somewhat surprisingly, neither group rejected the ideas of the other or even seemed aware of the contradictions within the movement. Instead, many, if not most, blurred the lines between the social and medical perspectives in their own writings, expressing elements of both approaches in their calls for reform.

By settling on a middle ground between the two approaches, rehabilitationists inadvertently slowed, but did not prevent, the full development of the medical model. In an age noted for its devotion to science and the expert, the slow growth of the medical paradigm demands an explanation. This explanation can be found by looking to the position of the "scientific experts" most directly connected to the rehabilitation movement—orthopedic surgeons.

In the first decades of the century, orthopedists lacked the credibility necessary to dominate the rehabilitation movement. Over the century or so prior to 1890, they gained recognition in the medical community as the specialists best suited to the care of cripples.[3] Despite their uncontested position in medical circles, they failed to gain preeminence in the rehabilitation movement until the conclusion of World War I. Known in the nineteenth century as "sawbones" or worse, early-twentieth-century orthopedic surgeons failed to earn unquestioned control of rehabilitation and were forced to share leadership with businessmen, social scientists, teachers, and other "progressive," reform-minded individuals. These individuals came together to answer the most fundamental questions concerning disability: Did older, nineteenth-century notions of divine causation still have validity in the twentieth century? Were cripples primarily a product of individual, physical impairment? Or rather, were they victims of stereotypes and social discrimination?

In cities such as Boston, New York, and Cleveland, reformers of the 1890s began to address these questions with unprecedented enthusiasm. The conclusions they reached rejected supernatural causes, explaining "disability" as a product of the interaction between physical impairment and social prejudice. The final explanation, while laced with contradictions, was a compromise between the opinions of social and medical rehabilitationists.

The nearly unanimous opinion among reformers that employment provided the best solution to the problem of disability also fit well with the development of a program planted on the middle ground. To rehabilitationists, the greatest problem facing the cripple was rejection from the workplace.[4] Enforced unemployment denied cripples access to something many considered the most fundamental right and responsibility of citizenship. To rehabilitationists and other Progressives, citizenship was a fairly uncomplicated matter, at least as it applied to males. It involved a give and take. The obligation of every male citizen was to work. Through work, men contributed to the economic well-being of the nation, set an example for younger generations, and symbolized the most prized aspect of the American character—independence. Without work, men became parasites feeding off the labors of others. Not only a duty, work also served as America's promise to its male citizens—a promise thought to benefit the individual in immeasurable ways.[5] In the words of one rehabilitationist, it provided "the only opportunity for real happiness." Only through employment could a man "look up at the sky every night and say 'I too, am doing my work in your world, O God!'"[6] To rehabilitationists, dependent cripples symbolized the antithesis of American citizenship, challenging America's identity as the land of opportunity. Such a situation necessitated reform.

The rehabilitationists' emphasis on employment led some to define "cure" as a physical improvement that increased an individual's chances of getting a job.[7] They even referred to certain aspects of rehabilitation itself as the "work cure."[8] The focus on work encouraged reformers to look beyond the disabled individual for an explanation of disability in society. This belief gained credence after a group of New York reformers canvassed local businesses and discovered that many employers assumed "that a cripple must be a beggar" and therefore denied job opportunities even to well-qualified, "reconstructed" cripples. The persistence of such beliefs convinced some advocates that rehabilitating the cripple required a change in cultural attitudes. "Until we can get public opinion more friendly towards the employment of cripples," wrote one rehabilitationist, "our placement cannot be extensive."[9] To achieve such a state of mind, social rehabilitationists made a top priority of convincing the public to hire cripples on equal terms with the nondisabled.

In the nineteenth century, Americans viewed cripples as members of the "afflicted" class—individuals suffering from divinely inspired physical conditions that left them dependent on the goodwill of more fortunate Americans.[10] Protestant religious doctrine reinforced the perception of the disabled person as dependent by teaching that a good Christian provided for "the lame, the halt and the blind," much as Jesus of Nazareth had done. The first institution created for crippled children in the United States fit well into this set of beliefs. During the Civil War, the New York Hospital for the Ruptured and Crippled became the first institution to address the problem of the crippled child. Construction of the hospital began after the dramatic appearance of disabled beggars on the streets of New York City in the early 1860s. The unique economic conditions produced by the war encouraged hundreds of disabled people—a startling number of whom were children—to beg for alms. Their presence so shocked and offended the sensibilities of some New Yorkers that an influential and well-to-do group united to create an institution designed to eliminate the problem.[11]

Dr. James Knight served as the first superintendent of the hospital. A model of medical conservatism during his twenty-four years as surgeon-in-chief,[12] Knight decried unproven or risky surgical procedures. He castigated those who practiced heroic surgery as "arrogant and mendacious exponent[s] of adventurous treatment"[13] and himself performed no more than seventy or eighty operations, mostly minor, on the approximately 180 children who entered the hospital during any given year. Yet he did treat his patients in other ways. He used orthotic devices to correct or brace disabled limbs, a dietary regime and physical exercise, as well as moral instruction, academic education, and vocational training to bring his pupil-patients into conformity with nondisabled norms.

Though considered something of a medical prude by more aggressive contemporaries and later rehabilitation-era orthopedists such as his successor Virgil Gibney, Knight constructed an institution that superficially resembled the Progressive Era hospital-school. His approach was not unlike that of the rehabilitationists in that he intended not only to provide crippled children with medical care but to prevent them from becoming mendicants by instilling in them the desire and skills to become moral citizens. But on closer examination, the comparison between Knight and the rehabilitationists breaks down. He set out less to "cure" children than, in a word frequently employed in his discharge reports, to "relieve" them. He attained relief through the use of minor medical procedures to ease painful or potentially dangerous conditions and through the use of educational, vocational, and moral training. If crippled children could be taught the immorality of begging while developing a small degree of earning capacity, he had fulfilled his mission and had relieved his charges.[14] Rarely did he achieve what rehabilitationists considered a cure—the conversion of the dependent cripple into "an earning, serving unit."[15] While rehabilitationists mirrored Knight's distaste for dependency, they carried this focus further, defining the problem of disability in terms of citizenship. In many ways, Knight's hospital foreshadowed the efforts of the rehabilitationists, but with less confidence, less public support, and a focus more narrowly trained on the individual. In this way, Knight contributed as much to the development of the medical model as he did to the rehabilitation movement. Though clearly an opponent of aggressive medical practices, and in fact, a man dedicated as much to education as to surgery, he nonetheless believed that the crippled child rather than society was most in need of repair. He made no apparent effort to change public attitudes toward employment of the cripple, nor did he agitate for any significant social change. In this sense, he differed from "adventurous" surgeons only in the means employed to correct the crippled child.

By the early twentieth century, the growing focus on correction of the individual exhibited by Knight and his more aggressive successors seemed to signal the coming of the medical model. Late-nineteenth-century changes in the medical profession supported this trend. Medical innovations from anesthesia to X rays provided surgeons with newfound respect. Meanwhile, the establishment of professional medical organizations, the creation and refinement of medical journals, the development of an increasingly specialized medical lexicon, and the reform of medical schools added great prestige to the medical profession. Such changes allowed physicians to gain unprecedented control over illness.[16] For their part, orthopedists established their own medical journals (including the *American Journal of Orthopedic Surgery*), surgical innovations, and institutions in which to perform their craft.

Beginning in the 1890s, individual philanthropists along with a number of organizations (most notably fraternal organizations such as the Rotarians and the Shriners) began working to create institutions that they believed would greatly improve the lives of crippled children; they then secured the help of orthopedists to achieve this goal.[17] The mostly nondisabled men and women who directed the rehabilitation movement not only worked with disabled children but also engaged in the accompanying effort to rehabilitate disabled military veterans injured in World War I and civilians injured in the "industrial army."[18] The institutions they created provided orthopedists with a base from which to develop their burgeoning specialty.

Of course, all this greatly benefited the orthopedists' reputation, a fact that would seem to suggest increased medical authority over physical disability, followed by the rapid emergence of a medical model to dominance in shaping societal understanding of disability. Yet certain events intervened that not only slowed the rise of the orthopedic profession and the development of the medical model but complicated both the rehabilitationists' agenda and public perceptions of disability. To begin with, doctors did not dominate rehabilitation. Many of the philanthropists and reformers who helped create the rehabilitation movement ended up sharing control with medical practitioners in each of its two main areas of work: hospital-schools and vocational rehabilitation. Leaders of the movement included businessmen, medical doctors, nurses, sociologists, bureaucrats, politicians, publicists, and even a few disabled adults.

Of those who came to the movement from outside the medical profession, Douglas C. McMurtrie and Joseph F. Sullivan were the most influential. The opinions of each, at least prior to 1920, reflect the social rehabilitationists' perspective. As a prosperous businessman in the craft of printing, McMurtrie's wealth and position allowed him to become a filter through which the vast bulk of information concerning the movement passed. His writings reflected the belief "that the greatest handicap is not a loss of limb or other disability but the weight of public opinion."[19] To him, the most important aspect of rehabilitation involved changing traditional attitudes toward disabled people. McMurtrie held the nondisabled primarily responsible for the dependency that characterized America's crippled population.

Sullivan expressed similar views, though he approached the subject from a vantage point that the nondisabled McMurtrie could not—as a self-proclaimed cripple. After contracting polio at an early age, Sullivan lost muscle function in both legs and one arm. Throughout his childhood, he met with great difficulty gaining physical access to school and social acceptance in the workplace. Perhaps this experience led him, unlike many of his contemporaries, to conclude that cripples comprised "a noble class of humanity" whose greatest need was opportunity.[20] Like McMurtrie, he entered the publishing profession. As an editor of small newspapers and magazines, and as author of numerous articles in larger publications, Sullivan served as an advocate for disabled children for over twenty years. During this time, he consistently argued that disability emanated from "a social arrangement that virtually condemns the cripple to mendicancy," rather than from the physical limitations of the individual.[21] To Sullivan and other, like-minded reformers, the problem of disability began in childhood—or, more precisely, in school.

Prior to 1920, Sullivan rarely wavered in his position that education and opportunity were the only tools needed for the success of the cripple. Nevertheless, he agreed with McMurtrie and other rehabilitationists that, in some ways, it was necessary to adapt the crippled child to an inaccessible world. The most significant way in which he voiced this belief was through his support of surgical intervention. In doing so, he failed to recognize that his support of orthopedic surgery not only aided the rise of that profession to greater status but unwittingly contradicted the social rehabilitationists' oft-repeated argument that "the great sufferings of crippledom" had little to do with one's "physical conditions."[22] Even an individual as self-consciously committed to social rehabilitation as Sullivan found his way to the middle ground between social and medical explanations of disability.

At the opposite end of the spectrum from Sullivan and McMurtrie, others in the rehabilitation movement placed little blame on society. Instead, they argued that the real source of disability lay in the physical and moral failings of the individual. Of those who expressed this opinion, many, if not most, came from a background in the medical sciences.[23] Medical rehabilitationists discovered a pathological process that explained the peculiar "mental kinks" they believed present in most individuals who lived with a disability for an extended period of time. Augustus Thorndike typified this outlook. As an orthopedic surgeon, he became familiar with the efforts around Boston (a leading city in the rehabilitation movement) to provide crippled children with industrial training. Within the industrial schools, he wrote, "all teachers realize the mental warp of the cripple, and struggle to overcome it."[24] To Thorndike and like-minded individuals, the cripple was a product of an ambiguous process of moral degeneration in which feelings of worthlessness, magnified by alcohol and reinforced by the pity of friends and families, produced a shiftless personality.

Charles H. Jaeger, a doctor who worked with both adult and child cripples, provides another example of the victim-blaming practiced by medical rehabilitationists. He explained the acquisition of a dependent spirit in a theory born of both the social and medical sciences:

Well-intentioned but ill-advised friends and relations coddle the patient. He is cared for and supported until he has lost his ambition to work. In his idle hours he seeks solace and companionship in the saloon. This environment still further aids in the moral decline [of the individual into dependency]. It is an easy step to beg for the money thus needed, and when he once finds out how profitable this is, he loses his desire to work.[25]

In the expression of their dependency theories, medical rehabilitationists conceived of dependency itself as something of a pathological process, through which the individual gradually became incapable of independence. Yet Thorndike's theory did not outwardly reject the assertions made by his counterparts, the social rehabilitationists. Though placing primary blame for the dependency that rehabilitationists equated with disability on the cripple, both Thorndike and Jaeger agreed that blame for the cripple's dependent status came "from both himself and the employer." Even to the staunchest of medical rehabilitationists, disability was understood as a product of individual failings coupled with a cultural understanding of disability that encouraged the dependency of the cripple.

Rehabilitationists of all stripes seem to have accepted that long-term disability created an entrenched and all-but-impossible sense of dependency in the individual. In turn, this belief led to the logical conclusion that, if long-term mendicant cripples made poor candidates for rehabilitation, then children made the best subjects. Further, the best subjects of all were those who lacked the dependency-generating comforts of the well-to-do. Thus, in the scheme of rehabilitation, poor children represented the best subjects, whereas affluent adults represented the worst. "These poor, neglected children," Jaeger concluded, "not spoiled by over-indulgence or schooled in depravity, have proven that, with a little care and effort expended along right lines, the problem of the cripple can be solved."[26]

Medical rehabilitationists had other reasons for the focus on indigent children. For one, children provided little resistance to medical authorities and therefore made ideal patients for a developing medical specialty that lacked the confidence of the American public. Their very dependency, their young ages, and the requirement of many hospital-schools that their parents give the institution temporary custody meant that orthopedists had broad control over the direction of their patients' medical regime. Thus, for orthopedists, indigent children made the ideal subjects for their developing medical specialty.

Rehabilitationists also focused on children because of the appeal children held for philanthropists. In their fund-raising campaigns, hospital-school administrators relied heavily on the sentimental appeal of their young charges, whether they were soliciting from wealthy philanthropists or state legislators. Thus, with the exception of the war years (1917–1919), when fears of an insufficient labor force encouraged Americans to rehabilitate adult males, children from working-class families provided the focus of rehabilitation efforts.

Rehabilitationists on both sides of the fence appeared oblivious to, or at least willing to overlook, the obvious contradictions that existed between the social and medical approaches to rehabilitation. In all their writings, Sullivan and McMurtrie never directly challenged the position of medical rehabilitationists.[27] For their part, Jaeger, Thorndike, and like-minded reformers never expressed opposition to the social rehabilitationists' position. Instead, all seem to have accepted without question the existence of a middle ground between the two perspectives in a move that, wittingly or not, kept the movement united. Apparently unrecognized by rehabilitationists on either side, however, was that in playing the role of the mugwump, each side effectively weakened its fundamental thesis. Calls for new medical facilities to treat crippled children weakened social arguments that claimed only society needed to change. Similarly, medical arguments blaming individual impairment for disability lost force in the face of assertions that social discrimination caused disability.

Further complicating matters, medical rehabilitationists typically presented one set of views in the popular media and another in trade and academic journals, where the only audience expected was other rehabilitationists. In the popular press, medical rehabilitationists exonerated the cripple of complicity in dependent status. A stream of articles featuring stories of successful cripples appeared in popular magazines such as *The Outlook, Ladies' Home Journal,* and *American Magazine.* Though not all such articles came from rehabilitationists, many did, and most such stories appeared between 1917 and 1921, at the peak of the rehabilitation movement.[28] These brief biographies detailed the great obstacles overcome by disabled individuals who had attained employment and generally supported the notion that society alone was responsible for the dependency of the disabled person. Given a chance, all cripples could succeed. Meanwhile, in journals intended primarily for other rehabilitationists, such as the *American Journal of Care for Cripples*, medical rehabilitationists contradicted such claims, placing blame for dependency and disability squarely on the individual. Indeed, the very efforts to reform cripples surgically and morally contradicted many of the claims made in popular magazines. The inconsistency of medical rehabilitationists served important functions. By presenting the cripple as a capable individual, rehabilitationists helped open up the job opportunities for cripples necessary for their vocational success; in locating fault in them, orthopedists justified their own work and the institutions they built.

Consensus as to the ultimate objective of rehabilitation—employment of the cripple—bound the two rehabilitation perspectives together. In fact, some went so far as to suggest that "productive workers . . . are no longer classified as cripples, and dare not be so regarded."[29] Virtually all rehabilitationists, no matter what type of institution they created, shared the common goal of employment for the cripple. Most agreed that to succeed required a combination of education and medical care.

Rehabilitationists initially placed primary emphasis on training the minds and bodies of young cripples through the hospital-school. Though boys were clearly the primary object of the rehabilitation movement, girls were included in numbers that in some institutions may even have exceeded those of their male counterparts. Given that the ultimate goal of the movement prior to 1920 was employment or preparation for employment, this is a somewhat surprising finding. Most Americans of the time still objected to the employment of large numbers of women. And, while girls were trained primarily for traditional women's jobs such as sewing and teaching, they were encouraged to continue through high school and even into college in a day in which the education of most girls from working-class families ended before high school.[30]

Why did rehabilitationists give such special consideration to crippled girls? The explanation lies in the very different conception of the roles of disabled and nondisabled women. It was widely believed that the crippled woman was unfit for marriage and thus would need to find some means of support. Writing in 1919 as a middle-aged woman, an anonymous cripple recalled the day some decades earlier on which she became engaged. The announcement "aroused a storm of disapproval and dismay; of pity for the man, pity for the woman and dire predictions for both." Relatives had long since explained to the would-be bride that "married life was too exacting" and that she was too "unattractive." Courageously, she rejected this advice and soon disproved the predictions of her relatives.[31] The story illustrates the difficulties faced by women who sought acceptance in the traditional role of housewife. It also helps explain the willingness of rehabilitationists to provide crippled girls with greater access to education.

For both boys and girls, then, rehabilitationists created the hospital-school. In all, U.S. rehabilitationists built some seventy institutions fitting the hospital-school mode over the thirty-four-year span between 1890 and 1924, and yet the history of these institutions has scarcely been touched upon.[32] Hospital-schools ranged in size from modest facilities of less than thirty "pupil-patients" to large institutions with hundreds of beds. Though diverse in their physical structure and mission, they shared a commitment to providing the crippled child with varying levels of both medical treatment and education. In the early years of the hospital-school, between roughly 1890 and 1915, education held an equal, if not superior, position to medicine on the agendas of many such institutions. During this time, few were willing to trust the fate of the crippled child solely to orthopedists, even though orthopedists generally conducted only those operations that posed little or no threat to the patient's life.[33]

Reformers employed the term *rehabilitation* to refer not only to the surgical and therapeutic treatment of cripples but to the rehabilitation of public attitudes toward disabled people.[34] In this important way they differed from their predecessors and complicated America's move toward the medical model. Those who emphasized the reshaping of public attitudes pointed to flaws in American society to explain the problem of disability. In doing so, they evinced the influence on the rehabilitation movement of emerging social sciences such as sociology and psychology. By the 1890s, researchers in the social sciences had concluded that childhood was a formative period in which social values were instilled—values that could not be easily replaced in later life.[35] Thus rehabilitationists demonstrated a particular concern with addressing the problem of idleness before it took root in the child. In studying the lives of children in the poorest areas of both rural and urban America, researchers discovered a number of factors that inhibited the child's growth into moral citizenship. A poor diet, unhealthy air, cramped living conditions, and disability all conspired to hinder the development of critical values in the working-class child.[36] Reformers intended to overcome such obstacles through the unique combination of medicine and education offered in the hospital-school.

For adults, a different institution was deemed necessary—vocational rehabilitation. The most important example was the Red Cross Institute for Crippled and Disabled Men in New York City.[37] This institute, which worked closely with the Surgeon General's Office during World War I, was created in 1917 as an experiment in the rehabilitation of adult male cripples. The "greater work" of the agency, headed by Douglas McMurtrie, was "in the abstract field of research and public education." The institute began its work with "a general educational movement . . . to create an enlightened public opinion towards the physically handicapped, so that they will be regarded from the standpoint of their capabilities rather than their disabilities. This is undoubtedly the most important phase of the whole question."[38]

To accomplish this goal the institute created a publicity service that regularly issued press releases to over eleven hundred newspapers nationwide, encouraging "comment that might be helpful to the cause of the disabled." A speakers bureau equipped with slides and film reels organized vast meetings at Carnegie Hall and the Hippodrome, canvassed hundreds of New York–area businesses seeking commitments to hiring cripples, and sent out a circular along with AT&T bills to over 1 million New York residents.[39] Through these and other publicity devices, institute leaders hoped to convince the public to consider the cripple a competent and capable citizen.

Despite placing primary emphasis on changing public opinion, the institute nonetheless ended up on the middle ground between social and medical rehabilitation with regard to adaptation. Outwardly, U.S. rehabilitationists claimed to use something known as the "American method" in making workplace adaptations. In the American method, "the cripple is regarded as the fixt [sic] element, and the device or method is adapted to the individual who uses it." This method stood in contrast to the European method, in which individuals were adapted to particular jobs, sometimes even using prosthetic devices that created a literal connection between man and machine.[40] The American method would seem to represent a social approach to the problem, since it required adaptation of a social barrier, while the European method more closely approximated a medical approach. In reality, however, American rehabilitationists hedged on their policy of not adapting men to jobs. The Institute for the Crippled and Disabled, for instance, maintained a workshop for the construction of artificial limbs, braces, and appliances in an effort to make cripples more employable. As an institute publication explained, "A limp is less objectionable to an employer than crutches."[41]

After 1920, vocational rehabilitationists drifted toward the medical model. During the 1910s, the Institute for Crippled and Disabled Men had been used as a training ground for those who would soon enter the mainstream workforce. Eventually this policy changed in a way that, to insiders, must have seemed subtle. In retrospect, however, the establishment of a sheltered workshop in May 1927 signaled a major shift in the institute's approach to rehabilitation. The workshop was intended as a way station of sorts between "homebound" workers and "regular employment."[42] Yet the move had tremendous symbolic significance. The increasing number of sheltered workshops that emerged around the country beginning in the Progressive era served as a symbol of the cripple's inferior status in the job market. It was, in effect, an admission by institute leaders that not all cripples were fit for regular employment, at least not without specialized training.

Though superficially a very different facility, the rehabilitation movement's other major institutional contribution, the hospital-school, was also built on rehabilitation's middle ground during the 1910s, then slipped into full embrace of the medical model in the 1920s. Rehabilitationists used the term *hospital-school* to describe institutions that combined varying degrees of education (moral, vocational, and academic), socialization, and medical practice. They were not purely medical institutions. Even the staunchest proponent of orthopedic surgery could agree that "the medical and surgical treatment of the physical ills of the body should always be supplemented by a similar effort to educate the mind of the cripple."[43] This idea was the backbone of the hospital-school, an institution unique to the rehabilitation era with a name that clearly illustrates the competing interpretations of disability that comprised the middle ground.

Not unlike institutes of vocational rehabilitation, hospital-schools were created to act as a temporary haven for crippled children from an outside world seemingly hostile to their very existence. Many attempted to create a physical environment in which the child could be entirely independent. In her 1914 study of institutions for crippled children, Edith Reeves placed great importance on the presence of adaptive equipment in evaluating such schools, while providing the modern observer with a glimpse into the workings of the hospital-school. Though few could afford to make all the adaptations Reeves applauded, institutions unencumbered by funding restraints created a few models that are most suggestive of what rehabilitationists hoped to accomplish.

During the 1910s, the Widener Memorial School for Crippled Children in Philadelphia set the standard of care. Thanks to the philanthropy of P. A. B.

Widener, who donated some $4 million to the institution, rehabilitationists were able to construct a prototype hospital-school that reflected the values of both social and medical rehabilitationists. Social rehabilitationists were no doubt pleased by the existence of a gymnasium equipped with the latest in adaptive equipment. Accessibility for mobility-impaired children was of prime concern. Elevators provided access to upper floors in the main buildings, and thresholds were eliminated from all doorways. Buildings were connected by glass-enclosed passageways that were heated in the winter. Adjustable desks and seats provided schoolchildren with accessible seating. Widener's medical facilities were also state of the art. Occasional use of the gymnasium for therapy rather than recreation, along with a surgical suite "comparable with those in the most completely modern general hospitals," reminded children that, despite the accessibility of their current accommodations, the burden of adaptation was ultimately theirs.[44]

Some institutions, such as the Van Leuven Browne Hospital School, the Minnesota State Hospital and School for Indigent Crippled and Deformed Children, and the Massachusetts Hospital School, maintained a strong, if not dominant, medical element. Of thirty-two institutions in a 1914 study of institutions for crippled children constructed during the rehabilitation era (1890–1914), all but one provided an orthopedic surgeon or other doctor with access to their pupil-patients. Some of these doctors were residents, though many others appear to have been visiting physicians.

In contrast to this medical presence, twenty-five of the institutions provided children with regular access to academic education, through resident teachers, visiting teachers, or nearby schools for crippled children. In addition, twenty-two of the institutions offered children some form of vocational training. These statistics suggest that the vast majority of the institutions created during the rehabilitation era supplied the basic ingredients of a hospital-school—institutions that included both education and medicine.

While physicians often became the most important individuals within such institutions, their authority did not go unchecked. To begin with, physicians ran relatively few hospital-schools. As of 1914, doctors held chief administrative positions at fewer than one-fourth of all such facilities. Statistics from that year reveal that doctors ran only seven of the thirty hospital-schools that provided the name of their superintendents. Of the twenty-three institutions with medical laypersons in charge, twenty-one superintendents were listed with the title Miss, Mrs., or Sister, while another two were listed as Mr. and Father.[45] The high number of women in charge of such institutions is probably explained by traditional gender roles. The assignment of women to the role of caregiver—whether as mother, educator, or nurse—made them the logical choice for the care of crippled children. Most administrators left few, if any, written records of their own ideological position within the rehabilitation movement. Still, it is clear that the majority worked to develop institutions that paid more than passing consideration to both the education and the medical treatment of the crippled child. They, too, seem to have sought out the middle ground.

The authority of the orthopedists within the rehabilitation movement was further limited by the poor reputation of the orthopedic profession. At the turn of the century, many Americans, especially members of the working-class poor families for whom most hospital-schools were constructed, shunned orthopedists as charlatans bent on turning crippled children into subjects of experimentation. And in fact, at teaching hospitals, which mostly served indigent populations and where most children were admitted, doctors referred to their patients as "clinical material."[46] Doubts concerning the efficacy of orthopedic treatment extended to the middle and upper classes and even plagued orthopedists themselves. Despite their faith in science, prior to World War I few rehabilitationists believed orthopedics was capable of curing the crippled child, though they proved far more willing to try than working-class parents wanted.[47] Within the medical establishment, the responsibility for treating crippled children had long since been conferred on the orthopedic surgeon. Yet, from the time the first orthopedic hospital for crippled children opened its doors in the United States during the Civil War, only the boldest of orthopedists were willing to make the claim of being able to fully cure physical disability. Most clung to the cautious path of medical conservatism first tread by James Knight and other nineteenth-century orthopedists who made relieving rather than curing their goal.[48]

Most hospital administrators also shunned orthopedists, though for reasons related to economics more than reputation. The early twentieth-century practice of orthopedics involved a time-consuming combination of surgery followed by months of therapy. In many cases, this formula had to be repeated several times to attain physical changes that, with some imagination, might be labeled a "cure." From the perspective of hospital administrators, the lengthy therapies and questionable results produced by such practices conflicted with the bottom-line exigencies of the modern hospital. Whereas nineteenth-century hospitals acted primarily as convalescent homes, the modern, twentieth-century hospital emerged as something of a profit-making enterprise. Though most hospitals still relied heavily on philanthropy, the efficiency-minded Progressive Era hospital administrator, who emphasized the bottom line, demanded an institution that did more than nurse the sick. Besides, philanthropists generally gave their support to hospitals with the highest reputations, and reputations were based largely on the number of patients "cured" in a given hospital. The skepticism of the public and the priorities of hospital administrators kept orthopedics on the periphery of medical respectability.[49]

The conclusion that medical practice did not dominate the hospital-school is further supported by an analysis of discharge policies in 1914. The conditions under which children were discharged demonstrated a commitment not only to medical care but to education and vocational training. Hospital-schools discharged pupil-patients for a number of reasons, but only five institutions established policies based purely on medical considerations.[50] Two others released children only if educational opportunities could be found elsewhere, while thirteen did so only after the pupil-patients were able to secure a job and find another home.[51] Flexibility was the key to most discharge policies. At the Widener Memorial School, for instance, where the parents of admitted children "signed an indenture binding [the] child over to the trustees of the institution until he shall reach his majority (21 years of age)," pupil-patients might gain an early release "if ready to begin wage-earning."[52] Similarly, at the Massachusetts Hospital School, children might be permitted to stay for long periods of time, even after all medical avenues had been exhausted, if it was thought the child could benefit from further education.[53] At the Minnesota State Hospital and School, discharge policies allowed pupil-patients to remain until "benefited as much as possible."[54] In this way, children could receive something more than medical treatment— they could be provided with the educational and vocational tools necessary to assume the responsibilities of moral citizenship.

Thus, circumstances conspired to prevent orthopedists from dominating the rehabilitation movement and, in the process, provided an opening for social rehabilitationists.[55] In this context, Sullivan, McMurtrie, and other social rehabilitationists found room for the expression of a perspective that challenged, however unintentionally, the basic tenets of the medical model. Yet none of these men committed himself to a position that denied medicine a role in solving the problem of disability. Even in the years prior to World War I, when orthopedic practice remained mired in doubts, the attitude expressed by social rehabilitationists toward medicine is best described as ambivalent. They neither promoted nor condemned surgical intervention.

Brad Byrom

By the mid-1910s, the middle ground began to shift toward the medical side of the rehabilitation movement. A growing number of reformers began emphasizing the importance of surgical and therapeutic intervention over education. The major reason for this change centered on the improved reputation of orthopedic practice. With its startling and unprecedented casualty rates, World War I produced a wealth of "clinical material" on which the orthopedist was able to develop his craft. Many of the casualties suffered impairment of one or more limbs—injuries that came to be referred to as "orthopedic handicaps." A number of American doctors, including such notable hospital-school orthopedists as H. Winnett Orr and Fred H. Albee, left for the battlefields of Europe even before the United States entered the war. The unusual circumstances surrounding battlefield surgery allowed orthopedists to develop innovative methods for repairing injured muscles, bones, and tendons. On returning to America, orthopedists brought with them greater knowledge, greater confidence, and, most important, greater respect in the eyes of their critics.[56] All that they lacked was clinical material. For many orthopedists, the hospitals that served America's disabled children would fill this need. The old strictures of conservatism that governed institutional practices in centers of orthopedics such as the Hospital for the Ruptured and Crippled loosened in the mayhem of total war.[57] From the outset of the rehabilitation era, orthopedic surgeons established their presence in hospital-schools, often without charge, thereby gaining a reputation as possibly the most philanthropic members of the medical profession.[58] This reputation combined with the newfound regard earned in World War I to help create a thriving medical specialty.[59]

Though it is difficult to gauge the exact level of involvement of orthopedists, the experiences of one asylum turned hospital-school and the pupil-patients there provide some indication of how changes in the orthopedic profession impacted on hospital-schools between 1900 and 1920. At the outset of its existence in 1907, the Van Leuven Browne Hospital School, much like other institutions for crippled children founded shortly after the turn of the century, was far less a hospital than a small asylum. Though doctors routinely visited and provided medical care, no surgeries were performed on the thirty or so pupil-patients living there until 1917.[60] This all began to change, however, with the conversion of Van Leuven Browne into the Michigan Hospital School. As the institution changed names, construction began on a new facility in the Michigan countryside that would increase capacity to two hundred pupil-patients. More important, a new administration allowed orthopedic surgeons, for the first time, to enter the lives of the children in the hospital-school.[61]

In 1919, a teenage girl wrote a note of thanks to her doctor and teacher at the Michigan Hospital School. The brief letter was relatively unremarkable, noting the educational and physical improvements she had made in her sixteen months at the institution. The letter appeared in the *Hospital School Journal* with a number of similar missives from other children who had been in the hospital-school. This teenage girl signed off with apparent affection: "I still remain a patient and a pupil,—Delphina."[62] Delphina entered the Michigan Hospital School at a time of transition. Neither completely a student nor exclusively a patient, her closing illustrates the tension within an institutional form that was neither fully hospital nor fully school, that accepted neither a social model of disability nor a medical model. By 1919, however, the experiences of pupil-patients like Delphina strongly suggested the direction in which hospital-schools, along with the American cultural definition of disability, was headed.

In 1913, another young pupil-patient named Edward Claypool had entered the same facility, then called Van Leuven Browne Hospital School. According to his own account, he had spent his first six years as a virtual prisoner in his home. Once at the institution, he reveled in the friendships and freedoms he discovered. Surrounded by other crippled children, living in a fairly accessible environment, and participating in both physical and intellectual activities designed for the physically disabled child, Edward gained access to a world from which he had previously been excluded. From the example of teachers and administrators at the small institution, two of whom were disabled themselves, he came to realize that a world of potential existed that he had never dared imagine. From the day he entered Van Leuven Browne in December 1913, he found that he "never again knew what it meant to be lonesome."[63]

But as Van Leuven Browne became a hospital-school, things began to change. The facility, which had once focused almost exclusively on educating and socializing disabled children, increasingly turned to medicine as a solution to the problem of disability. An orthopedic surgeon, William E. Blodgett, was enlisted and began a regular round of student examinations. Fortified by the increasing respect given to his profession as a result of World War I, he made regular use of surgery as a tool of rehabilitation. By 1918, surgery had become a part of the routine of daily life in the institution, now referred to as the Michigan Hospital School. Over the course of the next five years, Claypool underwent six surgeries aimed at allowing him to discard his crutches and braces. Yet, despite Blodgett's surgical efforts, at the age of fourteen Edward still required braces and crutches in order to walk.[64]

Changes in admission policies soon followed the upswing in orthopedic activity. Prior to 1920, most hospital-schools accepted all children regardless of whether or not their "condition" was amenable to surgical intervention.[65] By the 1920s, hospital-schools increasingly restricted entrance to those who could be aided by orthopedic surgery. The Michigan Hospital School exemplified such changes, deciding sometime after 1917 to accept only crippled children whom surgery would benefit. By 1924, the one-time Van Leuven Browne Hospital School had become part of the larger Michigan Children's Hospital. This final transformation reflected a larger national trend in which relatively small institutions that featured a mixture of education and medical care were absorbed or replaced by far larger, more exclusively medical institutions. Reflecting the same trend, whereas the *American Journal of Care for Cripples* (published 1914–1919) had focused on crippled children and primarily on their education, by the 1920s, periodicals such as the *Hospital School Journal* and the *Crippled Child* increasingly concentrated on curing cripples. Meanwhile, in terms of the cultural understanding of disability, the transformation of Van Leuven Browne signified the full emergence of the medical model of disability. With the coming of the medical model, social explanations of disability such as those that prevailed in the rehabilitation era virtually disappeared for the next half century. The experiences of Edward Claypool and others make it clear that with the increasing prestige and power of the orthopedic profession, the hospital-school, and American thought in general, was being pulled from the middle ground of the rehabilitation period toward the soon-to-be dominant medical model of disability. Joseph F. Sullivan provides the clearest sign of the medical model's ascendancy. By 1919 he devoted as much attention to the promotion of surgery as to education in his *Hospital School Journal*. He even wrote in favor of legislation "making it compulsory for parents to surrender their children to the authorities of the [Michigan Hospital School] when deemed expedient that the children might be treated in due time."[66] As the reputation of orthopedists improved, Sullivan and other social rehabilitationists who had once expressed ambivalence toward surgical intervention fell in line with the medical model.

1. The first institution referred to as a "hospital-school" was not created until after 1900. The first institution created in the mold of the hospital-school, however, was the New York Hospital for the Ruptured and Crippled, opened in 1863. This institution was followed closely by the New York Orthopedic Hospital, which opened in 1866. After this, no other significant institutions of this type were created until the 1890s. During this decade, several hospital-schools were created, including the House of St. Giles the Cripple in New York City (1891), the James Kernan Hospital and Industrial School near Baltimore (1895), and the State Hospital for Indigent Crippled and Deformed Children in St. Paul, Minnesota (1897). See Edith Reeves, *Care and Education of Crippled Children in the United States* (New York: Russell Sage Foundation, 1914); 168-233.

2. Social rehabilitationists and their counterparts, medical rehabilitationists, were separated not only by their competing explanations of the problem of disability but also by their backgrounds. Most social rehabilitationists did not come from a medical background, whereas many (though certainly not all) medical rehabilitationists did. Most rehabilitationists should be classified as neither, as they blended elements of each in addressing the problem of disability.

3. Little motivation existed for anyone to challenge the orthopedists' medical dominion over crippledom. It was commonly believed that cripples came primarily from the ranks of the poorest Americans, and therefore there was little profit to be made in caring for them.

4. The negative economic impact of unemployed disabled people is the topic of Garrard Harris, *The Redemption of the Disabled* (New York: D. Appleton and Company, 1919). Alice Willard Solenberger discusses the "Parasitic Cripple" and other types of unemployed crippled in *One Thousand Homeless Men* (New York: Charities Publication Committee, 1911), chaps. 3-6.

5. Numerous studies stress the importance of the work ethic in Progressive America. Among the most important of these are Daniel Rodgers, *The Work Ethic in Industrial America, 1850–1920* (Chicago: University of Chicago Press, 1978); and Herbert Gutman, *Work, Culture, and Society in Industrializing America: Essays in American Working-Class and Social History* (New York: Random House, 1977).

6. Elias Parker Butler, "Exit Mr. Tumult and Miss Shouting," *Carry On* 1 (October–November 1918): 12.

7. See, for instance, Harry E. Mock, "Reclamation of the Disabled from the Industrial Army," *Annals of the American Academy of Political and Social Science* 80 (November 1918): 29-34. Mock writes that a man is "disabled" only while "the doctor is helping cure him." Afterward, even if impairments remain, a man is "no longer classed as a cripple" if he "trains himself for work and becomes a productive citizen."

8. "The 'Work-Cure' for Crippled Soldiers," *Literary Digest* 62 (July 19, 1919): 24.

9. Gertrude R. Stein, "Placement Technique in the Employment Work of the Red Cross Institute for Crippled and Disabled Men," in Douglas C. McMurtrie, ed., *Publications of the Red Cross Institute for Crippled and Disabled Men* 1 (May 6, 1918): 10.

10. For a discussion of nineteenth-century views of disability, see Douglas C. Baynton, *Forbidden Signs: American Culture and the Campaign against Sign Language* (Chicago: University of Chicago Press, 1996), 102. The twentieth-century medical model of disability is discussed in Michael Oliver, *The Politics of Disablement* (New York: St. Martin's Press, 1990) 1–4; and Robert Bogdan, *Freak Show: Presenting Human Oddities for Amusement and Profit* (Chicago: University of Chicago Press, 1988), 274–78.

11. The "ruptured" were children with hernias.

12. The vast majority of surgeons, even in the rehabilitation era, were conservatives. Even Knight's successor, Virgil Gibney, was said to approach surgical intervention "with fear and caution." See Fenwick Beekman, *Hospital for the Ruptured and Crippled: A Historical Sketch Written on the Occasion of the Seventy-fifth Anniversary of the Hospital* (New York: privately printed, 1939), 47.

13. Ibid., 13.

14. Ibid., 29–47; Charles E. Rosenberg, *The Care of Strangers: The Rise of America's Hospital System* (New York: Basic Books, 1987).

15. Mock, "Reclamation of the Disabled," 30.

16. The standard history of medical professionalization in the United States is Paul Starr's seminal book *The Social Transformation of American Medicine: The Rise of a Sovereign Profession and the Making of a Vast Industry* (New York: Basic Books, 1982).

17. It should be pointed out that, while medical laymen were behind the creation of many such institutions, a number were created by orthopedists as well. See Katherine W. Ambrose Shrady, "The History of the Federation of Associations for Cripples," *American Journal of Care for Cripples* 1 (1914): 21.

18. Many of the most prominent reformers in the movement to aid crippled children, including Douglas C. McMurtrie and Dr. Fred H. Albee, were also leaders in the movement to rehabilitate America's soldiers.

19. Douglas C. McMurtrie, *The Disabled Soldier* (New York: MacMillan Company, 1919), 26.

20. Joseph F. Sullivan, *The Unheard Cry* (Nashville: privately printed, 1914), 37.

21. Joseph F. Sullivan, "A Plea to the Legislators of Michigan," *Hospital School Journal* 7 (November–December 1918): 4.

22. Ibid.

23. It should be pointed out, however, that not all doctors fixed the blame for disability wholly on the individual.

24. Augustus Thorndike, "Industrial Training for Crippled Children About Boston," *American Journal of Care for Cripples* 1 (1914): 19.

25. Charles H. Jaeger, "Trade Training for Adult Cripples," *American Journal of Care for Cripples* 1, 2 (June 1915): 68.

26. Ibid., 69.

27. Sullivan did challenge the idea that some individuals were beyond help and should be rejected by society as a result of physical inadequacies. See Joseph F. Sullivan, "Who Are the Unfit? A Question and a Reply to a College Professor," *Hospital School Journal* 9 (May–June 1921): 11.

28. The Surgeon General's Office and the Red Cross Institute for Crippled and Disabled Men each maintained a large publicity department that worked to encourage publications to produce just such types of articles. Examples include B. C. Forbes, "A Genius Who Never Walked a Step," *American Magazine* 89 (April 1920): 9–11; Norman Blake, "How One Man Overcame," *Ladies' Home Journal* 34 (November 1917): 64; Lacy Simms, "Useful as Other Men Are," *The Outlook* 120 (September 11, 1918): 54–57.

29. Charles A. Lauffer, "The Injured in Industry," *Carry On* 1 (June 1919): 11.

30. They also received training in a few occupations, such as stenography and secretarial work, that were transitioning to the women's sphere in the early twentieth century.

31. "What I Faced in My Life," *Ladies' Home Journal* 30 (February 1919): 13.

32. Not all these institutions were called hospital-schools. See Henry Howard Abt, *The Care, Cure and Education of the Crippled Child* (Elyria, Ohio: International Society for Crippled Children, 1924), passim.

33. Frederick Fox Cartwright, *The Development of Modern Surgery* (New York: Thomas Y. Crowell Company, 1967), 146–57. Instead, orthopedists focused largely on therapeutic measures such as bracing, stretching, and dieting, while other, social rehabilitationists worked to educate cripples and to alter public opinion concerning the cripple.

34. The double meaning of *rehabilitation* is illustrative of what separates this period from the subsequent period. Rehabilitation featured (and continues to feature) a focus on correcting the individual, by providing him or her with medical services or employment services. But to social rehabilitationists, the term also signified a rehabilitation of society and, in particular, social norms relating to disability. Though prior to the 1910s reformers did not employ this or any other specific term to describe their work (they spoke only of the "care, cure, and education" of crippled children), during World War I, as the movement peaked, *rehabilitation* gained widespread use.

35. Michael B. Katz, *In the Shadow of the Poorhouse: A Social History of Welfare in America* (New York: Basic Books, 1986), 115.

36. A few examples of studies that emphasized the problems presented by disability include Willard's, *One Thousand Homeless Men*; Nels Andersen, *The Hobo: The Sociology of the Homeless Man* (Chicago: University of Chicago Press, 1923); and F. C. Laubach, "Why There Are Vagrants" (published privately by the Municipal Lodging House of New York City, 1910).

37. Later referred to as the New York Institute for the Crippled and Disabled and today known as the International Center for the Disabled (ICD).

38. Howard R. Heydon, "The Supremacy of the Spirit," *Annals of the American Academy of Political and Social Science* 80 (November 1918): 55.

39. John Culbert Faries, *Three Years of Work for Handicapped Men: A Report of the Activities of the Red Cross Institute for Crippled and Disabled Men* (New York: Institute Crippled and Disabled Men, 1919), 70–75.

40. "Putting the Crippled on the Pay-Roll," *Literary Digest* 54 (March 10, 1917): 617–18.

41. Institute for the Crippled and Disabled, *Some Things a Ten-Year-Old Knows about Cripples* (New York: privately printed, 1928), 7.

42. Ibid., 9.

43. Newton M. Shaffer, M.D., professor of Orthopaedic Surgery, Cornell University, "On the Care of Crippled and Deformed Children," *New York Medical Journal* 68 (July 9, 1898): 37–40. Reprinted in William R. F. Phillips and Janet Rosenberg, eds., *The Physically Handicapped in Society* (New York: Arno Press, 1980), 38.

44. Reeves, *Care and Education of Crippled Children*, 171–83.

45. These statistics were derived from ibid., 141–201.

46. For an appraisal of working-class attitudes toward orthopedic surgeons, see "The Medical Department," *Hospital School Journal* 11, 1 (March–April 1923): 5–6; and Joseph F. Sullivan, "The Social Service Work of the M.H.S.," *Hospital School Journal* 8, 4 (February–March 1920): 5.

47. Many rehabilitationists did believe, however, that disability could, by and large, be prevented.

48. John Duffy, *From Humors to Medical Science: A History of American Medicine* (Chicago: University of Illinois Press, 1993), 200.

49. See Arthur J. Gillette, "The Advantage of a State Hospital for Indigent Crippled and Deformed Children in the Advancement of Orthopedic Surgery in the State," *American Journal of Orthopedic Surgery* 14, 5 (May 1916): 259–64 (also printed and circulated in pamphlet form); and Arthur J. Gillette, "Sixty Years of Surgery," *Hospital School Journal* 11, 1 (March–April 1923): 6.

50. These hospital-schools discharged pupil-patients after a cure was affected or after dispensary care could be substituted for institutional care.

51. Reeves, *Care and Education of Crippled Children*, 141–201. Seven institutions discharged children after they had been "benefited as much as possible," a policy description that is too vague to draw conclusions from.

52. Ibid., 175.

53. Ibid., 163.

54. Ibid., 166.

55. At least, this was the case until World War I, when the extensive experience gained by orthopedic surgeons in the war improved both the knowledge and reputation of orthopedic surgeons. See Cartwright, *Development of Modern Surgery*, 157.

56. In particular, Albee's bone-grafting procedure was perfected in Europe,

providing the orthopedist with a variety of new surgical options. See Fred H. Albee, *A Surgeon's Fight to Rebuild Men* (New York: E. P. Dutton & Co., 1943), 17.

57. Cartwright, *Development of Modern Surgery*, 157.

58. Reeves, *Care and Education of Crippled Children*, 28.

59. For the connections between war, surgery, and the crippled child, see Roger Cooter, *Surgery and Society in Peace and War: Orthopaedics and the Organization of Modern Medicine, 1880–1948* (Hampshire, England: Macmillan Press, 1993).

60. Most asylums and hospital-schools associated with a surgeon by 1910. Van Leuven Browne delayed its association with orthopedists because of a longstanding commitment to osteopaths.

61. See "The Medical Department," *Hospital School Journal* 11, 1 (March–April, 1923): 5; and "An Epochal Day," *Hospital School Journal* 8, 4 (February–March 1920): 3.

62. "As They Were and As They Are Now," *Hospital School Journal* 7 (May–June 1919): 3.

63. Edward Claypool, "What the Michigan Hospital School Has Meant to Me," *Hospital School Journal* 9, 6 (May–June 1921): 3.

64. Ibid.

65. I have arrived at his conclusion by comparing evaluations of admissions procedures in Reeve's 1914 study *The Care and Education of Crippled Children* with Abt's 1924 study *The Care, Cure and Education of the Crippled Child*.

66. Joseph F. Sullivan, "An Important Clause," *Hospital School Journal* 8 (September–October 1919): 3.

6

Cold Charity
Manhood, Brotherhood, and the Transformation of Disability, 1870–1900

John Williams-Searle

In March 1887, Barney Baldwin, a brakeman for the Louisville and Nashville Railroad, had his neck broken in an accident at Birmingham, Alabama. Like many other railroad workers during the Gilded Age, Baldwin survived the accident but was unable to continue working for the railroad. Moreover, he appears to have been uninsured through his labor organization, the Brotherhood of Railroad Brakemen (BRB).[1] He probably had few savings to fall back on, since brakemen were poorly paid. Unable to do manual labor and in need of costly continuing care, Baldwin's economic future was uncertain.[2]

Baldwin, however, chose to make the best of his misfortune. His distinctive injury allowed him to take up a new profession as a sideshow performer. The *Railroad Brakeman's Journal* matter-of-factly described Baldwin's "exhibition at a Chicago dime museum":

> His case attracts considerable attention from the medical, scientific and curious public. As he stands upon the platform with or without his head support it is evident that his neck is broken. When the support is removed his head hangs in a most helpless condition on his breast. His case is certainly a miraculous one.[3]

Baldwin's strategy to maintain his financial independence was unorthodox but not unprecedented among disabled railroaders. By relying on his remaining source of capital—his identity as a visibly disabled person in a culture eager to define the normal body—Baldwin managed to turn his disability into a wage.

Other railroaders also displayed their disabilities to achieve greater financial security and self-determination in their lives. Joseph Bellaire, for example, gained fame among railroaders as the "One-Fingered Fireman." He used his wages of identity to become a celebrity among railroaders, one of the most consistently noted figures in the monthly publication produced by the BRB. His notoriety protected him from being shuffled aside when his railroading career ended.

Although Baldwin's and Bellaire's choices of post-injury occupation were unusual—most disabled railroaders did not exhibit their injuries to the general public for gain—their dilemma was commonplace. Railroaders, whether injured, aged, or able-bodied, recognized that disability was a central issue in the life of the American railroad worker. It was a critical consideration of any organization that hoped to serve railroaders' collective needs. Yet, if disability was an issue that could rally men to the railroad brotherhoods, leaders soon discovered that debates over the care of disabled railroaders could also destroy organizational harmony.

Moreover, exploiting one's identity as a disabled railroader was a risky strategy during the latter decades of the nineteenth century, because the able-bodied members of the various labor organizations devoted to serving the running trades—known collectively as the railroad brotherhoods—were developing their own uses for their disabled brothers. Trainmen increasingly contested the meanings of disability in the work culture of railroading as they slowly confronted the dangers of their workplaces.

Railroaders in the 1870s believed that superior moral virtue, including courage, foresight, and bodily skill, defined independent manhood. They felt that men who made careful plans (fiscal and otherwise) mitigated dangers to themselves and their families. Railroaders scorned men who failed to take out insurance or who acted carelessly in the face of danger. Such men, even though they became physically and financially dependent, deserved little pity.

Why did working men conflate "independence" (demonstrated by control over one's body, one's household, one's workplace, and one's financial well-being) with "manliness"? Historian David Montgomery convincingly demonstrates that Gilded Age craftsmen organized not only over bread-and-butter issues such as wages but also to retain their traditional control and self-direction in the workplace. Michael Kimmel indicates that the primary fear among displaced artisans was the dread of being reduced to a wage slave.[4]

Economic productivity made for self-determination in a capitalist society. Limits on a man's ability to be economically productive, such as unemployment or injury, also imperiled his manhood. Railroaders, miners, and others in dangerous occupations recognized that a disabling injury posed a central threat to manliness as they understood it. Moreover, workers often equated the loss of economic productivity with other, much graver losses that struck at the heart of manhood and civic identity, though few said as much directly. They feared losing the ability to order their own affairs, to control the affairs of others within their households, and to claim the full citizenship that rested on these twin claims of mastery and self-mastery. Permanent, catastrophic injuries had the potential to do more than sever limbs or digits; they could rob a man of the ability to shape his destiny.

By the late 1880s, much of what American workingmen believed about the foundations of manhood was put to the test. Trainmen watched the rising injury statistics with alarm. Able-bodied railroaders faced constricted job markets that pitted the visibly disabled against those with no such outward signifiers. Employers pressured workers to bear the brunt of speedups and drives for efficiency, making arbitrary changes in the workplace over which workers had little say. These conditions prompted more trainmen to surrender a measure of their independence for a stake in protective collective action. As railroaders joined together to appeal for safer working conditions, they revised their previous perceptions of disability and reconsidered how best to address the needs of the disabled men in their ranks.

This essay examines how members of railroad brotherhoods struggled to situate the disabled trainman (as man, as injured, as brother) in the changing work culture of railroading between 1870 and 1900. I argue that the brotherhoods' evolving strategies for dealing with occupational injury reveal the difficulty with which able-bodied men acknowledged their own vulnerability in the workplace. Although brotherhood leaders initially tried to encourage self-reliance and self-insurance, they soon realized that workers (especially disabled workers) had limited individual resources with which to face catastrophic injury and an unlimited capacity for denial. To provide an effective remedy for the omnipresent hazards of their jobs, they would have to identify new, collective solutions. To provide these solutions, they first would have to acknowledge the real threat of disabling injury.

Railroaders' conflation of physical and economic independence with manliness, however, repeatedly undermined the ability of the railroad brotherhoods to respect or provide care for their disabled comrades. Eventually, the figure of the dependent disabled man in need of the group's protection became a powerful organizational tool, rallying able-bodied men to the cause of workplace safety, solidifying their commitment to oppositional craft-consciousness, and renewing their investment in a manly identity based on bodily wholeness and financial independence.

While the figure of the disabled worker was rhetorically useful to forge alliances among able-bodied trainmen, actual disabled men who continued to be economically productive presented troubling contradictions that threatened to undo the brotherhoods' ideas about manliness. Disabled men who continued to work and compete with the able-bodied for jobs challenged what able-bodied men thought they knew about what made a man a man. In so doing, they also tested the boundaries of brotherhood, fissuring class solidarity along lines of bodily wholeness. Able-bodied workers, sometimes within their own organizations and sometimes colluding with their employers, attempted to push disabled co-workers out of the workforce—in effect, exaggerating the economic preconditions for dependency.

Once disabled workers had been pushed to the economic margins, brotherhood members began to debate about how best to care for these dependent men. Arguments over the establishment of care facilities for the disabled railroad worker demonstrate that brotherhood members had an opportunity to transform protective fraternalism into a more comprehensive and socially radical idea of brotherhood. By placing injured workers at the center of their social vision and supplementing care habitually provided by the relatives of the disabled, the railroad brotherhood would have, in effect, become an extended family. Instead, when able-bodied brotherhood members eventually agreed to "protect" destitute disabled men, they did so in a way that served the ideological needs of able-bodied members at the expense of the disabled members.

When the railroad brotherhoods voted to support the privately funded Railroad Men's Home, their memberships endorsed a particular vision of the disabled trainman (economically and physically dependent, in need of group support, and dislocated from his own household—thus, demasculinized) that stood in stark contrast to able-bodied fantasies of manhood. Home directors initially supported rehabilitation and job retraining for residents, but they soon found out that able-bodied brothers were more interested in objectifying their disabled comrades. Although able-bodied railroaders mobilized as part of the railroad safety movement in the last decades of the nineteenth century to change the unsafe conditions that led to disabilities, they did little to defend their disabled comrades from economic marginalization. Instead, they used disabled trainmen to defend their ideals of (able-bodied) manhood.

To understand the tremendous changes in the meaning of disabling injury and the position of disabled trainmen in the work culture of railroading between 1870 and 1900, one must first briefly examine the context of those transformations. One of the biggest changes was the shifting relationship between masculinity, risk, and perceptions of disabling injury. Most railroaders in the 1870s and early 1880s exhibited the attitudes toward risk and disability that one might expect of men who had soldiered in and survived the Civil War. Trainmen during this era gauged masculinity and professionalism by one's response to workplace danger, viewing courage and controlled risk taking as sure signs of professionalism. Foolhardiness, evidenced by taking a risk that exceeded one's physical mastery of a dangerous situation or obeying a misguided order, demonstrated a lack of manly prudence.[5]

Trainmen's memoirs reveal that experienced workers dealt with danger through recognition and confrontation rather than by avoiding risk. Railroader O. H. Kirkpatrick explained, "The very nature of the trainman's work was so hazardous that it was only those who were disposed to take risks who got very far in their career."[6] During this time, in fact, most railroaders did not agitate for safety equipment, despite the rising casualty rates among railroad workers and the increasing availability of safety couplers and air brakes. Workers instead relied on their ability to work safely under dangerous conditions.

In part, the hiring climate of the time allowed them to maintain a degree of nonchalance. Even if they happened to be modestly injured on the job, trainmen with a slight visible disability (such as a missing finger) might return to work. Throughout this period, railroaders and employers alike often viewed a partial disability as a sign of experience. A brakeman's first crushed finger, for example, served as his "Red Badge of Courage" and helped mark his transition from greenhorn to experienced railroader.[7]

Some injuries were more serious, however, and trainmen found that the risks of their profession sometimes prevented them from being insurable through private companies. One engineer explained, "I did not receive a policy, simply because I was a Locomotive Engineer, which they classed as 'extra hazardous.'"[8] The railroad brotherhoods responded by developing their own insurance plans and charity funds. In 1867, the Brotherhood of Locomotive Engineers became the first to establish an insurance association. Their fund paid members for the loss of a hand, foot, or limb or for total blindness; survivors of trainmen who had died on the job received death benefits. Within two decades, every railroad brotherhood offered insurance policies. Members considered the insurance plans one of the central benefits of membership.[9] Some local divisions from among all the brotherhoods ran their own benevolent funds and looked to the welfare of their members, paying dues for out-of-work railroaders, providing food to struggling railroading families, and footing the doctor's bills for their disabled members.[10] It is no exaggeration to state that concerns about disability—whether expressed as the purchase of insurance for oneself or the provision of charity for another—played a central role in shaping the railroad brotherhoods in the last three decades of the nineteenth century.

In turn, the railroad brotherhoods became key institutions in the reinterpretation of the ideals of railroading manhood—a reinterpretation that struggled to harness productively the tensions between the stereotypical values of the itinerant "boomer" and those of the brotherhood member. According to railroader Charles Brown, the boomer was a man who "never stays any place on any one job long enough to get promoted, but keeps jumping around over the country from place to place . . . a happy-go-lucky, not caring-a-hang sort of cuss, here today, and there tomorrow, not giving a dang where he is."[11] Boomers also had a daredevil attitude toward risk and believed that the skillful disregard of danger was the sign of true manliness. Although husbands and fathers joined the ranks of the roving unemployed during the numerous economic downturns of the nineteenth century, the typical boomer was single and beholden to no one.

As economic and work conditions deteriorated in the late nineteenth century, however, railroad men began to change their attitudes toward risk, narrowly defining which confrontations with danger would bolster a man's professional reputation. The boomer ideal, once celebrated, faced competition in the work culture of railroading from the ideal of the brotherhood man. Skillful and brave, yet devoted to temperate living and the exercise of manly foresight, the brotherhood man kept his insurance paid up in case he was called on to sacrifice his life to save passengers and property.

The same conditions that prompted a reconsideration of the relationship between manliness and risk, not surprisingly, also prompted railroaders to take another look at the relationship between manliness and bodily wholeness. In part, economic competition fueled this refiguring. As hiring opportunities diminished, men with visible disabilities competed with the apparently able-bodied for limited jobs. Railroad brotherhoods, who had long conceived of themselves as providing reliable, sober, and competent workers to railroad companies, began to emphasize that disability was not a sign of experience and manliness but instead a marker of incompetence, dependency, and even immorality.[12] It was a short step, in ideological terms, from celebrating the manly skill of the professional to demonizing the unmanly ineptitude of the sot, the scab, and the "cripple."

All brotherhood publications periodically ran articles deriding the manliness, prudence, and competence of now-disabled men, but as the 1880s continued, the pieces ran much more frequently. For example, the *Railroad Brakeman's Journal* offered monthly cautionary tales about disabled brakemen who had let their membership in the BRB lapse or had failed their wives when they forgot to buy insurance. Some reports implied that a disabling injury was punishment for a brakeman's disdain for the protective aspects of the brotherhood.[13] While disabled men were never barred from membership on the basis of their injuries, monthly membership dues were an expense that many underemployed or unemployed disabled railroaders could not afford.

Even members in good standing, enrolled in the insurance program, faced nothing but suspicion when they attempted to claim the benefits due them. Able-bodied claims adjusters insinuated that injured men had contributed to their own misfortunes by lack of prudence, inept practice, or inebriation. Moreover, disabled claimants faced a gauntlet of forms, examinations, and quibbling to get the money that was owed to them. In 1889, Dr. F. M. Ingalls suggested that the BRB establish the post of medical director to prevent members from submitting fraudulent disability claims to the grand lodge. Ingalls argued that this practice was endemic and had cost the BRB $40,000 between January 1886 and July 1889.[14] Even if Ingalls's chief aim was to get himself installed as the chief medical examiner of the BRB, his accusations undoubtedly raised suspicions concerning the actual status of disabled brakemen.[15] Other railroad brotherhoods were similarly obsessed with guarding themselves against the chicanery of lightly injured cheats.

There were, to be sure, a few confirmed accounts of members taking advantage of brotherhood insurance plans by filing false disability claims. Yet the hysterical overreaction to false claims—brotherhood members jumped to the conclusion that all disabled men would exaggerate the extent of their impairment simply because an unscrupulous few did—resoundingly demonstrates that disabling injury and character were inextricably linked in the minds of the able-bodied.

The assault on disabled workers was not limited to their own fraternal organizations. Corporations rationalized their bureaucracies, pursued greater efficiencies, and established scientific management policies that systematically excluded even slightly injured workers from the running trades. By the end of the 1880s, companies manifested a mania for efficiency. Company managers feared disabled trainmen would work too slowly and would be more susceptible to injury. Managers also believed that employing disabled railroaders made passengers nervous; the image of railroader as risk taker was firmly fixed in the public mind, and some riders perceived that disabled men lacked either nerve or prudence.[16] Finally, L. L. Losey, chief claims agent of the Illinois Central railroad, explained that by rejecting disabled men, lines protected themselves "against fraudulent claims for pre-existing injuries which otherwise might be charged to an accident while in service."[17] He might have added that an unemployed disabled worker was far less likely to have the resources to bring suit for wrongful injury.

Railroad companies also took an increasingly hard line toward dispensing relief to their injured employees. Previously, managers had occasionally reassigned seriously disabled workers to lighter duties.[18] The Chicago, Burlington, and Quincy reserved work on the Chariton branch for old and disabled trainmen.[19] A few disabled men had also found work in company-established employee reading rooms. The Pennsylvania Railroad, for example, hired John Freed, an employee who had "lost a leg in the service of the company," to supervise the library at the company's railroad clubhouse in New York.[20] These cases represented only a handful of the men injured each year in occupational accidents, however. Managers, moreover, insisted that they had no duty to provide "charity" and could be rather harsh in their estimation of the skills of disabled railroaders. When an officer of the Chicago and Northwestern railroad refused to give a previously promised job to a disabled trainman, he tried to justify his decision when he explained, "He has trouble with cripples on an engine."[21] Disabled workers, for their part, often considered job preferences a matter of compensatory justice and bristled at the implication that they would stoop to taking a handout.

As time went on, managers explicitly linked the retention of disabled employees to an employee's "loyal" behavior. For example, in 1885, officers of the Chicago, Burlington, and Quincy Railroad (CB&Q) approved a payment of $41.50 to conductor J. M. Graham. Graham had lost an index finger while trying to couple an engine to his train; he also lost eighteen days' work during his recovery. CB&Q managers justified paying Graham a gratuity not because of any possible company liability but because he was "an old and faithful employee." Division Superintendent F. C. Rice made clear what constituted "good standing and faithful service" when he commented, "Should we ever have any trouble in the way of strikes Graham would be a man we could depend upon."[22] Railroad companies successfully pitted disabled workers against their able-bodied co-workers even as railroad brotherhoods were doing the same on the other side of the labor-capital divide.

Some railroaders further contributed to their disabled co-workers' problems by testifying to their incompetence in personal injury cases. After the drawbars of two cars crushed brakeman Andrew Reed's hand, for example, the rest of the train crew testified to Reed's ignorance of rail operations.[23] When the end of a brake rod impaled Edward Laughlin between two cars, he sued the Illinois Central, claiming that the bumpers of the freight cars were substandard and had misaligned, causing his injury. Trainmen who witnessed Laughlin's accident, however, testified that his skill and judgment had been wanting. The engineer of the train commented, "I have never saw such a coupling attempted since I have been railroading, when the cars were running as fast as those . . . Laughlin attempted to couple."[24]

The collusion between able-bodied railroaders and their employers to drive disabled trainmen from the workforce raises an interesting question: How were uninjured trainmen able to define their class interest in such a way as to place their injured co-workers temporarily outside the bounds of fraternity? The answer lies in the overwhelming power of a gender ideology that equated manhood with independence (bodily and financial). As railroaders struggled to retain control over their workplace in the face of railroad companies' increasingly rationalized management policies, they unwittingly acceded to the most exaggerated extension of manly independence and responsibility. To demonstrate their independent manhood, railroaders zealously guarded their control over how they should do their work. Although company officers issued their own work rules in an attempt to control the workplace, they became notable defenders of manly independence once a man became disabled, claiming that the injured parties bore full responsibility for their own mistakes. Courts joined employers in finding that men injured in a workplace over which they had diminishing control should still have been responsible for their own behaviors. Trapped by their own conflation of manhood and independence, able-bodied railroaders had to agree that injured workers had failed their responsibilities at work and had thus failed as independent men.[25]

This strand of reasoning is particularly apparent in court cases in which able-bodied crewmen testified against their now-disabled co-workers. Although employers undoubtedly used their formidable powers of coercion to procure favorable defense testimony in liability suits, workers themselves set the agenda for the type of testimony they delivered. Defense depositions reveal that trainmen embedded a discussion of character issues in their testimony on workplace competence. By joining their employers in making occupational disability a moral issue, able-bodied railroaders deluded themselves about their chances of injury, disguised the desperate need for safety reform, and denied the worth and manliness of their disabled co-workers.

Disabled trainmen faced either demotion to low-paying and low-prestige positions out of the public eye or outright dismissal. If they remained in the workplace, they faced the possibility of slurs, hostility, or shunning by their crewmates.[26] Judging from photographs of the era's train crews, men learned to keep their finger stumps and poorly healed legs hidden from view.[27]

Injured men also internalized their co-workers' poor opinions of them and their work. Joseph Dixon, a brakeman working in St. Paul, wrote to thank the BRB members for their help "while under the embarrassment of the loss of a foot."[28] Another brakeman, Peter Terboss, suffered a catastrophic injury that left him "a cripple"; he was unsure if brothers would see that he was still "able to work for the Brotherhood" if not for the railroad itself.[29]

Although railroad companies' discrimination against disabled railroaders was widespread at the end of the nineteenth century, the railroad brotherhoods did little to counter, and sometimes directly abetted, companies' programmatic attempt to rid themselves of disabled workers. The attempts to purge disabled men, however, did not solve the ongoing problem of workplace safety. More and more men fell prey to the misaligned coupler, the loose grab iron, and the low bridge. Brotherhood men soon had to face the uncomfortable notion that disabling injury visited one regardless of a man's character.

Accident statistics bore out this truth. In 1889, after the Interstate Commerce Commission (ICC) first issued national accident statistics and reported that one out of every twelve, or 8 percent, of all trainmen experienced a work-related injury, civic outrage began to build.[30] The ICC report even influenced President Benjamin Harrison's 1890 State of the Union address, when he urged safety-appliance legislation and recognized the risks railroaders encountered in their work: "It is a reproach to our civilization that any class of American workmen should, in the pursuit of a necessary and useful

John Williams-Searle

vocation, be subjected to a peril of life and limb as great as that of a soldier in time of war."[31]

Harrison's equation of workers and soldiers struck a chord with railroaders and the public alike. The *Railroad Trainmen's Journal* reprinted the relevant parts of Harrison's address, while commentators such as Congressman Henry Cabot Lodge wrote articles comparing the fates of railroaders and soldiers and decrying the dangers of the work.[32] The public became aware of what railroaders had known for decades: railroad employees, particularly those employed in the running trades, were routinely exposed to extreme dangers.

The president's address and the resulting public recognition of the problem influenced legislative action on employee safety, as Congress quickly held hearings to determine how to reduce the death and disablement of railroaders. Every congressional committee witness, it seemed, referred to workplace injury in tragic terms and pled with national officials to stop the maiming of the noble workingman. Helpless, hopeless disabled trainmen (and their struggling wives and families) became abstract figures of great rhetorical power, but disabled men themselves were rarely called to testify about their post-injury experiences.

In the end, the congressional hearings, the protests of the railroad brotherhoods—particularly the BRB—and the testimony of railroad safety advocates such as former Iowa railroad commissioner Lorenzo S. Coffin ultimately resulted in the passage of the federal Safety Appliance Act in 1893.[33] The railroading workplace grew marginally safer after the passage of the act. Despite these slightly improving conditions, however, railroaders realized that they could not rely solely on the machinery of the state to right the balance between workers and employers. They never assumed that the federal government would enforce the Safety Appliance Act without continuous agitation by the brotherhoods, nor did they assume that their employers would hasten to implement the act. This was a safe assumption, considering that in 1902, ICC secretary Edward A. Moseley guiltily admitted that no railroad company had ever been prosecuted for violating the Safety Appliance Act.[34]

Through the necessity of conveying the magnitude of harms rendered men by their careless employers, a notably softened view of the disabled man—quite at odds with the malingering drunkard who lurched through the pages of the brotherhood journals—began to enter able-bodied brothers' discourse on disability. Moving testimony about the consequences of dependency (always assumed as the end point of injury) stirred the sympathies of the able-bodied trainmen. Also, one imagines, the solid scientific data gathered on national injury rates countered the individual's impressionistic and local view of his profession's dangers. So large a problem could not be entirely a matter of character or carelessness. Some trainmen took the view that the disabled man needed the protection of his able-bodied brothers, just as the widows and orphans of their dead comrades did; both had been wronged by railroad companies. Others, however, hung onto a more negative view of disabled workers. Able-bodied trainmen would attempt to care for some of the thousands of permanently disabled men whom they assumed would be ignored by railroad companies and the state, but brotherhood solutions to the "problem" of the dependent disabled trainman mingled sympathy with contempt.

The first line of defense against dependence for the insured man was one's household. Railroaders knew that permanently disabled trainmen relied on their wives and children to take care of them when they could not return to wage work; they also had heard the sad tales of eviction when the mortgage was not paid. Brotherhood publications therefore focused considerable attention on the importance of home ownership, the smoothly functioning household, and, most important, the competent and companionable railroader's wife. The ideal locomotive engineer's wife was useful, helpful, and morally superior to the women of other classes. The author of an article published in the *Locomotive Engineers' Monthly Journal* advised those who were "looking for wives and companions, [to] turn from the fashionable, lazy and haughty girls, and select one from those who work for a living, and never—our word for it—will you repent your choice. You want a substantial friend and not a doll; a helpmate and not a mere help eat; a counselor and not a simpleton."[35] The ideal wife was as competent at home as her husband was at work. She would be able to meet all challenges, including that of caring for a permanently disabled spouse on the limited income provided by the brotherhoods' insurance plans.

The second line of defense was less reliable. Customary methods of relief, such as passing the hat at brotherhood meetings, might help supplement insurance.[36] When "the paper" circulated, managers and able-bodied trainmen wrote their names and a pledge amount to support an injured man. These temporary infusions of cash helped, but everyone knew that they could not substitute for a steady income.

Even when ideals of wifely solicitude and brotherly benevolence were met, they frequently were not sufficient to the needs of the injured man. Brotherhood journals noted with astonishment that a Brotherhood of Railroad Trainmen (BRT) member in good standing had been found living in the Cook County, Illinois, poorhouse.[37] Another man had to be removed from "an overcrowded and noisy boarding house"; a fellow trainman nursed him back to health.[38] Such cases tugged at the sympathies (if not the pocketbooks) of the brotherhoods. Railroad brotherhood journals began to float the question of residential care as a last resort for those men who had no homes, no families, and no friends. Advocates insisted that members should be able to rely on their other "family"—the railroad brotherhood—to supply care.

In response to the call for residential care, Dr. F. M. Ingalls, a member of the Brotherhood of Railroad Trainmen, established his own facility in 1890.[39] The Railroad Men's Home (also referred to as the Highland Park Home) in Chicago, Illinois, was privately owned but appealed to all the brotherhoods and private citizens for economic support. Ingalls wisely picked popular safety advocate Lorenzo Coffin to serve as the first president of the Home, and Ingalls himself served as a vice president.

Ingalls also quickly became the project's staunchest defender. The mere idea of institutional care for individuals with significant physical disabilities prompted considerable debate among all the railroad brotherhoods, particularly among members of the Brotherhood of Locomotive Engineers (BLE). Arguments for and against a greater involvement in residential care raged through the pages of the brotherhood journals for nearly a decade. The heated discussions reveal both the significance of disability in contesting models of manhood and the importance of disabled men in defining the boundaries of brotherhood. Above all, they demonstrate how much engineers and other trainmen disagreed about the meaning of disabling injury and the place that disabled trainmen were to occupy in the work culture of railroading.

Uppermost in the minds of critics was avoiding the appearance of charity. Although he recognized that the Railroad Men's Home was a "deserved success," the editor of the *Railroad Trainmen's Journal*, L. W. Rogers, pointedly questioned whether the private management of the Home indicated centralization of control as well.[40] He contended that the undemocratic way in which the Home had been organized betokened an overarching autocratic vision on the part of its founders. Rogers firmly believed that if the officers solicited for donations in railroad brotherhood journals, they also should allow the brotherhoods to supervise the Home. Rogers explained:

[A] representative of the home was before the BRT convention at Los Angeles, but only an endorsement and a donation was asked for. This would lead one to suppose that the originators of the movement have no intention of placing the home under the jurisdiction of the united organizations.[41]

If trainmen did not control the Railroad Men's Home, it became just another benevolent organization dispensing charity on terms over which railroaders had little say. The further implication was that only trainmen would be knowledgeable about what type of aid their disabled brothers required. The efforts of charity workers unfamiliar with the role of manliness in the work culture of railroading may have posed a significant threat to the manhood of disabled trainmen. Charity, then, even in a well-intentioned form, could undercut manly independence.

Ingalls quickly replied to Rogers's criticisms by reassuring readers that the Home would be skillfully run. In addition, he dismissed Rogers's concerns about the absence of brotherhood participation in the Home's establishment by commenting that had the developers of the Railroad Men's Home waited for the outcome of a parliamentary debate among the brotherhoods, "the railroad crossing and the poorhouse would be the alternatives of starvation for the poor unfortunate brothers."[42] Ingalls probably had a point, given his familiarity with the lengthy, circular, and often exhausting arguments that took place in the brotherhood journals. Despite Ingalls's best efforts, however, brotherhood members frequently criticized the Home throughout the next decade.

Organizers of the Railroad Men's Home attempted to situate their project in a way that would appeal to men who conflated manliness and economic independence. The prospectus of the Home published in the *Railroad Trainmen's Journal*, for example, stressed its rehabilitative character. Supporters went so far as to say that rehabilitated railroaders were likely to "get a better position than they had at the time of injury."[43] For boosters of the Home, economic productivity was the true measure of a man. In his defense of the Railroad Men's Home, Ingalls praised it for helping a disabled brother learn the jeweler's trade. He also commented that one resident was "undergoing a delicate and difficult surgical operation, which we hope will transform an entirely useless arm into one which will enable its possessor to earn a good living at any light trade."[44] Several years later, he reported that two residents had left "on account of their obtaining situations by which they can earn their own livelihood, having learned their trades while inmates of the institution."[45]

Despite these reassurances, some brotherhood members remained suspicious. They argued that the brotherhoods should retain complete power over a home intended to benefit their number. To achieve that objective, toward the end of the nineteenth century, BLE members held their own debate about whether to establish an exclusive home for disabled engineers on a piece of BLE-owned farm property in Mattoon, Illinois, known as Meadow Lawn.

Supporters and critics alike agreed that the proposed Meadow Lawn facility had to be self-supporting. Engineers feared that institutionalization would further unman their disabled co-workers; hence they constantly insisted that disabled brothers should have a critical role in their own care and support. One BLE member suggested having residents in charge of the home, so they would "feel [their] importance and responsibility." Independence and self-esteem would be further bolstered, argued this writer, if the home was not referred to by "the word institution, as it conveys the idea of being objects of charity."[46] One engineer from Cincinnati suggested that the BLE build an industrial plant on the Meadow Lawn property, where brothers out of work "on account of their age or other disqualifications . . . could be furnished employment."[47]

Most BLE members hoped that if the Meadow Lawn Home became a reality, it would serve only as a temporary retraining center that would quickly move disabled engineers from "unmanly" dependency to gainful employment in another occupation. Occupational rehabilitation, however, would be only part of the disabled railroader's restoration. Both to negate the common assumption that disabled railroaders had weak judgment and to assure potential residents that their manly prerogative to control their lives would not be denied them, Meadow Lawn supporters insisted that disabled trainmen would retain their independence. James Wood wrote that "everyone must be made to feel that they are at home, and not under iron rules, as would be the case in other institutions."[48] Brothers routinely feared that strict governance would undermine their independence and thus the manhood of engineers who had fought to be recognized as indispensable leaders of the train crew. This ideal of self-sufficiency, however, elicited some debate. Titus Hinchcliff realistically concluded, "We must not delude ourselves with the idea that because we have a farm of 256 acres of as fine land as ever laid out of doors we can put a colony of invalids on it and make it self-sustaining."[49]

How much additional care would be required? What would be the consequences of providing and paying for such care? These were thorny questions. Writers to the *Locomotive Engineers' Monthly Journal* worried that establishment of a BLE-sponsored home would undermine the organization's insurance program because members would rely only on the home to take care of them. One correspondent wrote, "Why need I join the Insurance or lay by a dollar for old age, the Brotherhood will care for me better than I can possibly care for myself."[50] Other BLE members argued that the funds devoted to Meadow Lawn would reduce the charity claims paid out to widows, orphans, and disabled brothers. R. W. Kelly explained, "Of the claims paid at our last convention 214 were widows, 32 were orphans and 152 incapacitated Brothers, a total of 398, located in 44 states and territories. Would we cut them off if we had a home?"[51] Some members feared that if the BLE ended charity payments in favor of establishing a home, brothers and their families formerly taken care of by the charity fund would immediately seek entrance to the home, overwhelming the institution's ability to care for anyone.[52]

One vocal group, harking back to notions that the disabled man was inherently less moral than the able-bodied, argued that unscrupulous engineers would exaggerate the extent of their disabilities to get free care and food at the Meadow Lawn Home. Some BLE members insisted, moreover, that if trainmen had been practicing the ideals of railroad manhood, they would scorn charity. According to member Cyrus E. Gallatin, brotherhood engineers came in two varieties. The diligent class included the man who worked to provide a home for his family, educate his children, and take care of his parents, while making every effort to plan for the future. Gallatin described the second class as those men "who will not work in bad weather if they can avoid it; who will not deny themselves anything they can get, and are decidedly improvident."[53] It was that lesser class of men, Gallatin implied, who were most likely to become disabled in the first place. He strongly urged the membership to vote against the creation of the Meadow Lawn Home: "I say, most emphatically, no! to a proposition that would compel members who are industrious and provident to provide a luxurious home for the shiftless and improvident."[54] Brother J. B. M. was even more blunt, accusing the proposed home of providing a refuge for "many engineers who have spent their earnings at gaming tables, saloons, and worse places."[55]

Many members echoed a common refrain when they complained that the home would make it difficult to discern the worthy from the trifling. The hostility exhibited toward their disabled comrades, when coupled with comments about unscrupulousness and assessments of moral worth, suggests that a fair number of BLE members retained the attitude that injured men had succumbed to the dangers of railroading due to incompetence and bad character. Some railroaders even believed that a work-related disability was merely divine retribution for a moral failing.[56]

Most opponents of the Meadow Lawn Farm, however, felt that establishing an exclusive engineers' home threatened the protective foundation of the BLE, because it would spread the financial resources of the organization too thinly. Moreover, the issue of who should care for the disabled trainmen threatened to destabilize domestic power relations by creating a new "superfamily" composed of brotherhood members. The two problems were intimately related in the mind of critics. They insisted that the Meadow Lawn Home would displace men from their rightful place as heads of their own households, thereby further eroding disabled workers' claims to full manhood and rendering themselves and their wives and children objects of charity.

Supporters of Meadow Lawn insisted that the operation of the home need not undermine the sense of manhood and independence that engineers derived as patriarchs. T. H. Hiner proposed that Meadow Lawn set up single-unit housing so that families could live together and not be divided. He explained that a family-centered approach would make Meadow Lawn superior to other fraternal homes:

> Do you, my Brother, want to go to a fraternal home somewhere, perhaps where you may never see the good, loving wife or dear children again; or would you rather go to the Meadow Lawn Home, where you can all be together, and where the measure of meal will not give out, where it costs nothing for rent, and you are a happy, unbroken family still?[57]

Hiner drove home his point by comparing the proposed family-friendly environment of Meadow Lawn to the men-only care provided by the Highland Park Home; there "families must be separated, and while the husband is enjoying the comforts of that home, the good wife may be starving."[58]

Naysayers, however, had a field day attacking Hiner's costly proposal. They scoffed at the notion that brotherhood men had the responsibility to support other men's families. They also complained that the extra expense of supporting the home would create hardships for engineers who were already paying mandatory insurance assessments and dues. Engineers feared that "direct taxation" of members would prevent young engineers from joining the ranks of the brotherhood and would ultimately threaten the future growth and stability of the BLE.[59]

Many members resisted what they perceived as the replacement of the natal family with a "brotherhood family." They complained that the BLE should not attempt to usurp the duties of railroading families to provide care for elderly and disabled relatives. Indeed, trainmen who opposed the home argued that engineers who could no longer pursue their profession because of disability or age would not want to leave the support of their friends and family to live among strangers. One engineer from Cedar Rapids, Iowa, confidently stated that his fellow engineers were "scattered all over the country, and the majority of them would much prefer to spend the remainder of their lives where they are acquainted and acclimated."[60] Another engineer explained, "Nothing on earth would tempt me to go to any home that would deprive me of my visits to my dear ones' graves."[61] According to these BLE members, a man—even a disabled man—would be diminished if removed from the context of his own home. In their vision of brotherhood, members' fraternal duties to one another were strictly limited to workplace concerns.

At the BLE's 1900 biennial convention, delegates finally settled the decade-long debate concerning the establishment of a home exclusively for engineers. They agreed to sell the Meadow Lawn Farm; the idea of the home died a quiet death. It is difficult to tell how many brothers agreed with Henry Hoppman's assessment that the resolution "was a stroke of wisdom and common sense, and does away with a very annoying question."[62] Correspondents to the *Locomotive Engineers' Monthly Journal,* or its editor, exhausted by a decade of debate, fell silent on the issue. In the year after the convention, not one letter referred to the late Meadow Lawn Farm. BLE members may have settled the issue of how to dispose of the Mattoon property, but repercussions continued to be felt regarding what the debate meant about the position of disabled engineers in the life of the BLE.

Faced with the possibility of making the BLE into something more than a fraternal-cum-labor association engaged in the protection of the narrow economic interests of approximately thirty thousand locomotive engineers, the BLE membership balked. Given the option of creating a new definition of brotherhood and contributing to the evolution of fraternalism, BLE members chose instead to limit the meaning of brotherhood to protection. Their debates over the character and needs of disabled railroaders, like their wavering support for their injured comrades, reveal that trainmen were not yet ready to abandon an individualistic notion of manly rights and responsibility in favor of a more fraternalistic conception. Although they were willing to recognize the need for care of disabled trainmen, they hesitated to commit themselves to an overarching fraternal vision that would have transcended individual responsibility and family-centered care. For the members of the

BLE who wanted to expand the idea of brotherhood, Meadow Lawn became the road not taken and a lost opportunity.

What role had disabled men themselves played in the debate? For the most part, it is difficult to know. Men rarely identified themselves as possessing a disability, for obvious reasons. Those few who did label themselves "old" or "crippled" staunchly opposed institutionalization, for equally obvious reasons.

Able-bodied trainmen were not as quick to reject the Railroad Men's Home, but neither were they enthusiastic. While brotherhood men agreed that someone should tend the unfortunate, they did not agree on who should foot the bill. Ingalls chided the railroad brotherhoods for not contributing more to the Railroad Men's Home, especially in light of the labor organizations' swelling treasuries: "The great growth of the several organizations is apparent from their reports, and if one and all would do their part by contributing their mite we could build and maintain a 'Home' for the unfortunate railway man that would stand out before the world a monument of organized labor."[63] Although Ingalls tried to stay optimistic, the fact remained that of the thousands of disabled railroaders, only five lived in the home in 1893.

There are several possible explanations for the home's lack of clientele. The organizers of the Railroad Men's Home rented a house in Chicago that President Lorenzo Coffin admitted was too small to handle increasing numbers of residents. In 1896, the Home's board of managers alleviated this problem when they bought a house in Highland Park, Illinois, on a lot that would provide plenty of room for expansion and would later allow them to build a second building on the property.[64] Admission standards may have excluded all but the most severely injured. Perhaps, however, the low enrollments give one an insight into the attitudes of disabled trainmen toward residential care. The Home remained the only facility in the nation devoted to the residential care of disabled trainmen, and thousands of men each year sustained traumatic injury, yet fewer than twenty (and often, fewer than ten) men lived there at any given time.

Proponents of the Home realized that acceptance (from both disabled workers and their able-bodied peers) would take time. In 1893, Coffin commented, "It is a work of time and patience, to educate men up to the proper point of caring for a fellow and brother railway man."[65] Coffin tried to elicit support by giving a human face to the home. He mentioned inmates by name, asking trainmen to consider what would happen if the home closed:

Shall this old engineer, Mr. Fish, now eighty-four years old; shall this conductor, Mr. Bangs, perfectly helpless; shall this fireman, Mr. Nace, with one leg; shall these helpless and suffering crippled men be turned upon the cold charity of the world, only to find their way, eventually, to the county poorhouse; from which we took our first inmate of the "Home," and who now is making a good living at the jeweler's trade, which the "Home" enabled him to learn? Already has the "Home" rescued three grand young men from hopeless dependency to self-sustaining independence.[66]

Coffin stressed the dual goal of rehabilitation and manly reinvigoration. Although he equated disability with "hopeless dependency," he also viewed dependency for some men as a temporary condition. The Railroad Men's Home would remake "men" of disabled railroaders by restoring their earning capacity. He recognized, however, that some men were too disabled or too old to return to the railroading workforce. Here, he appealed to anxiety and self-interest to elicit contributions to the home: "How soon some of these now contributing will be the suffering ones, none of us can tell."[67]

Although Ingalls reported that the Railroad Men's Home was a national success (despite having a membership of only three), his February 1893 quarterly report to the BLE's monthly journal indicated that members were once again wavering in their support of disabled trainmen. At one point, the BLE voted to recognize the Home only if it managed to get the endorsement of all eleven BLE divisions in Chicago. Considering the lack of unanimity among BLE members concerning the need for *any* home for disabled trainmen, this must have been a blow to the Railroad Men's Home's organizers.[68] When the BLE gave up on the idea of their own home at Meadow Lawn, however, divisions did send more disabled members to the Railroad Men's Home. In 1900, Highland Park housed twenty residents; seven of them were engineers.[69]

By 1900, all the railroad brotherhoods, the brotherhoods' ladies' auxiliaries, and the ladies' auxiliary to the Railroad YMCA supported Highland Park.[70] Voluntary donations from the brotherhoods, however, revealed seasonal fluctuations in generosity. Highland Park suffered from donation patterns that still plague charitable institutions. As the holiday season began, donations increased. In November 1899, the Home received $815 and brotherhood locals sent numerous boxes of groceries, canned goods, fruit, and cigars. During the month of December, brotherhoods and their ladies' auxiliaries were filled with the Christmas spirit, contributing $906 and many groceries.[71] Contributions declined thereafter, however, reaching a low of $127 in April 1900.[72] The receipts for the Railroad Men's Home in July 1900 also lagged, amounting to only $166.42. Lorenzo Coffin's dedication to the home project was readily apparent. To make ends meet during the lean summer months, he lent the home $250 and gave it "two fine shoats."[73]

Coffin expressed frustration over the brotherhoods' intermittent interest in and inconsistent funding of care for their own members. He began one angry letter by denouncing those who would deny the costly realities of disability: *"Why can not men understand? Or do they understand, and are they thoughtless and a little mean?"*[74] Coffin complained that brotherhood locals were more than willing to shuffle off their disabled men to the Home but refused to donate money to sustain its work.

When brotherhood members responded to the chronic underfunding of the Highland Park Home, they did so in ways intended to highlight the contrast between dependent disabled men and their independent selves.

On examination, the brotherhoods' fund-raising efforts confirm that able-bodied men had no interest in the work of rehabilitation, as the Railroad Men's Home's owners had hoped they would. Instead, visitors used the language of freakery and marginalization to interpret what little they saw of the lives of disabled residents. By fixing on residents' persons rather than on their personalities or skills, able-bodied railroaders were able to concentrate on the disabled workers' bodily limits and dependence while ignoring intellectual or physical possibilities for independence. Resting below the surface of these observations, however, was an alternate narrative of disability, an attempt by disabled men to demonstrate their skill and dignity despite the demeaning circumstances in which they found themselves.

One fund-raising event clearly illustrates this attempt to marginalize Home residents. On Wednesday, August 29, 1901, members of the Grand International Auxiliary (GIA) to the Brotherhood of Locomotive Engineers and members of the Chicago BLE divisions arrived by special train for a picnic to be held at the Highland Park Home. The GIA and BLE hosted the annual event to raise money for the home. Ideal weather greeted six coach loads of revelers as they disembarked from the train with their well-filled baskets. Oddly, few engineers attended the festivities, but one observer quickly explained their absence by noting that engineers could not get much time off since it was the railroads' busy time of the year. Judging from this BLE member's subsequent comments, however, some engineers may have preferred not to mingle with their disabled comrades. He observed of those railroaders present, "The majority were composed of those that have been 'laid on the shelf,' awaiting, as it were, the call of the Grim Reaper."[75]

After explaining that these official visits to the Home were to the residents "an oasis in their helpless and inevitably monotonous life," D. Neilson described the inmates.[76] First was Henry J. Ryan, severely burned in an accident involving a firebox. Neilson commented that Ryan was "a helpless cripple for life." His left arm was burnt off at the elbow, his right hand burnt to a stump, and his face, eyes, and ears scarred. For Neilson, however, Ryan was less a man than he was an object lesson, a symbol of the soullessness of the corporation that used a badly designed firebox. Neilson also felt he had to reassure readers that Ryan was an upstanding man and had not been responsible for his accident. He was a thirty-year railroading veteran who, in a previous mishap, had been rewarded with a medal by his passengers, whom he had saved at great risk to his own life. Readers may have missed this information, however, embedded as it was in a description of Ryan's extensive injuries.

Neilson continued to objectify his disabled comrades as he described the other residents. He referred to J. Stark, a quadriplegic former conductor, as the "heavy-weight" of the Highland Park Home. The "light-weight" Mr. Mathias, whose disability was old age and general debility, was also described solely in terms of his bodily attributes. One must situate Neilson's remarks in the context of the immense popularity of the American sideshow at the time. Spectators—middle-class gawkers, self-described rubes, anyone with the price of a ticket—used the sideshow to displace anxieties about their own identities, projecting their fears onto an exhibited person with a disability and thereby creating and policing the boundaries of "normality." Even sedate intellectuals, respectable ladies, and small children frequented so-called exhibitions, displays of the disfigured, disabled, or exaggerated bodies masquerading under the guise of scientific enlightenment. Nor was the taste in "freaks" limited to an urban audience; Midwestern county fairs commonly attracted spectators by presenting such oddities as "bearded women, five-legged calves, giants, dwarves, [and] learned pigs." Fair promoters quickly learned that fairgoers were so captivated by this mingled miscellany of animal and human "oddities" that the sideshow was instrumental to a county fair's financial viability.[77] When Neilson described Mr. Stark as a "heavy-weight" and Mr. Mathias as a "light-weight," he knew that hyperobese and anorexic persons were common sideshow attractions. He also knew that his readers would be able to identify these body types as outside normative bounds.

The novelty of the sideshow may have captured an audience's attention, but it is the underlying meanings embedded in freakery that help explain why spectators remained. Uniquely American ideas of democracy, which held that egalitarian individualism had leveled class distinctions, at least ideologically substituted a social hierarchy based on ability. In the United States, the inherited power of the old European order was replaced by the self-governing and self-made man. If status was theoretically no longer inheritable, how would Thomas Jefferson's "natural leaders" establish boundaries of power in which white male patriarchs would retain the most influential positions in society? The powerful in society accomplished this in part by creating an ideology of "otherness" that excluded African Americans, Native Americans, women, children, members of the working class, and people with disabilities from the nineteenth-century corridors of power. The freak show helped establish boundaries of social inclusion, allowing spectators to quell their status anxieties by gazing at people whose actual bodies had been defined as essentially un-American. According to Rosemarie Garland Thomson, "the freak soothes the onlookers' self doubt by appearing as their antithesis."[78]

Yet, for American workingmen like Neilson, the sideshow held an extra appeal. Like *Herrenvolk* republicanism, which reassured white members of the working class that, although downward social mobility was a constant threat, they could not lose their whiteness, the freak show promised spectators that their able-bodiedness would allow their social status to be above that of the "freak." The onlookers' unstable positions as citizens were, at least for the moment, secure.

Disabled trainmen, once revered as veterans, were now objects of pity and lessons of failed manhood. When Neilson turned his attention to J. Bellaire, he managed to convey the full breadth of the transition. J. Bellaire had been perhaps the best-known fireman of the Gilded Age. He had gained a national reputation as the "One-Fingered Fireman," and an earlier generation of railroaders had celebrated him for his ability to remain on the job despite his impairment.[79] Now, however, Neilson reduced him to a mechanical savant, another of the types of persons who found themselves on exhibit.

Since becoming a resident in the Highland Park Home, Bellaire had constructed seventeen miniature steam engines that were propelled by windmills. He proudly demonstrated the products of his ingenuity to visitors, perhaps as a way of displaying his ongoing usefulness and involvement in the work culture of railroading. Neilson, however, marginalized Bellaire and his accomplishments:

He has only one finger on a part of one hand; the other arm was amputated. He made all these [steam engines] himself. They are horizontal, upright, revolving, cylinder, oscillating and compound engines. They not only display considerable mechanical ingenuity, but are remarkable for being the handiwork of a man with only one finger, and prove that Mr. Bellaire is possessed of great patience and perseverance to accomplish so much, and so well, when so heavily handicapped as he unfortunately is.[80]

Although Bellaire's construction of miniature model steam engines required extensive technical knowledge and skill, Neilson attempted to trivialize his accomplishment to a form of toy making, a boyish pastime rather than a manly occupation. Bellaire's bid to be recognized as an engine designer and railroad craftsman had failed.

Neilson's other descriptions of the work undertaken by residents suggest that efforts at occupational rehabilitation had fallen by the wayside. Now, a resident's productivity in the Home seemed designed to infantilize and accentuate dependency. For example, men participated in embroidery and other needlework, in which they were "supervised by the Matron and the visiting Ladies." The managers of the Highland Park Home did not even conceive of textile work as potential employment for residents; rather, it became a way "to relieve the monotony of their lives."[81] This was hardly the occupational retraining promised by the founders of the Home. No longer did advocates of the Home mention that a disabled brother had learned a new trade and gone into business. Instead, residents of the Home lived under the gaze of their able-bodied comrades and reassured onlookers of their own normality.[82] The promise of rehabilitated manhood and reincorporation had been replaced by objectification.

At the turn of the century, the railroad companies' desire to be competitive through greater efficiencies and the railroad brotherhoods' efforts to maintain influence in the relationship between labor and capital by establishing a more responsible and rational model of railroading manhood undermined the status of disabled trainmen in the work culture of railroading. A physical disability no longer marked the skillful veteran and true railroading man. As a new meaning of disability emerged, spurred by railroaders' debates over the desirability of a Railroad Men's Home, it was increasingly clear that able-bodied trainmen had come to view their disabled brothers with pity and suspicion. Instead of being a source of cultural continuity and a rallying point for a general criticism of industrial capitalism, the disabled com-

John Williams-Searle

rade was now, for the able-bodied railroader, a warning. Capitalism had transformed disabled workers into useless men; the railroad brotherhoods facilitated this process by viewing their disabled members as less than men.

NOTES

I would like to thank Paul Longmore, Lauri Umansky, Bridgett Williams-Searle, Douglas Baynton, and the members of Dr. Baynton's seminar on the history of disability for their comments and assistance. The research contained herein was supported by funding received from the University of Iowa, the State Historical Society of Iowa, and the Newberry Library, Chicago.

1. The Brotherhood of Railroad Brakemen (BRB) began in September 1883 as a conservative fraternal and mutual benefit society. Many of the railroad trades initiated fraternal orders around this time, including the Brotherhood of Locomotive Engineers (1863), the Order of Railway Conductors (1868), and the Brotherhood of Locomotive Firemen (1873). Leaders of the BRB believed that fraternal ideals would foster cooperation between company officers and railroad trainmen. During the 1880s, brotherhood leaders in all the rail trades championed the insurance that their organizations provided and were leery of strikes, yet they recognized the advantageous possibilities of collective bargaining. By 1890, however, the Brotherhood of Railroad Brakemen had changed their name to the Brotherhood of Railroad Trainmen and had taken a more activist turn, its members in the vanguard of the battle to expose and rectify the unsafe working conditions under which railroaders commonly toiled. See Walter F. McCaleb, *Brotherhood of Railroad Trainmen* (New York: Albert & Charles Boni, 1936), 48–53; and Philip S. Foner, *History of the Labor Movement in the United States*, 2d ed., 10 vols. (New York: International Publishers, 1975), 2:247–248.

2. Lack of insurance was a common problem among brakemen, who were the lowest-paid workers among the running trades. At the end of the nineteenth century, brakemen typically made less than $2 per day. See "Wages of Railway Employees," *Reports of the Industrial Commission on Labor Organizations, Labor Disputes, and Arbitration, and on Railway Labor* (Washington, D.C.: Government Printing Office, 1901), 17:911.

3. *Railroad Brakemen's Journal* 4 (November 1887): 520.

4. David Montgomery, *Workers' Control in America* (New York: Cambridge University Press, 1979); and Michael Kimmel, *Manhood in America: A Cultural History* (New York: Free Press, 1996), 106.

5. For changing ideas of manhood during the Civil War, see Gerald F. Linderman, *Embattled Courage: The Experience of Combat in the American Civil War* (New York: Free Press, 1987), chaps. 8 and 9.

6. To support his claim, Kirkpatrick provided the example of Shorty, a brakeman

and inveterate risk taker. Shorty took risks "because he could no more control this desire than a sot can control the desire for liquor." Kirkpatrick portrayed Shorty as a genius brakeman, his risk taking a sign of skill: "I saw him perform hundreds of feats that required perfect timing, alerted reflexes, and the speed of lightning—where the slightest error in any particular would have ended in tragic death." Shorty's skillful disregard of danger led not to the grave, however, but to promotion and a long career as a conductor. See O. H. Kirkpatrick, *Working on the Railroad* (Philadelphia: Dorrance & Company, 1949), 116, 63, 65, 67. Kirkpatrick's comments stem from his observations as a railroader around the turn of the century.

7. James H. Ducker, *Men of the Steel Rails: Workers on the Atchison, Topeka, and Santa Fe Railroad, 1869–1900* (Lincoln: University of Nebraska Press, 1983), 55–56.

8. J. C. P. to BLE, Chicago, May 11, 1868, *Locomotive Engineers' Monthly Journal* 2 (1868): 164, quoted in Reed C. Richardson, *The Locomotive Engineer, 1863–1963: A Century of Railway Labor Relations and Work Rules* (Ann Arbor: University of Michigan, 1963), 132.

9. The Brotherhood of Locomotive Firemen (BLF) even originated, in 1873, as a benevolent insurance association, although disability insurance constituted a separate policy. The Order of Railroad Conductors (ORC) established an insurance fund in 1882; the Brotherhood of Railroad Brakemen (BRB) quickly followed suit in 1884. The Switchmen's Mutual Aid Association of North America established a locally administered guaranty fund for its members in 1886.

10. U.S. Interstate Commerce Commission, *Third Annual Report of the Interstate Commerce Commission, December 1, 1889* (Washington, D.C.: Government Printing Office, 1890), 387–390.

11. Charles P. Brown, *The Life Story of Chas. P. Brown as a Boomer Railroad Man* (Whittier, Calif.: Western Printing Corporation, 1929), 176; quoted in H. Roger Grant, ed., *Brownie the Boomer: The Life of Charles P. Brown, an American Railroader* (DeKalb: Northern Illinois University Press, 1991), xi.

12. An editorial in the *Railroad Brakemen's Journal* accused injured brakemen who claimed total disability of being frauds out to undermine the BRB. See "Total Disability Claims," *Railroad Brakemen's Journal* 4 (May 1887): 221. Railroad brotherhood leadership believed that their importance in the labor-capital relationship increased proportionally with their ability to provide highly skilled and loyal workers. For an early example, see Charles Wilson, "Annual Address," *Locomotive Engineers' Monthly Journal* 4 (November 1870): 487.

13. Of course, as a relatively young organization in need of funds, the BRB relied on these cautionary tales to scare brakemen into paying their dues and insurance assessments. The *Journal* reported in March 1888 that a former member had lost a leg in an accident on the Union Pacific railroad. The account concluded, "One thousand dollars would have been his had he remained in the Brotherhood." See "Crippled by the Cars," *Railroad Brakemen's Journal* 5 (March 1888): 127.

John Williams-Searle

14. Letter of F. M. Ingalls (Chicago, Illinois), in *Railroad Brakemen's Journal* 6 (September 1889): 403.

15. For other accusations of brakemen filing false disability claims, see "Misplaced Confidence," *Railroad Trainmen's Journal* 7 (August 1890): 480; and "Total Disability Claims."

16. Ducker, *Men of the Steel Rails*, 121–122.

17. L. L. Losey, "The Relations between the Surgical and Claims Departments of Railroads," pamphlet reprinted from the *Railway Surgical Journal* (March 1908), 3, Newspaper Clippings, 1899–1915, Illinois Central Archives, IC 2.9 v. 18, Newberry Library, Chicago.

18. Disabled trainmen might work at the less-demanding jobs of flagmen and watchmen, jobs that able-bodied railroaders scorned. O. H. Kirkpatrick criticized the work as "inconsequential" (*Working on the Railroad*, 117).

19. Walter Licht, *Working for the Railroad: The Organization of Work in the Nineteenth Century* (Princeton: Princeton University Press, 1983), 202.

20. "A Railroad Club House," *Locomotive Engineers' Monthly Journal* 24 (August 1890): 634. See also Ducker, *Men of the Steel Rails*, 44–45.

21. Appellant's Abstract of Record at 3, *Jessup v. Chicago & Northwestern Railway Company*, 82 Iowa 243 (1891).

22. F. C. Rice to J. D. Besler, March 30, 1885; J. D. Besler to Henry B. Stone, April 3, 1885, L. O. Goddard In-Letters: Miscellaneous, 1882–1896, Gratuities, CBQ 3G5.3, Chicago, Burlington, and Quincy Archives, Newberry Library, Chicago.

23. Appellant's Abstract of Record at 3–9, *Reed v. C., R. I. & P. R. Co.*, 57 Iowa 23 (1881).

24. Appellant's Abstract of Record at 23, *Muldowney v. Illinois Central Ry. Co.*, 36 Iowa 462 (1873).

25. John Fabian Witt argues that workers' desire to control their workplaces actually hindered workers' compensation reform in the nineteenth century; see his "The Transformation of Work and the Law of Workplace Accidents, 1842–1910," *Yale Law Journal* 107 (1998): 1467–1502. See also John Williams-Searle, "Courting Risk: Disability, Masculinity, and Liability on Iowa's Railroads, 1868–1900," *Annals of Iowa* 58 (Winter 1999): 27–77; and John Williams-Searle, "Broken Brotherhood: Disability, Manliness, and Safety on the Rails, 1868–1908" (Ph.D. diss., University of Iowa, forthcoming).

26. For example, "three-fingered Ike" was a slang term for a disabled brakeman. See Kirkpatrick, *Working on the Railroad*, 116.

27. For several examples, see "Elkhart Shop Crew, 1909"; "Elkhart Pattern Room, 1906"; and "L. S. and M. S. Shop Crew, 1885," in Visual Collection, National New York Central Train Museum, Elkhart, Indiana.

28. Letter of Joseph Dixon (Amboy, Illinois), in *Railroad Brakeman's Journal* 5 (November 1888): 499–500.

29. Letter of Peter Terboss (Hallstead, Pennsylvania), in *Railroad Brakeman's Journal* 5 (November 1888): 500.

30. Licht, *Working for the Railroad*, 190.

31. "President Harrison on Safety Appliances," *Locomotive Engineers' Monthly Journal* 24 (January 1890): 39.

32. *Railroad Trainmen's Journal* 7 (January 1890): 27; Henry Cabot Lodge, "A Perilous Business and the Remedy," *North American Review* 154 (1892): 191.

33. Mark Aldrich, *Safety First: Technology, Labor, and Business in the Building of American Work Safety, 1870–1939* (Baltimore: Johns Hopkins University Press, 1997), 33; "To the B. of L. E.," *Locomotive Engineers' Monthly Journal* 26 (March 1892): 262; Lorenzo S. Coffin, "Safety Appliances on the Railroads," *Annals of Iowa* 5 (January 1903): 561–582.

34. *Hearing before the Committee on Interstate and Foreign Commerce of the House of Representatives on the Automatic Coupler Bill, H.R. 11059* (Washington, D.C.: Government Printing Office, 1902), 33.

35. "She Works for a Living," *Locomotive Engineers' Monthly Journal* 4 (January 1870): 23.

36. All grades of employees, including railroad officers, subscribed to the frequently circulating papers. Some railroad officials recognized that their contributions could raise morale while narrowing the social divide between workers and managers. For one example, see James O. Fagan, *The Autobiography of an Individualist* (Boston: Houghton Mifflin Co., 1912), 134–135.

37. F. M. Ingalls, "The Home Again," *Railroad Trainmen's Journal* 8 (April 1891): 224.

38. Ibid.

39. It is no coincidence that Ingalls established the Railroad Men's Home at the start of the Progressive Era. A new popular interest in the scientific treatment of people with disabilities, combined with the increased practice of institutionalization during this era, undoubtedly affected the railroad brotherhoods' response to their disabled members. The professionalization of medicine that accompanied the Progressive Era also had an effect on how the brotherhoods perceived their disabled members. With the medicalization of disability, medical professionals tried to convince families that they were no longer qualified to provide the professional and specialized care and treatment that disabled men would need. See Paul Starr, *The Social Transformation of American Medicine: The Rise of a Sovereign Profession and the Making of a Vast Industry* (New York: Basic Books, 1982).

40. L. W. Rogers, "The Home," *Railroad Trainmen's Journal* 8 (March 1891): 156–157.

41. Ibid., 157.

42. Ingalls, "The Home Again," 225.

43. "The Brotherhood of Railway Employees' Home," *Railroad Trainmen's Journal* 7 (September 1890): 544.

44. Ingalls, "The Home Again," 224.

45. Ingalls, "The Brotherhood Home," *Railway Conductor* 10 (January 1893): 25.

46. James Wood, "No High-Salaried Officers for the Home," *Locomotive Engineers' Monthly Journal* 34 (March 1900): 167–168. Other brotherhoods shared this concern. The *Locomotive Firemen's Magazine*, for example, noted approvingly that the Miesse-Thorp Railway Brotherhood Hospital planned to use permanently disabled brotherhood men as male nurses. See "A Brotherhood Hospital," *Locomotive Firemen's Magazine* 14 (August 1890): 705.

47. "Build Some Kind of Plant on Farm," *Locomotive Engineers' Monthly Journal* 34 (January 1900): 35.

48. James Wood, "No High-Salaried Officers for the Home," 167.

49. Titus Hinchcliff, "The Farm and the Home," *Locomotive Engineers' Monthly Journal* 34 (February 1900): 107.

50. "The Home for Disabled," *Locomotive Engineers' Monthly Journal* 30 (April 1896): 291.

51. R. W. Kelly, "Opposed to Building the Home," *Locomotive Engineers' Monthly Journal* 34 (February 1900): 104.

52. "The Home a Debt on Our Children," *Locomotive Engineers' Monthly Journal* 34 (March 1900): 168.

53. Cyrus E. Gallatin, "Opposed to Meadow Lawn Home," *Locomotive Engineers' Monthly Journal* 34 (May 1900): 294.

54. Ibid.

55. "The Home a Disorganizer," *Locomotive Engineers' Monthly Journal* 34 (May 1900): 295.

56. They need not have worried that the doors of the Railroad Men's Home would swing wide. Its organizer, F. M. Ingalls, had been in the forefront of accusing disabled workers of exaggerating their injuries to get insurance money; his zealous policing of which railroaders were truly disabled may have ultimately restricted the number of men admitted into the Railroad Men's Home. See Letter of F. M. Ingalls (Chicago, Illinois), 403; see also "Misplaced Confidence," 480.

57. T. H. Hiner, "Facts and Figures for the Home," *Locomotive Engineers' Monthly Journal* 34 (February 1900): 101.

58. Ibid.

59. "A New Home Proposition," *Locomotive Engineers' Monthly Journal* 34 (February 1900): 99.

60. "Opposed to the Home Proposition," *Locomotive Engineers' Monthly Journal* 34 (January 1900): 30.

61. "Opposed to Building the Home," 104. Older engineers such as Harry C. Smith also worried about antagonizing younger BLE members. Smith explained, "The old fellows don't want a home where they know they are eating the bread of charity drawn from unwilling Brothers' pockets." It is unlikely, however, that all of Smith's older comrades agreed with his conclusion that "They would prefer the County [Poor] House, most likely" ("The Home," *Locomotive Engineers' Monthly Journal* 34 [March 1900]: 167).

62. "What Ought to Be Done," *Locomotive Engineers' Monthly Journal* 35 (October 1901): 618.

63. F. M. Ingalls, "The Brotherhood Home," 25.

64. Lorenzo Coffin, "The Home," *Locomotive Engineers' Monthly Journal* 30 (January 1896): 23.

65. Lorenzo Coffin, "Our 'Home,'" *Railway Conductor* 10 (March 1893), 100.

66. Ibid.

67. Ibid., 101.

68. *Railway Conductor* 10 (May 1893): 187.

69. "Highland Park Home," *Locomotive Engineers' Monthly Journal* 34 (March 1900): 176.

70. Highland Park was well known enough to receive donations from individuals and groups not directly associated with railroad organizations. In November 1899, a group from Fort Worth, Texas, describing itself as "families and friends of railroad people," donated money and a box of groceries to the home. See "Railroad Employees' Home," *Locomotive Engineers' Monthly Journal* 34 (January 1900): 35.

71. Ibid.; "Railroad Employees' Home," *Locomotive Engineers' Monthly Journal* 34 (February 1900): 111.

72. "Railroad Employees' Home," *Locomotive Engineers' Monthly Journal* 34 (June 1900): 357.

73. "Railroad Employees' Home," *Locomotive Engineers' Monthly Journal* 34 (August 1900): 577.

74. Lorenzo S. Coffin, "Railroad Employees' Home," *Locomotive Engineers' Monthly Journal* 30 (September 1896): 757.

75. D. Neilson, "Railroad Men's Home, Highland Park, Ill.," *Locomotive Engineers' Monthly Journal* 35 (November 1901): 671.

76. Ibid., 672.

77. *Iowa Homestead and Farm Journal* 17 (13 September 1872): 292, quoted in Chris Rasmussen, "Fairs Here Have Become a Sort of Holiday: Agriculture and Amusements at Iowa's County Fairs, 1838–1925," *Annals of Iowa* 58 (Winter 1999): 11.

78. Rosemarie Garland Thomson, *Extraordinary Bodies: Figuring Physical Disability in American Culture and Literature* (New York: Columbia University Press, 1997), 58, 64–65; David Roediger, *The Wages of Whiteness: Race and the Making of the American Working Class* (New York: Verso, 1991).

79. *Locomotive Firemen's Magazine* 14 (February 1890): 129.

80. Neilson, "Railroad Men's Home," 673.

81. Ibid., 672.

82. Leslie Fiedler, *Freaks: Myths and Images of the Secret Self* (New York: Simon & Schuster, 1978), 31.

7

The Outlook of *The Problem* and the Problem with the *Outlook*

Two Advocacy Journals Reinvent Blind People in Turn-of-the-Century America

Catherine J. Kudlick

"The specific difficulties that have depressed the Blind for centuries are to be lifted by an enlightened public sentiment and that strong arm of Congress," a new journal proclaimed in January 1900. "It is an age of great individuals and great achievements, and the Race is dwelling in the consciousness of an all-pervading intellectual and spiritual revolution."[1] Called *The Problem*, the upbeat and passionate publication out of Leavenworth, Kansas, was the official voice of the American Blind People's Higher Education and General Improvement Association (ABPHEGIA), a movement of blind intellectuals founded in the mid-1890s. D. Wallace McGill, its publisher-editor and the ABPHEGIA's recording secretary, had graduated from the Missouri School for the Blind in the late 1880s and become professor of Musical Theory and Psychology at the Kansas Conservatory of Music. He hoped his quarterly would spawn a movement "broadly national and ready for practical work." "The subscription list should contain a million names," he exhorted readers, for "no one can have knowledge while ignorant of the facts, and the facts about the Blind have never been circulated." Besides, he noted with characteristic verve, "who will remain in ignorance when Knowledge costs but a dime?"[2]

Though *The Problem* ceased publication just three years later, in 1903, in some ways McGill's dream of an organized movement working on behalf of blind people came true. By 1906 the ABPHEGIA became the basis of the American Association of Workers for the Blind (AAWB). In 1907 this highly organized and respected national group of professionals launched a new periodical, *Outlook for the Blind*. That publication would eventually become the organ of the American Foundation for the Blind (AFB), founded in 1921 and one of the leading blindness organizations to the present day. Like McGill, *Outlook*'s eclectic and passionate founder, Charles F. F. Campbell, had, according to one historian, "an unspeakable faith in the capacity of blind people to live dignified and useful lives."[3] *Outlook*'s inaugural issue promised "a forum for the free and open discussion of all topics concerned with work for the blind," declaring that "we have no theories of our own to advocate, no projects to exploit. Our only desire is to be of service to the great cause of helpfulness to the blind."[4] The new publication continued *The Problem*'s custom of relaying practical information, such as reports from institutions and organizations, proceedings from conventions and congresses, and a smattering of articles that showed blind people engaging in routine activities such as sports, cooking, and learning mathematics. *Outlook* even added a helpful feature: a listing of all recent publications available in various tactile formats. (Not until 1917 did Braille become the dominant system. This fact, and the enormous expense of producing embossed text, accounts for the ink-print format of nearly every magazine dealing with blindness at the time.)[5] Thus, *Outlook*, like *The Problem*, believed itself to be working for the great cause of improving the lives of blind Americans.

But in other ways, McGill's dream died with his quirky, spirited publication. Tellingly, *Outlook*'s first issue devoted several paragraphs to its origins without mentioning McGill or *The Problem*. Further underscoring the deliberateness of the omission, several writers—including the esteemed blind lawyer Edward J. Nolan, who had served as the ABPHEGIA's president in 1900 and wrote one of the pieces describing *Outlook*'s birth—contributed to both publications. For reasons that remain obscure, the blind leaders of the ABPHEGIA ceded their authority to the new AAWB, dominated by sighted professionals and a handful of blind fellow travelers like Nolan. The advent of the AAWB would create a rift in approaches to blindness that persists to the present day.[6]

Clearly, the role of sighted members in the ABPHEGIA had been an issue. Until 1905, the association had been dominated by blind people who, after finding themselves excluded from professional organizations such as the American Association of Instructors of the Blind, had needed a forum for exchanging ideas. "The consequence was just what might have been expected," Nolan told the mixed audience of blind and sighted members of the AAWB

Catherine J. Kudlick

in 1911; "the pendulum swung to the opposite extreme, and a society was formed which was intended to be, in effect, exclusively for the blind." Fortunately, he continued, good sense soon had won out because, "after some experience and deliberation," blind members came to realize that "we must call upon the assistance of our seeing friends; no matter what work might be undertaken, seeing people must bear a large share of the burden, and among the seeing people are many who are sincerely interested in the cause of the blind. It was, therefore, unfair to exclude them from our conferences."[7] Nolan believed inclusion of the sighted also made sound political sense, for membership increased from barely thirty in the ABPHEGIA in 1905 to over three hundred in the AAWB by 1911.[8] Thus, by the time of *Outlook*'s birth in 1907, a movement of blind people such as that depicted in *The Problem* no longer existed. Nothing comparable to it would reappear until formation of the National Federation of the Blind (NFB) in 1940.[9]

The Problem's demise did not result simply from sighted professionals taking over from blindness activists. The story is far more complex and interesting and has implications well beyond the blind community for thinking about American history and today's world. Although we can identify a "blind" perspective more often in *The Problem* and a "sighted" one more often in *Outlook*, blind and sighted people contributed eagerly to both publications and did not always take predictable stands. McGill duly rewarded sighted fellow travelers by naming them in "Our List of Honor." And, contrary to Nolan's implication that the ABPHEGIA excluded sighted people, membership consisted "of two classes, regnant and honorary, each class being equally open to both the Sighted and the Blind."[10] Meanwhile, *Outlook* used Helen Keller as one of its principal spokespersons and relied on blind men like Nolan as valuable contributors. Thus the differences between *The Problem* and *Outlook* reflected a struggle over how to define an identity for blind people. The presence of blind and sighted individuals on both sides of the debate indicates that we must explain the conflict as taking place not just between opposing groups but also within individuals themselves.

The complicated dynamics involved in the creation of blind identity developed within the context of other profound changes in Progressive Era America.[11] Identities of gender, class, race, and ethnicity all came into question as members of various groups challenged long-held values. Compounded by the violence of some suffragists, the "New Woman" seeking freedom and independence revealed just how charged gender roles had become.

Meanwhile, waves of new immigrants, labor unrest, and racial strife reinforced the fear that American society might never be the same. Dramatic advances in technology—from expansion of public transportation networks to the arrival of the telephone—altered the basic ways in which people interacted by creating new options for association. Capitalism itself entered a phase that required negotiating a different set of relationships between government and industry. These social and economic changes helped redefine politics in light of a growing role for public opinion. The same forces would reshape how society responded to blind people and how blind Americans understood themselves.

This new turn-of-the-century identity for blind people was simultaneously forged at a public and a private level. Publicly, the different paths taken by *The Problem* and *Outlook for the Blind* exemplified a passionate battle between two emerging groups in search of a voice in the Progressive Era political landscape.[12] One consisted of the forerunners of today's political interest group. They presented themselves as representatives of people who, based on what they did or who they were (laborers, women, African Americans, blind people), should not only enjoy a slice of the American political pie but also have a say in its ingredients. The other group comprised experts such as social workers, engineers, educators, and medical professionals. They claimed authority based on their advanced training and experience, which they enjoyed by virtue of their official paid positions. While some overlap existed between these groups, mostly they stood in opposition. This was particularly true in matters of disability, where few thought to question the idea of public custodianship until well into the century, and where the idea of a disabled person as an expert remains elusive in many quarters even today.

The Problem and *Outlook* contained elements of both voices, though each publication struck a different balance as it tried to find a position in the midst of the social, economic, and political upheaval. Considering the journals together reveals how culture, philosophy, professionalization, and education joined to create a new kind of politics defining a newly emerging social group. As with others who eked out an existence at the turn of the century, the blind people represented in these publications participated—sometimes deliberately, sometimes inadvertently—in debates over a variety of issues, many of them being consciously defined for the first time: What role should the state play? Should experts' voices outweigh those of their subjects? What did it mean to have a voice? And how might advocates use the new tools of mass culture to further a cause?

As the resolution of these issues helped create a new public identity for blind people, Victorian culture helped them shape a more private sense of themselves as men and women.[13] Discussions of topics ranging from education to homemaking explained the social roles of the sexes, conveying subtle messages about how blind people might not match these expectations. In its crudest form, Victorianism required that a man provide for his family by earning a living in the public sphere, while a woman managed the private world of domestic tasks by creating a secure home life and rearing children. Further, masculinity meant being strong and independent, while femininity meant being weak and dependent. Though recent scholarship has correctly noted the difference between the idea of separate spheres and how men and women actually functioned in daily life, it is useful to present it as the rough scaffolding that shaped gender ideals. Eager to enter mainstream American culture, many blind women and men—like many immigrants and African Americans—may have embraced these ideals with greater enthusiasm than people who took their social standing for granted. Some probably believed that fulfilling middle-class gender expectations might diminish the stigma of blindness, just as many black people and new arrivals hoped such conformity might pave over racial or ethnic differences.[14] Yet, at the same time, blindness—and disability more broadly[15]—undermined the rigid roles Victorian culture tried to assign to men and women.

The Problem's and *Outlook*'s respective creations of a public sense of blind identity would have fascinating links with a blind person's private sense of self. Though both publications devoted virtually all their space to matters of interest to men and seemed quite traditional in their ideals for men and women, they in fact offered varied messages about womanhood, manhood, and blindness. *The Problem* implicitly assumed that blind women, like every American female, experienced the vices and virtues of prevailing Victorian sexuality, whereas *Outlook* conspicuously avoided the topic. *Outlook* sanitized blind women, presenting them to showcase blindness professionals, while those in *The Problem* were women first and blind second.

That the differences between the two journals carried into discussions of private matters suggests important connections between blind people's public and private identities. Exploring the distinctive ways in which *The Problem* and *Outlook* portrayed these relationships illuminates how disability, nascent identity politics, professionalization, and gender came together a century ago to launch new possibilities for blind Americans. Scrutinizing the publications' role in creating an image and identity for blind people also raises broader questions about how studying disability can help scholars explain more fully turn-of-the-century ideas about identity, community, and politics.

The Problem and the American Blind People's Higher Education and General Improvement Association marked a dramatic departure from the past. A journal run by and for blind people was a long way from the pathetic, groping heroines of sentimental literature or the dreary beggars of the popular imagination, who sat like lumps on street corners.[16] The publication's wide mix of articles ranged from mini-autobiographical sketches by a blind bank president, a medical student, and a farmer to the texts of congressional bills to guarantee blind adults higher education.[17] McGill printed the ABPHEGIA's annual convention proceedings, the blind schools' alumni association reports, and debates on subjects such as the advantages and disadvantages of attending schools with sighted children (a precursor to today's "mainstreaming"), or whether Braille or New York Point offered a more efficient tactile reading system.[18] And pieces occasionally took up topics animating American popular culture, such as "Astrology" or "Oriental Psychology and Philosophy among Western Peoples."[19]

Some articles aimed to raise blind people's self-esteem. In a typical piece titled "How Shall the Blind Succeed?" Charles W. Gillilan of Shawnee, Oklahoma, described his experiences as one of the first blind students to graduate from a college alongside sighted peers. He offered many practical tips and kind words for the friends who helped along the way. "I found that it is necessary for one who is handicapped to exercise the creative side of nature," he explained. "One finds many difficulties which can be successfully met only by the genius of invention." But he also candidly warned: "Reader, you must not conclude from what I have said of my experience . . . that the blind person who enters college will find a bed of roses. If your ideal is high, you will experience moments of doubt and even despair, but if there is that in you which makes it impossible for you to yield even when the will is defeated and the heart is sick, then, I am ready to wager my life on your success. . . . Success is in store for the one who isn't afraid to suffer and work and wait."[20] Such articles reflected *The Problem*'s general philosophy of portraying blindness realistically, allowing a blind person to address other blind people frankly, while using this realism to improve the image of the blind.

To promote the ABPHEGIA and the cause of blind Americans, *The Problem*'s inaugural issue carried a "Personal Letter Addressed to the People of

Catherine J. Kudlick

the United States." It invited readers to send in any information they might have, particularly the names and addresses of any blind people.[21] "If you have ever known a blind person, or if any live in your community, will you not please investigate and give us all the information you can secure?" McGill pleaded. He also urged readers to make themselves known by writing "a personal letter either to me or to some other officer of the Association expressing interest in our work." Now and then the journal reprinted these letters or responded to them in columns with titles such as "Suggested Problems."

McGill's appeal coincided with a growing interest in the lives of blind people that would culminate in the federal government's publication of *The Blind in the United States, 1910.*[22] Since 1830, the U.S. Census had privileged blind Americans as a survey category. The introduction to the 1910 census marveled at how this population "has formed a regular feature of Federal census activities for a longer continuous period of time than any other inquiry except the decennial enumeration of the population." Only "the fundamental facts of sex, color, and age" extended further back in time in an unbroken series.[23] By 1880 and 1890, census takers received additional compensation for including supplementary information about members of "special classes" (soon to be known as the "defective, dependent, and delinquent classes"). A qualitative change in the information ensued when the 1900 census sought to include noninstitutionalized people with disabilities and asked blind people located by census takers to mail in (free of charge) follow-up questionnaires about the probable causes of their blindness, family relations, schooling, and employment.[24] Rather than relying on data from asylum directors and medical professionals as in the past, the Census Bureau turned to private individuals. Even if the absence of blind census takers and data interpreters still placed blind people in the passive role of subjects, the alterations indicated a realization of the need for more sophisticated information about blind people.

This climate of greater interest no doubt influenced McGill's new philosophy of blindness and blind people. While quantitative data could serve a useful purpose, *The Problem* explored qualitative ways in which blind Americans might have a real say in what society thought about them. The editors had to manage a tricky balance between welcoming sighted fellow travelers who contributed valuable articles and a tone that left no doubt about blind leadership. In 1896 the ABPHEGIA's Second Convention had resolved that no commissioner "shall serve who is not a thoroughly educated blind person of some experience."[25] Without making such a bald declaration, *The Problem* made its privileging of the blind perspective apparent by relying on the expressed interests of blind people themselves to determine the journal's content. For example, an important early article called for a variety of embossed-type periodicals devoted to "the non-partisan presentation of the most important facts of current news and current popular discussion" for blind readers.[26] Articles such as these, and *The Problem*'s very existence, empowered blind people both individually and collectively.

In general, *The Problem* conveyed an optimistic, inclusive picture of blind Americans.[27] McGill and his comrades envisioned a world where the sightless functioned on a par with the seeing, accordingly earning their rewards and punishments as human beings, not as *blind* human beings, with all laboring together to solve humanity's universal problems. As one editorial put it, "the difficulties of the Blind in particular are the difficulties of Humanity in general and by solving the Problem of the one, we solve the Problem of the other."[28] *The Problem* frequently referred to "the Great Human Family," "all thinking people," "all humanity," "all classes of people which taken together constitute the Race," "Humanity rather than a particular class." Even its title, *The Problem*, reflected not a negative view of blindness but the Progressive Era vogue for conveying a sense of optimistic urgency, much as the National Association for the Advancement of Colored People's (NAACP's) magazine *The Crisis*, edited by W. E. B. DuBois, would seek to motivate black Americans.[29] According to *The Problem*'s philosophy, then, blind and sighted had much to teach each other, and all of humanity would gain as a result. As one contributor asserted: "The public is beginning to see that being blind no longer means being an imbecile or idiot, and eventually we hope our worthy instructors will come to know that all our average sightless boys and girls ask is an equal chance with the sighted, and this being given, ability and merit will surely speak for itself."[30]

While Charles Campbell's *Outlook for the Blind* also presented a philosophy of helping Americans better understand the blindness world, it spoke *about* and *to* blind people more often than considering them as having voices in their own right. Whereas *The Problem* tended to refer to "blind people," *Outlook* spoke about "the blind," with even Helen Keller conveying this sense. At a time when blind people were just beginning to find a voice, *Outlook*'s first issue reprinted one of Keller's speeches, "The Heaviest Burden on the Blind."[31] Like so much of *Outlook*'s content, it presented a contradictory message about blindness. Keller simultaneously used images of weakness and strength, noting that "the men and women for whom I speak are poor and weak in that they lack one of the chief weapons with which the human being fights the battle. But they must not on that account be sent to the rear. . . . They must be kept in the fight for their own sake, and for the sake of the strong. It is a blessing to the strong to give help to the weak." Through Keller, *Outlook* presented an image of blindness that suggested dependence before independence and weakness over strength.

While McGill sought to create a forum for blind people to talk to one another and gain confidence in themselves as valuable contributors to solving humanity's problems, Campbell worked to change their public image. He highlighted the abilities of the blind by putting on display blind people and the accomplishments they learned from professional experts. *Outlook* sang the praises of state-of-the-art special education institutions and industrial homes for the blind, the experts' answer to the outdated nineteenth-century asylums.[32] Whereas McGill believed a positive image of blindness had to come from blind people themselves, Campbell assumed public perceptions must change before the blind could gain this self-confidence. Such differences in these editors' approaches and the resulting tone of their publications had important implications for the image of blind people and their sense of identity.

Campbell came to *Outlook* as the sighted son of Sir Francis Campbell, the celebrated blind head of Britain's Royal Normal College.[33] He traveled widely on the European continent and in the United States with the idea of becoming a teacher of the blind but quickly decided that bigger things could and must be done. Settling in the eastern United States, he eventually became director of several institutions for the blind and the editor of *Outlook*. Unlike McGill the intellectual, Campbell the entrepreneur saw a dual opportunity in publicizing blindness. Not only would publicity change the pathetic public image of blind people, but examples of experts teaching them to triumph over adversity could raise money for the cause. He experimented with various new media, touring North America with a series of a lantern-slide shows and "cinematographs" (early films) about blindness. *Outlook* was another foray into a modern medium, the slick professional journal pitched to interested experts and possible lay donors.[34]

But this modern approach could have consequences at odds with the interests that blind people had asserted in *The Problem*. The same financial realities that most likely helped bring down its predecessor forced *Outlook* to draw in money few blind people had. To make a case to professionals and a public that might willingly pay, *Outlook* sacrificed some of the independence it championed for the blind. After all, if blind people came off as competent and self-sufficient, why give the organizations helping them money? Thus, *Outlook* faced the challenge of simultaneously showing that blindness was pathetic and that blind people could be advanced. Further contributing to this tension was its complicated relationship to Progressive Era modernity. To keep its reputation as a voice for experts and to draw in philanthropic dollars, the journal needed to showcase its modernity through what teachers did for the blind, rather than what blind people ended up doing for themselves. These complex tensions appeared not only in the content of articles but in their tone. *Outlook*'s ability to walk this fine line accounts in large part for the publication's success and longevity.[35]

Catering primarily to sighted professionals and potential donors, *Outlook* came across as a glitzy magazine on the forefront of visual representations in print. Its photos of people and places, reproductions of Helen Keller's signature at the end of her letters, and advertisements for everything from carpentry tools to flour to women's furs made *The Problem* look dour by comparison. Intended to be read by eye and not by ear (as *The Problem* had been), the AAWB journal relied on visual cues and played with vision to create a sense of modernity in the blindness field. It also delivered news directed toward the (mostly sighted)[36] superintendents of schools for the blind and offered articles by physicians and ophthalmologists who wrote of blindness as a horror that might be cured through timely medical intervention or prevented by family planning to avoid the dangers of heredity. One of *Outlook*'s *causes célèbres* was a vociferous campaign against *ophthalmia neonatorum*, "babies' sore eyes," a campaign that resulted in the formation of the National Society for the Prevention of Blindness. Seen as a worthy cause by sighted donors, such an energetic crusade *against* blindness underscored *Outlook*'s complicated role as a vaunted champion of blind people.

Still, for the most part *Outlook*'s articles dealt with issues of interest to anyone concerned with blindness rather than its prevention. Campbell had a hard-edged appreciation for the possibilities and pitfalls blind people faced in modern America. In one early report, "Life among the Seeing," he laid down some of the ideas basic to his philosophy.[37] "The more one has to do with finding employment for the blind," he wrote, "the more evident it becomes that it is impossible to treat [them] as a class. The possibilities and qualifications of each person are so diverse that no sweeping generalization can be made." Even as his publication spoke for the interests and ideals of in-

Catherine J. Kudlick

stitutions for the blind, he championed situations where such institutions would be unnecessary. "Probably we all agree that a blind person earning a living wage side by side with seeing workers is enjoying a more normal life than if he were earning more in a subsidized institution for the blind," Campbell asserted. Working under institutional supervision might be good for some, particularly those who became blind later in life and "possessed but little initiative when they had their sight." But for the others he advocated government help in securing regular jobs. "If every state would make a systematic search and find even twenty or thirty such opportunities," he exclaimed, "how great would be the gain to the present limited number of occupations open to the blind." He thus argued for recognition of blind people in all their complexity while calling on government to take the lead in aiding their employment.

For all its attempts to appeal to professionals and donors, *Outlook* did not shy away from controversial issues. In April 1909, for example, it presented a debate about establishing a blind national college.[38] With the founding of special colleges for women, black people, and even deaf students in the decades since the Civil War, the idea of creating such a school for blind Americans resonated with broader national trends.[39] But the issue also had special significance for blind people because, as one participant noted, "it is fully recognized that it is by the brain rather than by the hand that the blind are most sure to succeed, and to none does a successfully pursued college course promise more than to the blind."[40]

Those in favor of a national college cited financial advantages. Some argued that the federal government would support an institution of higher learning for the blind just as it had with Gallaudet College, founded for the deaf in the 1860s. James J. Dow, superintendent of the Minnesota School for the Blind and *Outlook*'s most vocal advocate for a special college, believed the Gallaudet example set a precedent for federal support. Moreover, it "would be an enormous stimulus to the state institutions [like his] and would undoubtedly greatly enhance their efficiency and scope.[41] Others, such as the superintendent of the North Carolina School for the Blind and Deaf, believed a special college would better suit blind people's unique temperament. "There are advantages to be derived from pursuing one's studies in colleges for the seeing," he admitted, "but there are exceedingly few blind students who have the pluck and the cash to succeed thus.[42] For many proponents, money appeared as the big stumbling block to the ultimate goal of assimilation. "Many of the best students among the blind, as among seeing, are those in the poorest financial circumstances," the Iowa school's superintendent explained. "Many of these students would be glad to pursue a higher course of training, had they the opportunity to do so, but owing to their financial condition they are not able to provide means of support at a seeing college, nor are they able to secure the services of a reader.[43] As with calls for opening special colleges for other groups outside the mainstream, those seeking such institutions for the blind hoped a protected environment would offer the support that would enable their graduates to enter the world with greater confidence and competence.

But by far the greater number of participants in the debate attacked the idea of a special college. Both sighted experts and blind graduates feared that blind people might become isolated as a class. S. M. Greene, superintendent of the Missouri School for the Blind, argued that "it is necessary for the blind student to mingle with the sighted in order to obtain true proportions for life adjustment."[44] Putting it more bluntly, the superintendent of Colorado's School for the Deaf and the Blind said that "our folks are [already] blind enough and peculiar enough after twelve or fifteen years of association in a school for the blind." He echoed one blind graduate's assertion that "every educator of the blind knows the deleterious effect of collecting the blind together in isolated groups.[45] Albert B. Irwin, a blind man who had earned a master's degree at Harvard, explained that "a College for the Blind would but deepen the ruts out of which its students must be got before they can hope to succeed in the world with the seeing.[46]

The debate over higher education was one of the few times blind people had a real voice in *Outlook*. Averaging about four times longer than those submitted by blindness professionals, their letters contained some of the journal's most eloquent and passionate words. All of the blind contributors had earned degrees from universities and given the matter serious thought based on those experiences. For example, with his Harvard degree, Irwin was in a particularly good position to point out that "if the public is slow to recognize a new college at best, how much slower would this recognition come to a special institution?" "Unless a college degree carries with it a large measure of public confidence," he argued, "it is going to lack much of its value to the blind person who needs something to offset the burden of proof which invariably rests upon him.[47]

Newel Perry made an especially well documented case against special institutions.[48] After attending the University of California at Berkeley and earning a doctorate in mathematics from the University of Munich, he drafted the blueprint for New York state's 1907 law providing blind college students with scholarships to hire readers. In the debate over a blind college, he cited detailed census figures and financial data and outlined economic, political, and social reasons for his opposition. Since no top-rank scholars would choose to teach in such a place, "a national college for the blind would at best be a second-rate school." Perry, like the other blind contributors, defended his experience of attending college along with sighted students. Blind people's passionate and eloquent participation in the debate showed that, even without *The Problem*, they still had much to say on their own behalf.

The debate over a special blind college printed in a professional journal provided surprising possibilities for fostering a sense of collective identity among blind Americans. *Outlook* seemed open to presenting views from a variety of sighted and blind perspectives that did not always adhere to its philosophy. In addition, by representing disagreements among sighted professionals, the AAWB organ inadvertently created a wedge for blind people to participate as equals in an ongoing debate. When the experts had not yet agreed on an issue, they seemed more willing to listen to firsthand experiences. Moreover, at a time when no other widely circulating periodical touted itself as expressing the views of blind people themselves, *Outlook* unintentionally provided a valuable service of putting them in touch with one another and conveying a sense that a critical mass of potential leaders did exist. Articulate responses from men such as Perry, Irwin, and Nolan provided a positive image of blind Americans to sighted and blind alike at the same time that they made blind people aware they were not alone. But while *Outlook* had clearly involved them in certain discussions, it would never fulfill *The Problem*'s mission to speak of and for blind people. It is revealing, for example, that the journal grouped their responses together at the end of the discussion, only after sighted professionals had weighed in with their opinions.

Despite the blind contributors' criticism of separate schools, they in fact owed their own activism to their experiences in such places, because more than any other factor the special schools fostered a sense of community among blind people. Before the universal use of Braille, efficient public transportation, and inexpensive, widely available, reliable telephone service, those schools provided rare opportunities for blind people to meet and connect. These students not only learned the occupational and living skills in the official curriculum but also developed their perspectives regarding blindness and the social situation of blind people. In such environments it was only a matter of time before blind men began to form a sense of community that often continued after graduation. Correspondence among the alumni of one such school had led to the founding of the ABPHEGIA and *The Problem.*[49]

Debates such as the ones over a special college notwithstanding, blind people contributed infrequently to *Outlook*, with the conspicuous exception of Helen Keller. The blind-deaf superstar has long been a sore point with some blind people, partly because she created an unattainable ideal and partly because, like *Outlook* itself, she cloyingly evoked pity. Even more disturbing for some, she depoliticized disability, avoided promoting collective action by blind people, yielded power to condescending sighted professionals, and failed to challenge prejudice and discrimination as her socialist leanings might have promised, all the while playing the part of the saintly blind virgin. As her biographers have observed, it is nearly impossible to separate her own motives and ideas from those of the people around her. Not only did she always learn and communicate through intermediaries, she faced difficult financial circumstances that required her to temper her views about everything from politics to blindness so as not to alienate her benefactors. At the root of all discussions about Keller is the question of whether she was a thinking person in her own right, an issue that also haunts nearly all discussions of disability both past and present.[50]

Not surprisingly, then, Keller conveyed a contradictory message about blind people and her own role as a spokeswoman. After describing weakness as one of "The Heaviest Burdens of the Blind," she explained that "the help we give the unfortunate must be intelligent." "Pity and tears make great poetry but they do not make model tenement houses, or keep children out of factories, or save the manhood of blind men."[51] For Keller, as for many Americans, the real problem lay in idleness, the solution in jobs. Even if the state provided the capital and basic job training, the local community must "meet him with a sympathy that conforms to the dignity of his manhood and his capacity for service." Predictably, she favored special institutions: "the true value of a school for the sightless is not merely to enlighten intellectual darkness, but to lend a hand to every movement in the interests of the blind." Yet she also saw no need for the blind to be segregated from the seeing throughout life, for "the city of the blind is everywhere." Just like sighted people, blind ones suffered their defeats and savored their victories, contrary to the wild success and hopeless failure assigned them by popular imagination. "Like the seeing man, the blind man may be a philosopher, a mathematician, a linguist, a seer, a poet, a prophet," due to his individual capacity, not some mythic insight born of blindness. "If the light of genius burns within him, it will burn despite his infirmity, and not because of it." Yet, after so carefully affirming blind people's diversity, she ended by resorting to stereotypical pity. "I appeal to you, give the blind man the assistance that shall secure for him complete or partial independence. He is blind and falters. Therefore go a little more than half way to meet him. Remember, however brave and self-reliant he is, he will always need a guiding hand in his."

Thus, Keller's view of blind people—the one *Outlook* placed before the American public in its first issue—was full of contradictions. The sightless were strong, ambitious, and diverse but also weak, lazy, and likely to play the few roles society had assigned to them for centuries. Their personal strength should garner respect, but society should come to them "more than half way" and extend that ubiquitous "guiding hand." Even her sympathy with blind people and her role as their spokeswoman cut both ways as she simultaneously presented herself as a fellow blind person and as one who looked down on them.[52] Keller's article would never have appeared in *The Problem* because at bottom she denied agency to the blind people she championed. Help, according to *Outlook*'s most prominent blind spokeswoman, must come from outside before it could come from within. Further, the idea of a single blind individual speaking for all blind people would have been unthinkable for a journal run by and for blind people, even if it was one man's brainchild. McGill had made *The Problem* a forum for blind people to speak in a variety of voices on many topics, some not even about blindness. It had demonstrated blind people's heterogeneity without any one person like Keller having to announce it.

Keller's contradictory feelings about blind people and her role as spokeswoman no doubt influenced her conflicted approach to gender in "The Heaviest Burden on the Blind." She was the only prominent blind woman writing in either *The Problem* or *Outlook*, and one of the few people to mention women in matters not directly concerning what were thought of as women's issues. Moreover, she displayed sensitivity to the importance of manhood for blind men, a feeling surely enhanced by the common characterization of disability as feminine.[53] In America, which acknowledged the relationship between disability and gender only implicitly, Keller's willingness to mention gender at all was significant. And yet she clearly held a traditional view of women's and men's places in society. Like all the writers in both *The Problem* and *Outlook*, when she addressed the need for education and jobs, she spoke about and to blind *men*. "I can tell you of blind men who of their own accord enter the sharp competition of business and put their hands zealously to the tools of trade," she declared. "It is our part to train them in business, to teach them to use their skills carefully."[54] Whether craft skills or works of genius, such pursuits bolstered a blind man's place in the world, countering the assault from the weakness attributed to disability. Because blindness only compounded a woman's femininity, Keller implied, it was more important to preserve the blind man's threatened manhood. By choosing male occupations as her examples, by highlighting the stresses of blind men, and even by mentioning women in passing, Keller reinforced traditional gender roles.

As Keller's observations suggest, gender expectations lie at the root of many discussions about blindness and disability, influencing the blind person's sense of self.[55] Beginning with Aristotle, western thinkers have drawn unflattering parallels based on the premise that female bodies were inferior copies of the male. Ideas about women and disability have reinforced each other, as images of weakness and dependence invoked images of femininity. Blindness may have forced men who otherwise might have taken their masculinity for granted to consider consciously the notion of their manhood and the social expectations attached to it. If a blind man led a useful life (such as those engaged in the various jobs recounted in *The Problem*'s mini-autobiographies), his blindness could be presented as of little or no significance. But more often, it seemed to threaten manhood by keeping an individual dependent. Not only were most blind men thought incapable of earning a living sufficient to provide for a family, but—in an era before widespread programs to teach mobility and independent living—many believed they could not travel without assistance. For blind women, meanwhile, disability compounded the disadvantages already associated with being female—helplessness, dependence, frailty—but without a social payoff, for even in a world that celebrated female virtues, it made women *too* feminine. And since few believed blind women could run a household and provide a home environment for a husband and children, they were deemed unmarriageable, cutting them off from a major avenue of social participation. Blindness undermined manhood and redefined womanhood in unsettling ways.

The Problem and *Outlook* approached gender differently, even as each helped reinforce unique aspects of the status quo. A close analysis of an article about homemaking from each publication reveals those differences and may deepen our understanding of the relationships among blindness, gender, and creating a sense of both public and private identity.

Writing in *The Problem* in fall of 1900, Lillian M. Hinkle attempted to answer the question she was most frequently asked: "How is a sightless woman practically useful?"[56] She responded enthusiastically with the optimistic though cautious "In most every womanly line." Condemning the state schools for the blind for giving children "a common education without any practical sensibility," she argued for the value of home teaching. But this could succeed only if parents played an active part, which led her to the focus of her story, Mrs. Blanche Elmaker Logan of Kansas City, Kansas, the very model of a modern blind homemaker. Hinkle found her to be "a self-poised womanly woman, ready for all emergencies, keen in all perceptions, alive to all business ventures, and yet purely emotional and aesthetic . . . one of the most perfect home-makers I ever knew." Mrs. Logan kept a clean house, raised several children (being "a wonderful mother . . . strict yet kind, and ever patient"), and proved "fully competent to converse intelligently on any subject from science or poetry to the humor of a Dickens character." Her sighted husband, Professor W. J. Logan, principal of the Kansas School for the Blind, "has ever been proud to introduce her to people in any station in life, no matter how lofty that station may be because of her great womanly self possession."

A decade later in *Outlook*, Miss Elizabeth C. Cory, a teacher of Domestic Science at the Missouri School for the Blind, gave her answers to the questions: "Can a Blind Girl Learn to Cook? If so, how is she taught?"[57] In some respects, her description of her Domestic Science course seems more helpful than Hinkle's pep talk in *The Problem*. Step by step, she took the high school–age girls through the two-year course aimed at creating a meal, from learning about food and nutrition to lighting the gas stove. "At first they do it with fear and trembling," she explained, "but they soon gain confidence and learn to regulate the gas burner putting the hand above the blaze and turning it up or down." They also learned to label and measure ingredients "by using the cup, spoon and knife in much the same way that the seeing girl would, with the exception that the blind girl must get used to lifting the cup to feel how heavy it is, learn that half a cup of sugar will not be as heavy as a whole cup, and learn that one-fourth of a cup of milk will weigh less than a third of a cup, etc." In the second year, they mastered canning, pickling, and jelly making, organizing a kitchen, setting a table, and cleaning up. After learning "to use up left-overs so that nothing will be wasted," in the grand finale the girls served a four-course meal to invited guests. "Great care is taken to make the work practical," Cory concluded, "that it may be of lasting use."

Though both articles dealt with blindness and domesticity and both were written by sighted women who explained how blind women could fulfill social expectations, their tone and presentation reveal two very distinct underlying philosophies. By celebrating the values of home teaching, Hinkle suggested that not everyone looked to schools staffed by experts as the best means of educating blind students, especially in matters of daily life. *The Problem* approached domesticity from the standpoint of a blind woman having achieved the ideals of the sighted world. She won respect not as a blind person but as a woman who did things well. Hinkle noted that the fact that friends "come to her with a sense of extreme pleasure rather than curiosity is an appreciated compliment to Mrs. Logan." In contrast, *Outlook* focused on the accomplishments of the teacher, the expert without whom the students' achievements would have been impossible. Cory made clear that she devoted much energy to this class, with comments such as "We spend considerable time in practice of that kind." The article even included girls' testimonies about how much they had learned. While Cory did not overtly brag, the article underscored the value of a trained teacher in an institutional setting. Her invitation to visit the school, the staged dinner at the end of the course, the entire article celebrated visibility and display, even a kind of showmanship that used the pupils to demonstrate their teacher's success. Photos of the pupils proudly posing in the kitchen and in front of the set dining-room table presented the blind girls as spectacle for the sighted world. *Outlook*'s use of display again illustrated what was being done *for* the blind rather than *by* them.

The distinction between "by" and "for" the blind basic to the philosophical differences between the two advocacy journals yielded different ideas of womanhood. Though Hinkle's article never showed Mrs. Logan leaving home, it conveyed her sense of independence and assertiveness as she went about her daily chores. Her determination and interest in manly things such as business never eclipsed her femininity. Moreover, while Logan's domesticity was chaste, like that of any good turn-of-the-century housewife, the presence of a husband and children hinted at her undeniable sexuality. Consider Hinkle's verbal portrait of domestic bliss:

> One of the most beautiful home pictures I ever beheld I saw one Autumn evening in the sitting room of the Logan home. It was after the Professor's

Catherine J. Kudlick

school hours and he was seated before the fire reading the current news from the daily papers to his wife, while she was busily engaged crocheting her little child an artistic wool jacket. To perfect the scene, the little daughter of eighteen months sat at their feet playing with her kitten, and the occasional fondling of a devoted parent gave a rich "Be of good cheer" spirit of expression to the whole.[58]

Even if parts of Hinkle's sketch make today's feminists cringe, her portrait was, in fact, quite radical. Not only did it show a competent and independent blind woman comfortable with herself, but it spurned contemporary prescriptive literature that urged blind girls never to marry and certainly never to raise children.[59] This contrasted sharply with images of Helen Keller or the prim girls in Cory's cooking class.

Unlike *The Problem, Outlook* offered no hints of sexuality in its portrayals of domesticity. It put Cory's class on display, but the photos did not suggest availability or invite desire, the usual goals associated with women and display in the nineteenth century. "Station B of the Poultry Class at the Missouri School for the Blind" would probably have aroused passion in few readers of any journal, let alone *Outlook,* as it showed a blind young lady in Victorian dress standing in the middle of a chicken coop. A second picture posed girls in a large kitchen wearing white hats and aprons and conveys the brisk efficiency of Domestic Science. Only a third photograph, set in a middle-class home, might suggest the lure of feminine adolescence. Decorated with heavy framed pictures, plants, and solid wooden bookcases filled with ink-print books (not tactile ones), the image, titled "Dining Room for Domestic Science Pupils at Missouri School for the Blind," displays two rigidly poised girls standing on either side of a table set with cloth and crystal. Like the girls in all the other pictures, the matronly one on the right does not look at the camera, while the more youthful one on the left seems as if she might scold the viewer if given the chance. To be sure, some of the missing allure might arise from the absence of eye contact, one of the earliest steps in seduction. Without it, the sighted viewer of such photos might infer a lack of interest.[60] But even (and especially) taking this into account, the fact remains that blindness has influenced how we approach the possibilities for womanhood. Thus, the young lady in the chicken coop confirms what the lack of eye contact has already prepared readers to believe: the girl is not available. None of the pictures is fetching because *Outlook* did not believe blind girls should be fetching, not even in that subliminal way so central to

Victorian fantasy. And though Cory's account described teaching girls at the age when most popular magazines surely would be extolling how such courses prepared them for matrimonial duties, she never mentioned marriage. Instead, she noted examples of girls planning to return to their families and share their skills with relatives. *Outlook* never intended these girls to grow up to be Mrs. Logans.

This brings us once again to the underlying differences between *The Problem* and *Outlook*. It raises the question of a possible relationship between the journals' philosophies about blindness and their approaches to the possibilities of womanhood. Did an implicit link between disability and the feminine influence how they understood and presented each idea? And what are the implications for a public sense of blind identity? *The Problem*'s desire to demystify blindness and blind people surely contributed to its eagerness to create a normal portrait of gender roles. If Mrs. Logan could fulfill a traditional feminine ideal, some of this respectability might rub off on blindness, or at least help dilute the negative images associated with it. In addition, because *The Problem* appeared more comfortable with blindness, it depicted various unorthodox possibilities for a disabled woman. *Outlook* had to tread more carefully. Just as a positive image of competent and independent blind people might have alienated possible donors, a traditional feminine role undermined the publication's raison d'être. Running a household and raising children of her own suggested that a woman such as Mrs. Logan could function without *Outlook*'s subscribers. Nor could a journal that took on the cause of eliminating *ophthalmia neonatorum* (a form of blindness linked to venereal disease) allow its depictions of women even to hint at sexual possibility. Though most blindness is not inherited, suggestions of a blind woman's sexuality might also have evoked the possibility of tainting the human race. Like their counterparts in other fields, *Outlook*'s professional readers were surely aware of the scientific literature on eugenics that flourished in the Progressive Era, which placed much blame on irresponsible sexual conduct.[61] In addition, mention of sex would have been highly improper in a professional forum commanding public respect. Thus, to lend an aura of respectability to blind people, *Outlook* seized on one aspect of Victorian womanhood, chastity, while *The Problem* stressed another, domesticity.

At the same time, the links each journal drew between women and disability helped complicate ideas of gender and feminism. In contrast with the prim veneer of *Outlook*'s cooking students, *The Problem*'s championing of marriage and child-rearing for blind women was a radical act in terms of disability but not for womanhood. Blindness aside, Mrs. Logan fulfilled the most conservative ideals that could undercut women's social and political gains. *Outlook*, meanwhile, offered a vision of womanhood that linked her more directly to the professional and public realm. Though *Outlook* never intended it this way, it suggested a possibility whereby a blind woman might define herself in a way other than that imposed by being a daughter and, later, a wife. In an era that offered few options for independent women, blindness, like invalidism, might open up possibilities for reflection and individual action not available to women following a traditional path.[62] Moreover, by putting female students on display, *Outlook* provided a public image of women engaged in having a professional education. Even if the journal did not promise blind women careers beyond returning home as spinsters to perform a minimum of household chores, it showed them learning the latest innovations in Domestic Science from experts. In some ways, few presentations of womanhood could be more modern.

As the two articles about homemaking show, *The Problem* and *Outlook for the Blind* differed dramatically in their underlying philosophies, approaches, and tones. *The Problem* urged blind people to help themselves and one another; *Outlook* celebrated seeing experts who provided help because they knew best. McGill's journal sought to create a sense of community *of* blind people; Campbell's asked the sighted community to provide help *for* them. That Wallace McGill was blind while Charles Campbell was sighted surely played an important part in establishing this difference from the beginning. Just as men and women or white and black people understood their options differently based on their experiences, sighted and blind people inhabited distinct worlds. Growing up blind, attending special schools, and living with the constant need to prove himself to skeptical sighted people, Professor McGill no doubt learned lessons that Campbell could only imagine. As much understanding and concern as Campbell had for blind people, he oriented himself toward the sighted world. Everything he did, including editing *Outlook*, passed through this filter. And even if either man had been intellectually or temperamentally so inclined, the social and political climate would not have allowed a blind man to publish a journal for experts, nor would it listen to a sighted one who spoke radically about options for blind people.

Yet the two approaches to blindness did not neatly divide between good modern blind people and reactionary sighted professionals who relegated the blind to dependency. Neither blind nor sighted individuals automatically adopted either view of blind identity. Representatives stood on both sides, everyone earnestly believing himself or herself to be acting for a better world. Moreover, both McGill and Campbell were modern men who brought new ideas about blind people and blindness into an emerging modern political culture. The substantial differences in their approaches reflect the fact that each seized on a different aspect of this modernity to further the cause of improving blind people's lives. McGill drew on the powerful current of shared group interest espoused by a journal dedicated to political and social change. Like African Americans and women, he sought a new way to empower citizens who had never before dared to claim power. Campbell used modern media such as photography and the journal itself to solicit the goodwill and financial support that would help keep the cause (and the publication) alive, thus revealing his understanding of public opinion as a new resource. Both approaches would have unintended and sometimes negative consequences: *The Problem* failed to garner sufficient political or monetary support, while *Outlook* gained these things at the expense of a movement organic to blind people themselves. Yet each journal contributed much to changing the landscape on which the identity of blind Americans would develop.

By dominating the blindness field over the next generation, *Outlook* associated blindness with professionals keen on making an impression on mainstream American society. But it did not destroy a movement *of* blind people. Instead, it showed them that not everyone who claimed to be acting in their best interests came with the same spirit and assumptions. *Outlook* put an end to the naïveté evident in *The Problem* to such an extent that when the founders of the National Federation of the Blind launched a new movement a generation later, in 1940, they brought a mistrust of sighted blindness professionals with them. *The Problem* had shown what was possible; *Outlook* demonstrated that such dreams could never be taken for granted.

This look at two advocacy journals raises intriguing ideas about the factors affecting personal and group identity and the possibilities for change. Like socioeconomic class, race, gender, ethnicity, and sexuality, disability is but one identifying element that determines how we respond to our political and social environment. The story becomes particularly interesting when two or more of these elements combine. Which factor prevails under which sets of circumstances, and what determines this prevalence? Is there a hierarchy among these elements, or does a new hierarchy reconstitute itself each time they come into proximity? Like the representatives of so many other groups coalescing at the turn of the century, publications such as *The Prob-*

lem and *Outlook* played with this hierarchy as they tried to find a place in the evolving social and political order. Both introduced blindness as a factor to consider along with an already-recognized one, such as gender. More important, both assumed blindness would be *the* defining factor in a person's life. For one of the first times in history, these journals argued that this characteristic, always understood as personal and private, might have significant political ramifications. In effect, people like McGill, Campbell, and all those who spoke out in their publications were coming to articulate a reciprocal relationship between a person's sense of self and the wider world of interest groups and experts. Once the equation had been drawn, the "all pervading intellectual and spiritual revolution" promised by *The Problem* had begun.

NOTES

Special thanks to Anita Baldwin, Lucy Barber, Larry Glickman, Gil Johnson, Kim Nielsen, Barbara Pierce, Harold Snider, Clarence Walker, and the editors for comments, suggestions, and lively discussion.

1. *The Problem* 1:1 (January 1900): 1.

2. Ibid., 3. In 1895 a group of graduates of the Missouri School for the Blind founded the Missouri National College Association for the Blind. In 1896 they changed the organization's name to the American Blind People's Higher Education and General Improvement Association. Unfortunately, no circulation or publication figures have been found to indicate the extent of *The Problem*'s readership.

3. Frances A. Koestler, *The Unseen Minority: A Social History of Blindness in the United States* (New York: David McKay Co., American Foundation for the Blind, 1975), 482.

4. *Outlook for the Blind* 1:1 (April 1907): 3.

5. The one notable exception was the *Mathilde Ziegler Magazine*, a publication designed to make literature and news items available to blind readers through several forms of embossed type. It was founded the month before *Outlook for the Blind*, in March 1907, and continues to be published today.

6. The differences between the National Federation *of* the Blind and the American Foundation *for* the Blind embody this today. As for the early years of the AAWB, most standard histories of the organized blind movement pass quickly over it. See Floyd Maston, *Walking Alone and Marching Together: History of the Organized Blind Movement in the United States* (Baltimore: National Federation of the Blind, 1990), 6; Harry Best, *Blindness and the Blind in the United States* (New York: Macmillan, 1934), 619; Koestler, *Unseen Minority*, 14–15. The primary sources offer a bit more information, but none of it sufficient to reconstruct the history fully. See *Bulletin of the Missouri National College Association for the Blind* (1895), Supplement (1897); Edward J. Nolan, "Historical

Sketch of the Association," in *The Saginaw Conference: Origin, Constitution, Proceedings, Papers, and Compiled Discussions: American Association of Workers for the Blind, Eighth General Convention* (Hartford, August 22–25, 1905), 48–51; Edward J. Nolan, "A Brief History of the American Association of Workers for the Blind," in *Proceedings of the Eleventh Convention of the American Association of Workers for the Blind* (Overbrook, PA, 1911), 14–16. Nolan's defensive account of the early years of AAWB suggests that the history might, in fact, have been acrimonious. "The history of this Association has been remarkably free from discord, factions and unpleasant incidents," he told delegates to the 1911 meeting of the AAWB.

7. *Proceedings of the Eleventh Convention*, 15.

8. Ibid.

9. For an in-house history of the NFB, see Matson, *Walking Alone and Marching Together*.

10. *The Problem* 1:1 (January 1900): 4.

11. See Steven J. Diner, *A Very Different Age: American in the Progressive Era* (New York: Hill and Wang, 1998); Robert H. Wiebe, *The Search for Order, 1877–1920* (New York, 1967); John Whiteclay Chambers II, *The Tyranny of Change: America in the Progressive Era, 1890–1920* (New York: St. Martin's, 1992); Alan Dawley, *Struggles for Justice: Social Responsibility and the Liberal State* (Cambridge, Mass.: Harvard University Press, 1991); Daniel T. Rogers, "In Search of Progressivism," *Reviews in American History* 10:4 (December 1982): 113–32.

12. For an interesting discussion of the professions from a contemporary, see Abraham Flexner, "Is Social Work a Profession?" *Proceedings of the National Congress of Charities and Correction* (Chicago, 1915), 576–91.

13. On Victorianism and gender in America, see Carroll Smith-Rosenberg, *Disorderly Conduct: Visions of Gender in Victorian America* (New York: Knopf, 1985); Robyn Muncy, *Creating a Female Dominion in American Reform, 1890–1935* (Oxford: Oxford University Press, 1991). On undoing separate spheres in an earlier period, see Linda Kerber et al., "Beyond Roles, Beyond Spheres: Thinking about Gender in the Early Republic," *William and Mary Quarterly* 46 (July 1989): 564–85.

14. This is one of the main pillars of Kevin G. Gaines's book *Uplifting the Race: Black Leadership, Politics, and Culture in the Twentieth Century* (Chapel Hill and London: University of North Carolina Press, 1996).

15. The relationship between blindness and disability is problematic in that the thrust of much contemporary activism is to decouple this association, a stance that has many intriguing implications that lie beyond the scope of this essay. I link them here because they remain intertwined in the public—and, to a lesser extent, the intellectual—imagination.

16. Mary Klages, *Woeful Afflictions: Disability and Sentimentality in Victorian America* (Philadelphia: University of Pennsylvania Press, 1999); Jessica Langworthy, "Blind-

ness in Fiction: A Study of the Attitude of Authors toward Their Blind Characters," *Journal of Applied Psychology* 14:3 (June 1930): 269-86.

17. The bill in question was House Bill 4347, introduced December 15, 1899. It died in committee.

18. On what is sometimes called "the war of the dots," see Koestler, *Unseen Minority*, 37-39. Until Braille was adopted as the universal system for tactile reading, debates raged within the blindness community regarding the best method. At the height of the controversy in the early years of the twentieth century, at least five different systems operated simultaneously, each one requiring a different set of reading skills, thereby creating the tactile equivalent of a Tower of Babel for blind people. Moreover, the confusion limited the number of books blind people could read, since valuable time and money were wasted on reproducing one book in multiple formats rather than many more books in a single format. "In order to avail himself of the full range of literature (which at best is woefully limited)," Major Migel, the founder of the AFB explained, "the blind reader must learn and keep well up in, all these codes. How long would our seeing friends stand for such a state of affairs in ink type?" (quoted in Koestler, *Unseen Minority*, 36). The two leading contenders among the systems were Braille and New York Point.

19. *The Problem* 3:4 (October 1902): 85-89; *The Problem* 1:1 (January 1900): 24.

20. *The Problem* 1:1 (January 1900): 18.

21. Ibid., 7.

22. Department of Commerce, Bureau of the Census, *The Blind in the United States, 1910* (Washington, D.C.: Government Printing Office, 1917).

23. Ibid., 11.

24. Ibid., 319-24.

25. *The Problem* 1:1 (January 1900): 12.

26. *The Problem* 1:2 (April 1900): 41.

27. One interesting exception was "How Things in This World Look to a Blind Man by John Curruth, Blind Man Who Now Sees" which, despite subheadings such as "Yellow Nauseated Him," extolled the glories of regained vision. See *The Problem* 4:4 (October 1903): 95-99.

28. *The Problem* 1:1 (January 1900): 17.

29. Charles Flint Kellogg, *NAACP: A History of the National Association for the Advancement of Colored People*, vol. 1: *1909-1920* (Baltimore: Johns Hopkins University Press, 1967), 149-54. DuBois's objective had been to found a magazine that would "ring true on the problem of human rights to all men, be beautiful, be entertaining, and also incidentally give this Association the widest publicity of any similar organization in the world" (152). As Gaines has argued in his *Uplifting the Race*, however, this idea of uplift was complex and even contradictory because of the conflicts between class mobility and race embedded within it to reinforce notions of patriarchy. The

comparison with the situation of blind people raises intriguing questions about class and gender dynamics that are unfortunately beyond the scope of this essay.

30. Lilian M. Hinkle, in *The Problem* 1:4 (October 1900): 76.

31. *Outlook for the Blind*, 1:1 (April 1907): 10–12.

32. On institutions for the blind in the nineteenth century, see Best, *Blindness and the Blind*; Klages, *Woeful Afflictions*, esp. chaps. 2 and 5. For the early history of American institutions more generally, see David J. Rothman, *The Discovery of the Asylum: Social Order and Disorder in the New Republic* (Boston: Little, Brown and Co., 1971).

33. Koestler, *Unseen Minority*, 482–84.

34. On the use of photography in the Progressive Era, see Robert Westbrook, "Lewis Hine and the Ethics of Progressive Camerawork," *Tikkun* 2:2 (April/May 1987): 24–29.

35. *Outlook for the Blind* became *The New Outlook for the Blind* in 1951 and since 1977 has lived on as the American Foundation for the Blind's *Journal of Visual Impairment and Blindness*.

36. Unfortunately, no statistical information exists regarding the number of blind men who found themselves in such leadership positions. Even today, anecdotal evidence suggests that the numbers of blind directors of institutions and service organizations remain very small.

37. *Outlook for the Blind* 2:1 (April 1908): 23–28.

38. *Outlook for the Blind* 3:1 (April 1909): 17–23.

39. Helen Lefkowitz Horowitz, *Alma Mater: Design and Experience in the Women's Colleges from Their Nineteenth-Century Beginnings to the 1930s* (New York: Knopf, 1994).

40. *Outlook for the Blind* 3:1 (April 1909): 18.

41. Ibid.

42. Ibid., 19.

43. Ibid.

44. Ibid., 20.

45. Ibid., 19, 23.

46. Ibid., 23.

47. Ibid.

48. Ibid., 21–22.

49. The school in question was the Missouri School for the Blind. See Nolan, "Historical Sketch of the Association," 48–50. The role of special schools in the development of a community has been more thoroughly explored with respect to people with other disabilities, particularly deaf people. In this book see Susan Burch, "Reading between the Signs" (chapter 8). Also see John V. Van Cleve, ed., *Deaf History Unveiled: Interpretations from the New Scholarship* (Washington, D.C.: Gallaudet University Press, 1993); John V. Van Cleve, ed., *Gallaudet Encyclopedia of Deaf People and Deafness* (New York: McGraw-Hill, 1987); John V. Van Cleve and Barry Crouch, *A Place of Their Own: Creating the Deaf Community in America* (Washington, D.C.: Gallaudet University Press, 1989).

Catherine J. Kudlick

50. Dorothy Herrmann's *Helen Keller: A Life* (New York: Knopf, 1998) raises the question of Keller's agency throughout. See also Joseph P. Lash, *Helen and Teacher: The Story of Helen Keller and Anne Sullivan Macy* (Reading, Mass.: Addison Wesley, 1997); and Klages, *Woeful Afflictions*, particularly chaps. 8 and 9. As for Keller's relationship to her benefactors, see Herrmann, *Helen Keller*, 234–36; and Kim Nielsen's essay "Helen Keller and the Politics of Civic Fitness" in this book (chapter 10).

51. *Outlook for the Blind* 1:1 (April 1907): 10.

52. Dorothy Herrmann suggests throughout *Helen Keller* that Anne Sullivan had a phobia about disabled people, which may have influenced some of Helen Keller's own ideas.

53. Rosemarie Garland Thomson, *Extraordinary Bodies: Figuring Disability in American Culture and Literature* (New York: Columbia University Press, 1997), chap. 2.

54. *Outlook for the Blind* 1:1 (April 1907): 11.

55. Garland Thomson, *Extraordinary Bodies*, 19–21. For a discussion of current attitudes about the relationship between women and disability, see Michelle Fine and Adrienne Asch, eds., *Women with Disabilities: Essays in Psychology, Culture and Politics* (Philadelphia: Temple University Press, 1988).

56. *The Problem* 1:4 (October 1900): 74–76.

57. *Outlook for the Blind* 4:4 (January 1911): 165–69.

58. *The Problem* 1:4 (October 1900): 75.

59. Catherine J. Kudlick, "The Helpless and the Hopeless in Cross-Cultural Context: Images of Blindness and Gender Stereotypes in Late Nineteenth Century France and America" (paper presented at the Berkshire Conference of Women Historians, June 1999).

60. For a discussion of eye contact from the perspective of a blind person, see Georgina Kleege, *Sight Unseen* (New Haven: Yale University Press, 1999), chap. 5.

61. For a discussion of this literature, see Martin Pernick, *The Black Stork: Eugenics and the Death of 'Defective' Babies in American Medicine and Motion Pictures* (Oxford: Oxford University Press, 1996), 72–73.

62. Maria Frawley, "'A Prisoner of the Couch': Harriet Martineau, Invalidism, and Self Representation," in David T. Mitchell and Sharon L. Snyder, eds., *The Body and Physical Difference: Discourses of Disability* (Ann Arbor: University of Michigan Press, 1997), 174–88.

8

Reading between the Signs
Defending Deaf Culture in Early Twentieth-Century America

Susan Burch

No topic has received more attention in Deaf history than education and Deaf schools. During the early twentieth century, a struggle for control of deaf education pitted supporters of communication in sign language and of employment of Deaf teachers against oralists who advocated banning sign, requiring deaf people to learn speech, and providing instruction only by hearing teachers. The Deaf community led the fight against oralism. To the community, the residential schools represented the original "places" of a distinct Deaf culture. Graduates had gone to considerable effort to preserve this real as well as symbolic center of the culture. Yet, even within the schools, hearing educators had intended to assimilate deaf people to society rather than separate them from it. Early educators, who were often ministers, wanted to recruit deaf people into Christianity by giving them the ability to read the Bible. By the Progressive Era, educators of the deaf extended this goal, seeking to assimilate deaf people into mainstream (hearing) America. Comparable to the rhetoric of other educators regarding ethnic minorities and new immigrants, hearing professionals frequently asserted the need not simply to assimilate but to control deaf students.[1]

Historians have commonly assumed that oralism triumphed in early twentieth-century deaf education. In fact, Deaf people demonstrated consistent agency in their fight to maintain a role in Deaf education. Most advocates for the traditional Deaf values of communicating in sign language and employing Deaf teachers gained limited recognition from their intellectual critics or from the broader society. In many ways, the battle over the schools proceeded by attrition: as oralism rose, Deaf people became marginalized from a traditional "place" of culture. The oralists, however, never succeeded as completely as their propaganda might suggest. Deaf people not only resisted pure oralism; they managed to participate in teacher qualification programs, influence faculty and administrators, increase the use of sign language in schools by the 1940s, and transmit positive cultural views of Deafness within the schools. In doing so, they broadened their strategies to defend their culture, fostered greater unity within the Deaf community, and maintained a separate communal identity.

Ironically, the battle over the schools also fostered a particular ideological bond between the Deaf community and the hearing world. As oralism rose, so did the percentage of female teachers in deaf education. In part reflecting a general trend in the teaching profession, this feminization of the deaf teaching corps met with opposition from the Deaf community. Deaf resisters to oralist education often employed the same gender stereotypes as the oralists who championed a maternalist approach to deaf education. Thus, although the struggle to defend sign language united the Deaf community in many ways, that unity came at a price to Deaf women.

The debate over communication methods long predated the establishment of the first school for the deaf in America. Ancient philosophers such as Plato and Aristotle pondered whether deaf people could learn speech or process knowledge. By the sixteenth century in Europe, some deaf pupils were receiving instruction through sign language. In mid-eighteenth-century France, sign-based education became well established and began to spread to other European countries, while private tutoring in late eighteenth- and early nineteenth-century England and Germany evolved into schools that implemented oral and lipreading techniques. In America, most schools founded between 1817 and the 1860s adopted the French method of sign-based teaching. No classes formally taught signs; teachers and students simply used them as the language of instruction and communication. As a result, the language and the method became a central part of the developing Deaf culture. The schools not only fostered a common sign language across the nation, they also provided Deaf people a self-contained and supportive environment. New "places" for Deaf people sprang from the schools, beginning with alumni associations, churches, and Deaf publications. In 1864, Deaf people gained the opportunity for advanced education with the establishment of Gallaudet College, to date the only liberal arts university in the world exclusively for the deaf. By the mid–nineteenth century, Deaf cultural self-awareness was established and expanding.

During the late nineteenth and early twentieth centuries, several develop-ments created a more hospitable climate in the United States for pure oral-ism. Progressives sought the reform *of* education and reform *through* educa-tion. Advances in biology and other disciplines further inspired a movement for "new education." This approach relied heavily on pure and applied sci-ences and viewed the objective of education as preparation for life, empha-sizing vocational training and practical subjects such as mathematics.[2] By the late nineteenth century, oralism began to displace sign language as the primary method used in American schools. Led by the charismatic and influ-ential Alexander Graham Bell, oralists argued for the "restoration" of deaf people into mainstream American society, a goal viable, they said, only through speech and lipreading training. Oralists also drew on other contem-porary concerns to generate public support for their agenda.

In the wake of the recent Civil War, and in the midst of an unprecedented influx of immigrants, political and social reformers sought to integrate America's marginalized communities and to create cultural cohesion by en-forcing a common spoken language, English, and by fashioning a cohesive national plan of schooling for young citizens. Oralists crafted their rhetoric to match this mainstream ideal. Equating language with acculturation, Bell declared that "for the preservation of our national existence," Americans must share the same language.[3] Contending that speech training would make deaf people less pitiable, oralists tied speech to normality.[4] N. F. Walker, a superintendent of various deaf schools during his long career, claimed, "The deaf who make English their medium of thought are less pe-culiar and less suspicious than those who do not. . . . They have the view-point more largely of the great mass of people among whom they must live. . . . They are broader in their vision."[5]

By the turn of the century, the pure oral argument had other support. The rise of the medical professions and promotion of the sciences buttressed oral programs. Scientists, doctors, and oral educators had similar goals and ap-proaches to eliminating the handicap of deafness. Medical professionals often focused more on prevention and cures for deafness, but their research on hearing aids and other tests to detect and correct deafness enhanced oral-ists' efforts to eliminate social and educational barriers for deaf people. Both groups sought to *normalize* deaf people according to mainstream values. En-abling deaf people to talk and, in the ideal outcome, to hear better would supposedly "restore" them to the broader world. Medical doctors tested and sought to preserve residual hearing. Departments for auricular training that utilized and developed hearing became a common part of deaf education. This emphasis on the physical condition of deafness also united oralists and medical specialists, thereby creating a broad and powerful network.

Oralists had financial resources as well. Supported by Bell's monetary reward for winning the French Volta prize and further buttressed by his profits from the telephone patent, organizations for the promotion of speech and lipreading blossomed from the late nineteenth through the early twentieth century. Other wealthy benefactors such as Andrew Carnegie and Thomas Edison took an interest in Bell's experiments and joined the leading oral association, the American Association for the Promotion and Teaching of Speech to the Deaf (AAPTSD). The National Education Association, the foremost educational organization by the early 1900s, also advocated strong oral training. Such financial and public support enabled oralists to initiate a massive publicity campaign. Frequent recognition in mainstream publications and professional journals, public speaking tours, and meetings with influential politicians inundated homes, as well as doctors' offices, school board meetings, and state legislatures' appropriations committees, with an oralist view of deafness.

The majority of Deaf people consistently opposed pure oralism, supporting variations of the "combined method" of instruction that emphasized oral training for all students and signed communication for those incapable of success in speech. Edward Miner Gallaudet, the hearing president of Gallaudet College and the most recognized opponent of pure oralism, joined the Deaf community in advocating for the combined method. The flood of oralist publicity frustrated Deaf people. Particularly irritating were public presentations of oral "successes," deaf people who could articulate clearly and lip-read with facility. Deaf people often condemned the deceptiveness of this oralist public relations tactic. Most oral "successes," they noted, were postlingually deaf, were often hard of hearing rather than profoundly deaf, and had intense coaching before presentations. Thus, many had already been able to speak well before their hearing loss and could read lips more readily than the average prelingually Deaf person.

The effectiveness of oralist propaganda fueled its expansion in deaf education. Because oralism demanded one-on-one work with students, the number of oral teachers mushroomed; they naturally supported the oralist agenda. Moreover, many oral advocates rallied for the establishment of nonresidential schools or day schools so that deaf children could spend greater time with their families. Many parents welcomed this idea. Parents often felt estranged from children who lived in residential schools and who preferred the company of other Deaf people. The possibility of maintaining a constant home life with their children and communicating with them in the parents' own (spoken) language seemed to minimize their children's deafness. Oralists' promise that deaf children could speak pulled at the heartstrings of parents who wanted to hear their children's voices, who wanted their children to be "normal" like them. Thus, many parents flocked to the oralist cause. Indeed, perhaps more than any other element in the debate, the issue of family exacerbated tensions as Deaf adults fought with hearing parents over the fate of children who were not theirs by blood but, Deaf leaders argued, by culture.

One of the leading oral schools for the deaf, the Clarke Institution for Deaf-Mutes in Northampton, Massachusetts, focused on "family" in another way. Clarke's success particularly threatened Deaf people's argument for sign language in deaf education. Like other oral programs, Clarke's, led by the indomitable Caroline Yale, promoted speech and lipreading as skills intended to liberate deaf children from their disability and return them to society. It also emphasized the ideals of a Christian family, described teachers as surrogate mothers, and portrayed the school as a family-like environment. In addition, the female instructors at Clarke and other oral schools were thought to personify the traits desirable in the ideal deaf student, and particularly the ideal deaf female. Recognized for their charity, patience, sweet disposition—in short, their maternalism—these educated hearing ladies set an example for their female pupils. They sought to indoctrinate specific hearing behaviors into the girls, including appropriate laughter, speech, breathing sounds, and other social etiquette. As hearing women who promoted oralism, they literally spoke to (and embodied for) young deaf girls the social expectations of the broader community The maternal overtones of the school not only soothed parents' concerns about the welfare of their children but also reflected broader trends in education.[6]

By the turn of the century, women had entered schoolteaching in substantial numbers. As World War I ended, nearly nine out of ten teachers were women, and in the 1930s, women still constituted four-fifths of the teaching force. This disproportion occurred in part because women often earned half the pay of men, and when they married, they were required to resign, thus enabling schools to hire new, lower-paid women to fill positions.[7] The demographics of oral programs also helped produce the preponderance of female teachers, because oralists encouraged enrollment of younger students. Believing that speech education should begin as soon as possible, oral adminis-trators urged parents to register children as young as three or four. The argu-ment followed that women, as natural mothers, were naturally fitted to teach little children. The Clarke school set up its own teacher-training pro-gram in 1892 with the support of the AAPTSD and closely aligned itself with public schools. The program promoted even greater numbers of female teachers. A report of the National Association of the Deaf noted that of sev-enty-seven teachers sent out by Clarke's training facility, only two were men. As one observer quipped, "Almost to a woman they are women."[8]

The Clarke example suggests an additional motivation for the expansion of oralism. The network of Clarke-trained teachers strikingly resembled the contemporaneous settlement-house movement led by Jane Addams. Both movements, oralism and aid to poor immigrant communities, enabled edu-cated women to enter a secure, respected profession and a virtually all-fe-male environment. That the Clarke school was located directly across the street from Smith College and showed considerable interest in graduates of Smith and other Ivy League women's colleges further suggests a conscious decision by Caroline Yale and her followers to establish a dominion of fe-male reform and employment.[9]

The success of the Clarke school and other pure-oral programs increas-ingly threatened Deaf adults' place in deaf education. Oralism's demand of more time for one-on-one speech training not only reduced the amount of time available for academic work but required inexpensive teachers who could work with younger pupils. This produced a rapid influx of hearing women into schools. As hearing women came to dominate deaf teaching, a more spirited competition arose among Deaf people for the remaining in-structional positions. In this struggle, Deaf men faced the double insult of watching opponents of their culture weaken the ties between the schools and the Deaf community and of having women, viewed as the inferior sex, replace them at work.

While Deaf men lashed out at this trend, the feminization of the profes-sion ultimately displaced educated Deaf women to an even greater extent, depriving them of both educational and career opportunities and social choices. Unlike teachers in mainstream society, hearing female educators (and social workers) for the deaf presented a behavioral model and not a ca-reer archetype for young deaf girls. In addition, not only oralists but Deaf men encouraged hearing female teachers to exemplify ideal feminine traits to deaf girls. In articles in Deaf community publications and in speeches at

Deaf conferences, adult Deaf men frequently praised such feminine characteristics. Thus, as mainstream society opened up more opportunities for women in general, it closed doors for Deaf women. Meanwhile, male leaders of the Deaf community urged Deaf women to remain at home and allow Deaf men to demonstrate their abilities as workers. The rise of oralist female teachers and the response of Deaf men narrowed Deaf women's vocational options and their ability to achieve self-sufficiency.[10]

Further complicating the interplay of gender ideology with Deaf identities, Deaf men and hearing supporters of sign language shared with oralists many assumptions about women. In 1891, one year before the Clarke school launched its teaching-training program, Gallaudet College opened its Normal (Teaching) Department, partly to counter the threat of staunch oralism but also to resist the feminization of the teaching profession. E. M. Gallaudet himself argued that the latter development "is to be regretted upon very high grounds . . . women are naturally fitted by talent, tact and patience to teach little children; but when they [the students] are older they need sterner attributes of men, more logical faculties and stricter sense of justice that are masculine traits. The Normal Department at Gallaudet has done something to start this improvement. Of their graduates more than 82% have been men."[11] Yet, if Gallaudet's Normal Department sought to prevent hearing women from taking over deaf education, it failed to guarantee Deaf men a role in the schools. The program limited admission to hearing graduate students.

As a result, whether oralists or supporters of the combined method, school administrators were typically hearing men, while women remained as teaching faculty. Continuing the metaphor of traditional "families," the men generally managed the schools, but the women/"mothers" did the primary rearing of the students. Writers in both Deaf publications and oralist journals revealed the emergent composition of the faculties by describing all teachers as "she." The language used to describe administrators and teachers during this period also indicates the gendering of the schools' hierarchies. State school superintendents, all but two of whom were men, were often described as strong, honest, intelligent, and, occasionally, stubborn. Ideal teachers were said to demonstrate particularly feminine traits, such as charity, attention to moral behavior, kindness, sensitivity, and a strong nurturing nature. Gender ideologies dominant in both the oralist movement and the Deaf community may have helped contribute to the displacement of Deaf adults, men and especially women, from deaf education and to the larger presence of hearing people, both male and female.

Oralism, like mainstream education, exploited (hearing) women in order to achieve its agenda. As they struggled to attain an independent livelihood and higher social status for themselves, those women contributed to the disempowerment of Deaf people (men and women). Deaf men sought to defend their livelihoods, status, and identities not only by battling oralism but by utilizing sexist ideas regarding both hearing women and Deaf women. Deaf women, having the most limited option of any of these groups, sought to defend Deaf education, sign, the Deaf community, and Deaf men from both oralism and displacement by hearing teachers, but in so doing they themselves were forced into even more subordinate roles.

Across the United States, oralism gained ground in the first decades of the twentieth century. In 1911, the state of Nebraska instituted a legal mandate for oral education at its residential school. The Nebraska state school had originally maintained a combined program, but in 1910, two parents of deaf children petitioned the governor to convert the school to pure oralism. They recruited other parents and began a campaign to lobby the state legislature to require the reorientation. Superintendent R. E. Stewart, who opposed the bill, was replaced by Frank Booth, an ardent supporter of pure oralism and former administrator at the American Association for the Promotion and Teaching of Speech to the Deaf. The Nebraska oral law mandated that all children admitted to the state school would be trained in the oral, aural, and lipreading methods to the exclusion of the manual alphabet and sign language. Only children deemed incapacitated by mental defect or malformation of the vocal chords would be taught in a manual department.

An outraged Deaf community responded. George Veditz, former president of the National Association of the Deaf (NAD), published a scathing commentary on Nebraska's law. He encouraged the NAD to commit strong financial support to reverse the decision.[12] Deaf leaders challenged the law several times, offering bills to the legislature that would return the combined method to the school. These campaigns failed, but leaders continued to rally support from various other school superintendents and to expand their fund drive.[13]

Another major setback for the Deaf community occurred in the late 1920s. The Nebraska conversion helped inspire New Jersey's superintendent, Alvin Pope, to apply a pure oral program at the state school in Trenton. Pope, who had earned his graduate degree at Gallaudet College, had worked at the Nebraska school under Superintendent Booth and had become an ardent oralist. Ascending to the superintendency at New Jersey in 1917, he became the first administrator there to call for the exclusive use of speech. Rather than seeking a legislative mandate, as had happened in Nebraska, he opted to convert his school's program gradually. For years Deaf faculty, and particularly George Porter, the popular editor of the school's paper, the *Silent Worker*, resisted Pope's policy. In 1929 the superintendent responded with a swift and potent new plan. He implemented a pure oral program, fired five Deaf teachers, and stopped the publication of the *Silent Worker*. Although the Deaf community responded with outrage, leaders in the state and national associations were unable to unite and effectively counter the measures at New Jersey.[14]

Both Nebraska and New Jersey exposed in an obvious and focused way oralists' dominance. The Deaf community found itself outfinanced, outpublicized, and outmaneuvered. Nebraska oralists undercut the community's power, largely ignoring its pleas and restricting its exposure in mainstream publications. Under the administration of Superintendent Booth, the Nebraska school's newspaper published only positive articles about oralism, excluding Deaf people's perspectives altogether. Most other schools with strong oral programs likewise suppressed commentary on methods. Because school papers had long functioned as a treasured place for Deaf cultural expression, this censorship particularly epitomized to Deaf people the repressive nature of oralism.

Along with the repression of Deaf perspectives, Deaf advocates charged oralist teachers with abusing deaf students who failed to match up to oralist demands. Albert Ballin's experience as a student in the New York Institution for the Deaf's strong oral program was not uncommon. Students who could not achieve advanced speech and lipreading, he recounted, often found themselves labeled as "oral failures" and ridiculed as "born idiots" or "dummies." Teachers sometimes suggested that they were the "offspring of degenerate foreigners," "a product of the slums," or "vicious by nature." On occasion, he said, these students were physically punished.[15]

In response to the repression of sign and the suppression of Deaf opinions, Deaf people continued to seek avenues to express their perspectives. Often they turned to independent Deaf newspapers such as the *Deaf-Mute's Journal* and *American Deaf Citizen* to express their views candidly. Some leaders initiated letter-writing campaigns and met personally with parents as well as politicians to address the Nebraska law. While unable to convince political leaders or staunch oralists of the legitimacy of their claims, they did establish a new dialogue with some parents and gained greater recognition for their position.[16]

Although Nebraska, New Jersey, and other schools remained purely oral in theory and policy, oralists never fully realized their goals in fact. Deaf students proved quite adept at limiting pure oralism. For example, when Superintendent Pope began reducing manual programs at New Jersey in 1917, students protested, appealing to the State Board of Education. Often the most effective mode of resistance was less obvious. Although direct comments by students during their time at the schools have largely been lost, reminiscences and evidence from faculty members illustrate the ability of students to subvert oral goals and create spaces of Deaf culture even within the seemingly hostile school walls. Teachers and observers at the Nebraska and other schools conceded that the children picked up sign language from each other. Upon graduation, the overwhelming majority joined the adult Deaf community.[17]

Because of administrators' central role in the methods debate, the selection of school superintendents became a major concern to the Deaf community. If they could gain access to these administrators, Deaf adults hoped to move beyond merely commenting on and advising about educational policies to actually influence the decisions of those who had a more recognized "voice." The extreme examples of Nebraska and New Jersey exemplified Deaf people's deepest fears about the leadership of schools. The Deaf community found it impossible to remove Pope or the oral method from New Jersey in 1929. Yet that year nevertheless marked the start of a slow decline in pure oralism, as Deaf people began to mount successful efforts to secure superintendents more receptive to Deaf interests.

To take one important example, during the 1930s the Georgia Association of the Deaf (GAD) succeeded in ousting the state school's staunchly oral administrator. GAD president James Stalling campaigned for most of the decade against Superintendent James Coffey Harris. The GAD confronted the methods issue directly, arguing that the oral program at the school had produced substandard results: no students had achieved high enough academic levels to gain admission to Gallaudet College for more than fifteen years, and many students had been expelled from the Georgia school for "failing" to achieve sufficient oral skills.[18] The end of Harris's term at Georgia was particularly sweet for Deaf people. Not only had they successfully convinced state administrators to recognize the limitations of pure oralism; they helped secure a new superintendent, who demonstrated greater interest in the experience and opinions of the community. Clayton Hollingsworth, a Gallaudet Normal Program graduate, addressed a GAD conference before the beginning of the school term, thanking the Deaf community for its activism and pledging his support of the combined method.[19] By 1939, students were again using sign language in their classes. The results demonstrated the benefits of the combined method. Some students showed greater academic progress in one semester than previous students had in years of training under the oral method. Meanwhile, Deaf state associations in Illinois, Idaho, Louisiana, and Texas mounted and won similar campaigns.[20]

While these schools represented important counterpoints to the failures at Nebraska and New Jersey, other institutes demonstrated in sometimes more subtle, sometimes more vigorous ways the limited success of the oralist campaign. Active resistance to pure oralism even erupted at times. The vast majority of schools adhered to the combined method even at the height of the pure oral movement. All of the residential schools employed oral training, but the insistence that some departments use signed communication in the classrooms, as well as the opportunity for students to enter such departments with relative ease, suggests that many teachers gave more attention to individual students' needs than to oralist principles. In addition, the residential schools in Arkansas, Colorado, Iowa, Maryland, and Missouri enjoyed generally positive relations between administrators, head teachers, and the Deaf community. Meanwhile, other states repelled attempts to expand oralism. In California and Ohio, considered bastions of Deaf culture, the schools and communities went even further: Superintendents Elwood Stevenson and J. W. Jones, both hearing, outspokenly supported employing Deaf teachers, maintaining the place of sign language in their schools, and combating legal discrimination against Deaf people.[21]

These developments were important to the Deaf community, who recognized that pure oralism promoted a negative view of Deaf people. At bottom, oralism altered the character of the schools by vilifying sign language and promoting the image of nonvoicing Deaf people as "oral failures," somehow defective, deviant, even un-American. The continued hiring of combined-method advocates as superintendents preserved a philosophical and cultural perspective that gave Deaf people not only more effective education but a more positive identity. Throughout the first half of the twentieth century, Deaf people used the means at their disposal to address their marginalized place. But they did more than confirm their identity among themselves. At times creating or re-creating avenues of influence at the schools, they limited the hegemony of hearing people over them.

While Deaf advocacy played a central role in undermining the spread of pure oralism, changes in the education profession and society contributed to the Deaf community's success as well. In education, pedagogical theorists called for a more child-centered approach. Before the turn of the century, policymakers preferred well-defined directives issued from above by educational authorities over heeding those who experienced the application of methods. In short, the burden of proof was on the students rather than on the pedagogical ideas. This pattern characterized deaf education too, as the methods debate shows. In the early 1900s, however, theorists began to reverse this approach in general education. Insisting that pedagogy must prove its value, they stressed the importance of children's background, identity, and needs. Rather than expect students to accommodate theories, schools should accommodate pupils. Meanwhile, though oralist ideas remained dominant in deaf education through the 1920s, arguments began to appear that took a modified position. By the 1930s, presentations at professional conferences revealed a noticeable shift. The influence of John Dewey's educational philosophy, with his emphasis on the necessity to respond to the individual child's needs and abilities, had infiltrated deaf education, thereby weakening the oralist position.

Progressive educational theories also promoted scientific measurements of school programs, again stressing results rather than abstract theories. Both oralists and combined-method advocates welcomed this scientific focus, each believing that empirical data would end the methods debate in their favor. Because the people who developed sign-language education were religiously motivated, New Jersey superintendent Alvin Pope argued, that method was fundamentally antiscientific. In contrast, he claimed, oralism was a more reasonable method, its only major limitation being the prevalence of lesser-trained women in the field. He further suggested that because psychologists had attributed emotional strain in certain children to learning two languages, sign-language use in schools should be discontinued.[22] Deaf leaders countered that objective studies would demonstrate that combined-method students learned more and better, whereas pure-oral students had underdeveloped skills.[23]

Throughout the first half of the twentieth century, scientists and educational specialists used a plethora of tests on deaf students, but the most revealing appeared in the 1920s with the invention of the audiometer, which tested frequency and extent of hearing. Although primitive electric hearing aids had been employed at the turn of the century, accurate testing for residual hearing lagged far behind. Successful experiments with the audiometer had significant implications for deaf pedagogy. In 1924 and 1925, using audiometers, educational specialists Rudolph Pinter, Herbert Day, and Irving Fusfeld conducted a study of twenty-nine schools for the deaf. They found that the residual hearing of residential students in primarily combined-method programs was lower than for those at exclusively oral day schools. Day-school students also had greater range of hearing than for residential students.

The study's scientific conclusion reinforced what Deaf people had claimed all along: speech ability depended directly on the age at which deafness occurred, the degree of residual hearing, and the length of training in speech. But the information and conclusions from this and other studies rarely influenced mainstream educational commentary. Such findings failed to stop the well-established oralist media machine. Nonetheless, the new data did enable the Deaf community to use scientific studies to refute exaggerated oralist claims and to "prove" the limitations of pure oralism—indeed, of oralism in general. This research also empowered Deaf people to reject the common label of "oral failure." Of additional importance, the survey helped touch off a new movement that would bring both sides together.

If the opposing camps in Deaf education agreed on little else, they concurred on the critical need to change public perceptions of Deafness, to get rid of outdated and biased labels, and to classify the degrees and types of deafness. As scientists improved studies of hearing abilities, a reinvigorated movement toward reclassification began in earnest. The Deaf community, oralists, medical professionals, and educators joined the effort for various reasons. Deaf people resented terms such as *deaf and dumb* and *deaf-mute* for the social implications of inferiority and deviancy, while oralists found those labels distasteful because they denied what oralists perceived as the true ability of deaf people to speak. Throughout the early twentieth century, both Deaf and oralism advocates editorialized on and discussed the need to educate mainstream society about the inappropriateness of such terms. Deaf leaders and educators also chided their own community for including the offensive labels in their commentaries. In addition, the NAD and numerous local chapters of Deaf associations published pamphlets and established publicity committees in an effort to inform the public about deafness and preferred terminology.

The issue remained important to interested Deaf and hearing people, but not until the 1930s did a strong push for an alternative nomenclature develop in educational circles. Leaders at the Conference of Executives of American Schools for the Deaf (CEASD) met in 1936 and agreed to cooperate with the American Otological Society to standardize definitions of deafness. In their report to Convention of American Instructors of the Deaf (CAID) in 1937, the group strongly recommended dropping a number of terms, including *deaf-mute, deaf and dumb, semi-mute, mute,* and *deafened.* Into the 1940s, professionals moved to replace the old terminology with current classifications.[24]

Advocates for deaf education and the community pushed for broader recognition of deaf education's legitimacy, calling for removal of *dumb* and *mute* from the names of schools. They also began a long campaign, often led by state Deaf associations, to transfer all deaf schools from Departments of Welfare and Charity to Departments of Education or Special Education. Enlisting parents as well as educators and administrators, Deaf leaders made significant progress; by 1934, only two schools were still called asylums, and forty-two residential schools had been reclassified as educational institutions.[25]

The place of Deaf teachers in schools, however, created fractures within the coalitions and remained one of the most problematic aspects of deaf education. Historians have correctly noted that oralism's rise repressed the Deaf community in many ways. Most obvious, oralism denied employment to educated Deaf people as teachers in the state schools. This, in turn, implicitly and sometimes explicitly, reinforced the patronizing social perception of Deaf people as inferior, dependent, even mentally deficient. In addition, the exclusion of Deaf role models from the schools inhibited transmission of Deaf cultural values. Several subtle factors, however, previously neglected by scholars, reveal an important negotiation between the Deaf community and the schools. Deaf people fought to defend employment of Deaf teachers. Teaching was not only a traditional and well-respected profession for educated Deaf people; it was also the most obvious means of intergenerational cultural transmission. Deaf leaders further recognized the need to keep Deaf community members at schools to counter the implications of oralist rhetoric. Pure-oral zealots never achieved their goal of eradicating Deaf teachers or Deaf culture from the schools. The staying power of Deaf instructors attests to the tenacity and capabilities of individual teachers, as well as to the influence of their community. Indeed, more than half of Gallaudet College's graduates between the world wars—and sometimes as many as three out of four—returned to schools as teachers of deaf children. These improved opportunities resulted largely because of social, economic, and demographic conditions, partly because CAID opened teacher qualification and certification to Deaf teachers, and partly because the combined method became entrenched at schools.[26] Despite the hostile oralist environment for Deaf faculty, these teachers were passionately committed to their community. Gallaudet graduates, more than most Deaf people, had other, better-paying career options, such as printing or small businesses. Their decision to return to the schools, often their alma maters, even at the price of lower incomes reveals the enduring desire to maintain and advance the Deaf community and its culture. While not all the Deaf teachers stayed on, they carried on an important tradition in the community and influenced numerous young people.[27]

More important than sheer numbers and percentages was the influence individual Deaf teachers had at schools. As administrators and community advocates had commonly noted, Deaf teachers demonstrated the greatest commitment to the life of students outside the classroom, often attending athletic games and association meetings and counseling students. It was this profound bond between young Deaf people and Deaf role models that oralists most feared and opposed and that supporters of the Deaf community most lauded.

Moreover, Deaf teachers subverted oralism. Philosophically and practically, they rejected pure oral training and often praised sign language, not only for its expediency but for its legitimacy as a language and its humanizing effect. Francis Fox of the New York School for the Deaf was renowned for his confrontations with oralists and his unwillingness to allow hearing educators to dominate professional discussions and policymaking. In articles and at conferences, he challenged the oralist premise that education and language were synonymous. His popularity as a signer clearly had an impact on his students; one claimed, "He taught us to 'hear' the beauty of sign language and the expression contained in it, thus brought home a new idealism."[28] Fox and other teachers frequently declared their commitment to the moral rectitude and positive work ethic of students. Oralists also supported this indoctrination into "normalcy," but Deaf teachers added an important subtext: not only were Deaf people upstanding citizens like everyone else; they were intellectual and cultural equals. Even Deaf teachers who did not become active community leaders served as important role models for deaf children by implicitly contesting oralists' labeling of the youngsters as "failures" and mainstream society's stigmatizing of them as "other." Students passionately testified how Deaf teachers, much more than hearing instructors, inspired them. To take just one example among an immense number, when Gallaudet College professor John Hotchkiss died, his former students wrote: "We not only liked him—we loved him. . . . He got into the game and was not ashamed to be one of us. . . . He was more than a teacher. He was a comrade. He stood by the students in particular and the deaf in general."[29] Refuting negative stereotypes of their community in both mainstream society and especially in the oralist movement, Deaf teachers offered students valuable and valued role models of how to live as Deaf adults.

This ability of Deaf teachers to influence generations of students remained constant even as hearing women dominated at schools. Within and outside the classroom, Deaf students naturally flocked to Deaf teachers for advice and easy communication. Most residential schools still had several Deaf teachers on staff, even during the height of strong oral programs. Several schools were recognized as bastions for Deaf teachers. Indiana, for example, consistently maintained a large number of Deaf instructors, as did California, where Deaf teachers received salaries equal to their hearing peers.[30] Deaf men also held administrative positions as deans, principals, and head teachers; others served as unofficial advisers to superintendents.

Deaf teachers managed to subvert oralism and influence their students in another important realm. At strong oral schools, most Deaf teachers were relegated to vocational and manual departments rather than to traditional academic classes. Many historians, and indeed, many Deaf people at the time, viewed this as deflating Deaf teachers' status, but the situation was more complex than that. Since the 1820s, vocational training had stood at the center of deaf education as a means to ensure graduates' employability. Deaf schools pioneered the field of vocational education. Thus, throughout the nineteenth century, the alumni enjoyed advantages over their hearing peers, who usually had little or no comparable experience. Concern over Deaf students' ability to become self-sufficient united oralists and combined-method advocates. As a result, in the twentieth century, even as traditional academic departments were downsized to accommodate courses on lipreading and speech, vocational training was expanded. In 1905, fifty-four of the fifty-seven schools had vocational departments. This represented 95 percent of the schools, up from 83 percent a quarter century earlier.[31]

Although, by the early 1900s, more Deaf students had access to vocational training, broad transformations in industry and schooling reduced the advantage such education had offered to previous generations. In factories, machines replaced manpower; occupations became more subdivided and specialized. Meanwhile, progressive educators, interested in the employment and assimilation of immigrants and other minorities, concluded that vocational training could instill important cultural values about work. The American Federation of Labor and the National Association of Manufacturers joined forces to demand trade instruction in schools. Theodore Roosevelt's and Woodrow Wilson's presidential administrations advocated and even mandated vocational and industrial training in public schools.[32] As these developments quickly advanced, deaf education began to fall behind. P. N. Peterson, an instructor of "sloyd" (basic handwork for children) at the Minnesota school, lamented in 1914, "Schools for the Deaf were the pioneers among educational institutions in industrial training. . . . Manual training for the hearing is comparatively new, but it is progressing rapidly. The schools for the deaf are in danger of losing their leadership if, indeed, they have not already done so." CAID president J. W. Blattner agreed, recognizing that public schools had surpassed deaf schools in vocational training because the former applied scientific methods in the shop, linked vocational with literary work, standardized the former, and awarded it credits toward the high school diploma. He also recognized, as did most educators and Deaf community members, that equipment and financial support for training in deaf schools lagged far behind that in hearing schools and in the outside world.[33]

Despite these significant setbacks, the continued importance of vocational training had positive effects on Deaf teachers and schools. Because industrial teachers earned less than academic instructors, schools often hired Deaf men. By 1940, roughly two out of five vocational teachers at residential schools were Deaf.[34] Their presence may also suggest unspoken recognition of sign language's superiority in deaf education. Most administrators certainly recognized the importance of vocational training, as virtually every CAID conference called for improved and expanded facilities. Superintendents also gave Deaf industrial instructors strong support, focusing on their success as tradesmen and mentors. The Deaf community, knowing the key place of vocational training in the schools, often focused its effort to maintain Deaf teachers on expanding their role in this department. Unnoticed by oralists then or by historians since that time, the staffing of vocational departments had significant cultural undercurrents. As pupils divided most of their in-class time between the industrial and oral departments, they undoubtedly moved back and forth between two diametrically opposed views of Deafness and learning. Although

Deaf vocational teachers and oral teachers sought the same goal—to produce self-sufficient students—the former ultimately undermined oralism by communicating with their students in signs. In addition, the Deaf adults and the deaf students worked together on the students' most pressing need: qualifying them for employment after graduation. As a primary arena in which Deaf students could mingle with Deaf adults, vocational classes represented a central Deaf "place" within the schools.[35]

On the surface, much remained the same at the schools between the 1890s and the beginning of World War II. Teachers, administrators, parents, and the Deaf community continued to debate the methods issue, and oralism still played a central role. Nevertheless, oralism never eclipsed manual communication. By the end of the 1930s, sanctioned sign-language use was on the rise. This was largely due to Deaf people's active maintenance of their language and the increasing number of Deaf teachers and Gallaudet-trained hearing teachers at the schools. Scientific studies also helped by legitimating what Deaf people had always known: sign-language use did not impede English acquisition, and combined-method students competed on a par with, and sometimes surpassed, pure-oral-trained pupils. While the subtle shift of recognition never converted ardent oral supporters to the opposition, Deaf people achieved a number of successes against repressive programs. Under pressure from the Deaf community and its allies, various states ousted oralist superintendents, and some schools staved off pure-oral programs. The loss of Nebraska and New Jersey to pure oralism stood as a reminder of the hostile environment in which Deaf people functioned, and professionals and parents frequently ignored Deaf people's opinions. But the Deaf community continued to express its views, to challenge discrimination, and to clarify and pursue its goals. Using educational issues to catalyze local and national campaigns, it sometimes created sophisticated and effective networks with parents, politicians, and specialists. In the schools, Deaf teachers and hearing allies also exerted their influence. As role models, Deaf teachers subverted negative images of Deaf people perpetuated by oralists and offered viable and vibrant alternatives for the students. They also continued to communicate in signs and often introduced students to the broader Deaf community. While vocational training offered fewer advantages to Deaf students than it had in the nineteenth century, it served as an important place for Deaf cultural transmission. The interplay among cultures, perceptions of Deafness, and training for adult life was a defining experience for most Deaf people.

NOTES

1. This is a study of Deaf culture in contrast to deafness. The latter is an audiological condition; the former refers to a particular group of people who share American Sign Language (ASL) as a primary means of communication, associate primarily with other Deaf people, often attend Deaf residential schools, join social and political clubs that promote Deaf cultural awareness, read Deaf-produced publications, share a common folklore, and often see themselves as separate from mainstream society.

2. See Lawrence Cremin, *The Transformation of the School: Progressivism in American Education, 1876–1957* (New York: Alfred A. Knopf, 1961), 85, 94.

3. Alexander Graham Bell, "Is Race Suicide Possible?" *Journal of Heredity* 11 (1920): 340.

4. For more on this argument, see Douglas Baynton, *Forbidden Signs: American Culture and the Campaign against Sign Language* (Chicago: University of Chicago Press, 1996).

5. N. F. Walker, "Use of English in Schools for the Deaf," *CAID Proceedings* (1920): 34–37. Also see G. Hudson-Makunen, "The Medico-Education Problem of the Deaf Child," *Volta Review* 12 (1911): 221.

6. Margaret Winzer notes that, in contrast, manual schools—at least in the nineteenth century—were masculine in tone, strictly regimented and institutionalized. See Margaret Winzer, *History of Special Education* (Washington, D.C.: Gallaudet University Press, 1993), 129; Baynton, *Forbidden Signs*, passim.

7. Dominic W. Moreg, *Schools in the Great Depression* (New York: Garland Publishing, 1996), 7; "Salaries and Contracts," *American Annals of the Deaf* (1920): 253. In one essay titled "Tomorrow's Teacher of the Deaf," the director of the Division of Exceptional Children in Milwaukee, S. S. Slaughten, referred to all teachers as "she" (*Volta Review* 37 [August 1935]: 470).

8. "Female Teachers," *National Association of the Deaf Proceedings* (1907): 27. For more on Caroline Yale, see H. William Brelje and Virginia M. Tibbs, *The Washington State School for the Deaf, the First One Hundred Years, 1886–1986,* (n.p.) 110; Mary E. Numbers, *My Words Fell on Deaf Ears* (Washington, D.C.: Alexander Graham Bell Association for the Deaf, 1974), passim.

9. The Seven Sister Schools appreciated Caroline Yale as well. She was awarded honoree degrees from Wesleyan in 1896 and Mt. Holyoke in 1927. The Clarke school also enjoyed the patronage of President and Mrs. Calvin Coolidge. Mrs. Coolidge had taught at Clarke for two years, and the first couple spearheaded the Coolidge Endowment Fund, which reached $2 million by 1929 and was used for research, new construction, and teacher support. See Winzer, *History of Special Education*, 243. The desire to secure greater opportunities for their sex, common during the broad Progressive Period, appears to be another motivation of many oral educators. See, for example, Robin Muncy's *Creating a Female Dominion in American Reform, 1890–1935* (New York: Oxford University Press, 1990), and Katherine Kish Sklar's works on Jane Addams.

10. It is important to note that hearing teachers did not necessarily intend this, or intend this in the explicitly gendered way in which the result manifested. Other social factors influenced this situation as well.

11. Irving Fusfield, "Is the Male Teacher Becoming an Extinct Species?" *American Annals of the Deaf* 66 (1921): 29–31.

12. George Veditz, "The Nebraska Iniquity," *Deaf-Mute's Journal* (18 May 1911): 2.

13. "Nebraska," *National Association of the Deaf Proceedings* (1913): 19; "Nebraska Parent's Letter to NAD," *National Association of the Deaf Proceedings* (1913): 93.

14. For more about the New Jersey situation, see Robert Buchanan, "The Silent Worker Newspaper, 1890-1929," in John Van Cleve, ed., *Deaf History Unveiled* (Washington, D.C.: Gallaudet University Press, 1993), 172–97; Susan Burch, "Biding the Time: American Deaf Cultural History, 1900 to World War II" (Ph.D. diss., Georgetown University, 1999), 70–74.

15. After graduation, Ballin dedicated much of his life to promoting sign language and demonstrated a keen interest in various issues affecting the Deaf community. See Albert Ballin, Deaf Biographical Files, Gallaudet University Archives, Washington, D.C.

16. "The Nebraska Oral Law," *National Association of the Deaf Proceedings* (1915): 27, 29–31. See also the publication of the Nebraska Association of the Deaf, the *Silent Facts*, established in 1919.

17. For example, Magdelene Pickens, "An Institutional Study of the Nebraska School for the Deaf" (Social Research Project, University of Omaha, 1947), 27; Charles Rawlings, "A Survey of Facilities for the Education of the Deaf in Nebraska," *American Annals of the Deaf* 83 (1938): 442–43; George Porter, "The New Jersey Muddle the Result of Too Much Meddle," *American Deaf Citizen* (6 December 1929): 1, 3. See also Buchanan, "Silent Worker Newspaper," 172–197.

18. "Abolition of the Sign-Language Protested," *American Deaf Citizen* (7 August 1931): 2; "Georgia Head Still Opposes Signs," *American Deaf Citizen* (20 January 1933): 1; *American Deaf Citizen* (24 March 1933): 1; "Georgia Association Prepares," *American Deaf Citizen* (18 June 1937): 1. Deaf commentary on Harris became particularly frequent and colorful in the 1930s. In one article, a Deaf writer likened Harris's brand of oralism to his middle name, Coffey (coffee): too much of it gave everyone mental constipation (*American Deaf Citizen* [27 April 1934]: 2).

19. "Georgia Convention a Complete Success," *American Deaf Citizen* (9 July 1937): 1; "I Have Asked the Deaf," *American Deaf Citizen* (18 March 1938): 4.

20. For examples from other states, see *NAD Bulletin* (June 1935); *NAD Bulletin* (January 1935): 3; Convention of American Instructors of the Deaf, "School Items," *American Annals of the Deaf* 74 (September 1929): 419; "Daniel T. Cloud Named Superintendent of Local Deaf School by Emmerson," (Jacksonville, Illinois) *Daily Journal* (30 July 1929): 12 and passim; Patrick James Dowling, "A History of the Illinois School for the Deaf" (master's thesis, Gallaudet College, 1965), 54, 73; "A Turn for the Better in Illinois," *American Annals of the Deaf* 74 (1929): 418–20.

21. For example, see Elwood Stevenson's 1940 National Association of the Deaf speech "The Education of the Deaf," in Caroline Burnes and Catherine Ramger, *History of the California School for the Deaf, Berkeley, 1860–1960* (Berkeley: California School for the Deaf, 1960) 109; *NAD Bulletin* (April 1935): passim; J. W. Jones, *Education of Robert, a Deaf Boy: Out of Darkness into the Light* (Columbus: State School for the Deaf, 1925), 62; "Deaf Teachers," *American Annals of the Deaf* 53 (1908): 274; J. W. Jones, "News and Comments," *Silent Courier* (15 October 1914): 3.

22. Alvin Pope, "Scientific Spirit," *American Annals of the Deaf* (1928): 312–16, 323.

23. See, for example, Alvin Pope, "Scientific Spirit," *American Annals of the Deaf* (1928): 323.

24. "Report of the Conference Committee on Nomenclature," *American Annals of the Deaf* 83 (1938): 1–3. Although overly optimistic, scholar Harry Best noted in 1943 that society and specialists demonstrated greater sensitivity by avoiding terms such as *deaf and dumb* and *mute*. He added that a recent White House Conference on Child Health and Protection had included the modified definitions of deafness and hard of hearing. See Harry Best, *Deafness and the Deaf in the United States* (New York: Macmillan, 1943), 123–24.

25. See, for example, E. A. Fay, *Progress in the Education of the Deaf* (Washington, D.C.: Bureau of Education, 1914), 454–55. Changes in teacher certification also held great importance for the Deaf community. For more on this subject, see Burch, "Biding the Time," 93–105.

26. This included an increased number of schools for the deaf and admissions to Gallaudet, as well as the personal intervention of administrators and faculty to help talented Deaf men and women find employment at the schools.

27. Of 422 Gallaudet graduates between 1915 and 1940, 228 (54 percent) became teachers. See I. Fusfeld, "Professional Preparation and Advancement of Deaf Teachers," *American Annals of the Deaf* 86 (1941): 422–23. See *List of Students by Degree, Date, and State* (Washington, D.C.: Gallaudet College, 1944–45), 13–14; Harley Drake, "The Deaf Teacher of the Deaf," *American Annals of the Deaf* 85 (1940): 148–49.

28. Merv Garretson, speech at the Fanwood School, May 1, 1998, in Biographical File: Francis Fox, Gallaudet University Archives, Washington, D.C.

29. F. A. Moore, "Doctor John Burton Hotchkiss: A Tribute," *Silent Worker* 35, 4 (January 1923): passim. The entire issue of the *Silent Worker* was dedicated to Hotchkiss; the outpouring from colleagues and students is particularly moving. See also George Veditz, "John Burton Hotchkiss," *Jewish Deaf* 8, 9 (January 1923): passim.

30. *Tale of Two Schools: The Indiana Institution and the Evansville Day School, 1879–1912* (n.p., 1993); Michael Reiss, "Student Life at the Indiana School for the Deaf during the Depression Years," in Van Cleve, ed., *Deaf History Unveiled*, 198–223; Winfield Runde, "The Deaf Teacher," *North Dakota Banner* 53, 4 (January 1944): 3–4.

31. Ronald Emery Nomeland, "Beginnings of Vocational Education in Schools for the Deaf" (master's thesis, University of Maryland, 1967), 20.

32. Cremin, *Transformation of the School*, 50. Attendance in American high schools generally jumped after 1880, partly in response to all states adopting child labor laws by 1920. Moreover, the high school diploma had become a terminal degree for Americans, and vocational training to enter the job market became particularly important. See Arthur F. McClure, James Riley Chrisman, and Perry Mack, *Education for Work: The Historical Evolution of Vocational and Distinctive Education in America* (Madison, Wis.: Associated University Press, 1985), 28.

33. P. N. Peterson, "The Ideal or Practical—Which?" *American Annals of the Deaf* 59 (1914): 135–42; J. W. Blattner, "Vocational Education," *Convention of American Instructors of the Deaf Proceedings* (1920): 154–59.

34. Leonard Elstad, "Normal Training of Deaf Teachers," *Convention of American Instructors of the Deaf Proceedings* (1935): 195; Best, *Deafness and the Deaf*, 573.

35. Most programs focused on male students and funded male-oriented job training, such as carpentry, shoemaking, and farming. Classes for girls enforced the expectation of their primary role as mothers and wives, teaching them cooking and sewing skills. While cosmetology and simple secretarial courses may have offered limited access to self-sufficiency, Deaf women clearly suffered the additional disadvantage of an educational system that downplayed academics and tangible skills to find well-paying work.

9

Medicine, Bureaucracy, and Social Welfare

The Politics of Disability Compensation for American Veterans of World War I

K. Walter Hickel

World War I proved crucial in the development of disability as an expansive but contested category for distributing welfare payments to many Americans. The war's human toll necessitated new approaches to defining disability and to managing its social and economic consequences, problems basic to modern social policy and social citizenship in many western countries. While provisions for disabled veterans and their dependents built on Civil War–era military pensions, the only previous form of large-scale disability benefits, they also reflected Progressive Era beliefs about the shared responsibility of individuals, employers, and the state in ameliorating the impact of industrial capitalism and industrial warfare on families. Like other Progressive reforms such as public hygiene programs, workmen's compensation, and child labor laws, wartime disability policy reconceived the relationship between people, their bodily and mental capacities, and the physical and social environment. Its ideological and political configuration became an archetype of twentieth-century social policy.[1]

At the center of wartime disability policy was a conflict over the meaning of disability itself that has shaped the politics and administration of Social Security Disability Insurance and other disability benefits up to the present. In regulating access to benefits, federal lawmakers defined disability as functional impairment, a declension from a normal body or mind that reduced one's capacity for productive labor. They expected modern medical science's precise clinical techniques to measure this reduction. Physicians, who approached disability in terms of diagnosis, prognosis, and treatment, became the gatekeepers to benefits. World War I veterans benefits legislation thus was a crucial step in the codification, institutionalization, and reification of this medical conception of disability in regulating access to welfare payments.

Yet, from the start, that medical conception proved contradictory and controversial. In examining veterans for service-related disability, physicians routinely applied not medical criteria but cultural and racial values. They regarded certain diseases as prevalent, if not congenital, among particular racial groups. For instance, they considered black Americans biologically predisposed to tuberculosis, despite the absence of clinical studies demonstrating this. Such cultural and racial views of disease, though medical fictions, had real consequences, because in attributing a medical condition to congenital weakness, low standards of personal hygiene, or moral degradation, rather than to military service, physicians invalidated the disability claims of many black veterans. The latter understood this prejudicial logic quite well and objected to it.

While physicians claimed identification of impairment as a medical prerogative, they admitted that evaluating it as a disability required an abstraction from a medical examination's results. Moreover, they could not explain this abstraction in medical terms. Instead, they had to couch it in the language of disability law and the arithmetic of disability rating schedules, the complicated numerical tables that officially measured the severity of a disability. Yet law and disability ratings were the domains of legislators and benefits administrators, not physicians. Meanwhile, benefits administrators sought to reconcile legal and bureaucratic constraints with the demands of a powerful veterans lobby and with their own professional ambition to create as large a clientele as possible for the programs they oversaw.

Veterans themselves articulated a social conception of disability that firmly placed disabled people in the social context of their relationships and needs. To them, modern medicine and bureaucratic government were only two elements of this context, and not the most crucial. They gave greater weight to the structure of local labor markets, job requirements, racial segregation, and social norms ascribing to men their roles as workers, providers, and citizens. To veterans, disability touched on all of these institutions and relationships, rather than merely denoting the medical condition of an individual isolated from society or a purely legal entitlement to benefits.

The differences among medical, bureaucratic, and social conceptions of disability became politically charged when veterans complained about unfair rulings on their claims, physicians asserted their professional authority, and lawmakers and officials sought to mediate through legislative and administrative intervention. These political tensions revealed disability as an artifact of capitalist democracy, resonating throughout its economic, social, and political relations. Conflict over the definition of disability and the level of benefits disabled persons could claim exposed the divergent interests and relations of power between employers and employees, skilled and unskilled workers, elected legislators and career bureaucrats, physicians and patients. Such conflicts also indicated that World War I veterans welfare programs perpetuated racial segregation and sought to ensure both the social protection of white veterans and their racial supremacy, for officials reinforced inequities of race and class in administering disability benefits. As a result, as a means of compensating individuals for the human cost of modern industrial warfare and production, disability benefits quickly became—and have remained—contested.[2]

Some 930,000 World War I veterans applied for disability benefits during the first five years after the November 9, 1918, armistice.[3] One of them, Charles M. Geter, with just five years of schooling, had worked before the war as an iron molder and night watchman in Augusta, Georgia, shifting casually between semiskilled and unskilled jobs to eke out a $15-a-week wage. Gassed in the Argonne Forest, he showed symptoms of pulmonary damage later diagnosed as chronic bronchitis and "weak lungs" and was awarded compensation. In spring of 1920, he began training to rehabilitate him first as a machinist, then as a cabinetmaker. Geter appreciated the compensation payments and the small wage from the training workshop, not least because he had married in February and now had a wife to support. But by April 1922, complications arose with the return of warm weather. The "poorly ventilated" workshop turned "very hot," and Geter grew "very anemic." In May, his breathing became difficult enough for the local Veterans Bureau's medical officer to refer him to its tuberculosis hospital in Lake City, Florida. Restless after five months' hospitalization and no confirmed recovery, Geter left the hospital in October 1922 against doctors' advice. That action disqualified him from further vocational training, although he retained his compensation. By May 1923, he came to regret cutting short his treatment, but, he explained, he could not return to the hospital because in his absence his compensation was insufficient to support a wife and aged parents who were "entirely dependent upon me." In a final setback, a medical examination in 1925 concluded that his pulmonary problems and newly diagnosed psychoneurosis warranted only the lowest rate of compensation and were only temporary. Shortly afterward, his compensation payments stopped.

The benefits Geter drew for five years, including disability compensation, vocational rehabilitation, and hospital care, had been established in an omnibus law, the War Risk Insurance Act of 1917.[4] Congress aimed to replace traditional veterans benefits, and especially Civil War military pensions, with a more rational, equitable, and modern system of provision. The linchpin of the diverse measures created by the act was the promise of financial compensation for those among the total of 5 million American World War I servicemen who had a disability.

Compensation would provide a margin of financial security for disabled veterans in a labor market that systematically discriminated against them and would allow them to withdraw from the labor market altogether if their disability was severe. "The least efficient workman is the first to be dropped from the payroll," rehabilitation specialists warned. "The very fact that the [service]man is disabled increases the danger of his belonging to this class." Employment and wage discrimination, lawmakers foresaw, would intensify due to the economic dislocation of war and to demobilization. In fact, that dislocation produced a wave of strikes in 1919, one of the largest in American history, and the brief but severe 1920–21 recession. Rather than be relegated to menial jobs, as had often been the lot of disabled people, veterans with diminished capacity for wage labor would live in a manner that preserved their dignity as defenders of a proud nation.[5]

Congress granted compensation to officers, enlisted men, and members of the all-female Army and Navy Nurse Corps who had incurred a disability in or as a consequence of their World War I service, whether caused by injury, disease, or aggravation of a previous medical condition.[6] Compensation did not indemnify patriotic sacrifice or physical or mental suffering; it reimbursed potential future income loss due to service-related impairment and the disadvantage it caused the veteran in the labor market. At least, that was how the War Risk Insurance Act construed disability. Nonetheless, during the 1920s, Congress came to regard compensation as recompense for military service, uncoupling it from veterans' income potential.

In contrast to military pensions or workmen's compensation, the reduction in earning capacity was to be calculated not with regard to a veteran's prewar or current occupation but as the "average" reduction in earning capacity veterans with a specific disability would likely sustain in any and all "civil occupations," skilled or unskilled, manual or intellectual. Nor did claimants' actual earnings matter either at the time they applied for compensation or while they received it. A finding of disability by itself entitled them to compensation.

Since the reduction in earning capacity varied with the type and severity of each impairment, disability was expressed as a percentage representing the deviation between the productive capacity of an imagined healthy and normal person and the residual capacity of the disabled veteran. For example, a veteran whose capacity to work efficiently—and thus whose income potential—was reduced by 40 percent received a disability rating of 40 percent. To aid calculation of this percentage for "specific injuries . . . of a permanent nature," a disability rating schedule provided a comprehensive index of amputations, injuries, diseases, and mental disorders. It assigned percentages to each according to the purported impact on the veteran's ability to work. The agencies that administered the War Risk Insurance Act, the Bureau of War Risk Insurance and its successor, the U.S. Veterans Bureau, were to develop the schedule.

A temporary or permanent war-related disability rated at 10 percent or more and not due to "willful misconduct" entitled an individual to compensation. Neither veterans' actual income nor (unlike Civil War pensions) former military rank were considered, only the degree of their disability and (again unlike pensions) the number of their dependents. For temporary total disability, these rates ranged from $80 a month for a veteran with no dependents to $120 for a similarly disabled man who was married, had two or more children, and had two dependent parents.[7] Total permanent disability included loss of both hands or both feet, the sight of both eyes, the loss of one hand and one foot and other such combinations, and the state of being "helpless and permanently bedridden"; it was assessed at a flat $100 per month.[8] Compensation for partial temporary and partial permanent disability was to be calculated as a percentage of the compensation for total temporary and total permanent disability respectively. Again, this percentage was to equal the reduction in earning capacity attributable to the disability. For example, a veteran without dependents with a temporary disability rated at 20 percent (that is, an earning potential reduced by 20 percent) received $16 per month, 20 percent of the $80 paid to an unmarried veteran with a total temporary disability.

Disabled World War I veterans compensation drew on three related but distinct concepts: a clinical and environmental explanation of the causes of disability, an understanding of dependency that reflected the political economy of industrial capitalism, and the principle of workmen's compensation. All three concepts were hallmarks of the Progressive Era.

Until the late nineteenth century, disability and its economic effects of unemployment, poverty, and dependence were often regarded as a preordained fate, a divine stigma incurred at birth, or a result of individual moral flaws and self-destructive habits such as criminality, alcoholism, and sexual promiscuity. Reflecting this view, government agencies and private charities directed their attention to disabled children. For adults disabled later in life, benefits remained very limited. Most important, since the colonial era, soldiers visibly disabled during military service had been entitled to military pensions. St. Elizabeth's Hospital, founded in 1852 in the nation's capital, provided custodial care for mentally ill sailors and soldiers and local residents, while Freedmen's Hospital, founded in 1865, offered Washington's black and indigent white population medical care, including long-term care for tuberculosis patients. Both hospitals were federally funded. Apart from these provisions for certain clearly defined social groups—children, veterans, and residents of the District of Columbia and its vicinity—no government entities above the local level regarded disability as their responsibility.[9]

Beginning in the 1890s, and influenced by Louis Pasteur's and Robert Koch's epidemiological studies, public health officials, social scientists, employers, labor leaders, and politicians in industrializing nations gradually rejected the moral understanding of disability. They began to locate its causes not just in the trauma of warfare but in the effects of infectious disease, crowded and unsanitary living quarters, ignorance of the laws of hygiene, and the health risks of factory production, conditions affecting both children and adults. This shift in the perception of disability from personal fate to social contingency was, writes Seth Koven, "part of a larger trend away from explanations of social problems that focused on innate or moral failings of individuals, toward one that focused on social, environmental, and epidemiological factors."[10] Disability compensation under the War Risk Insurance Act reflected this trend. It took a no-fault approach to claims adjudication. Administrators did not ask whether a veteran could have done anything to avoid the injury or infection that caused the disability, as long as it did not result from willful misconduct such as self-mutilation.[11] Searching for biological or etiological, not moral, causes, medical examiners recognized a widening range of diseases as sources of disablement. Thus, War Risk Insurance embraced the new social and environmental conception of disability and envisioned an activist role for government in alleviating its effects.

In War Risk Insurance as in other Progressive social policies, the medical and social redefinition of disability also converged with changing understandings of dependency. As Nancy Fraser and Linda Gordon have argued, by the 1890s preindustrial reciprocal relationships of dependency and protection between tenant and landlord had been superseded by the contractual market relations of wage earner and employer. Meanwhile, traditional associations between personal independence and ownership of productive property gave way to the ideology of the "living wage": under conditions of industrial capitalism, white workers would gain economic independence by earning wages sufficient to support their families, irrespective of their actual subordination to employers. Dependency became a status appropriate only to white women, to black people, and children.[12]

During the Progressive Era, the distinction between the "natural" dependency of women and children on a male breadwinner and the "unnatural" dependency of white men on public charity was enshrined in public policy. During the first two decades of the twentieth century, many municipalities and states implemented mothers pensions and female and child protective labor laws, while initiatives to establish old age, unemployment, or health insurance for purportedly independent male industrial workers all failed.[13] But this gender and racial distinction in the meaning of dependency made urgent the need for administrative techniques to separate the few adult white males unemployed through no fault of their own (such as industrial accidents) from the majority of poor, unemployed white men whose failure to earn a living wage stemmed from laziness and other moral faults. The former merited public aid; the latter did not. The medical and environmental conception of disability gave physicians and benefits administrators new, powerful diagnostic and social-scientific tools to distinguish the deserving from the undeserving poor.

In addition, War Risk Insurance likened service-related injuries and medical conditions to the results of industrial accidents and occupational disease. In that sense it paralleled another formative Progressive social policy: workmen's compensation. Progressive reformers intent on ameliorating the most detrimental effects of industrial capitalism on workers and their families focused on work-related injuries and illnesses. In alliance with labor unions, they scored one of their greatest successes when, between 1908 and 1920, they persuaded Congress and forty-five state legislatures to adopt workmen's compensation laws to rectify the shortcomings of common-law employer liability in securing relief for industrial accident victims. These laws varied considerably in detail, but every one replaced expensive litigation and sometimes large, but always uncertain, rewards with efficient administrative proceedings and guaranteed payments to all federal and industrial workers injured on the job. Industrial accident commissions, not courts, would arbitrate claims according to a written disability rating schedule, published rates of payment, and a no-fault approach that did not try to make the worker personally responsible for his disablement. To cover the cost of disability benefits, employers would buy industrial accident insurance and society at large would pay slightly higher prices for goods.[14]

These elements of workmen's compensation all became part of War Risk Insurance. Soldiers were disabled in the service of their "employer," the nation-state, and had a claim to indemnification similar to that of industrial workers under workmen's compensation laws. Veterans disability compensation would ensure guaranteed benefits at rates published in advance of military service and possible disablement; it would replace the sometimes larger but less-predictable payments under the Civil War pension system, a system Progressive reformers thought as arbitrary as liability law. Advocates of War Risk Insurance regarded the pension system as corrupt and wasteful precisely because it was "based on the principle of gratuities and political favor rather than on a sense of social justice and mutual obligation." Attributing the latter advantages to social insurance in general and workmen's compensation in particular, they designated disability provision as compensation, not pensions.[15] Lawmakers applying the principle of workmen's compensation to the problem of World War veterans disability expected compensation to prove more rational and equitable than Civil War military pensions. But their expectation soon met disappointment. Just as workmen's compensation laws failed to make good on their promise to limit court litigation and contain conflict between employers and disabled workers, veterans disability compensation quickly became contested and politicized, the very shortcomings for which the new law's framers criticized the military pension system.[16] The dispute arose from the divergent objectives of Veterans Bureau physicians, benefits administrators, and veterans, and from their divergent conceptions of disability.

The laws and regulations enjoined Veterans Bureau physicians and officials to conceive of disability as a medical category. Eligibility for benefits derived not from a veteran's own contention of inability to work or from social values defining the physical and mental capacities expected in a healthy adult male but from identification of an objective impairment by individual medical examination and diagnosis. This medical determination of disability had a long precedent in nineteenth-century procedures for awarding veterans disability pensions. The General Law Pension System of 1862, the statute governing disability benefits for Civil War veterans, required a medical finding of impairment. Workmen's compensation laws also adopted a clinical definition of disability, although they applied to private employer-employee conflict only, not to public benefits. The War Risk Insurance Act again reified the medical conception of disability in regulating access to benefits. The effectiveness of this conception soon became apparent: of 940,000 compensation claims adjudicated by June 30, 1924, Veterans Bureau doctors disallowed over 485,000. In almost all these cases, they thought the medical evidence of impairment, and especially of its origin in military service, insufficient.[17]

Because physicians later came to be seen as a driving force in the expansion of Social Security Disability Insurance benefits (created in 1954), the mechanism by which the medical conception of disability led to restriction of World War I disability benefits requires explanation. "Early in 1918 everyone thought of the disabled man in terms of amputations or blindness," officials recalled. "Little thought was given to the effects of tuberculosis, heart lesions, or the many types of war neurosis." Yet these three types of impairments alone eventually accounted for almost half of all compensation claims, while not more than five thousand American servicemen underwent amputations and fewer than two hundred were blinded.[18] After the war, bureau physicians, benefits administrators, and Congress began to recognize an increasing range of injuries, diseases, and infections as grounds to award compensation. Propelling the increase, officials admitted, were scientific, political, and bureaucratic dynamics that "could not be foreseen or predicted with any considerable degree of accuracy" in 1917.[19] To identify the many medical causes of disability, by the early 1920s the bureau not only relied on its own twenty-two-hundred staff physicians but hired no fewer than twenty-six-hundred private physicians throughout the country on a fee-for-service basis as so-called Designated Medical Examiners.[20]

The reliance on medical diagnosis alone to initiate the process toward a disability rating gave these physicians inordinate power and discretion to limit the number of successful claims.[21] The Veterans Bureau's first director, Charles R. Forbes, remarked that "almost every act of the Bureau is based on a medical opinion . . . and its huge expenditures are undertaken on the advice of our doctors."[22] The chief of the Medical Division declared: "Nothing is more important than the ratings so far as this Bureau is concerned, since

K. Walter Hickel

the making of the rating is the lever which starts in motion the entire machinery of the Bureau."[23] Until 1924 medical referees, physicians specializing in medical disciplines such as surgery or psychiatry, working in the Bureau's fourteen district offices, assigned disability ratings. That year, Claims and Ratings Boards in the roughly one hundred, newly created regional offices took over this function. Though these boards comprised claims administrators and rehabilitation officials as well as physicians, they used the results of medical examinations and thus the medical conception of disability as the basis for their decisions. Historians who have studied professionalization in medicine during this period have overlooked the role of physicians in the adjudication of disability claims under War Risk Insurance. That role obviously augmented physicians' professional authority by giving them jurisdiction over a large new clientele, disabled World War I veterans.[24]

The Veterans Bureau's disability rating schedule was both the apotheosis of the medical paradigm of disability and the source of physicians' institutional power. The schedule symbolized the link between veterans disability compensation and workmen's compensation. The state industrial accident commissions that administered the latter had devised such schedules to ensure consistent, rational, and incontestable disability ratings based on medical science. The framers of the War Risk Insurance Act hoped that a comprehensive, scientific, written disability rating schedule would introduce consistency and predictability into the award process. They believed the schedule would do away with the favoritism, arbitrariness, and spectacle of pension bills for individual veterans that had marred administration of the General Law Pension System.

Medical officials considered the schedule indispensable, scientific, and esoteric. Because their claims to professional authority and autonomy rested on their expertise in interpreting and applying the rating schedule, they guarded it closely. Responding to a request for a copy of the schedule, the director of the Bureau of War Risk Insurance explained that it was "confidential" and "not for publication at this time," ostensibly because it was "subject to revision at any time." Even members of Congress found their requests for a copy rebuffed. Frank T. Hines, the Veterans Bureau's second director, informed Congressman Victor Berger that the schedule "is highly technical in character and can only be explained by persons thoroughly versed in the law and regulations under which the Bureau operates. It is regretted that the requested copy cannot be furnished you." Physicians were so intent on maintaining control over the schedule that they resisted making it available even to other Bureau officials. "At present there is the utmost secrecy about the table and the Medical Division will not let it get out even in the Bureau itself," complained one assistant director.[25]

The Bureau kept the schedule secret in an effort to isolate the disability rating process from political interference by congressmen friendly to the powerful American Legion (founded in 1919) and other veterans organizations. Furthermore, it wanted to maintain the mystique of scientific objectivity in the rating process. Not least, one suspects, Bureau physicians carefully concealed the ratings they assigned to particular impairments for fear that veterans might use such information to tailor their claims, rehearse for their medical examinations, and receive a higher rating. During the 1960s, the fear that claimants would manipulate the process of medical discovery on which disability ratings rested made the Social Security Administration reluctant to publish its Social Security Disability Insurance disability standards. That controversy repeated almost verbatim the earlier debate over publication of the Veterans Bureau disability rating schedule.[26]

Under congressional directive, the Veterans Administration finally published a second edition of its disability rating schedule in 1933. Over eighty pages long, it listed hundreds of medical conditions, many with austere clinical descriptions of symptoms of varying severity. It assigned most conditions a specific percentage figure. It made medical expertise and medical constructions of disability paramount in awarding compensation.

But the schedule also declared that, separate from and in addition to "a clear presentation of the clinical manifestations of the underlying pathology," disability ratings required "evidence of actual impairment of function, affecting the industrial adjustment of the individual."[27] Impairment became disability, and thereby grounds for an award of benefits, only as it affected a veteran's employment prospects and limited his capacity for wage labor. To produce a rating, impairment must be linked to economic and social variables that described the claimant's position in labor markets and occupational hierarchies, in short, his position in the larger social structure. "All activities of the Bureau and, in fact, the Bureau itself is builded [sic] primarily upon medical and medico-legal grounds," one of the Bureau's medical officials reiterated. Those grounds involved "the extent to which physical infirmities, anatomical losses and mental disturbances interfere with vocational pursuits, industrial activity and social adaptation." Though physicians may not have connected medical science with economic and social considerations, disability ratings merged them.[28]

A disability rating supposedly measured the degree to which functional impairment hindered two essential activities of adult males in a capitalist society: waged labor and support of dependents. Disability, declared one official, "will be assessed, as it should be, with reference to the whole range of activities, economic and social, . . . personal and public, in which the normal man may or must participate."[29] The criteria applied in rating disability for purposes of compensation often combined unrelated measures developed by different types of experts in their respective and disparate intellectual and practical disciplines—not just physicians but also lawyers, administrators, vocational specialists, social scientists, and legislators. Their often unrelated and countervailing approaches support Jerry L. Mashaw's point that disability rating requires "a translation of clinical evidence into functional limitation, a translation that corresponds to the expertise of no known profession."[30]

The complications and contradictions arising from a simultaneously medical, legal, and social definition of disability became graphically apparent at one of the first stages in the compensation award process: determining whether or not a claimant had incurred an impairment in military service. The War Risk Insurance Act made this determination a necessary precondition for an award of compensation, just as workmen's compensation laws required a determination that a worker's injury or disease had been incurred in the course of his work. Under both laws, physicians made this determination. It proved difficult. According to the War Risk Insurance Bureau's director, it represented "the most serious difficulty" in adjudicating claims. The problem arose because the majority of veterans filed claims several years after their discharge from the military. In many cases, their service records showed no evidence of disease or injury. To expedite compensation claims, the War Risk Insurance Act provided for certificates at the time of discharge or in the year after, stating that an individual had a condition likely to result in disability in the future; but few had obtained such certificates.[31] As of July 1, 1920, military physicians had issued only 6,646 certificates, a number far below veterans' rate of injury and disease.[32]

Even if a medical examination revealed that a claimant was presently sick or injured, in many cases it failed to yield definite indication that the condition originated in military service. In particular, "medical cases," veterans with physiological diseases rather than anatomical damage or loss, presented "an amazing number of complications" because the precise cause and course of many diseases were highly variable and complex and were too little studied.[33] Given the state of medical science, a retrospective determination of service origin in these cases involved as much conjecture as scientific in-quiry, even if Bureau physicians never openly admitted it.

The disjuncture between the legal requirement of a disability's service ori-gin and the ability of physicians and veterans to provide unambiguous med-ical evidence of service origin was often great. From June 1925 to June 1926, medical examiners rejected 15,000 of 20,600 claims solely because they con-cluded the disabilities had not resulted from military service.[34] Legislators and Veterans Bureau administrators decided they must bridge the disjunc-ture to avoid confining compensation benefits to a limited number of veter-ans who had left the service already visibly disabled. The problem grew more serious as more time elapsed between the war's end and the filing of a claim. Congress and Bureau officials addressed this difficulty through legal means that revealed disability to be a political, social, and bureaucratic construct, rather than a medical finding. They thus inadvertently created the kind of inconsistency and special legislative provision that Progressive reformers had thought marred the Civil War pension system.

First, Congress passed legislation positing a conclusive presumption of service origin for certain of the most complicated medical conditions affect-ing veterans. It singled out tuberculosis and neuropsychiatric disorders be-cause it rightly assumed that, given popular fears of contagion and mental illness, these posed particularly high barriers to employment. The 1921 act establishing the Veterans Bureau stipulated that all veterans who, within two years of discharge, developed active tuberculosis or neuropsychiatric dis-orders rated at not less than 10 percent were presumed to have incurred their impairments in military service. They would automatically receive compen-sation without further medical inquiry. In later acts, Congress lengthened the time frame of this provision from two years to six, though only for tuber-culosis. As a result, during the 1920s tuberculosis alone accounted for al-most a fourth of compensation awards and neuropsychiatric disorders for another fourth.[35] Moreover, the World War Veterans Act of 1924 awarded $50 a month for life to all veterans with arrested tuberculosis, whether it ac-tually limited their capacity for labor or not. That stipulation completely by-passed the rating schedule on which awards officially rested. It meant that by 1927 more than a third of total compensation payments went to veterans with a single disease, active or arrested tuberculosis. Despite the intentions of the War Risk Insurance Act's framers, compensation had become reim-bursement for military service rather than for disability and its economic ef-fect on veterans.[36]

Claimants with tuberculosis or neuropsychiatric disorders still had to undergo medical examinations, but the law now left physicians no authority to interpret the origin and development of these diseases and fixed the conclusions of medical findings regarding awards.[37] Legislative fiat could define disability if that simplified administrative procedures, made a welfare provision more widely accessible and therefore more credible, and satisfied a constituency as well organized and powerful as veterans. After all, the Veterans Bureau's first director had committed it to the maxim that "doubts are to be resolved in favor of the ex–service man, and the presumption is always in favor of the claimant."[38]

In addition to creating various statutory definitions of eligibility, the Bureau sought to resolve problems in the medical determination of impairment through administrative procedure. A 1925 regulation allowed ratings for separate noncompensable disabilities (those rated below 10 percent) to be combined into one rating that *would* entitle the veteran to compensation. Here, disability became a purely arithmetical calculation, entirely disconnected from medical standards.[39] In addition, a 1923 regulation called for reexamination of all veterans drawing compensation for temporary disability "with a view of putting them on a permanent basis wherever possible." The impetus was not medical but political and administrative, namely, "relieving the claimant of the necessity of frequently reporting for examination, and producing in the mind of the claimant a certain realization that a definite amount of money was coming to him periodically." Officials expected this change to dispose veterans more favorably toward the Bureau, a compelling political objective in the context of the fiscal retrenchment and antigovernment rhetoric that characterized the Republican administrations of the 1920s.[40]

Administrative rules that allowed lay observers familiar with the claimant to present evidence also had a great impact on adjudication of claims and on the underlying definition of disability. Lay evidence had as long a provenance in veterans disability claims procedures as medical examination. Most notable, the Civil War General Law Pension System had permitted it. That system required a medical examination to ascertain the fact of present disablement and the disability's origin in military service. But if, as often happened, no continuous medical record existed, lay evidence of a veteran's incapacitation during military service and the years since discharge was admissible to help him establish his eligibility. Former comrades, neighbors, employers, and other witnesses without medical training could offer such evidence in the form of *ex parte* testimony.

The Bureau of War Risk Insurance and the Veterans Bureau adopted this administrative practice in order to make disability compensation more flexible and amenable to veterans' needs. "If the claimant can submit affidavits from disinterested parties testifying to the fact that he did suffer from a disease or disability while in the military service, . . . such evidence will be accepted," the director of the Bureau of War Risk Insurance ruled. Application forms introduced in 1928 asked claimants to list the names and addresses not only of all physicians who had treated them since their discharge but of "other persons who know any facts about any sickness, disease or injury which you have had in active service or since discharge" and who might help establish the distant origins of disability in a war that had ended ten years earlier.[41] By itself, though, lay evidence did not validate a claim of disability. Bureau officials always sought verification from physicians who might have treated the veteran since his discharge and thus could attest "that at the time of his discharge the claimant did suffer from the disabilities claimed."[42] Many veterans, however, did not consult physicians even when they became sick, because they could not pay the fees, because no physician was available in their community, or because they distrusted physicians' remedies. Many doctors whom veterans did consult failed to keep records of their examinations and could not recall the results, had moved away, or had died. Even if physicians could provide the results of examinations, these frequently proved inconclusive because of the obscure etiology of many diseases. Thus, given claimants' often incomplete, indeterminate, or altogether irrecoverable medical histories, their claims might be developed, if not finally resolved, by stepping outside the confines of professional medical discourse and technique and drawing on the observations of knowledgeable laymen.

Staff physicians especially accepted lay evidence in neuropsychiatric cases, which made up almost a fourth of all claims and troubled physicians even more than cases of organic disease.[43] In these cases, physicians themselves applied nonclinical examination criteria. Many psychiatric and neurological disorders, such as epilepsy or the newly recognized phenomenon of shell shock or other psychoses, severely tested and often eluded the diagnostic and therapeutic techniques of psychiatry and neurology, medical disciplines still in their infancy as the war ended. Bureau physicians also considered neuropsychiatric disorders easy to feign and in certain instances related to the pathology of venereal diseases, specifically syphilis. These disorders thus raised suspicions of malingering and illicit sex, suspicions encouraged by the War Risk Insurance Act and its stipulation that "willful misconduct" invalidated a veteran's claim. Disability benefits, like other Progressive social provisions, aimed to enforce conventional norms of personal demeanor, family relations, and sexual behavior. In the final analysis, private morality played as big a part in the Progressive definition of disability as did medical science and diagnostics.[44]

In establishing a veteran's psychiatric profile, along with clinical categories such as depression and neurosis Bureau psychiatrists routinely applied nonclinical criteria, including such social and cultural artifacts as "social conduct," "appearance," "spontaneity of speech," and "school knowledge."[45] "Constitutional Psychopathy," the Bureau's medical director explained, involved "an indisposition to govern [oneself] according to accepted standards of right and wrong"—purely moral, not medical, criteria.[46] A San Francisco district office psychiatrist considered some veterans' "inability to adapt themselves to their environment" and refrain from "breaking established customs" to be signs of mental illness.[47] In identifying such purportedly abnormal behavior, a Veterans Bureau psychiatrist suggested that a "good lay description of the man, his difficulties, his reactions, etc., is often better than the 'cut and dried' report of a medical examiner."[48] Mental impairment, the psychiatrists implied, was not exclusively a clinical condition, to be established only by a medical specialist, but a deviation from accepted norms of social behavior and self-discipline that laymen could gauge as well.

Designated medical examiners also relied on nonclinical and lay evidence in rating disability. Bureau officials charged that these local contract physicians allowed "personal equations to enter into consideration [of disability claims], and a physician being acquainted with the claimant's general reputation in the community . . . the estimate of disability would be colored by these prejudices" to the veteran's disadvantage. Nonetheless, "many civilian practitioners have been, to say the least, most lenient in the reporting of cases of claimants who are simply exaggerating the most trivial complaints into major disabilities." To prevent personal antipathy or favoritism from entering into the disability rating process, officials in 1922 divested the examiners of authority to render disability ratings and reserved that power to staff physicians, though they, too, were prone to apply social and cultural criteria.

Nonclinical standards of evaluation pervaded compensation claims procedure at many turns. Bureau officials espoused a concept of disability officially based on medical science but that in fact blended clinical evidence with normative judgments of private morality, idealization of the work ethic, and racial stereotypes in an uneasy and often contradictory combination.[49] Bureau physicians asserted that disability lay within the domain of modern clinical medicine, removed from the experience and analytical capacity of politicians, lay witnesses, or the veterans themselves. In contrast, other officials felt much less certain that determination of an impairment's service origin and its rating as a disability were medical processes at all. Disability rating, admitted a lawyer for the Bureau, "while perhaps the most important, is, at the same time, the most unsatisfactory of all the work which the Veterans Bureau is called upon to perform—unsatisfactory in that the ratings rest, in their adoption and application, largely upon matters of judgment and opinion." Judgment and opinion were the defining characteristics not of medical science but of political conflict.[50]

For their part, veterans and the lay witnesses who testified for them articulated a social and cultural understanding of disability that diverged from the clinical framework invoked (if not consistently applied) by Veterans Bureau physicians. Veterans resisted the medical paradigm of disability. Finding the new language of clinical medicine abstract and confounding, they used it only with difficulty in making their claims. They adopted instead the political language of citizenship and entitlement. They insisted that disability was actually construed in the context of individual needs and social norms—as claims administrators admitted openly and Bureau physicians conceded inadvertently—and that the federal government owed them recognition as defenders of the nation.

Craig West offered a case in point. A black veteran from Birmingham, Alabama, West had been a farmer and unskilled laborer before his military service. After a medical examination in 1924, his disability rating for tachycardia (rapid heartbeat) was reduced to less than 10 percent, resulting in withdrawal of his compensation and cancellation of his vocational training. "I have been unable to follow any work long enough to make anything like a living since my return from service," he protested. "It seems strange how those doctors can just give a man such little attention and report on his condition."[51]

In filing a claim for reinstatement of his compensation and continuation of his vocational training, West provided testimony from several laymen sympathetic and familiar with his condition. The owner of the shop where he had been in training stated that West "very often showed signs of suffering and at times was compelled to go home" in the middle of the workday. West's wife, his landlord, a boyhood neighbor, and a fellow veteran all agreed he had been unable to perform "manual labor more than half of the time" since his discharge and was, in fact, "totally incapacitated for such labor." Nonmedical testimony about his incapacity for the physically demanding unskilled or semiskilled occupations available to him seemed to West a convincing basis for his claim. But knowing that medical evidence carried particular weight with Bureau officials, he provided an affidavit by a local physician, stating that his heart problems "render the said soldier totally disable[d] for the performance of manual labor. He has to have an attendance [*sic*] with him all the time as he can not do anything of himself." All this evidence notwithstanding, in September 1925 a designated medical examiner found West's symptoms "entirely subjective" and denied his claim. Unwilling to accept either this decision or the medical conception of disability underlying it, West pursued his claim for several more years, but without success.

In the minds of veterans, their relatives, their neighbors, and fellow workers, disability remained a social concept, understood only partially in medical terms. Rather, it was a concept influenced by notions about an individual's prerogatives and obligations toward his dependents, his local community, and the state. At its root were expectations about the level of assistance and the rewards a man should receive for a life of labor, moral integrity, and patriotic loyalty in a just and democratic society. Reinforcing these expectations, the men who filed for War Risk Insurance benefits had undergone the first nationwide conscription in American history. Because the state had compelled them to submit to the risk of disablement on the battlefield, they felt strongly that it should compensate them.

"I can't work to support my family and I now feel that I am intitled [*sic*] to some means of support," explained Everett Taylor, a white farmer from Grand Saline in northeast Texas who was diagnosed with mitral stenosis, a narrowing of heart passages. A month later and still not better, he felt even more convinced of the justice of his claims: "I feel that I am worthy, and am entitled to everything that can be done for me." Charles Geter, the veteran from Augusta, protested the termination of his compensation by explaining that he could not return to his prewar occupation as an iron molder, "as the Forman [*sic*] which I was with for six years before enlisting in service says he will not employ me as he knows I am not able to work." Many disabled veterans thought themselves incapable of working, especially full time and in the low-skilled manual occupations to which their limited education and the structure of local economies often restricted them. Veterans who did consider themselves capable of working knew that disparaging images of disabled people harbored by employers and other workers reduced their job opportunities. While they did not call for laws banning workplace discrimination, they did insist that War Risk Insurance fulfill its purpose of allowing a disabled veteran to withdraw from the labor market and yet support his dependents in dignity if the obstacles to employment proved too high.[52]

In their claims, veterans conflated notions about their social roles and responsibilities with the specific social relations in which they lived, relations shaped by the availability and nature of work in particular localities, prevailing standards of living, and the needs of dependents. "The Bureau is in no position to ascertain the true merits of all claims, due to their ignorance of local conditions," declared the Union, South Carolina, American Legion Post. Its members resolved that "all claims for disability presented by veterans of the World War be first referred to a designated committee of the Local Post . . . for investigation; and that the findings of said committee shall be final and conclusive as to the merits of the case." Other veterans similarly complained about "paper ratings" made in the Bureau's fourteen district offices far from a claimant's place of residence, ratings based on written reports of medical examinations alone. Decentralization of claims adjudication to some one hundred regional offices in 1924 eased such complaints but never answered them fully.[53]

Veterans believed that identification and assessment of disability required personal knowledge of the particular social context in which a person lived: his family, community, and economic options. Compared to such knowledge and evidence, centralized medical or administrative authority was at best irrelevant, at worst the cause of injustice. Claimants and their allies collected evidence that focused on their capacity to conform to work and family roles sanctioned by society, using medical testimony if available but moving beyond the medical paradigm of disability as necessary.

The resolution adopted by the American Legion's Union Post had no effect; Veterans Bureau physicians and administrators retained all authority to rule on claims. Nonetheless, arguments that ability to work required consideration not just of medical indicators but also of labor markets and employment practices proved hard to dismiss. They emerged time and time again in adjudication of claims. Often, the very officials charged with administering benefits articulated these arguments. In 1921, the assistant director of the Veterans Bureau, who had complained of excessive secrecy about the rating schedule, criticized disability ratings as "based upon narrow professional medical analysis, rather than upon what the [War Risk Insurance] Act calls for—industrial disability," the inability of people with impairments to find stable, well-paying jobs. He urged revision of the table, "not only by doctors, but by a committee to consist of at least one attorney, some laymen and if possible a practical business man." Almost two decades after World War I, this tension remained unresolved. As a review of Veterans Administration procedures by the U.S. Attorney General's office pointed out in the late 1930s, "the complaint is somewhat general [among claimants] that the Administration tends to rely too heavily on medical evidence, . . . at the expense of other types of evidence, such as that submitted by the veteran's fellow members in the community." The report concluded that "affidavits of laymen in the veteran's community attesting to his total inability to work are often dismissed without discussion in the face of a . . . medical report which finds no serious disease."[54]

Disability was at once a medical construct established by physicians and a social construct established by legislators, administrators, and veterans within the social relations of labor, families, and local communities. The nature and implications of this ambivalent meaning became most evident in the adjudication of black veterans' claims. Racial segregation and hierarchy were integral to the social relations within which disability was diagnosed, interpreted, and experienced, most obviously in the South. The welfare policies adopted to benefit World War I veterans sought to bolster both the well-being and the racial privilege of white veterans.

During the war, black leaders such as W. E. B. DuBois had called on black Americans to "close ranks" and stand behind the nation's war effort, expecting that loyalty in wartime would give them an undeniable claim to full citizenship. Heeding this call, black Americans participated fully in the war effort. But their patriotism did not have the effect DuBois had expected. Determined to maintain patterns of racial subordination during the upheaval of war, white Americans aggressively asserted their racial supremacy, most dramatically through violent "race riots" and lynchings. Congress, controlled by southern Democrats, and the Wilson administration, led by the first southern-born president since the Civil War, further exacerbated racial tension and inequity by enforcing segregation throughout the federal government and the new conscript army and by opposing antilynching laws.[55]

Given the depth of officially sanctioned racial animosity under the Wilson and subsequent Republican administrations, it is unsurprising that the distribution of disability benefits became racially biased as well. Disability benefits paid to black veterans could potentially undermine racial inequality rooted in labor markets, income distribution, and the relationship between the state and racially defined groups of citizens. Compensation could amount to several times the $30 a month black agricultural laborers earned in the South and could more than equal the $500 to $600 annual income of black families in small southern towns.[56] Benefits enabled black disabled veterans to forgo poorly paid, menial jobs; gave them a measure of financial independence; and conferred on them a status of clients of government services equal to that of white veterans. For these reasons, such compensation became controversial and enmeshed in the politics of racial subordination, especially in the South, where four out of five black veterans lived. While fewer than half of all veterans who sought compensation received it, the very claim of black disabled veterans was often contested.

Veterans Bureau physicians and administrators defined disability with reference to medical characteristics they thought innate to each race and that distinguished racial groups of veterans from one another. In particular, white physicians interpreted the increased mortality rate of black Americans since emancipation as a sign of both congenital weakness and lack of self-discipline, which became apparent once they had been loosed from the medically and morally beneficial discipline of slavery.[57] Sharing this racial ideology of disease, Bureau physicians, for instance, contended that "tuberculosis is in the colored race as a whole" and that its progress "is usually much more rapid in negroes than whites, and the mortality much higher." Likewise, they attributed disability among "Spanish-American" veterans in New Mexico to "racial lack of stamina" that made them especially susceptible to the tuberculosis four in ten had contracted.[58]

Bureau officials neither had available nor felt a need for surveys that would have linked increased risk of tuberculosis among certain groups to housing conditions, medical care, or other environmental and social factors. Rather, most physicians took on faith the racial basis of disparities in infection and morbidity rates. These assumptions were pernicious because they tended to invalidate black veterans' claims: if disease derived from racial biology and congenital weakness, it was less likely to have originated in military service. Though not written explicitly into War Risk Insurance policy, these ideas shaped its local administration.[59]

Bureau officials in the South evoked racialized conceptions of disease to cast doubt on black veterans' claims, insinuating that these claims were dubious and needed careful screening. "The majority of the disabilities of the southern negro," falsely declared the manager of District 5 (the Carolinas,

Georgia, Florida, and Tennessee), "are traceable to venereal diseases, and, in the majority of instances, existed prior to enlistment." Disregarding that black veterans, like their white counterparts, predominantly claimed compensation for tuberculosis and neuropsychiatric disorders unrelated to venereal diseases, the official questioned the service origin of their disabilities. He also suggested that they likely resulted from the veterans' own culpable immoral behavior. Both findings served as official grounds for denial of benefits.[60]

Similarly, when a medical examiner diagnosed syphilis in Prince Willis, a black veteran living in Tuskegee, Alabama (location of the only Veterans Bureau hospital open to black patients), and recommended hospitalization, the district official dismissed the advice. Without himself examining Willis, he declared categorically that the "condition for which he is in need of treatment is not due to military service . . . [but] is due to claimant's own willful misconduct." Contrary to that ruling, in several cases the Bureau recognized syphilis as compensable because aggravated by military service. Syphilis, like all other diseases, required individual medical examination and etiologic study.[61] Such misconstruction and misadjudication of black veterans' claims drew on moral standards of responsible behavior with clear racial inflections and indicated the hostility many southern Veterans Bureau officials felt toward black veterans as clients of the nation-state. As one official reported, local Bureau of War Risk Insurance representatives in the South, "who are of course always white, will not, as a matter of principle, forward us all necessary evidence to complete the negro's claim. As a general rule, the fact that the claimant is a negro in their eyes is sufficient evidence that he is not in need of Government assistance."[62]

Black claimants understood best the combined effect of unofficial but pervasive discrimination and a racialized understanding of disability. James E. Sanford, who received vocational rehabilitation at Hampton Institute in Virginia, said that his interactions with local designated medical examiners and Bureau physicians, all of them white, "convinced [him] that . . . not one cares to serve the colored men." He charged that physicians received black veterans in their offices only on certain days and only at night, after they had served all white patients. Demeaning as such rituals of racial discrimination were, they were not as disconcerting as the "certian antimidation [*sic*]" "always . . . confronting a Colored man, when he makes an appeal for information or the request of an application blank for compensation." Such intimidation was "as constant, day and night, as the color of his flesh." Warning that the white official "to who the man applies, assumes the roll of judge and juror," Sanford concluded, "we are invariably received and treated as a colored man and not as a disabled soldier." Still, he refused to forgo the disability benefits to which he clearly felt entitled, and he "frequently" advised his black comrades on how to file compensation claims.[63]

The experience of War Risk Insurance shows that disability represents an inference made from an often uncertain medical finding of impairment (especially in cases of chronic disease and mental disorder), according to changing and socially contingent legal and administrative standards. As social constructs, disability and the standards by which it is inferred are deeply contested. Assertions of expert knowledge by Veterans Bureau physicians, the bureaucratic and political imperatives that guided claims administrators in awarding benefits, and the self-images, needs, and social relations of the veterans themselves produced divergent, even irreconcilable conceptions of disability and friction in the administration of disability benefits. Workmen's compensation laws and Social Security Disability Insurance replicated this pattern.[64] Under those programs, too, examining physicians sought to devise medical criteria for measuring the degree of disablement and thus for regulating access to benefits. As Deborah Stone has pointed out, such criteria were "full of errors of reification and false precision."[65] Administrators sought to liberalize admission requirements in order to create a larger clientele of beneficiaries and justify annual appropriations. In the process, they devised regulations that attenuated medical standards of evidence and at times circumvented them altogether. Finally, claimants argued that their inability to work and provide for dependents arose from employment requirements, the structure of local labor markets, discrimination against workers perceived to be disabled, and racial inequality as much as from bodily or mental incapacity. They insisted on recognition of their claim to benefits even if a medical examination could not conclusively establish an impairment. Disability policy has yet to reconcile these conflicting perspectives.

NOTES

1. Historians of World War I, Progressivism, and twentieth-century social welfare have made only cursory references to War Risk Insurance as a progenitor of modern social and disability policy. See James Leiby, *A History of Social Welfare and Social Work in the United States* (New York: Columbia University Press, 1978), 158; Neil A. Wynn, *From Progressivism to Prosperity: World War I and American Society* (New York: Holmes

and Meier, 1986), 123; Claire H. Liachowitz, *Disability as a Social Construct: Legislative Roots* (Philadelphia: University of Pennsylvania Press, 1988), 33; Theda Skocpol, *Protecting Soldiers and Mothers: The Political Origins of Social Policy in the United States* (Cambridge: Harvard University Press, 1992), 632 n. 107. Deborah A. Stone, *The Disabled State* (Philadelphia: Temple University Press, 1984), 72-84, the best account of War Risk Insurance and its administration, is based largely on George J. Goldsborough, Jr., William G. Tinsley, and Arnold C. Sternberg, *The Social Security Administration: An Inter-Disciplinary Study of Disability Evaluation*, 2 vols. (Washington, D.C.: George Washington University, 1963), which, despite claiming an interdisciplinary approach, is mainly a legal and case history of disability adjudication. Other surveys and studies of welfare policy ignore War Risk Insurance entirely. See Michael B. Katz, *In the Shadow of the Poorhouse: A Social History of Welfare in America* (1986; rev. ed., New York: Basic Books, 1996); James T. Patterson, *America's Struggle against Poverty, 1900–1994* (Cambridge: Harvard University Press, 1994); Edward D. Berkowitz and Kim McQuaid, *Creating the Welfare State: The Political Economy of the Twentieth-Century Reform* (rev. ed., Lawrence: University of Kansas Press, 1992).

2. For a discussion of medical and social conceptions of disability in the context of industrial capitalism, see Michael Oliver, *Understanding Disability: From Theory to Practice* (New York: St. Martin's Press, 1996), 32–52; Michael Oliver, *The Politics of Disablement: A Sociological Approach* (New York: St. Martin's Press, 1990), 46–94; Colin Barnes, "Theories of Disability and the Origins of the Oppression of Disabled People in Western Society," in *Disability and Society: Emerging Issues and Insights*, ed. Len Barton (London: Longman, 1996), 43–57; Simi Linton, *Claiming Disability: Knowledge and Identity* (New York: New York University Press, 1998); and Rosemarie Garland Thomson, *Extraordinary Bodies: Figuring Physical Disability in American Culture and Literature* (New York: Columbia University Press, 1997), 37–50. For the contest over definition in administration of workmen's compensation and Social Security Disability Insurance see Stone, *Disabled State*, 90–139; Edward D. Berkowitz, *Disabled Policy: America's Programs for the Handicapped* (Cambridge: Cambridge University Press, 1987), 20–40, 105–51; Martha Derthick, *Policymaking for Social Security* (Washington, D.C.: Brookings Institution, 1979), 302–12.

3. Number of claims for disability compensation in *Annual Report of the Director, United States Veterans Bureau, 1923* (Washington, D.C.: Government Printing Office [hereafter GPO], 1923), 1; for this and the next paragraph on Charles M. Geter: "Supervision Reports"; Geter to Sub-District Manager, Savannah, May 4, 1923; Geter to [U.S. Veterans Bureau] Insurance Division, Sept. 19, 1925, all in file "Geter, Charles M.," box 22, Regional Office Training Case File, 1918–1928, Records of the Veterans Administration, Record Group (hereafter RG) 15, National Archives, Washington, D.C. (hereafter Sample Training Case File).

4. For the text of the War Risk Insurance Act, passed October, 6, 1917, see 40 *Statutes at Large*, 398. For its compensation provision, see *The War Risk Insurance Act,*

with Amendments prior to April 1, 1923 (Washington, D.C.: GPO, 1925). For a detailed discussion of the War Risk Insurance Act as a progenitor of modern social provision in the United States, see K. Walter Hickel, "Entitling Citizens: World War I, Progressivism, and the Origins of the American Welfare State, 1917–1928" (Ph.D. diss., Columbia University, 1999).

5. Elizabeth G. Upham, "The Absorption of Handicapped Labor into Industry," *Vocational Summary* 2 (July 1919): 44–45. For the dislocation of labor markets and patterns of employment that shaped the economic and social context for wartime disability provision, see William J. Breen, *Labor Market Politics and the Great War: The Department of Labor, the States, and the First U.S. Employment Service, 1907–1933* (Kent: Kent State University Press, 1997); Joseph A. McCartin, *Labor's Great War: The Struggle for Industrial Democracy and the Origins of Modern American Labor Relations, 1912–1921* (Chapel Hill: University of North Carolina Press, 1997); David Brody, *Labor in Crisis: The Steel Strike of 1919* (New York: Harper & Row, 1966); and Carol Marks, *Farewell— We're Good and Gone: The Great Black Migration* (Bloomington: Indiana University Press, 1989), 80–136.

6. By 1924, twenty-three hundred of the thirty-five thousand former members of the Army and Navy Nurse Corps, as well as the all-female Navy "Yeomanettes," had applied for compensation, half of whom had their claims recognized. Three hundred female military personnel had died in the war, and their survivors were drawing compensation as well. See Frank T. Hines to General Federation of Women's Clubs, Sept. 8, 1924, 2, file "[Compensation and Claims] September 1924," box 88, Directors' Files, 1917–1934, Records of the Veterans Administration, RG 15, National Archives, Washington, D.C. (hereafter Directors' Files).

7. If a serviceman died from such injury or disease or became incapacitated compensation from $25 to $75 was to go to his dependents, calculated according to their number and relationship to the soldier. For example, the widow was to receive compensation of $25 monthly until her death or remarriage if she had no children and up to $52.50 if she had four children or more.

8. The rate for permanent total disability was lower than the maximum rate for temporary disability because the War Risk Insurance Act provided for additional (though voluntary) insurance up to $10,000 in coverage in cases of such permanent total disability.

9. William H. Glasson, *Federal Military Pensions in the United States* (New York: Oxford University Press, 1918); James W. Trent, Jr., *Inventing the Feeble Mind: A History of Mental Retardation in the United States* (Berkeley: University of California Press, 1994); *Report* no. 741, "Transfer of Freedmen's Hospital," Committee on Education and Labor, 87th Cong., 1st sess., July 19, 1961, 2; Frank Rives Millikan, "Wards of the Nation: The Making of St. Elizabeth's Hospital, 1852–1920" (Ph.D. diss., George Washington University, 1990).

10. Seth Koven, "Remembering and Dismemberment: Crippled Children, Wounded

Soldiers, and the Great War in Britain," *American Historical Review* 99 (October 1994): 1175-76. On the nineteenth-century understanding of disability and its gradual change, see also Stone, *Disabled State*, 90-97; Douglas C. Baynton, *Forbidden Signs: American Culture and the Campaign against Sign Language* (Chicago: University of Chicago Press, 1996), 15-26, 34-38; Philip M. Ferguson, *Abandoned to Their Fate: Social Policy and Practice towards Severely Retarded People in America, 1820-1920* (Philadelphia: Temple University Press, 1994), 5-7, 32-34, 50-60, 98-104, 113-16. Ferguson stresses that severely retarded people gained little from the reconceptualization and medicalization of their disability and remained isolated in asylums.

11. How many veterans had their compensation claims denied on the grounds of willful misconduct is not clear from available statistics.

12. This and the following paragraph are largely based on Nancy Fraser and Linda Gordon, "A Genealogy of *Dependency*: Tracing a Keyword of the U.S. Welfare State," *Signs* 19 (Winter 1994): 319-23.

13. For a systematic elaboration of gender distinction in Progressive social policy, see Skocpol, *Protecting Soldiers and Mothers*, 155-479.

14. Stone, *Disabled State*, 97-99; Berkowitz and McQuaid, *Creating the Welfare State*, 46.

15. Samuel McCune Lindsay, "Soldiers' Insurance versus Pensions," *American Review of Reviews* (October 1917): 402. Under the General Law Pension System established in 1862, Union veterans received monthly payments for service-related permanent total disability—defined as inability to perform any kind of manual labor—ranging from $8 to $30, as well as for a number of enumerated disabilities such as loss of limbs, according to military rank. Rates were raised steadily over the following decades, until by World War I pensions ranged from $24 a month for disability "equivalent to the loss of a hand or a foot," to $30 for inability to perform manual labor, to $55 for the loss of an arm at the shoulder, to $72 for such a degree of helplessness as to require the regular aid of an attendant, to $100 for blindness or the loss of both arms or feet. See Glasson, *Federal Military Pension*, 132, 267, 270. The substantially lower rate for inability to perform physical labor than for loss of an arm represented the kind of inconsistency in the pension system Progressive reformers and War Risk Insurance proponents criticized.

16. On the increasingly complex, adversarial, and legalistic process by which disability claims were negotiated under state workmen's compensation laws, despite the premise that these laws would make litigation unnecessary, see Walter F. Dodd, *Administration of Workmen's Compensation* (New York: The Commonwealth Fund, 1936), 214-337; Berkowitz, *Disabled Policy*, 20-30.

17. Number of disallowed compensation claims calculated from figures in *Annual Report of the Director, United States Veterans Bureau, 1924* (Washington, D.C.: GPO, 1924), 14. More than 237,000 veterans were drawing compensation by 1924. Average monthly disability compensation was $37, the average compensation payment to survivors, $25.

18. On the role of physicians in expansion of disability benefits after World War II, see Stone, *Disabled State*, 148–52; quotation from Federal Board of Vocational Education, *Fifth Annual Report* (Washington, D.C.: GPO, 1921), 29.

19. Federal Board of Vocational Education, *Fifth Annual Report*, 29.

20. Figures on medical examiners in R[ichard] G. Cholmeley-Jones [director of the Bureau of War Risk Insurance] to Royal Meeker, Feb. 26, 1921, 7, file "General Activities," box 6, Directors' Files; figure on staff physicians from "Report of Conference of District Managers, Chiefs, Medical Divisions, Chiefs, Rehabilitation Divisions," Sept. 18–22, 1922, transcript of proceedings, 15, box 39, Directors' Files. In one year, July 1921–July 1922, Veterans Bureau designated medical examiners and staff physicians conducted 387,747 examinations of veterans; see "Medical Division," June 15 [*sic*], 1922, 4, file "Speeches—General, 1922," box 42, Directors' Files.

21. Moreover, a veteran would forfeit his compensation for as long as he refused to submit to a periodic medical examination, administered to confirm that he continued to have a disability. The claimant also could be asked to submit "to any reasonable medical or surgical treatment" that might alleviate his disability. If he refused, his compensation was not affected, but he could not claim additional compensation for any resulting deterioration in his condition.

22. Charles R. Forbes, in "Report of Conference of District Managers," 15.

23. E. O. Grossman to Director [Veterans Bureau], May 7, 1925, file "Ratings," box 111, Directors' Files.

24. Information on medical referees in *Annual Report of the Director, United States Veterans Bureau, 1924*, 37; on establishment and composition of Claims and Ratings Boards, see Section 7151, attached to U.S. Veterans Bureau, Regulation no. 74, Aug. 12, 1924, file "Claims—General, August 1924," box 88, Directors' Files. Paul Starr, *The Social Transformation of American Medicine: The Rise of a Sovereign Profession and the Making of a Vast Industry* (New York: Basic Books, 1982); Rosemary Stevens, *American Medicine and the Public Interest: A History of Specialization* (rev. ed, Berkeley: University of California Press, 1998); and James G. Burrow, *Organized Medicine in the Progressive Era: The Move towards Monopoly* (Baltimore: Johns Hopkins University Press, 1977), do not mention the role of physicians in administering disability compensation for World War I veterans or workmen's compensation. Dodd, *Administration of Workmen's Compensation*, 295–303, 409–18, details the role of physicians in monitoring occupational health, in diagnosing work-related health problems for purposes of awarding workmen's compensation, and as expert witnesses in workmen's compensation litigation but does not relate this role to the professional authority and identity of physicians.

25. Cholmeley-Jones to Meeker, 2, 12; Frank T. Hines to Victor Berger, Dec. 28, 1926, file "Adjudication Service," box 126, Directors' Files; Leon Fraser, "Memorandum for the Director," July 2, 1921, 2, file "Medical Division, 1920–21," box 26, Directors' Files.

26. I am indebted to Edward Berkowitz for pointing out this analogy. For a de-

scription of the debate over the publication of disability standards under Social Security Disability Insurance, see Stone, *Disabled State*, 120–22.

27. *The United States Veterans' Administration Schedule for Rating Disabilities*, 2d. ed. (Washington, D.C.: GPO, 1933), 3.

28. "Medical Division, U.S. Veterans' Bureau," draft of speech, June 28, 1922, file "Speeches—General, 1922," box 42, Directors' Files.

29. Garrard Harris, *The Redemption of the Disabled: A Study of Programmes of Rehabilitation for the Disabled of War and of Industry* (New York: D. Appleton, 1919), 189.

30. Jerry L. Mashaw, "The Definition of Disability from the Perspective of Administration," in *Disability Policies and Government Programs*, ed. Edward D. Berkowitz (New York: Praeger, 1978), 167.

31. According to the original act, application for compensation had to be made one year after discharge—unless the veteran procured a medical certificate within the year stating that at the time of discharge he had already sustained an injury or contracted a disease likely to result in disability or death—but not later than five years after discharge. Once the veteran had secured such a certificate, he or his survivors could apply for compensation within five years of the onset of disability or of his death. These restrictions once again distinguished compensation from the pension system, which allowed claims decades after the soldiers' discharge, a policy the framers of the War Risk Insurance Act thought had contributed to the corruption of the system. Later amendments to the act, however, liberalized stipulations for filing claims, and veterans brought claims throughout the 1920s.

32. "Medico-Military Activities during World War to July 1920," n.d., 7, file "Medical Division, 1920–1921," box 26, Directors' Files.

33. Harris, *Redemption of the Disabled*, 59.

34. *Annual Report of the Director, United States Veterans Bureau, 1926* (Washington, D.C: GPO, 1926), 243, table 68.

35. The nearly forty-six thousand cases of tuberculosis among recipients in 1925 constituted 21.7 percent of all compensation cases; while neuropsychiatric disorders accounted for 21.1 percent of compensable cases. *Annual Report of the Director, United States Veterans Bureau, 1925* (Washington, D.C.: GPO, 1925), 20. The World War Veterans Act, June 7, 1924 (43 *Statutes at Large*, 607), made the presumption of service origin rebuttable by "clear and convincing evidence" in the case of neuropsychiatric impairment, but the presumption remained in place with bureau physicians bearing the burden to prove that such impairment was *not* of service origin. The act also created a conclusive presumption of service origin for spinal meningitis and a rebuttable presumption for paralysis agitans, encephalitis lethargica, and amoebic dysentery, all diseases whose etiology perplexed physicians. Stipulations reviewed in Frank T. Hines to Senator Frank B. Willis, Nov. 26, 1927, 3, file "Adjudication Service," box 126, Director's Files.

36. Gustavus A. Weber and Laurence F. Schmeckebier, *The Veterans' Administration:*

Its History, Activities and Organization (Washington, D.C.: The Brookings Institution, 1934), 131–32; proportion of compensation payments to tuberculous veterans given in Hines to Willis, 3.

37. Recognizing the windfall of compensation that veterans with these enumerated diseases, and especially with tuberculosis, stood to gain, Hines warned that "Congress must necessarily expect from sources outside the Bureau strenuous effort to secure special consideration for those veterans having other injuries and diseases than those covered by the special statutory provisions of the law." See Hines to Willis, 4.

38. Charles R. Forbes, "Memorandum for Assistant Director, in Charge of Compensation and Insurance Claims Division," June 15, 1921, file "Chief [Compensation and Claims Division]," box 21, Directors' Files. For the role of veterans organizations, especially the American Legion, in pressuring the Veterans Bureau to award benefits more generously and relax evidentiary standards, see Katherine Mayo, *Soldiers What Next!* (New York: Houghton Mifflin, 1934), 50–66, 148–77; William Pencak, *For God and Country: The American Legion, 1919–1941* (Boston: Northeastern University Press, 1989), 171–89.

39. "Address of General Frank T. Hines at the Fifth Annual Convention of the Disabled Veterans of the World War," June 24, 1925, 12, file 060.01, box 106, Directors' Files.

40. *Annual Report of the Director, United States Veterans Bureau, 1924*, 15–16; *Annual Report of the Director, United States Veterans Bureau, 1925*, 21. Further resulting from this regulation, permanent disability ratings (total and partial) increased from 19 percent of all ratings on June 30, 1923, to 49 percent two years later, ensuring that a greater number of veterans would draw compensation for a longer period of time, and often for life.

41. Cholmeley-Jones to Meeker, 10–11; Section 13c, U.S. Veterans Bureau Form 526—Revised February, 1928, "Application for Compensation of Veteran Disabled in the World War," copy in box VB 2, Veterans Bureau, 1921–1930, Publications of the U.S. Government, RG 287, National Archives, Washington, D.C.

42. Cholmeley-Jones to Meeker, 10–11.

43. *Annual Report of the Director, United States Veterans Bureau, 1925*, 20. Despite the large number of veterans with neuropsychiatric disorders, the Veterans Bureau offered them only limited services. None of the U.S. Public Health Service and naval hospitals that the Bureau of War Risk Insurance took over between 1919 and 1921 and converted to use as World War I veterans hospitals specialized in psychiatric treatment. Veterans requiring such care had no option but to seek admission to the Bureau's general hospitals, where they were informally placed in improvised psychiatric wards without sufficient trained personnel and appropriate resources. Not until the second half of the 1920s did the Bureau began to build officially designated psychiatric hospitals for the care and institutionalization of veterans with neuropsychiatric impairments.

44. On the development of psychiatry after the turn of the century, see Gerald N. Grob, *Mental Illness and American Society, 1875–1940* (Princeton: Princeton University Press, 1983), 108-43; and Elizabeth Lunbeck, *The Psychiatric Persuasion: Knowledge, Power, and Gender in Modern America* (Princeton: Princeton University Press, 1994), 46-77; on images of venereal disease at the time of World War I, see Allan M. Brandt, *No Magic Bullet: A Social History of Venereal Disease in the United States since 1880* (New York: Oxford University Press, 1987), 115-21.

45. These and other criteria are included on a form used in compensation claims procedures by the Bureau of War Risk Insurance, titled "Preliminary Neuro-Psychological Examination"; copy in file "Storm, Burton H.," box 32, Sample Training Case File.

46. E. O. Grossman to Director [Veterans Bureau], Dec. 3, 1924, 2, file "[Compensation and Claims] Dec. 1924," box 85, Directors' Files.

47. [J. H. Evans], "The Training of Youths with Low Mental Capacity," n. d., 3, 5, file "J. H. Evans," box 24, Executive Office General Correspondence, 1919-1924, Rehabilitation Division records, Records of the Veterans Administration, RG 15, National Archives, Washington, D.C. (hereafter Rehabilitation Division records).

48. Dr. F. M. Barnes, "N. P. Considerations in Advisement," *Rehabilitation Manual, District 9* (St. Louis: n.p., 1923), 5, copy in box 2, Miscellaneous File, 1919-1925, Rehabilitation Division records.

49. Frank T. Hines to Joe Sparks, March 21, 1923, 2, file "Ratings," box 68, Directors' Files; Charles R. Forbes to Adjutant, American Legion, Louisiana, Oct. 27, 1921, file "District No. 6," box 31, Directors' Files.

50. J. Altheus Johnson to Director [Veterans Bureau], February 1924, 1, "Col. Boughton's File," box 89, Directors' Files.

51. For this and the following paragraph, see Craig West to Department Bureau War Risk Insurance [Veterans Bureau], April 4, 1924; affidavits; and examination reports all in file "West, Craig," box 29, Sample Training Case File.

52. Everett Taylor to Karl C. Kunsenmueller, Dec. 20, 1923; and Everett Taylor to W. R. Lee, Jan. 18, 1924, 3, both in file "Taylor, Everett Lee," box 74, Sample Training Case File. (Taylor's file contains numerous letters in which he complained about delay or nonreceipt of compensation payments.) Geter to Sub-District Manager; and Geter to Insurance Division. Since compensation was a gratuity, it was not adjudicable in court; veterans could challenge rulings on their compensation claims only through formal appeal to the District and Central Boards of Appeal.

53. Resolution cited in Frank T. Hines to Commander, Union Post No. 22, Feb. 2, 1924, 1, file "Claimants, General Material, Jan., Feb., 1924," box 88, Directors' Files; discussion of "paper ratings" in *Annual Report of the Director, United States Veterans Bureau, 1924,* 3.

54. Fraser, "Memorandum for the Director," 2; Attorney General's Committee on Administrative Procedure, "The Veterans' Administration," n.d. [1939-1940], 46, copy in box 128, Directors' Files.

55. Mark Ellis, "'Closing Ranks' and 'Seeking Honors': W. E. B. DuBois in World War I," *Journal of American History* 79 (June 1992): 96–124; Emmett J. Scott, *Scott's Official History of the American Negro in the World War* (1919; reprint, New York: Arno Press, 1969); Desmond King, *Separate and Unequal: Black Americans and the US Federal Government* (New York: Oxford University Press, 1995), 9–35; William B. Tuttle, Jr., *Race Riot: Chicago in the Red Summer of 1919* (New York: Atheneum, 1970); Claudine L. Ferrel, *Nightmare and Dream: Antilynching in Congress, 1917–1922* (New York: Garland Publishing, 1986).

56. Gilbert C. Fite, *Cotton Fields No More: Southern Agriculture, 1865–1980* (Lexington: University of Kentucky Press, 1984), 98; Ruth Reed, *The Negro Women of Gainesville, Georgia* (Athens: Phelps-Stokes Fellowship Publications, n.d. [1920]), 30.

57. John S. Haller, Jr., *Outcasts from Evolution: Scientific Attitudes of Racial Inferiority, 1859–1900* (1971; reprint, Carbondale: Southern Illinois University Press, 1995), 40–60, 176–77; George M. Fredrickson, *The Black Image in the White Mind: The Debate on Afro-American Character and Destiny, 1817–1914* (1971; reprint, Middlebury: Wesleyan University Press, 1987), 228–55.

58. Dr. H. A. Pattison to R. G. Cholmeley-Jones, Sept. 28, 1920, 4, file "Tuberculosis Section, 1917-1921," box 30, Directors' Files; Federal Board of Vocational Education, *Fourth Annual Report* (Washington, D.C.: GPO, 1920), 351, 349.

59. The Veterans Bureau did not compile statistics on the filing and rejection of claims by the claimant's race. Still, evidence from Veterans Bureau files, though anecdotal, indicates that the racial identity of a claimant figured prominently in the adjudication of his disability claim.

60. M. Bryson to Asst. Director [Rehabilitation Division], March 23, 1921, 1, box 104, District Files, 1918-1925, Rehabilitation Division records, Records of the Veterans Administration, RG 15, National Archives Regional Branch, East Point, Georgia.

61. Veterans Bureau director Hines told the director of the New York Department of Health, Division of Venereal Disease, that "venereal diseases not innocently acquired exclude a claimant from medical care and treatment as well as from compensation," but veterans "whose condition was noted at the time of enlistment and was aggravated by stress of service (as distinguished from the natural progress of the disease) are entitled to benefits." See Frank T. Hines to Dr. Joseph S. Lawrence, Jan. 22, 1924, 1, file "Claimants, General Material, Jan., Feb., 1924," box 88, Directors' Files. Veterans who acquired a venereal disease through sexual contact with their wives while they were in military service were entitled to benefits as well. Venereal disease clearly did not allow summary judgment but had to be examined in the light of each case.

62. Relief Officer, District 6, to Manager, Montgomery, Alabama, Sub-District, May 17, 1923, file "Willis, Prince," box 31, Sample Training Case Files; George Fell to G. F. Saxton, Sept. 21, 1920, file "Investigation Division, Aug.–Dec., 1920," box 33, Directors' Files. To understand better the impact of racial imagery on disability claims adjudication, one might consider Jerry Mashaw's explanation that it "is quite

K. Walter Hickel

easy to imagine . . . social conditioning that would induce a belief that white, male family heads have strong attachments to the work ethic. That belief would quite likely create a propensity for deciders [claims adjudicators] to treat the disability claims of this group of applicants as peculiarly credible. If one assumes . . . that the disability judgment depends in large part on whether the claimant has tried or is willing to try 'hard enough' to be self-sustaining, then being black or female could very easily turn out to be an influential factor in disability determinations." See Mashaw, "Definition of Disability," 162–63.

63. All quotations in this and the following paragraph from James E. Sanford to Dr. J. R. A. Crossland, Nov. 10, 1921, box 1, Correspondence of J. R. A. Crossland, Negro Section, Training Sub-Division, Rehabilitation Division records.

64. On the tension between medical diagnostics as a means of restricting access to Social Security Disability Insurance benefits and the legal, political, and economic dynamics toward an expansion of these benefits, see Berkowitz, *Disabled Policy*, 105–51, and Stone, *Disabled State*, 107–86.

65. Stone, *Disabled State*, 116.

10

Helen Keller and the Politics of Civic Fitness

Kim Nielsen

Helen Keller is a historical figure known around the globe, whose story tends to begin and often end with the moment when Anne Sullivan pumped water onto the seven-year-old girl's hand and the manual alphabet became Keller's main means of communication.[1] The Helen Keller who appeared at rallies of striking workers seems like a different person. The iconography that maintains our shared cultural memories of her generally omits her political life and politicized activities, particularly her interest in radicalism and her critique of capitalism. Born in 1880, Keller first considered politics during her years at Radcliffe College, 1900–1905.[2] She remained an active and visible participant in the American left until the early 1920s, when she was in her early forties. Her interest in socialism began when she read H. G. Wells's utopian novel *New Worlds for Old*. Then, under the intellectual guidance of John Macy, a Harvard lecturer and the spouse of her teacher Anne Sullivan Macy, she went on to read more about politics. Joining the Socialist Party of America in 1909, she became an advocate of female suffrage, a defender of the radical Industrial Workers of the World, and a supporter of birth control and assistance for the unemployed. She criticized World War I as a profit-making venture for industrialists and urged working-class men to resist the war. She supported striking workers and jailed dissidents and expressed passionate views about the need for a just and economically equitable society. She blamed industrialization and poverty for many of the disabilities of the American working class. Speaking before the U.S. Senate Foreign Relations Committee in 1921, she encouraged diplomatic recognition of the newly created and highly controversial Soviet Union.[3] She called on the nation's political leaders to consider her opinions.

Helen Keller insisted she was a good citizen. As such, she felt she had the right and obligation to participate in the civic realm—to have and express political opinions, to attempt to convince others of those opinions, to be a public presence, and to vote. Her political participation presumed her own civic fitness. But being born a white woman did not guarantee to her the citizenship she desired. Citizenship is a legal status of rights and obligations shaped by such factors as gender, race, class, sexuality, and our bodies. At the same time, it is a mutable and participatory state of being. One can be a good citizen, a bad citizen, a full or second-class citizen.[4] It is in the civic realm that the quality and nature of one's citizenship are assessed.

Until her death in 1968, Keller encountered the common beliefs that she was disqualified from civic life and full expressions of citizenship not only by her gender but, even more, by her disability. These ideas of "civic fitness"—historical and cultural definitions of who is fit for civic life and the relationship of those definitions to our bodies—shaped her political life. Adopting varying strategies and political choices in her efforts to claim civic fitness, Keller had to remain ever mindful of the fluid politics of the body that policed the boundaries and possibilities of her civic action. Her citizenship was limited not by her disability but by the ways in which contemporary society interpreted her disability. Her claims to civic fitness were frustrated by a set of cultural values that deemed the disabled body unable to meet the individual and personal demands of a body politic that depended on self-government, self-determination, and individual autonomy. Had she been male, her claims to civic fitness would still have been sifted through these societal interpretations of disability, but differently. In the eyes and laws of the society in which she lived, Keller's gender and disability, taken together, virtually nullified much of her citizenship status.

By her political expressions, Keller indicated that she assumed herself fit for participation in civic life; yet she did acknowledge external and internal limitations on that participation. But those limitations were not her deafness or blindness. In her political writings from approximately 1900 to the mid-1920s, the limitation she acknowledged was that of being female—the *gendered* body. When protesting the arrest and conviction of a defender of union activists, she discussed the tenuousness of her political participation by saying, "I have arrived at this conclusion with some hesitancy. For a mere woman, denied participation in government, must needs speak timidly of the mysterious mental processes of men."[5] Discussing her reluctance to speak about the conditions of poverty that contributed to blindness, she wrote:

Moreover, the subject was one of which a young woman might be supposed to be ignorant, and upon which, certainly, she would not be expected to speak with authority. It is always painful to set one's self against tradition, especially against the conventions and prejudices that hedge about womanhood.[6]

Though Keller acknowledged that the barriers rooted in her gender caused her to hesitate in her civic expressions, she insisted that it should not be so. Just as paternity did not "incapacitate" the bodies of men for citizenship, she argued that the possibility of maternity should not render women's bodies unfit for citizenship.[7] She failed to mention the citizenship of the disabled body.

The identity politics Keller tried to espouse was gender based. Leaning toward a gender essentialism, she argued that women had unique knowledge, responsibilities, and skills that gave them political energy. This sense of obligation and mission was common among the early generations of female college students in the United States.[8] She argued that if given the vote, women would "use the ballot to prevent war and to destroy the ideas that make war possible."[9] Women, as "the natural conservationists," needed to "face questions that men alone have evidently not been quite able to solve."[10] Women could do this, Keller insisted, because they had a stronger "social consciousness" than men; consequently, many social problems could be solved "only with the help of women's social experience."[11] In her effort to position herself as a political actor who centered her political identity in her gender, Keller joined a wide array of early twentieth-century female activists. Her declaration that "woman's place is still in the household. But the household is more spacious than in times gone by" echoed the sentiments of many other women interested in the tasks of politicized domesticity.[12] In this period many women, from a wide political spectrum, used gender-based arguments to justify and explain their political sensibilities and to claim civic fitness.[13]

Perhaps Keller embraced a gender-based political identity strategically, to claim civic fitness by acknowledging the metaphorical disability of gender rather than the physical impairments of blindness and deafness, because she thought this would least limit her. By claiming a *gendered* body, she may have sought to seize control of how she defined herself and others defined her. Again, however, in the eyes and laws of the society in which she lived she was not simply female, for she embodied both a gender and a disability status.

When Helen Keller referred to her disability, she claimed it as a source of her civic awareness but did so in ways that implicitly undercut disability as a viable political category for both herself and others. Consider, for example, her views concerning the connection between citizenship and work. Male claims to full citizenship derived in significant measure from men's paid productive employment, whereas economically dependent individuals were deemed disqualified from citizenship. Common prejudices thus regarded blind people as civically unfit because they presumably could not work. Keller's own work as a writer and public speaker not only was very important to her, as meaningful work is for many people, but she used it as a tool to claim full and equal citizenship. Work also gave her a means to distinguish herself from the many unemployed blind people who were devalued by society as unproductive and dependent. For example, in 1907 she wrote that it was "our part" to train blind men in the ways of business.[14] At the same time, like other advocates for blind people throughout the twentieth century, she sought to refute the biases that blind people were incapable of paid employment and therefore incompetent for full citizenship. In 1904 she argued that the "idle adult blind" were "citizens" who were "a public or a private burden, a bad debt, an object of pitying charity, and an economic loss." But work would raise blind people from "dependence to self-respecting citizenship" and allow them to become "useful blind people." Therefore, states and other civic entities could best help blind people by establishing employment agencies and work training programs. She suggested that state agencies encourage the public to employ blind individuals as "piano tuners, notepaper embossers, shampooers, masseurs, chairmakers, brushmakers, tutors, singers, church organists, tea tasters."[15] Efforts to free blind people from economic dependency would enable them to become good citizens.

But this strategy of embracing the culturally dominant assumption of a relationship between paid employment and good citizenship placed Keller in several quandaries at once. The distinction she drew between a useful and a dependent citizenry implied that unless and until blind people engaged in paid work, they were not and could not be good citizens. That dichotomy also undermined her own claims to civic participation, because she was not as economically self-sufficient as she desired and claimed to be. In the 1904 speech quoted above, she said that she had found "abundant work" and that it was a "blessedness." Keller had excelled in her college writing courses; the publication of *The Story of My Life* (her autobiography, as much as one can write an autobiography at twenty-three years of age) was a success; and she considered herself a professional writer. Yet the money she earned was not enough to support herself and Anne Sullivan in the fashion both desired, and so the pair had to depend on the philanthropy of the wealthy for their daily needs. Keller wanted to write on subjects other than her own disability, but editors tended to be uninterested in other subjects.[16] Money was a constant stress. Helen Keller was, in fact, not an economically self-sufficient citizen.

Keller's linkage of paid employment and good citizenship also was awkward because of the tangled knot of gender, race, class status, and disability. She tried to claim that, because she earned money, she was a good and useful citizen. Yet, for women, such a claim was complicated. In the framework of turn-of-the-century citizenship, productive and self-supporting work made men civic agents. In contrast, dependency implied virtue for able-bodied, middle-class white women. For able-bodied black and poor white women, dependency marked a problem to be fixed by work. For women with disabilities, regardless of color, dependency exaggerated and contributed to the interpretation of their disability as debilitating and socially discrediting.[17] Successful use of wage earning as a measurement of good citizenship might have aided Keller as an individual, but it reinforced her status as aberrant, in terms of her gender and class background, and distanced her from other people with disabilities. Furthermore, when she listed possible occupations for people with disabilities, she generally listed male trade occupations. What were women with disabilities to do? Their civic claims were complicated not only by their gender, and sometimes by their race, but also by the limited employment possibilities for many people with disabilities. Other white women and many black women used either actual or metaphorical maternalism to claim good citizenship. But this claim, too, was unavailable to many women with disabilities, because of the belief that they could not and should not bear children. Keller's 1904 assertion that her good citizenship rested on her economic independence was made when few options existed on which to base her citizenship claims.

While Keller asserted her qualification for full citizenship by declaring that her disability did not prevent her from achieving economic self-sufficiency, she also argued that her experience of disability in itself enhanced her civic fitness. For example, in a 1912 letter about striking mill women in Little Falls, New York, she wrote, "I, deaf and blind, have been helped to overcome many obstacles. I want them to be helped as generously in a struggle which resembles my own in many ways."[18] The solidarity she expressed with those in poverty, the empathy she felt for industrial workers, she partially credited to her disability. Her disability, she insisted, along with her well-trained mind and her female sensibility, gave her both political insight and a heightened awareness of human struggle. She made the same assertion when she titled her 1914 collection of political essays and speeches *Out of the Dark: Essays on Physical and Social Vision*. In other words, her disability uniquely enhanced her citizenship.[19]

This strategy had the serious limitation of grounding the claim for a disability-enhanced citizenship in a private experience of overcoming obstacles rather than in a politically understood shared experience of discrimination. Unlike late twentieth-century disability rights activists who asserted solidarity with other oppressed people because of comparable histories of oppression—a political experience—Keller asserted empathy with poor and working-class people due to a shared experience of overcoming—a physical and psychological experience. Because of the emotive and personal grounding of this claim to citizenship, the political insights she attributed to her disability left her little room for further political theorizing. She expressed empathy for the poor and the working class but could not go beyond this to suggest a shared *political* experience of oppression, unfulfilled citizenship, or the denial of rights. Nor did she ever suggest that the poor and the working class, grounded in their experiences of struggle, might understand issues of disability.

When Keller did try to politicize disability, she described it as a personal affliction spawned by social and economic injustices that produced physical impairment. She blamed impairments on the unsanitary tenements of urban poverty, unsafe and unregulated industrial conditions, and other economic inequalities. In this analysis, disability was not a political category of its own but a consequence of class inequalities. As long as "ignorance, poverty, and the unconscious cruelty of our commercial society" remained, she argued, "will there be blind and crippled men and women."[20] These impairments were preventable. They would be eliminated if the working class only had greater power. This analysis parallels Marx's assessment of the oppression of women under capitalism. He argued that the "real" problem was capitalism. As soon as capitalism was dismantled, the oppression of women and its accompanying problems would disappear. By taking this approach, Keller primarily focused on the evils of capitalism, and impairments appeared only as a by-product. She did not examine the socially constructed experience of disability. She did not call attention to societal prejudice and discrimination against people with disabilities. She did not assert that people with disabilities had rights. The community she called to action and indignation by politicizing the issue of disability was the working class, not people with disabilities. These efforts to politicize disability are interesting because her own disability was not related to urban poverty, industrial conditions, or any other economic inequality—rather, it was due to a feverlike illness and the limited medical resources available to her relatively well-to-do family in 1881. Nonetheless, her attempt to politicize disability should not be dismissed as the efforts of someone overly focused on economics. Instead, she appears to have been exploring, with only limited success, the political theorizing of disability while leaning heavily on the political insights of the radicalism with which she was most familiar. Keller never sought to use disability as a political category.

Her most frequent allusions to disabilities in this period occurred in accusations that not she but those indifferent to the problems of modern society were the truly disabled. In 1913 she asserted:

> It seems to me that they are blind indeed who do not see that there must be something wrong when the workers . . . are ill paid, ill fed, ill clothed, ill housed. Deaf indeed are they who do not hear the desperation in the voice of the people crying out against cruel poverty and social injustice. Dull indeed are their hearts who turn their backs upon misery and support a system that grinds the life and soul out of men and women.[21]

Similarly, she labeled the *Brooklyn Eagle* "socially blind and deaf" for its support of capitalism and its opposition to socialism.[22] When Keller was on the vaudeville circuit, she combined humor with the same political thread, stating that she had a "fellow-feeling" for President Warren G. Harding, for "he seems as blind as I am."[23] And in criticizing the U.S. court system, she wondered "what surgery of politics, what antiseptic of common sense and right thinking, shall be applied to cure the blindness of our judges and to prevent the blindness of the people who are the court of last resort?"[24] Keller used disability as a metaphor of obtuseness about injustice, echoing biblical metaphors, in an effort to explain social *ills* to others. But this commonplace rhetorical use of disability to represent deficiency of understanding or defectiveness of humanity bought into an understanding of disability as both debilitating and dehumanizing. That rhetorical move also narrowed the possibilities of her own political expression, leaving her again unable to claim disability as a legitimate political grouping, or as the base for legitimate political interests.

Many who disagreed with Keller's politics clearly understood disability as debilitating, for they questioned her capabilities and attacked her political colleagues for misleading and manipulating her. According to her political opponents, her blindness and deafness rendered her politically disabled and thus incapable of independent and reasoned political opinions—unfit for civic life.[25] At first the press blamed Anne Sullivan and John Macy for filling Keller's head with leftist nonsense, calling them "enthusiastic Marxist propagandists." And when a letter and donation Keller sent to the National Association for the Advancement of Colored People (NAACP) became public knowledge, an Alabama newspaper attributed it to the couple's Yankee influence.[26] But Sullivan and Macy were soon replaced, as Keller's political opponents repeatedly imputed her political beliefs to the influence on her of the larger radical movement, the effects of her disability, or both. For example, when it was rumored that Schenectady, New York's socialist city government would soon appoint Keller to the public welfare board (this never came to pass), critics wrote: "It would be difficult to imagine anything more pathetic than the present exploitation of poor Helen Keller by the Socialists of Schenectady."[27] Another journalist wrote that Keller's socialism was due to "the manifest limitations of her development."[28] Her critics apparently could not conceive of her as capable of independent political thought and so presumed that someone must have manipulated her.

In the 1910s, Keller tried to confront the politics of civic fitness head on. "I plead guilty," she said, "to the charge that I am deaf and blind," but she adamantly declared herself capable of understanding contemporary events— "I claim my right to discuss them."[29] She read extensively in braille (in several languages), was familiar with contemporary thinkers, and had magazines and newspapers from all over the world read to her. In fact, she insisted, "I have the advantage of a mind trained to think, and that is the difference between myself and most people, not my blindness and their sight."[30] To those who would pity her, she rejoined, "I do not want their pity; I would not change places with one of them. I know what I am talking about." She rejected those who imagined her "in the hands of unscrupulous persons who lead me astray and persuade me to espouse unpopular causes and make me the mouthpiece of their propaganda." In a wonderful twist that emphasized her gender, disability, and the ways in which she relied on different senses than her detractors did, she argued that she had skills—skills unique to a woman with a disability—that they did not have: "Let them remember, though, that if I cannot see the fire at the end of their cigarettes, neither can they thread a needle in the dark."[31] Keller claimed the right to political opinions and insisted that her opinions were as well reasoned, if not better reasoned, than those who thought of themselves as "normal" and "whole."

Despite her vigorous claims of civic fitness, Keller remained fairly isolated from possible political and ideological allies—men and women—even during the early radical phase of her life and career. During her years at Radcliffe, due to her interest in radicalism and reform, she met many leading female activists and knew of many others. What differentiated Keller was her relative lack of involvement in the close networks of club women, settlement-house workers, peace advocates, union organizers, social scientists, and legislative campaigners. She met political women, corresponded with them, occasionally spoke in public forums, but remained on the sidelines of the rich emotional and organized public work of radical and reformist women. Activist women who encountered her tended to use the extravagant language employed by Emma Goldman, who praised her for having "overcome the most appalling physical disability."[32] Just as Keller was to serve as a superstar for the American Foundation for the Blind—one whose personal appeal could solicit funds, whose presence could draw an audience, whose public image could incite renewed passion for the cause, and whose words could guarantee media attention—so she served for the left of the early twentieth century. For Goldman, as for many others, Keller's disability made her an inspirational novelty but not a comrade.

After the early 1920s, Keller distanced herself even further from radical politics. She rarely mentioned it publicly, as her activism around these issues diminished. One reason for this was financial. Keller and Sullivan needed cash, and Sullivan and the American Foundation for the Blind (AFB) thought her politics jeopardized the public approval on which their livelihood depended. Founded in 1921, by 1924 the AFB provided the bulk of the two women's income. The conservative businessmen who largely led the AFB did not take kindly to Keller's political views.[33] The antiradicalism and conservatism of the period also may have prompted her political cautiousness. Others who had expressed sentiments similar to hers were deported, arrested, or pressured into silence. Antiradicalism sought to enforce a conservative definition of who was a good citizen—and contested notions of good citizenship included not only ideology but race, gender, and physicality.[34] Keller may also have become more circumspect politically because of Anne Sullivan's health, which had deteriorated and was in periodic crisis throughout the late 1910s and 1920s. With Sullivan unable to join her on speaking tours, Keller's activities were restricted. She worried greatly about her good friend, who had never approved of her political radicalism.[35] Finally, in the face of organized antifeminism and dissension within the progressive female community, with a united feminist cause unclear, many women limited their political activities. Keller may have felt the same pressures.

Some evidence also indicates that Keller altered her political behavior in response to stereotyped and limiting public perceptions of her disability. In 1924, Wisconsin senator Robert La Follette received the presidential nomination of the Farmer-Labor ticket. A month later Keller wrote to him, apologizing for her tardiness but explaining that she had hesitated to write because of her fears of what newspapers opposed to him would say about his movement and its manipulation of her if she endorsed him publicly:

> It would be difficult to imagine anything more fatuous and stupid than the attitude of the press toward anything I say on public affairs. So long as I confine my activities to social service and the blind, they compliment me extravagantly, calling me "archpriestess of the sightless," "wonder woman" and "a modern miracle." But when it comes to a discussion of poverty, and I maintain that it is the result of wrong economics . . . that is a different matter! . . . I do not mind having my ideas attacked and my aims opposed and ridiculed, but it is not fair fighting or good argument to find that "Helen Keller's mistakes spring out of the limitations of her development."

The quandary she found herself in, Keller wrote, "explains my silence on subjects which are of vital interest to me."[36] Keller's political opponents succeeded in doing what her blindness and deafness had not: they robbed her of her political voice, denying her the full exercise of citizenship.

Keller did not buy into the contention that her disability disqualified her for civic fitness; nor did she acquiesce simply in order to protect her livelihood. The numerous obstacles caused by interpretations of her disability made the political participation she desired increasingly difficult on myriad private and public levels. The antiradicalism of the 1920s went hand in hand with growing national concern about the state of the U.S. body politic. Immigration restrictions made it increasingly difficult, particularly for a person with a disability, to become a legal citizen.[37] The growing popularity of eugenic sentiments reflected the sharpened concern about the physical "fitness" of American citizens. Medical and educational experts increasingly viewed people with disabilities as within the realm of their expertise and sought to "cure" or to "shelter" them in medical arenas. This context, coupled with the content of her political views, limited the effectiveness of Keller's claims to civic fitness.

As a result, and in contrast to Keller's political involvement during the first two decades of the century, by the mid-1920s, as she reached her mid-forties, she narrowed her political activities to focus on the American Foundation for the Blind. In some ways this concentration served her well. On behalf of the AFB she traveled, raised funds, lobbied political leaders as well as state and national legislatures, and became an international star. She made a comfortable living, visited over twenty foreign countries, met innumerable international figures, and was considered by the State Department one of the most effective public representatives of the United States. In Eleanor Roosevelt's words, she was "a goodwill ambassador of the U.S."[38] The AFB relied extensively on Keller for fund-raising and political lobbying, confident that her signature at the bottom of a fund-raising letter, a personal letter from her, or a personal appearance could raise large sums of money or sway a legislature.[39]

The political identity Keller embraced, somewhat reluctantly, after the mid-1920s was that of a blind person whose civic interests and knowledge revolved around blindness. Her experience had taught her that public expression of a broad-ranging civic fitness was difficult and made narrow by anti-radicalism and by public expectations of what someone with her disability should be. This was, quite literally, a politics of the body. Helen Keller seems to have escaped one stereotype only to move to another: from the politically manipulated and publicly pitied deaf-and-blind young virgin to the politically safe but glorified superblind saintly spinster. Both stereotypes emphasized her *difference*, separating her from a normal social network.

The experiences of the early 1920s taught Keller difficult lessons about definitions of civic fitness and the politics of the body. One response to these lessons appears to have been that for the rest of her life she avoided political activities, and even AFB travel and fund-raising, that involved substantive work. For example, in 1938, President Franklin Roosevelt invited Keller to serve on the Committee on Purchase of Products Made by the Blind. Keller and both of the Roosevelts had corresponded since at least 1931.[40] This federal committee, created as part of the New Deal effort to resurrect the economy and provide financial support to citizens, facilitated the federal government's purchase of supplies made by blind workers—cotton mops, corn brooms, whisk brooms, cuspidor mops, deck swabs, cocoa mats, pillowcases, triangular oil-treated mops, wall and ceiling fans, and mattresses.[41] The invitation provided an opportunity to help implement many of the work opportunities she had advocated, work opportunities endorsed by the

AFB.[42] With the exception of the War Department, all federal divisions had given their official nods to Keller's appointment. Keller accepted but then declined the federal post. Writing to President Roosevelt, she explained:

> I accepted this offer with the understanding that no work would be involved. Now, however, I have learned that it would mean attending countless meetings, constant travel, detailed routine for which I have neither the professional experience nor the comprehensive knowledge required. Therefore, embarrassed and troubled as I am, I must withdraw my consent.[43]

Still recovering emotionally from the death of Sullivan in 1936, and still adjusting to the assistance of someone other than Sullivan, Keller may not have known how to manage the obligations of a federal committee. And given the past history of her political involvement, she may have feared active participation.

After the 1920s, there were only two major exceptions to the narrowing of Keller's political interests—neither of which included the wide-ranging public activism of her earlier life. In 1940, she served as honorary chair of the American Rescue Ship Mission, using her influential name to raise funds. The Vichy government of France had expressed a willingness to let refugees leave concentration camps, and Latin American countries were willing to open their doors if others would pay for the refugees' transportation costs. When Eleanor Roosevelt and others learned of communist support for the effort, they notified Keller. Keller resigned, but anticommunists publicly criticized her and other members of the committee, and Keller's file in the Military Intelligence Division of the War Department had its first entry since 1919. The incident also added weight to the "pertinent information" the Federal Bureau of Investigation kept on Keller. Perhaps the FBI gave her the biggest political endorsement she received after the 1920s, when it monitored her activities throughout the 1940s and 1950s.[44]

The other exception to Keller's political inactivity came in 1948, when she considered endorsing Henry Wallace's presidential campaign and served as a sponsor of the Committee of One Thousand's criticism of the House Un-American Activities Committee (HUAC).[45] These also earned her a note in her Military Intelligence Division file, pressure from friends on various sides of the issues, and pressure from the AFB. The AFB's Robert Irwin warned her that her interests might cause HUAC to investigate the Foundation. He then had a letter sent to contributors, reassuring them of Keller's patriotism and declaring that "naturally some of the Socialistic and Communistic leaders have taken advantage of her interest in the humanitarian side of their professings." Irwin expressed the AFB's concern about Keller's politics more bluntly in a letter to AFB president William Ziegler: "Helen Keller's habit of playing around with Communists or near-Communists has long been a source of embarrassment to her conservative friends."[46] In the end, Keller refused to lend her name to the Wallace campaign, explaining that she could not do the thorough examination of Wallace she desired. To her friend Jo Davidson, a Wallace supporter, she wrote, "Lovingly I envy you the gift of carrying on two or more diverse kinds of work at once."[47] For Keller, the citizenship she sought, one in which she could carry on the "diverse kinds of work" she believed in, was nearly impossible.

Keller had become a transnational sacred image for the AFB, with vaguely New Deal–ish but rarely specified or acted-on political interests. This innocuous statement she wrote to Eleanor Roosevelt exemplifies the political sentiments she stated publicly: "Until we realize that we are all bound together—that we live by each other and for each other, we cannot create a better, more advanced world for our children to be born in."[48] Presumably frustrated, angered, and exhausted by the metaphorical, social, and physical barriers imposed on her politics during the first two decades of the twentieth century, Keller hesitated to pursue again a broad-ranging, active citizenship. Public assumptions about the civic unfitness of a person with her disability frustrated the political expressions she sought. Consequently, in this period of her life, she adopted an identity politics that revolved around her disabilities and that was inherently passive. Keller's political efficacy derived from her status as a sacred image, to be pitied and glorified, and to whom the public would pay little attention if tarnished. What she had discovered by the 1920s, and what the AFB knew, was that her claims to civic fitness undermined that sacred image and rendered her ineffective as a fund-raising tool. For example, when national newspaper columnist Westbrook Pegler attacked Keller's earlier politics in a 1947 column, AFB donations went down, and AFB leader Robert Irwin felt it necessary to send an appeasing letter to possibly offended contributors.[49] The political choices she made and did not make from the late 1920s until her death in 1968 resulted from conclusions she had come to at a time when she felt she had few options.

The choices Keller made within this increasingly narrow framework illustrate the limitations it imposed on her capacity for political analysis. For example, contrast her actions during the Great Depression with that of other people with disabilities. While she said little publicly about the economic realities of the Depression, she initially refused to lend her name and persona to the AFB's Talking Books campaign to purchase huge numbers of phonographs for blind people. When AFB Director M. C. Migel telegraphed his request in 1933, she replied that talking books were a luxury that blind people could go without while 10 million people were out of work.[50] This gave her a chance to refuse Migel while contrasting her politics against his. But the incongruity of this fairly privileged deaf-blind woman, who had access to nearly any reading material she desired, referring to talking books as a luxury while setting the interests of poor and working-class people above and against those of blind people is striking. When Keller spoke on behalf of the Social Security Act, she pled for a special allowance for the "Negro-blind" and the "deaf-blind" because they were the "hardest pressed and the least cared-for" of blind people.[51] A self-conscious Southerner, she knew that racism limited the access of disabled people of color to services, and that deaf-blind people were surely more devalued than people with disabilities regarded as closer to "normal." This argument revealed her knowledge of the intersection of racism and disability, while pulling on emotional heartstrings.

In contrast to Keller's response to the Depression, other people with disabilities laid claim to their stake in citizenship. The National Association of the Deaf, state associations of Deaf people, and the League of the Physically Handicapped protested the disability-based discrimination of the Works Progress Administration (WPA) and similar work-relief programs.[52] Large numbers of disabled people wrote to Roosevelt, emphasizing their economic productivity and requesting exemptions for people with disabilities from rubber-tire and gasoline rations, so that they could maintain the jobs that kept them out of poverty and off relief rolls. Though these actions represent radically different ideas about disability and the citizenship of people with disabilities, they all represent actions that went beyond the scope of Keller's political vision.

As Keller moved away from radical politics and toward the American Foundation for the Blind, she adopted a politics of disability in line with AFB ideology and further isolated herself from other people with disabilities. This politics was consistently conservative, consistently patronizing, sometimes repugnant. It assumed disability to be inherently debilitating. Her alliance with the AFB in the last half of her life highlights her disability politics from this period, but her earlier discussions of disability also provide insight into her analysis of disability's political implications. Throughout her life, whether seeking citizenship as a radical, as an AFB ambassador, or as a woman of compassion and reason, she lacked a politicized consciousness of disability. One of her first public speeches, delivered in 1896 when she was sixteen years of age, touted the value of speech for deaf people.[53] Then and thereafter, she sided with oralists such as Alexander Graham Bell and opposed the Deaf community's defense of American Sign Language.[54] And at the height of her involvement in radical politics, she supported eugenic and euthanasia policies to prevent the birth and sustenance of children with significant disabilities, a position that accorded with the eugenic thought of both radicals and conservatives of her era. In reference to a widely publicized case in 1915 in which a doctor withheld life-saving treatment from a disabled infant, she expanded on her linkage between citizenship and economic self-sufficiency, saying: "Our puny sentimentalism has caused us to forget that a human life is sacred only when it may be of some use to itself and to the world."[55] In her later years, unlike activists in the politicized groups of disabled people that existed during her lifetime (such as the National Federation of the Blind or the League of the Physically Handicapped), Keller never referred to discrimination against disabled people, called for antidiscrimination laws, or went beyond legislative lobbying and fund-raising for AFB programs. The work programs she referred to were sheltered workshops condemned by the activist disability movements, and particularly by the organized blind movement, as exploitative and segregated. The NFB, for example, criticized the AFB's ideology of paternalism in the 1940s—AFB leadership was dominated by sighted professionals and philanthropists—and many of the programs it advocated. Whether or not Keller was aware of criticisms of the AFB is unclear.

What is clear is that Keller's highly public persona of disability limited not only her political options but the effectiveness of the attempts of others to define disability as a legitimate political category. As the power of professionals increased in the lives of disabled people and in public understandings of disability—and the AFB certainly is representative of such a professional grouping—Keller acquiesced to the increasing medicalization of people with disabilities and demonstrated a continuing inability to understand disability as a political category.[56]

Aided and encouraged by Sullivan and the leadership of the AFB, Keller avoided contact with other people with disabilities throughout her life. She repeatedly turned down requests to speak to groups of Deaf people or other groups of disabled people. None of her close friends was disabled. Her isolation is in sharp contrast to the politicized groups of people with disabilities that existed during her lifetime, based in friendships and social networks formed in educational institutions. Keller relied on Sullivan to communicate news and information to her. It seems unlikely that Sullivan or other of Keller's supporters, such as Alexander Graham Bell, would have volunteered knowledge of such networks. While Keller insisted on getting information and taking action regarding female suffrage, radical politics, oral speech, and Swedenborgianism, against Sullivan's wishes, she seems to have made no inquiries or efforts to learn about disabled professionals, disabled tradespeople, or simply other adults with disabilities living on their own. For instance, she appears to have had no contact with the American Blind People's Higher Education and General Improvement Association, the turn-of-the-century network of blind professionals and intellectuals of her own generation who published *The Problem* (the publication described by Catherine J. Kudlick in this volume). Nor did she link with the blind school alumni associations, the state associations of organized blind activists that emerged in the 1930s, or the National Federation of the Blind, founded in 1940, who admittedly were a generation younger.

After Sullivan's death in 1936, Keller continued in this pattern. Her isolation contributed to her inability to successfully politicize disability as an issue of rights, prejudice, or discrimination. It limited her own actions. She never experienced or saw herself as part of a minority or oppressed group, only as an individual who had difficulties. Though her visit to World War II veterans with disabilities shows some knowledge of a parallel experience, she felt compelled to choose between aligning herself with deaf or blind people. For her to have argued that blind people comprise a political category, such as class, and then to have asserted that the myriad disability experiences result in a shared political identity would have been truly revolutionary.

Keller failed to move beyond her political individuality also because, like other disabled superstars, she became mired in the performance and ideology of perpetually overcoming her disability. This allowed her to escape the role of a housebound invalid but depoliticized disability by relegating it to the realm of coping and personal character. Keller had initially tried to reject both the invalid and overcomer roles—not by confrontation but by claiming the female role. This rejection did not work for her because no one saw her as "simply female," and because the female role itself implied a kind of "invalidism." Neither could she develop a public image comparable to that of Franklin Roosevelt—that of a disabled person who physically, psychologically, and morally triumphed, with courage and cheer and by sheer individual will, over daily adversity and returned to "normal" social networks.[57] Unlike Roosevelt, her disability was her public image, performance, and role—to remain in character, she kept continually "overcoming." Although she distanced herself from others with disabilities, defined herself politically in terms of gender, and often met with criticism from those who saw her as civically unfit because of her disability, the novelty of her disability and the star status she achieved created for her a public space and voice.

Though this may have been a lonely public space, it had the benefit, though twisted and double-edged, of making her the mythological person she remains in much of the public imagination. It provided her with financial benefits, international travel, public attention, and the status of an international star. It enabled her to remain unique, garnering attention to both herself and Anne Sullivan. It created a career for the two of them when few were available to women. An alliance with other people with disabilities would have destroyed her public image as a one-of-a-kind miracle. Given the limited practical or theoretical options perceptible to her, her isolation from other people with disabilities, and her inability to politicize disability, her career can be explained as a pragmatic choice. This choice, however, helped frustrate, and would continue to frustrate, the efforts of disability activists to make the theoretical and political moves that Helen Keller found difficult.

Given Keller's early radicalism and political engagements, her failure to adapt radical or progressive analyses to the situation of blind people or others with disabilities is frustrating to the contemporary observer. A complex and tangled knot of economic, psychological, cultural, gender, and political factors constricted her. At the center of this failure is the reality that everything she had—her education, her home and material goods, international travel, access to famous people, her own international fame, and the emotional center of her life, Anne Sullivan (whose reputation Keller took responsibility for after Sullivan's death in 1936)—depended on and had always depended on the *role* of Helen Keller. To adapt radical or progressive analyses to people with disabilities would have been the undoing of Keller as an individual performance and would have made her one of a social class. Anne Sullivan, Alexander Graham Bell, the Perkins School for the Blind, and the AFB worked to construct the persona of Helen Keller, but Keller herself embraced and worked hard to maintain her public image. From the moment Anne Sullivan entered her life, throughout her years as a child at Perkins, and throughout her years of national and international travel, she more or less consciously fashioned herself as a public figure whose persona depended on—quite literally as well as figuratively—her marked *difference* and distance from others with a disability, as well as from those who considered themselves "able" and "normal."

The one exception to Keller's isolation from other people with disabilities occurred during and immediately after World War II, when she received a great deal of press for visiting soldiers who had become disabled during the war. The press coverage of these events portrayed her as the ultimate model for the soldiers to emulate, ignoring the implications of their age and gender differences. In the visits, she apparently did not discuss increased federal funding for people with disabilities, vocational rehabilitation or employment prospects, or education for the newly disabled men; nor did she discuss the discrimination they would face. In essence, she did not turn these visits into the politicized events they could have been. She did not thereafter extend her contacts to include involvement with civilians with disabilities. Keller's actions portrayed disability as a personal tragedy that occurred to disconnected individuals, with neither group nor political consequences, rather than the induction of those individuals into the social identity of a stigmatized group.

The question of Keller's impact and whether anyone actually listened to her political views remains. She seems to have served the same purpose, in a much less sophisticated form, for the early twentieth-century left as she did for the AFB. She drew people, funds, attention, media, and she garnered excitement. The left, those opposed to the left, and the AFB all seem to have equally ignored her claims to individual civic fitness; and, with her cooperation, each group used her image as a useful tool. As a "good" person with a disability—cheerful, moral, and nonthreatening—and as a woman, she seems to have been expected to utter platitudes. These were encouraged by the left and accepted by the AFB. It is ironic that those opposed to her politics seem to have taken her claims to civic fitness more seriously than those in agreement, for they felt her public statements and ideological incursions dangerous enough to challenge. When her platitudes became more specific and she applied them to the political arena, she broke the boundaries of gender and ability that policed her body and thereby challenged the body politic.

The ideology of liberal individualism—self-government, self-determination, and individual autonomy—permeated the national context in which Keller's contested claims to civic fitness took place. Each of these prongs of liberalism establishes what the self can do for the self as the grounding of citizenship. Because of this, liberal individualism blurs easily into the over-comer image that many public people with disabilities, such as Franklin Roosevelt, embraced in the twentieth-century United States. If overcomers could not govern their own bodies, they could at least transcend their physical limitations by sheer will and thereby prove their personal autonomy and social validity. Helen Keller's claim of civic fitness, in contrast, was limited by an interpretation of her disability that assumed her body and self were not and could not be self-governing, self-determined, and autonomous. These principles of liberal individualism, as Rosemarie Garland Thomson has pointed out, are in conflict with disability: "Disability's indisputably random and unpredictable character translates as appalling disorder and persistent menace in a social order predicated on self-government . . . physical instability is the bodily manifestation of political anarchy." The disabled body purportedly lacked civic fitness not only because of its perceived debilitating nature but because it contradicted the tenets of liberal individualism. Helen Keller's body did not neatly fit. Her political body represented an unstable character, a body and person neither self-governed nor autonomous. In Keller's case, her claims to civic fitness and her political body were doubly disturbing. Not only was her body the "bodily manifestation of political anarchy," but she embraced ideologies considered by many Americans to be the literal equivalent of anarchy.[58] The politics of the body merged with the politics of politics to limit profoundly Helen Keller's claims to civic fitness.

NOTES

1. The complexity, depth, and range of the questions raised by Keller's political life and public image preclude full discussion in this essay. Part of my intention here is to point to areas needing further research and debate. I intend to explore these questions further in *The Radical Lives of Helen Keller*, a book in progress with New York University Press. This essay benefited greatly from the wisdom and patience of Cathy Kudlick, Paul Longmore, Anthony Quiroz, Lauri Umansky, and Nathan Tuff. I am grateful to them. The Franklin and Eleanor Roosevelt Institute graciously provided funding for research at the Franklin Delano Roosevelt Library. I also wish to acknowledge the Schlesinger Library, Radcliffe Institute, Harvard University, for providing permission to reprint from Mary Elisabeth Dreier Papers.

2. Keller claimed politics to be a part of her life earlier. In 1896, at sixteen years of age, she addressed a Philadelphia crowd on the value of oral speech to the deaf. The benefits of speech that she detailed included telling stories to her siblings, reading to

her mother, and discussing "the political situation" with her father. See "Address of Helen Keller at Mt. Airy" (July 8, 1896), in Lois Einhorn, *Helen Keller, Public Speaker* (Westport, Conn.: Greenwood Press, 1998), 80.

3. Helen Keller, "A Plea for Recognition of Soviet Russia" (1921), in Philip S. Foner, ed., *Helen Keller: Her Socialist Years* (New York: International Publishers, 1967), 104–106.

4. As Joseph Shapiro and others have shown, the disability rights movement also uses the language of citizenship in protests against "second-class citizenship." See Joseph P. Shapiro, *No Pity: People with Disabilities Forging a New Civil Rights Movement* (New York: Random House, 1993).

5. Helen Keller, "An Appeal to Reason" (1910), in *Out of the Dark: Essays, Letters and Addresses on Physical and Social Vision* (New York: Doubleday, 1914), 30.

6. Helen Keller, "The Truth Again" (1909), in *Out of the Dark*, 178.

7. Helen Keller, "Why Men Need Woman Suffrage" (1915), in Foner, ed., *Helen Keller*, 67.

8. On the first generation of female college students, see Helen Horowitz, *Alma Mater: Design and Experience in the Women's Colleges from their Nineteenth-Century Beginnings to the 1930s* (New York: Knopf, 1984); and Rosalind Rosenberg, *Beyond Separate Spheres: The Intellectual Roots of Modern Feminism* (New Haven: Yale University Press, 1982).

9. Keller, "Why Men Need Woman Suffrage," 67.

10. Helen Keller, "The Modern Woman," (1912) in *Out of the Dark*, 43.

11. Helen Keller, "Why Men Need Woman Suffrage," in Foner, ed., *Helen Keller*, 67.

12. Keller, "Modern Woman," 76. Keller's words are similar to those of Jane Addams. For example, Jane Addams, "Why Women Should Vote" (1910), in Christopher Lasch, *The Social Thought of Jane Addams* (New York: Bobbs-Merrill, 1965), 143–151.

13. For varying definitions, analyses, and uses of gender-based arguments such as maternalism, see Seth Koven and Sonya Michel, "Womanly Duties: Maternalist Politics and the Origins of Welfare States in France, Germany, Great Britain, and the United States, 1880–1920," *American Historical Review* 95 (1990): 1076–1108; Theda Skocpol, *Protecting Soldiers and Mothers: The Political Origins of Social Policy in the United States* (Cambridge: Harvard University Press, 1992); Kathryn Kish Sklar, "The Historical Foundations of Women's Power in the Creation of the American Welfare State, 1830–1930," in *Mothers of a New World: Maternalist Politics and the Origins of the Welfare States*, ed. Seth Koven and Sonya Michel (New York: Routledge Press, 1993), 321–342; Eileen Boris, "What About the Working of the Working Mother?" *Journal of Women's History* 5 (Fall 1993): 104–109; Molly Ladd-Taylor, *Mother-Work: Women, Child Welfare, and the State, 1890–1930* (Urbana: University of Illinois Press, 1994); Linda Gordon, *Pitied but Not Entitled: Single Mothers and the History of Welfare, 1890–1935* (New York: Free Press, 19994); Gwendolyn Mink, *The Wages of Motherhood: Inequality in the Welfare State, 1917–1942* (Ithaca: Cornell University Press, 1995); Linda Gordon, "Putting

Children First: Women, Maternalism, and Welfare in the Early Twentieth Century," in *U.S. History as Women's History: New Feminist Essays*, ed. Linda Kerber, Alice Kessler-Harris, and Kathryn Kish Sklar (Chapel Hill: University of North Carolina Press, 1995), 63–86; Felicia A. Kornbluh, "The New Literature on Gender and the Welfare State: The U.S. Case," *Feminist Studies* 22/1 (Spring 1996): 171–197; Lisa D. Brush, "Love Toil, and Trouble: Mother hood and Feminist Politics," *Signs* 21 (Winter 1996): 429–443; Sonya Michel and Robyn Rosen, "The Paradox of Maternalism: Elizabeth Lowell Putnam and the American Welfare State," *Gender and History* 4 (Autumn 1992): 364–386.

14. In *Outlook for the Blind* 1/1 (April 1907): 11, Keller wrote: "I can tell you of blind men who of their own accord enter the sharp competition of business and put their hands zealously to the tools of trade. It is our part to train them in business, to teach them to use their skills carefully."

15. Helen Keller, "Our Duties to the Blind" (1904), in Einhorn, *Helen Keller, Public Speaker*, 82–87. See also Helen Keller, "The Heaviest Burden of the Blind" (January 15, 1907), in Einhorn, *Helen Keller, Public Speaker*, 88–90.

16. Joseph Lash, *Helen and Teacher: The Story of Helen Keller and Anne Sullivan Macy* (New York: Addison-Wesley. 1980), 363.

17. For more on gender, work, and citizenship, see Linda K. Kerber, *No Constitutional Right to Be Ladies: Women and the Obligations of Citizenship* (New York: Hill and Wang, 1998), chap. 2.

18. Helen Keller, "The Worker's Right," (1912) in *Out of the Dark*, 35.

19. Eleanor Roosevelt made a similar claim about Franklin Delano Roosevelt. Responding to a question about the consequences of FDR's "illness" on his "mentality," she said, "Anyone who has gone through great suffering is bound to have a greater sympathy and understanding of the problems of mankind." See Hugh Gregory Gallagher, *FDR's Splendid Deception* (New York: Dodd, Mead and Co., 1985), 95.

20. Helen Keller, "The Conservation of Eyesight" (1911), in Einhorn, *Helen Keller, Public Speaker*, 91–92.

21. Helen Keller, "A New Light Is Coming" (1913), in Foner, ed., *Helen Keller*, 53.

22. Helen Keller, "How I Became a Socialist" (1911), in Foner, ed., *Helen Keller*, 28.

23. Einhorn, *Helen Keller, Public Speaker*, 107.

24. Keller, "Appeal to Reason," 33.

25. The most recent biography of Helen Keller equally devalues Keller's political interests by explaining them not as ideology or genuine interest but as "an acceptable outlet for the rage and anger that she seldom permitted herself to express about the fate that had left her disabled and helpless." See Dorothy Herrmann, *Helen Keller: A Life* (New York: Alfred A. Knopf, 1998), 175; Herrmann expresses similar sentiments on page 204.

26. Keller, "How I Became a Socialist," in *Out of the Dark*, 20.

27. Ibid.

28. Ibid.

29. This is, as far as I can determine, the only time Keller used the word *right* in reference to herself.

30. Keller, "New Light Is Coming," 52–54.

31. "Strike against War" (January 5, 1916), in Foner, ed., *Helen Keller*, 75–81.

32. Emma Goldman, *Living My Life* (New York: Ams Press, 1970), 648–649.

33. Frances A. Koestler, *The Unseen Minority: A Social History of Blindness in America* (New York: David McKay Co., 1976), chap. 2.

34. For example, see Kim Nielsen, *Women against Women: Anti-Radicalism, Gender and the First Red Scare* (Columbus: Ohio State University Press, forthcoming).

35. Though Sullivan and John Macy initially were blamed for Keller's activism, Sullivan never approved of Keller's socialism, suffrage advocacy, or other political interests. Her disapproval may have been compounded by the fact that Keller was first introduced to radicalism by Macy, her estranged husband. See Herrmann, *Helen Keller*, 178, 204–205; Lash, *Helen and Teacher*, 454–455.

36. Helen Keller, "To Senator Robert M. La Follete," (1924) in Foner, ed., *Helen Keller*, 113.

37. Douglas Baynton, "The Inspection Line: Detecting Disabled Immigrants at the American Border, 1882–1924" (paper given at the 1999 Organization of American Historians, in author's possession).

38. Einhorn, *Helen Keller, Public Speaker*, 23. M. C. Migel, president of the American Foundation for the Blind, tried in 1949 to convince Eleanor Roosevelt to use her influence to allow Keller to address the United Nations Assembly on "labors to be undertaken on behalf of the sightless of the world." See M. C. Migel to Eleanor Roosevelt, Franklin Delano Roosevelt Library. Courtesy of the American Foundation for the Blind, Helen Keller Archives. In 1960, former labor leader Mary Elisabeth Dreier wrote to Keller: "When you went abroad, and to the east, I had thought what a wonderful thing it would be if they made you an Ambassador of the United States. The government has been insensitive, and normally would be, I presume to such an idea." See Mary E. Dreier to Helen Keller, July 13, 1960, Mary Elisabeth Dreier Papers, Schlesinger Library, Cambridge, MA, box 10, folder 166.

39. For example, see Koestler, *Unseen Minority*, chap. 6.

40. Keller knew the Roosevelts well enough to know that for a message to reach FDR quickly or to be considered seriously, it was best to go through Missy LeHand, FDR's private secretary. When Anne Sullivan died, Keller telegrammed LeHand with the funeral information. See telegram from Helen Keller to Missy LeHand, October 20, 1936, President's Personal File #2169, Helen Keller, Franklin Delano Roosevelt Library.

41. "Report of Purchases Made under the Schedule of Blind-Made Products," May 27, 1940, FDR Papers as President, Official File, #3303, Committee on Purchase of Products Made by the Blind, Franklin Delano Roosevelt Library.

42. Koestler, *Unseen Minority*, 219.

43. Helen Keller to Franklin Roosevelt, July 15, 1938, FDR Papers as President, Official File, #3303, Committee on Purchase of Products Made by the Blind, Franklin Delano Roosevelt Library. Courtesy of the American Foundation for the Blind, Helen Keller Archives.

44. Military Intelligence Division of War Department, National Archives, Washington, D.C. Keller does not have an official FBI file but is cross-referenced extensively in the files of other individuals and organizations. My 1997 appeal for information on Keller, under the Freedom of Information Act, netted a review of 118 pages and the release of 44 pages.

45. Being a sponsor meant that her name went on the letterhead and that she signed her name to fund-raising appeals.

46. Lash, *Helen and Teacher*, 702–704.

47. Ibid., 705.

48. Helen Keller to Eleanor Roosevelt, February 8, 1939, Eleanor Roosevelt papers, series 100, file Kar-Kelly, Franklin Delano Roosevelt Library. Courtesy of the American Foundation for the Blind, Helen Keller Archives.

49. Lash, *Helen and Teacher*, 703.

50. Koestler, *Unseen Minority*, 138.

51. Ibid., 184.

52. Paul Longmore and David Goldberger, "The League of the Physically Handicapped, 1935–1938: A Case Study in the New Disability Historiography" (unpublished article in author's possession).

53. "Address of Helen Keller at Mt. Airy," 80.

54. Keller learned oral speech despite the disapproval of Sullivan. Sullivan's disapproval appears not to have been motivated by disability politics but an effort to maintain her own connection to Keller. For an analysis of the debate over oralism versus sign language, see Douglas Baynton, *Forbidden Signs: American Culture and the Campaign against Sign Language* (Chicago: University of Chicago press, 1996).

55. Martin S. Pernick, *The Black Stork: Eugenics and the Death of "Defective" Babies in American Medicine and the Motion Pictures since 1915* (New York: Oxford University Press, 1996), 6, 71, 92, 103.

56. For a discussion of the medicalization of disability, see Robert Bogdan, *Freak Show: Presenting Human Oddities for Amusement and Profit* (Chicago: University of Chicago Press, 1988), 278.

57. For further insights on FDR, see Gallagher, *FDR's Splendid Deception*.

58. Rosemarie Garland Thomson, *Extraordinary Bodies: Figuring Physical Disability in American Culture and Literature* (New York: Columbia University Press, 197), 42–44.

Images and Identities

Part III

11

Martyred Mothers and Merciful Fathers

Exploring Disability and Motherhood in the Lives of
Jerome Greenfield and Raymond Repouille

Janice A. Brockley

By the time thirteen-year-old Raymond Repouille died, his father, Louis Repouille, had already tried to kill him twice. Raymond's mother, Florence Repouille, barely managed to save him each time. Both the New York City Children's Court and the family doctor knew about the previous murder attempts. When Louis Repouille, a white immigrant from the Dutch West Indies, finally succeeded in murdering his son in 1939, he did not expect punishment for his crime. He was right. Despite Florence Repouille's denunciations, he received two years of probation and served no time in prison. Repouille had been encouraged by another murder committed earlier in the year. Louis Greenfield, a Jewish immigrant from Austria, had killed his son Jerome, or Jerry. Greenfield had been acquitted entirely of his son's death. Raymond's and Jerry's murders present a fascinating puzzle: Why would these fathers correctly feel that they could kill their sons and receive only tolerance and even social approval? The answer to this question lies in the complicated emotions and ideas surrounding disability and motherhood in the 1930s. By exploring Raymond's and Jerry's deaths, we can gain insight into their lives and the social and cultural dilemmas that surrounded children with disabilities and their families.

A growing literature on disability studies demonstrates that society and culture shape the social meaning of the experience of disability. Historians and other scholars describe how cultural interpretations frame physical and mental conditions.[1] In the 1930s, intellectual disability triggered an array of cultural associations ranging from perverted deviance to angelic innocence. Frequently, discussions of intellectual disability included images of horror and distortion manifested physically, especially for those with more severe disabilities. Popular discussions of intellectual disability constructed it in two ways: The body could be seen as physically incompetent, a reflection of the mind's vacancy, or it could become dangerously healthy, an exemplar of the dangers of the body without a mind to control it. The body thus became a reflection of the mind.

Physical disability, while stigmatized, was not as disturbing as intellectual disability. People like Raymond were clearly at the bottom of a hierarchy of stigma. In line with this hierarchy, those physical disabilities that appeared to have an intellectual component, such as cerebral palsy and epilepsy, were also some of the most stigmatized.[2]

In practice, physical and intellectual disabilities could be hard to separate: Whether a disability originated in the body or mind could be almost impossible to distinguish. With few ways to measure the brain directly, mental capacity had to be judged by action or communication. In Raymond's case, he had only limited ability to move his limbs, presumably because of the same brain damage that caused his intellectual disability. His intellectual capacity therefore had to be judged by his physical control and ability to communicate. Once the judgment of his intellectual capacity was made, however, it dominated perceptions of Raymond. He was primarily an "imbecile." Implicitly, his physical limitations were the result of his "imbecility." Intellectual disability took priority over physical disability. Nonetheless, Raymond's physical disabilities played a significant role in his life experience, shaping the care he received and perceptions of his life. His father and newspaper articles about his murder frequently referred to Raymond as "just a dead body lying around."[3] His immobility was an important proof of the totality of his disability and the invalidity of his life.

Scholars in disability studies point out not only that cultural assumptions shape our perceptions of disability but also that social arrangements actually shape what is considered a disability. The availability of services, the structures of buildings, the distribution of income, and many other factors all transform human variation into disability.[4] Scholars have had a harder time applying this model to people with severe intellectual disabilities. It is all too easy to see people with severe disabilities as automatically excluded from society. By carefully examining the lives of people like Raymond Repouille, however, we can begin to analyze how a lack of social support encouraged a perception of people with severe disabilities as burdens, incapable of having rewarding relationships. We can see how cultural stereotypes obscured Raymond's representation in newspapers, in the minds of social service workers, and in the courtroom. The same stereotypes facilitated his eventual death.

In 1939, two adolescent boys with disabilities were killed by their fathers in New York City: Raymond Repouille and Jerome Greenfield. Raymond was unable to use his limbs, was blind, and was severely retarded.[5] Jerome, or Jerry, Greenfield was first described as an "incurable imbecile who had fits."[6] Later descriptions fluctuated. It is almost impossible to get any clear sense of Jerry's disabilities because his father's skilled defense attorney and the newspapers used his body to dramatize a series of anecdotes about the dangers of intellectual disabilities. Some descriptions emphasized his physical debility: He was "partially paralyzed and to the end could not walk without help" and was subject to "painful convulsions."[7] The same newspapers, however, could also emphasize his dangerous physical ability and "his continued physical development," as a result of which "the child was becoming a menace and might attempt a sexual assault on his own mother."[8] Jerry's physical reality was permanently obscured behind the stories his body was used to tell.

The newspaper coverage of Raymond's and Jerry's deaths fit into a popular debate over mercy killing in newspapers and magazines in the mid- to late 1930s.[9] In these years, the euthanasia movement gained new prominence. It failed to achieve euthanasia legislation, but the cause seemed to have both professional and popular support.[10] Jerry's and Raymond's deaths, therefore, fit neatly into a contemporary popular debate.

The powerful narrative of mercy killing camouflaged the similarities between the killings of these disabled children and other types of child death and abuse and obscured the surrounding issues and events. Louis Greenfield and Louis Repouille told the police and reporters that they killed their intellectually and physically disabled sons out of mercy.[11] The newspapers reported that Jerry and Raymond were hopeless, without any potential for development or education. The public discussion of the cases took for granted that their parents had only three choices: to care for their sons without help, to confine them to a custodial institution, or to kill them.

Police interviews and newspaper articles open a window into the lives of two families of youths with severe disabilities. They reveal troubled relationships between parents and experts, divisions between parents, cultural discomfort over motherhood, and the effacement of some children from society. The archival records also demonstrate the tangled and violent relationships within the Repouille family. At times, Raymond seemed almost incidental to his own murder. Newspapers and experts simplified these tangled issues into a dichotomy between the irrational mother who refused to release her child to an institution or to death and the rational father who killed to protect his family. These stories display the limits of assistance from outside experts, who were willing to extend only certain kinds of help, on their own terms. They also point out the difficult position of mothers, who were utterly essential to the functioning of the private nuclear family and deeply distrusted by experts at the same time. Given the devaluation of Jerry's and Raymond's lives, their mothers' devoted care appeared less reasonable to the courts and newspapers than their fathers' drastic actions.[12]

The Deaths of Jerome Greenfield and Raymond Repouille

In their cold-water flat near Harlem, Raymond Repouille's parents, Louis and Florence, followed the accounts of Jerry Greenfield's death with interest. The story received front-page coverage from the beginning. January 13, 1939, the morning after Jerry's death, the front page of the *Daily Mirror* announced that "Pity Drives Dad To Kill Sick Son" below a picture of the "agonized father" being booked at the police station.[13] Under the blaring headlines, the reporters described how Louis Greenfield, a forty-two-year-old milliner and Jewish immigrant from Austria, sent his wife, Anna, to work without him and killed their son with two handkerchiefs soaked in chloroform. Louis Repouille had already tried to kill his son and saw Jerry's murder as a justification of his actions. Repouille, a hospital elevator operator, later remembered that "the minute the case came out, I told . . . [Florence] he wouldn't get anything, he would get away with it."[14] Repouille was right. As the Greenfield story unfolded slowly over the following months in the newspapers, popular sympathy stayed firmly with the suffering father. The district attorney indicted Louis Greenfield for first-degree manslaughter, the lowest charge possible. His attorney, the famous and skillful Samuel Leibowitz, argued that Greenfield was not guilty because of "'defective reason'—after years of physical and mental torture caused by the suffering of the boy."[15] Medical and parental testimony described Jerry as a "'vegetative organism' who had to be watched every minute he was awake ... [and who] had grown into a 'tremendous man' with uncontrolled instincts."[16] Amid "the sniffling and sobbing of spectators and several members of the jury," Greenfield testified that he had suffered for years until "God's will" guided him to kill Jerry.[17] The jury acquitted Greenfield. "I should never have been put on trial," Greenfield told reporters after the trial. "The lawmakers should have been put on trial. The people whose laws condemned my son to live and condemned my wife and myself to life with him. Jerry should have been put to death at birth."[18] Now that Jerry was dead, he and Anna were "planning to adopt a child, about two or three years old, to take his place just as soon as we establish our new home."[19] The trial ended, therefore, with the couple apparently joyfully planning to reconstitute their family.

The Greenfield killing had special meaning to Florence and Louis Repouille because of their family situation. Raymond was the eldest of their five children.[20] He was thirteen and what the newspapers described as "blind, crippled, and feeble-minded."[21] Florence had already managed to save her son twice from Repouille's murder attempts. On both occasions, Florence had called in neighbors and medical aid but not the police. About six months before Raymond's death, Repouille told Florence "he had chloroform in the house. He would give him a little bit and he would put him out of his sufferings."[22] Florence searched the apartment for the chloroform without success.

The family was under another source of stress at the time. Repouille had frequently visited charity organizations to complain about Florence's drinking and neglect of their children, charges that the social workers were unable to substantiate. In August 1939, Repouille complained again and asked for the children other than Raymond to be committed to an orphanage or some other form of public care. It is not clear why he thought this would be possible. The case went to the domestic relations court. The probation officer sent by the court could not find any evidence of misbehavior by Florence but did note Florence feared that Repouille would "kill the cripple child" and had tried to twice before, though not recently. The case file stated that Repouille apparently felt "that he was justified in attempting to kill his child because of the fact that it is a helpless cripple."[23] Florence also complained that Repouille abused her. To alleviate these problems, the court ordered the Repouilles to institutionalize Raymond, and Ethel McDougall, the court probation officer, planned to give Florence some advice on budgeting. Florence, however, resisted any attempt to institutionalize Raymond and felt that the court was against her. She and Repouille fought over money, Florence's supposed drinking, and what should happen to Raymond. Tensions between husband and wife seemed to be reaching a crisis.

On October 12, 1939, Repouille stayed home from work. Around noon, Florence took Jeanette, the baby, for a walk, leaving her keys at home. She went around the corner and stood for a few minutes. Then "[a]ll of a sudden I said, 'My God, Louis is up to something.'"[24] When she got home, the apartment door was locked and Repouille did not answer when she knocked. She said, "Oh, my God, I betcha now he is going to kill that kid."[25] She ran downstairs to the neighbors for help. One neighbor called the police. The police broke into the apartment and took Raymond to the hospital, but they were too late. He was dead.

More than a year's delay followed between Raymond's death and his father's trial. At the trial in December 1941, Repouille, a less persuasive man than Greenfield, could not maintain the smooth, selfless image that the former had successfully presented. Though his attorney, Paul O'Dwyer, was a successful advocate for a variety of liberal causes in New York City, Repouille created many of his own problems.[26] His testimony contradicted his claim that his mind "went perfectly blank" when he killed Raymond. His admission that he had struck his wife on at least twenty occasions and the social worker's testimony that he had tried to institutionalize all of his children except the youngest further damaged his credibility. The jury convicted him of manslaughter in the second degree, but he received a suspended sentence of five to ten years. Repouille, however, was indignant that he had been found guilty. Six years later, he lost his appeal to become a citizen because of his conviction. However, the U.S. Second Circuit Court of Appeals decided that when the period of the sentence had passed, he could reapply for citizenship without prejudice. "It is reasonably clear," Judge Learned Hand observed, "that the jury which tried Repouille did not feel any moral repulsion at his crime."[27] After all, Hand continued, Repouille committed the crime "to help him[self] in . . . [his other children's] nurture which was being compromised by the burden imposed upon him" by Raymond.[28] "[O]nly a minority of virtuous persons would deem the practice morally justifiable, while it remains in private hands," Hand stated, but

there are great numbers of people of the most unimpeachable virtue, who think it morally justifiable to put an end to a life so inexorably destined to

Janice A. Brockley

be a burden to others, and . . . condemned to a brutish existence, lower indeed than all but the lowest forms of sentient life.[29]

Hand compared Repouille's actions to the civil disobedience of the abolitionists protesting against slavery. In the end, he concluded that however morally justified Repouille's actions might be Repouille must wait until the end of his parole period before applying for citizenship. Hand's opinion, however, left no doubt where his sympathies remained.

"Perverse Tendencies" and "Vegetative Organisms": Describing Disability

The coverage of the "mercy killings" drew on a series of cultural images of disability. In the Greenfield trial, the images presented were carefully crafted. Leibowitz was a famous lawyer who had developed his skills and reputation defending infamous criminals and employed his talents as a showman and a lawyer to great effect. Repouille was never able to maintain a comparable facade. Although he was white, he was a poor immigrant from the Caribbean who lived in a largely African American neighborhood. He was often contradictory and shocking: He told newspaper reporters to take pictures of him with his dead son on his lap; he informed the police that previously he had threatened to kill Raymond to punish his wife but that the actual killing was different and committed solely out of mercy; and he admitted that he had attempted to institutionalize his "normal" children. Florence refused to defend her husband and freely told the police and reporters that his actions were unjustified. In light of all this, it may seem surprising that so many people believed Repouille's claim that he killed Raymond solely out of mercy.

Given the unconvincing narrative he presented and the constant contradictions made by his wife, why *did* so many people believe him? The answer lies in the cultural frames placed around disability in the 1930s. Parents, the courtroom witnesses and spectators, and the newspapers applied a wide range of meanings to Raymond's and Jerry's physical and intellectual impairments. Many of these images were contradictory: Jerry was both a pitiful imbecile who could not leave his apartment alone and a dangerous potential rapist and murderer. Such cultural constructions had a powerful life of their own and did not even have to be called upon specifically: culturally trained spectators would supply them automatically. When the police interviewed McDougall, the Repouille family's social worker, they asked if she knew why Repouille had tried to kill his son:

A: It was always by inference, that he wanted to relieve the child of suffering.
Q: Did she [Florence] ever say that to you? Have you a single notation, anywhere that the child was suffering?
A: No.
Q: In other words, what you have just given me was something you were imagining yourself from all the facts in the case?
A: Inferences from the facts.[30]

The image of the suffering, disabled child was so potent that McDougall was unable to imagine an alternative explanation.

The least-threatening popular and medical image of an intellectually disabled person, especially for an intellectually disabled male, was that of a permanent and innocent child. Without mature reason and intelligence to guide them, mental defectives would not be able to control their impulses and passions. Therefore, mental defectives should ideally be like Victorian children, innocent of sex, violence, and other negative adult emotions.[31] The stereotype of the mental defective as a neutered, angelic child remained powerful between the 1930s and 1950s and still has resonance today. Nevertheless, it did not appear in the coverage of these mercy killings—only its dangerous counterimage manifested itself.

One of the most potent charges leveled against Jerry challenged this safe, asexual image. The dark obverse of the child image was the primitive, violent, sexual child's mind in an adult body—male urges set free.[32] In this theory, mentally deficient males would never achieve adulthood and thus could not control their primal urges. They would be unable to attract sexual partners, but they would still have passion and desire. Consequently, they posed the threat of sexual deviancy, rape, or violent crime. This fear drew on broader ideas about *physical* disability as well. In popular culture, the disabled body either eliminated or perverted the sexual drive. Movie images of physical disability reinforced this stereotype. Disabled characters in films of the 1920s and 1930s alternated between the sweet, sexless innocent and the vindictive villain who sought to avenge his symbolic castration and lack of sexual potency.[33]

The denunciations of Jerry fit easily into this long line of popular representations of people with disabilities as a social threat. In this interpretation, Greenfield protected society by killing his son. The trial testimony and courtroom arguments worked to elaborate these fears. In these fantasies, Jerry's body, which at other moments was portrayed as weak and pitiful, became threateningly strong and menacing. Undoubtedly drawing on popular concern over sexual psychopaths who were unable "to repress or to sublimate their overly active sexual impulses," the biographer of Greenfield's attorney, Samuel Leibowitz, claimed that "nature had been cruel enough to develop fully the sex urge within him [Jerry], and that having no mind to control this urge, it was possible that it would lead him to assault, rape, or kill."[34] Dr. I. Newton Kugelmass, Jerry's physician, testified at the trial that he had urged the parents to sterilize Jerry to "protect the mother from unwarranted offenses and lessen the possibility of perverse tendencies which the boy had undoubtedly experienced."[35] *The Sun* and the *New York World Telegram* made the implied charge explicit and accused Jerry of threatening to assault his mother. What Kugelmass meant and how his comment related to Jerry's behavior is unclear. In an advice manual, Kugelmass suggested sterilization of all mental defectives.[36] He, like some other psychiatrists, may have seen sterilization as therapeutic surgery or a standard precaution, or he may have worried about a more common "perversion," namely, masturbation.[37] Regardless of what he meant, his comments were enough to trigger a set of cultural associations that needed no further elaboration or explanation to take flight. *Who* Jerry was and what he *had done* was hidden behind *what* he was and what he *might do*.

The other set of cultural frames focused on the problem of suffering.[38] The press, parents, and court testimony seldom described Raymond or Jerry as suffering physically. Despite the frequent use of the words *suffering* and *mercy*, few descriptions of physical pain were provided. Instead, the boys' fathers, the newspapers, and the courts portrayed Raymond and Jerry as "suffering" by virtue of their disabilities.

Because of their disabilities, society defined Raymond's and Jerry's lives as not worth living. The press and others frequently described Raymond in particular as virtually dead: "just a dead body lying around."[39] Raymond was so severely disabled that he did not qualify as a living person. Such rhetoric could be flexible: Leibowitz similarly described the infant Jerry as "[j]ust a lump of flesh in a crib."[40] This rhetoric rested on a set of assumptions about what constituted an acceptable life. More than any other group, "idiots," or people with severe mental and physical disabilities, were stigmatized as inhuman. In this view, Raymond lacked the attributes of real life, namely, intelligence and consciousness. Implicitly, life was only worth living if a person could fulfill certain basic social goals. For those without these abilities, life itself became a form of suffering. Their fathers did not have to demonstrate that Raymond and Jerry wished to die or would have chosen to be killed. Their lives by definition were not worth living: hence their consent or wishes as individuals were irrelevant, presumably because they were considered incapable of generating or expressing them. The issue was not what Jerry and Raymond *wanted* but what was assumed to be best for them and for those around them.

Most of the discussions of suffering in the newspaper coverage did not focus on Jerry and Raymond. It quickly became clear that their families were the real victims. The families' suffering took a variety of forms: The most obvious was simply enduring Jerry's and Raymond's presence. Scholars argue that in the 1920s and 1930s, physical disability became a form of visual pornography.[41] The newspapers teased the readers with references to and descriptions of Raymond's and Jerry's bodies, but the press never published pictures of either Raymond or Jerry. The ultimate example of disability as obscenity appeared in an article in the *Daily Mirror*. The paper announced that Greenfield possessed more than one hundred pictures of Jerry that he would show to the jury. Leibowitz claimed, "There are not 12 American citizens to be found who, after seeing these pictures, would not declare the father's act justified."[42] The pornography of the disabled body transformed mementos of a child into a justification of his death.

Articles also dwelt on the suffering of the families in enduring the youths' need for care and their drain on financial resources. The coverage of their murders emphasized the unusual financial and social burdens Raymond and Jerry posed in a way that ignored both the general realities of life for working-class families and the lack of "normal" community resources for disabled children. The press and the courts naturalized Greenfield's and Repouille's desperation, transforming their anguish into the automatic result of their sons' disabilities. The description of Repouille as "frantic with poverty and despair" seemed to blame Raymond and overlooked the realities of life for an immigrant family living on the wages of an elevator operator in Depression-era New York City. Similarly, the coverage of the Greenfield case described a family steadily deteriorating under an intolerable burden. Jerry may well have been a major financial burden. The last ten years of his life, however, occurred during the Great Depression, when many small-business men suffered. The national financial crisis undoubtedly helped shape the difficulties that confronted both families. The press coverage also ignored the impact of a lack of community resources to assist either family. No newspaper, commentator, or witness ever pointed out that a daily school program or household help might have eased Anna's and Florence's burdens without requiring institutionalization of their sons. In these constructions, the parents more than their children obtained "mercy" through the "mercy killings." The villains were Raymond and Jerry, not the social situation that surrounded them.

None of this implies a public consensus on the use of euthanasia. In 1939, opinions remained divided.[43] Some commentators specifically feared that the Repouille and Greenfield cases might lead to growing public tolerance of euthanasia.[44] The cases do demonstrate a widespread willingness to accept that certain types of existence inevitably created suffering not just for the individual but also for the people around him or her. In the stories of "mercy killings," euthanasia functioned as just another method of removing the disabled person from view. For many commentators and spectators of the cases, institutions might well have been a preferred solution. The opponent of euthanasia who protested that an "idiot child may have fond parents who want him alive, even if it were in a distant institution" was not necessarily in conflict with Repouille's and Greenfield's sympathizers.[45] The public support for Repouille and Greenfield expressed not a consensus that euthanasia was desirable but a belief that families had to be protected from the burden of disability.

Dangerous Mothers

Intimate emotional relationships, however, opened the possibility of an alternative construction of disability. Florence's testimony to the police about Raymond demonstrated how someone could see him as both severely disabled and fully human. She did not deny the severity of his disabilities and conceded that he could not speak or see or move around. Nor did she expect him to live a "normal" life span. She emphasized, however, the ways in which Raymond interacted with her and his environment: He had all the attributes of personhood.[46] He could, after all, "understand quite a bit."[47] He liked ice cream and fruit. Sometimes she would play games with him. Most of all, Florence felt that Raymond loved her and could not survive for long in an institution. "He was attached to me," she explained. "He couldn't see me but he knew I was next to him."[48] For Florence, Raymond was a complete and beloved person in a way that accepted his disabilities. Her description also emphasized the ways in which he was a participant in their mutual relationship, rather than the passive recipient of instinctual mother love.

Raymond and Jerry could not easily represent themselves. Raymond could not speak, and Jerry was unintelligible to anyone but his parents. The two people who knew them most intimately and had the best right to speak for them were their mothers. Ironically, that close emotional connection was used to discredit the two mothers in the courtroom, in the newspapers, and in the minds of experts, including their social worker and physician. The people who had the greatest opportunity to know Raymond and Jerry were the people who had the least opportunity to describe them.

Florence and Anna were undermined by popular and professional suspicions of motherhood. Advice manuals and psychologists since the 1920s had been warning that all mothers ran the risk of spoiling their children for independence and adult relationships.[49] What was a problem for mothers of "normal" children was an overwhelming danger for mothers of disabled children. The apparently innate dependence and vulnerability of children with disabilities made it even more likely that mothers would succumb to the impulse to keep their children perpetual infants. This did not mean that women should leave the home. Private nuclear families required the full-time labor of a wife and mother.[50] Families with disabled children could be even more demanding of maternal labor. Anna "watch[ed] him [Jerry] all day, help[ed] him dress, . . . took him for walks and attend[ed] to the simplest matters of his personal hygiene.[51] Florence said that she could not leave Raymond alone to have the surgery she needed, but her reasonable fear of Repouille's murderous impulses might have been a large part of her reluctance. These women's labor made it possible for their sons to stay out of institutions. Writers on handicapped children, however, were very suspicious of maternal motives, warning against spoiling children and keeping them dependent. In this view, a mother's efforts to keep her child at home might reflect her own emotional gratification from her child's dependence.[52] The *New York Herald Tribune* referred to Jerry as the "burden his mother insisted on carrying"—a description that summed up much of the criticism.[53]

Like other mothers, Anna and Florence were operating in a vacuum of social support. In reality, public institutions could not begin to take all the people who were intellectually disabled in the United States. Most facilities were overcrowded, with long waiting lists. Limited funding and the realities of institutional life made these facilities grim places to live, especially for the most disabled residents, those like Raymond and Jerry. Both Raymond and Jerry had spent short periods in institutions before being removed by their parents because of their ill health, apparent neglect, and unhappiness. Neither young man was eligible for any kind of public education. Blaming mothers for their "excessive devotion" obscured the real social problems that made that devotion necessary. In these cases, "excessive devotion" translated into an unwillingness to accept the neglect and abuse of a public institution, the only help offered by the community.

The social work system shared this critique of motherhood and disability. When Repouille turned to the city's social welfare system to bring his wife under control, the domestic relations court had two visions of the family to choose between: Repouille's unsubstantiated portrayal of Florence as a drunken and neglectful mother versus Florence's description of Repouille as a violent man who abused her and wanted to kill Raymond. The court ignored Repouille's violence and found no evidence of neglect or drinking by Florence. Instead, the probation officer decided that the "main difficulty in this case seems to be Raymond the crippled boy," who absorbed all of Florence's attention and disrupted the home.[54] The court blamed Repouille's admitted violence on its targets, Raymond and Florence. Their intimacy and inadequacies caused him to abuse them.

The court's interpretation was not inevitable. Repouille's and Florence's testimony allow us to construct an alternative narrative that focuses on Repouille himself as a deeply frustrated man with social ambitions. He wanted to become an American citizen and resented Florence's revelation of their immigrant status to the police and social workers. While Greenfield's part ownership of his business might stand for the moderate success of an immigrant, Repouille was still struggling. He worked steadily and turned over his wages to his wife but was able to afford only a cold-water flat on the outskirts of Harlem. Florence remembered that he had resented her pregnancy with Raymond, their first child, because it meant that she had to give up her well-paying job. According to Florence, her husband's violence began after she quit work and they had Raymond and their other children, which undoubtedly strained the family's resources. Florence's statement to the police suggests that Repouille's resentment of Raymond began well before the revelation of his disability and even before his birth. Raymond and Florence presented obvious targets for his frustration and violence.

Social service agencies, however, seemed unable to respond to such issues. Historian Linda Gordon describes a similar pattern in her study of family violence in Boston in this period. Social workers would ignore the husband's violence while attempting to "fix" the more available wife.[55] In this case, Raymond, also a victim of violence, became the primary focus of social intervention. Yet Florence, too, remained a target of both her husband and the social workers, through Raymond. While her husband threatened to kill Raymond, the social workers demanded that he be put away. As Ethel McDougall, the social worker, explained:

> Mrs. Repouille . . . had claimed that if Raymond was taken away from her she would break up her home and place all the other children—we felt she did not mean this, but that after Raymond was placed, she would realize that the other children had a claim upon her affection and care and she would then make a better adjustment as a mother.[56]

Not surprisingly, Florence felt that "the court wasn't on her side, was against her."[57]

The focus on Raymond and Florence's relationship is unaccounted for by the children's court records or the social workers' statements. After examining the records, it is difficult to see how Florence was failing as a mother. The social worker cited problems of cleanliness and money management, but she said that the apartment rooms "were not dirty; were cleaned up as much as possible; the paint was dirty and because of that gave the appearance of being upset."[58] The case record noted that social workers found no evidence that Florence drank or neglected any of her children. The Catholic charity worker who had earlier visited "felt that there was a possibility of fantasy on the man's part."[59] Raymond was not a major financial drain. The social worker, Florence, and Repouille all reported that the pair constantly fought about money but the only recent expenses for Raymond were for ice cream and fruit. The children's court judge, however, stated that the other children needed to be protected from Raymond and from Florence's "excessive love" for him.[60] Since the social worker and court made no specific accusations against Florence, it appears that, to them, Florence's love for Raymond was by its very nature excessive and dangerous to the family.

Raymond was thus blamed for the Repouille family's problems. The flaw in this judgment revealed itself when the family remained troubled after his removal. Less than a month after Raymond's murder, Florence went to the police to complain that her husband was threatening to beat her and that he had gone to the children's court to see if he could have the other children put away. She also said that she was "afraid to go to sleep at night with Mr. Repouille around."[61]

Conclusion

The Repouille and Greenfield trials could have followed a different pattern. The murder of James Fitzpatrick by his stepfather, Lawrence Rougeau, four days after Raymond's murder presents an alternate model.[62] Rougeau, apparently inspired by the earlier killings, claimed he feared that his stepson was beginning to show the initial signs of insanity, like his mother, who had recently been committed. The newspapers and police, however, rejected Rougeau's attempt to define James as a mercy victim. They described a blond, blue-eyed child who was "familiar to neighbors as a lively, 'normal' child."[63] One paper even published a picture of the attractive little boy, which they had not done for Raymond or Jerry. The coverage of Rougeau was unsympathetic and sarcastic. One paper remarked that he "seemed rather surprised today because nobody seemed to approve of his drowning of his stepson."[64] Rougeau's legal treatment was strikingly different as well. He plead guilty to second-degree murder. The district attorney informed the judge that such a plea would "insure such medical treatment for the defendant as he may require and remove the defendant from society, where he was a menace to himself and others."[65] In contrast, Repouille and Greenfield were charged with manslaughter, despite the months they spent planning the deaths of their sons. Neither man went to prison or was forced to have psychological treatment. Something was unmistakably different in the first two cases from the third. In the words of the *New York Herald Tribune*, the Greenfield case "inspired only universal pity for the harassed father," and the Repouille killing, though troubling for several reasons, had "undertones of the deepest tragedy." The Rougeau murder, by contrast, was a story "of unmitigated sordidness, which would seem to present none of the justification and evoke none of the compassion which were factors in the other two."[66]

The discussions of Jerry's and Raymond's murders separated out a single disruptive element—the disabled child. The implication was that the child's limitations created the tragedies that followed. Jerry's and Raymond's disabilities obscured all the complexities that contributed to their deaths. Family violence, poverty, inadequate social services—all became reflections and inevitable results of disability, rather than independent factors in the young men's murders. If the disabled child was the problem, there was no reason to look at the social structures in which the families lived. In this way, arguments for mercy killing and euthanasia that claimed to be social reforms simply left the responsibility in the hands of the family to choose between private care and drastic action, equating individual remedy with social change. Even for those who did not accept the validity of euthanasia or mercy killing, the accounts of the mercy-killing cases presented moral dramas in which a severely disabled child destroyed a family, leaving no apparent solution but death. Onlookers might describe the event as a tragic crime or a justified act, but either way, the disability served as the only possible explanation. The story of Raymond's death suggests that murdering a disabled child might not always be so different from other forms of child abuse. The similarities, however, were hidden behind the discourse of disability, which stated that "mercy killings" were essentially about disability. The implicit moral of these dramas was not necessarily that euthanasia was acceptable but that disability made it impossible for some people to share "normal" families and "normal" lives.

NOTES

1. Charles E. Rosenberg, "Introduction: Framing Disease: Illness, Society, and History," in Charles E Rosenberg and Janet Golden, eds., *Framing Disease: Studies in Cultural History* (New Brunswick, NJ: Rutgers University Press, 1992), xiii–xxvi.

2. For examples, see Ellen Dwyer, "Stories of Epilepsy, 1880–1930," in Rosenberg and Golden, eds., *Framing Disease*, 248–72; Philip M. Ferguson, *Abandoned to Their Fate: Social Policy and Practice toward Severely Retarded People in America, 1820–1920* (Philadelphia: Temple University Press, 1994); and Steven Noll, *Feeble-Minded in Our Midst: Institutions for the Mentally Retarded in the South, 1900–1940* (Chapel Hill: University of North Carolina Press, 1995), 109.

3. "Nature of Petition: Neglected Children" (carbon copy of Children's Court Case

File, in future cited as C.F.), Louis Repouille Case File, Municipal Archives of the City of New York, 4.

4. Michael Oliver, *The Politics of Disablement: A Sociological Approach* (New York: St. Martin's Press, 1990), 11.

5. I use the term *severely disabled* to indicate that Jerry and Raymond and others like them were put in a separate category and treated differently from individuals who were considered to be less disabled. In the course of this essay, I use the terms that many people find offensive, such as *mental defective*. I use these terms to indicate the historical categories and attitudes.

6. "Bronx man Kills Imbecile Son, 17," *New York World Telegram*, 12 January 1939.

7. "Mercy Slayer Says he Acted on 'God's Will,'" *New York Herald Tribune* (hereafter *NYHT*), 11 May 1939; "'Better Off Dead,'" *Time*, 23 January 1939.

8. "Mercy Killing Jurors Weep," *New York Sun*, 11 May 1939.

9. Martin Pernick, *The Black Stork: Eugenics and the Death of "Defective" Babies in American Medicine and Motion Pictures since 1915* (New York: Oxford University Press, 1994), 160–61.

10. Stephen Kuepper, "Euthanasia in America, 1890-1960: The Controversy, the Movement, and the Law" (Ph.D. diss., Rutgers University, 1981), 95–140; Pernick, *Black Stork*, 161–62, 163–67.

11. Louis Greenfield and Louis Repouille will be referred to by their last names because they share the same first name. All other family members will be called by their first names to distinguish them from Louis Greenfield and Louis Repouille.

12. My analysis of mercy killing was strongly influenced by "'Lives Not Worth Living,'" in Jenny Morris, *Pride against Prejudice: A Personal Politics of Disability* (London: Women's Press, 1991), 39–63; and Nat Hentoff, "The Awful Privacy of Baby Doe," in Alan Gartner and Tom Joe, eds., *Images of the Disabled, Disabling Images* (New York: Praeger, 1987), 161–75.

13. "Pity Drives Dad to Kill Sick Son," (New York) *Daily Mirror* (hereafter *DM*), 13 January 1949. See also the *new York Times* (hereafter *NYT*), *New York Sun, Brooklyn Eagle*, (hereafter *BE*), *Daily Mirror, Daily News*, and *New York Herald Tribune* between January and May 1939. Only direct quotations will be cited.

14. "Louis Repouille Statement," part I (hereafter L.R.I.), Louis Repouille Case File, 17.

15. "Father on Trial as 'Mercy Killer,'" *NYT*, 9 May 1939.

16. "3 Broken Lived Related by Wife of Mercy Killer," *NYHT*, 10 May 1939.

17. "Mercy Slayer Says He Acted on 'God's Will,'" *NYHT*, 11 May 1939.

18. "Mercy Killer, Freed by Jury, to Rest, Then Adopt a Child," *BE*, 12 May 1939.

19. Ibid.

20. See the Louis Repouille Case File and the *New York Times, New York Herald Tribune, New York Sun, New York World Telegram, Daily News*, and *Daily Mirror* between October 1939 and December 1947. Only direct quotations will be cited.

21. "Boy Cripple, 13, Is Put to Death By His Father," *NYHT*, 13 October 1939.

22. "Florence Repouille Statement," part I (hereafter F.R.I.), Louis Repouille Case File, 77.

23. C.F., 2.

24. F.R.I., 82.

25. Ibid.

26. Paul O'Dwyer, *Counsel for the Defense: The Autobiography of Paul O'Dwyer* (New York: Simon and Schuster, 1979).

27. *Repouille v. United States*, 165 F. 2d 152 (2d Cir. 1947).

28. Ibid.

29. Ibid.

30. "Statement of Ethel McDougall," part I (hereafter E.M.I.), Louis Repouille Case File, 7.

31. For examples of this image, see Alexander Johnson, "Children Who Never Grow Up," *Survey* (1 December 1922): 310-16; and Edgar A. Doll, "Children Who Never Grow Up," *Hygeia* 12 (June 1934): 534.

32. For discussions of passionate masculinity in this period, see Gail Bederman, *Manliness and Civilization: A Cultural History of Gender and Racism in the United States, 1880–1917* (Chicago: University of Chicago Press, 1995), 92–109; E. Anthony Rotundo, *American Manhood: Transformations in Masculinity from the Revolution to the Modern Era* (New York: Basic Books, 1993), 252–58; and Peter N. Stearns, "Men, Boys and Anger in American Society, 1860-1940," in *Manliness and Morality: Middle-Class Masculinity in Britain and America, 1800–1940*, ed. J. A. Mangan and James Walvin (Manchester: Manchester University Press, 1987), 75–91.

33. Martin F. Norden, *The Cinema of Isolation: A History of Physical Disability in the Movies* (New Brunswick, NJ: Rutgers University Press, 1994), 105–6.

34. Quentin Reynolds, *Courtroom: The Story of Samuel S. Leibowitz* (New York: Farrar, Straus & Co., 1950), 172; Estelle B. Freedman, "'Uncontrolled Desires': The Response to the Sexual Psychopath, 1920–1960," *Journal of American History* 74 (1987): 91, 83–106.

35. "Boy Slain by Father Menace, Doctor Says," *NYT*, 10 May 1939.

36. I. Newton Kugelmass, *The Management of Mental Deficiency in Children* (New York: Grune & Stratton, 1954).

37. Joel T. Branslow discussed the use of vasectomy to treat mental illness in "In the Name of Therapeutics: The Practice of Sterilization in a California State Hospital," *Journal of the History of Medicine* 51 (1996): 29–51, and in *Mental Ills and Bodily Cures: Psychiatric Treatment in the First Half of the Twentieth Century* (Los Angeles: University of California Press, 1997), 54–70.

38. See Pernick, *Black Stork*, 89-97; and Kuepper, "Euthanasia in America," 95-127.

39. C.F., 4.

40. "3 Broken Lives."

41. Robert Bogdan, *Freak Show: Presenting Human Oddities for Amusement and Profit* (Chicago: University of Chicago Press, 1988), 275–78; Pernick, *Black Stork*, 121–25; Rosemarie Garland-Thomson, *Extraordinary Bodies: Figuring Physical Disability in American Culture and Literature* (New York: Columbia University Press, 1997), 75–78.

42. "'Mercy Killer' Bases Defense on Pictures," *DM*, 19 January 1939.

43. Kuepper, "Euthanasia in America," 95–168; and Pernick, *Black Stork*.

44. "Mercy Killings in New York" (clipping), Louis Repouille Case File; "Euthanasia and the Law," *NYHT*, 16 October 1939.

45. Leo Kanner, "Exoneration of the Feebleminded," *American Journal of Psychiatry* 9 (1942): 21.

46. My discussion of Florence and Raymond's relationship was shaped by Robert Bogdan and Steven Taylor, "Relationships with Severely Disabled People: The Social Construction of Humanness," *Social Problems* 36 (1989): 135–48.

47. F.R.I., 32.

48. Ibid., 85.

49. Christina Hardyment, *Perfect Parents: Baby-Care Advice Past and Present* (New York: Oxford University Press, 1995), 189–92; Peter N. Stearns, *American Cool: Constructing a Twentieth-Century Emotional Style* (New York: New York University Press, 1994), 165–71.

50. Ruth Schwartz Cowan, *More Work for Mother: The Ironies of Household Technology from the Open Hearth to the Microwave* (New York: Basic Books, 1983); Linda Gordon, *Pitied But Not Entitled: Single Mothers and the History of Welfare* (Cambridge, MA: Harvard University Press, 1994).

51. "3 Broken Lives."

52. For examples, see John Ruhräh, "The Parent and the Handicapped Child," *Hygeia* 12 (October 1934): 902; and Ethel Horsefield, "Suggestion for Training the Mentally Retarded by Parents in the Home," *American Journal of Mental Deficiency* 46 (1941–42): 533–37.

53. "3 Broken Lives."

54. C.F., 3.

55. Linda Gordon, *Heroes of Their Own Lives: The Politics and History of Family Violence, Boston 1880–1960* (New York: Penguin Books, 1989), 281–82. See also David Peterson del Mar, *What Trouble I Have Seen: A History of Violence against Wives* (Cambridge, MA: Harvard University Press, 1996), 115–34.

56. E.M.I., 19.

57. Florence, quoted by McDougall, E.M.I., 16.

58. E.M.I., 13

59. Ibid., 6.

60. C.F., 4.

61. "Mrs. Repouille," 1 November 1939, Louis Repouille Case File.

62. On October 16, 1939, Rougeau's story was covered by the following newspapers: *The Sun, New York Times, Daily News,* and *Daily Mirror.*

63. "Stepfather Slays Boy, 5, by Drowning," *NYT,* 16 October 1939.

64. "Lays Killing of Son to Fear of Insanity" (clipping), n.d., Laurence Rougeau Case File, New York Municipal Archives.

65. "Recommendation," by Thomas E. Dewey, District Attorney, Lawrence Rougeau Case File.

66. "Euthanasia and the Law."

12

Blind and Enlightened

The Contested Origins of the Egalitarian Politics of
the Blinded Veterans Association

David A. Gerber

Positive stereotypes can be as big a burden to bear as negative ones.[1] For those who choose to conform to them, they set impossible standards and impose narrow goals. Such is the case, for example, with the cliché that the blind are capable of deeper wisdom than the sighted by virtue of their liberation from the distraction of visible, surface impressions that hide the actual nature of things and people. Blind disability activists denounce this flattering stereotype, just as they denounce negative stereotypes of the blind as helpless or doomed to live in existential and cognitive darkness.[2] I do not wish to argue that stereotypes serve as an effective basis for analytical thinking. The history of the blinded American veterans of World War II, however, does suggest that blindness incurred in adulthood was instrumental in influencing a significant, progressive reorientation in deeply held beliefs. Certainly, this is what members of the founding cohort of the Blinded Veterans Association (BVA) offer when asked about the origin of the BVA's strong organizational commitment, from the moment of its birth, to fighting racial, religious, and ethnic prejudices. Blindness, they told me in oral history interviews, in a variety of ways led them directly to their egalitarianism.[3]

The oral history testimonies of blinded veterans of World War II about this politics may at one and the same time get the narrative history of that commitment wrong, while expressing nonetheless what is, for these men, a larger symbolic truth. Regardless of whether their organization was actually born without prejudice, as they contend, or whether it arrived at its politics through internal struggle, which I believe more plausible, the experience of confronting and adjusting to blindness did require the white Christian majority of these men to shed many of the social attitudes and assumptions about Others that they had taken for granted prior to becoming disabled.

The BVA was founded in March 1945 at Old Farms, the U.S. Army's blind rehabilitation facility located at Avon, Connecticut. Its founders were some one hundred men, then undergoing mobility and orientation training, who had been blinded in combat or by accidents and disease while serving in the U.S. Army and Air Force during World War II. (Navy and Marine blinded servicemen were rehabilitated separately at the Philadelphia Naval Hospital, but many of these veterans, too, soon joined the BVA.) By 1948, the BVA represented some 850 (60 percent) of the 1,400 American servicemen who became visually impaired as a result of the war.[4] The BVA sought to ensure that blinded veterans received the material and medical assistance they needed from the Veterans Administration (VA) to make an effective, practical transition into civilian life. Ultimately, the veterans hoped to reclaim conventionally valid social identities and civic dignity. The BVA aimed to stimulate self-help and solidarity among the men and to combat any discrimination against them in employment and in public accommodations that would block their reentry into civilian life.[5] Its founders feared that through demoralization and discrimination, the blinded veterans would come to share the fate of the civilian blind. Very few of these men had had any actual contact with civilian blind people. Yet they harbored many fears, based partly on the actual lowly status of the blind and partly on their own prejudices. Blind people, they believed, were inevitably reduced to dependent, socially marginal denizens of sheltered workshops; blind people, they understood, received pity and charity but lost their social roles and self-respect and, with these losses, their claims to civic dignity.[6] Thus, although the BVA adopted admirably universalistic goals in its fight against racial and disability discrimination, its ideology sought on a very basic level to separate the blinded veterans from the civilian blind.

From its inception, the BVA took a strong stand against racism and anti-Semitism. Both of these forces were pervasive in American society, if unacceptable to many thoughtful Americans as consciousness dawned of the terrible consequences of Nazi racist anti-Semitism.[7] Its politics of inclusion and egalitarianism would put the BVA in the progressive forefront of veterans groups in encouraging equality and mutual understanding among Americans, both in its own ranks and in society. A 1946 survey of the seven major veterans organizations found a complex, contradictory pattern of official silence, formal tolerance, and local discrimination, especially regarding African American membership. While the largest veterans organizations—the American Legion, the Veterans of Foreign Wars, the American Veterans of World War II, and the Disabled American Veterans—did not bar blacks, they never forced the issue of open membership on their local posts. In large part, they feared that the membership would become divided by such insistence. As a consequence, blacks were mostly excluded or allowed to organize separate chapters, depending on the section of the country and the state of local white opinion. Mixed posts were rare. Several smaller veterans organizations (the American Veterans Committee, the Veterans League of America, and the National Conference of Union Labor Legionnaires) shared liberal or moderately leftist convictions; as national policy, they spoke out for civil rights legislation, and the American Veterans Committee strongly encouraged open membership and mixed local affiliates. No record of formal anti-Semitism in veterans organizations exists. Anecdotal evidence, however, suggests its presence in the local posts of the largest groups, as in voluntary associations and semipublic institutions throughout American society. The continuing existence of the separate Jewish War Veterans of America, established in 1896 by Civil War veterans, speaks to the reaction of Jews to the hostility they faced in mixing with Christian veterans, as well as to specific Jewish cultural and political needs.[8]

In both word and deed, the BVA's founders took the opposite course, encouraging equality and inclusion among the membership and speaking out against segregation, discrimination, and intolerance. Individual BVA chapters were integrated by race, ethnicity, and religion, with Jewish, African American, Japanese American, and Mexican American men represented alongside white Christians. From the BVA's earliest years it included a rabbi as well as a priest and minister among its national chaplains. Its leadership ranks, too, were inclusive from the beginning. Pincus Hoffman, a Jew who had been snow-blinded while stationed in the Aleutian Islands, chaired the BVA's founding meeting. Hoffman was elected the association's first vice president, then became its secretary and treasurer, and served on the national board of directors in later years, just as would other Jewish members. Vasco DeGama Hale, a Connecticut African American who was blinded, partially deafened, and lost one hand and four fingers of the other hand in a training accident, was chosen national secretary by a vote of the entire membership in 1951; as such, he sat on the national board of directors. James W. Hope, an African American from North Carolina, had been on the board of directors a few years before Hale began to serve.[9]

Just as the BVA fought to have guide dogs admitted to public places and denounced discrimination in employment against the blind, it spoke out in support of passage of civil rights legislation for African Americans, again in contrast to most other veterans organizations.[10] Whenever possible, the BVA combined its disability politics and its antiracist commitment, sometimes going to considerable lengths to make its political point. One noted instance was widely reported in the press in 1946. When Sergeant Isaac Woodard, an African American with four years of military service, was blinded as a result of a gratuitous, savage beating by civilian police in South Carolina, the BVA called for the prosecution of Woodard's attackers. At an early opportunity after Woodard's convalescence, the BVA inducted him into its ranks at an impressive ceremony at its New York City headquarters, to which it invited the press.[11] The commitment to the values of equality, inclusion, and solidarity that the BVA displayed in its embrace of Woodard is effectively symbolized by its official insignia, adopted in 1947: a large, six-pointed military star containing two masculine hands, one of them dark in color and one of them light, grasped in friendship and solidarity; just above the star are a cross and a star of David.[12]

Nothing in the general and, as observers have remarked, greatly diverse political, social, ethnocultural, and regional backgrounds of the BVA's early membership prior to blindness[13] would have led one to predict so forthright a stand against the prejudices deeply embedded in their society and in other veterans organizations. There is certainly no evidence of prewar political, let alone antiracist, activism among those who founded and led the early BVA. We are naturally led to inquire what there was in the experience of these men—an experience of military service, traumatic injury, blindness, rehabilitation, and group formation—that produced their egalitarianism.

We are not the first to make this inquiry. No analytical history of the BVA exists to assist us, and the BVA's official record (its two in-house histories written in the 1990s for fund-raising purposes[14] and its monthly publication, *The BVA Bulletin*) is silent on the subject, as if to say the organization was born, without birth pains, with its politics. A sighted friend of the BVA at the time of its founding, however, the novelist Baynard Kendrick (1894–1977), did attempt to explain the relation between the blinded veterans' experience and their politics.

In my research, I encountered Kendrick through a neglected feature film, *Bright Victory* (1951).[15] At moments, with surprising effectiveness for a Hollywood melodrama, this film attempted to link the story of the blinded veterans' antiracist commitment with their experience of injury and rehabilitation. The movie itself was based on an equally obscure novel, *Lights Out* (1946),[16] which was written by Kendrick, who is remembered today among devotees of the mystery as the creator of the detective Duncan Maclain, a combat-blinded veteran of World War I whose acutely developed, compensatory sensorium is the source of his ingenious but usually plausible investigative talent.[17] Both *Bright Victory* and *Lights Out* trace the spiritual journey of Larry Niven, a young blinded veteran whose unreflective racism, the result of his Florida upbringing, is gradually transformed into a commitment to racial equality as he painfully embarks on the path to rehabilitation at army hospitals and at Old Farms. In these institutions, he is surrounded by veterans of all races, ethnicities, and religions. Each veteran, whatever his background, seems equally traumatized by losing his sight. All of them need the practical assistance and moral support of one another to save them from giving in to helplessness, dependence, and despair. Niven must fight two battles simultaneously—one against his own deeply ingrained racial prejudices and the other against the suicidal despair and self-hatred with which he initially confronts his blindness.

Both *Lights Out* and *Bright Victory*, the latter with a more upbeat title designed to attract the mass audience for Hollywood entertainments, are for the most part highly conventionalized products of mid-century, middlebrow, mass culture. They combine the well-trod paths of romantic entertainment with a moralistic exploration of a significant social problem. Racism is not understood in the book or the movie in terms of structural forces, conflicting political and economic interests, and differentials in power between significant social groups. Instead, within the strictures of bourgeois ideology, it appears as the dilemmas and reactions of individuals. Within these conventions, individuals resolve social problems by adjusting as individuals, usually at some level through heterosexual bonding; and they do so in ways that work to reestablish the legitimacy of the status quo.[18] A melodramatic romance of the boy (Niven) gets girl (Judy), boy loses girl, and boy and girl are reunited variety pushes the plot along in both the book and the movie. Larry Niven eventually finds love, after rejecting Judy because of his initial fear of dependence and because he believes Judy mistakes love for the pity she might feel for him. Similarly, he eventually finds the capacity to love himself as a blind man, after being tempted by suicide. Moreover, Niven grows to love his friend Joe Morgan, the blinded African American veteran whom he at first rejects after learning of Morgan's color. If the plotting is predictable, so, too, is Kendrick's work as a technician

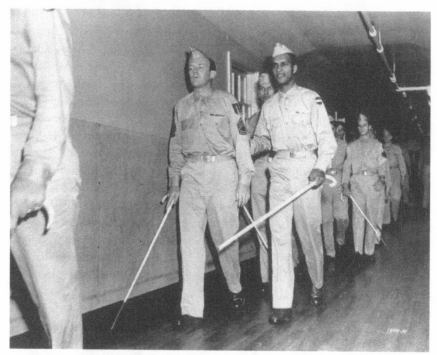

Figure 12.1. In *Bright Victory* (1951), the southern-born blinded veteran Larry Niven (Arthur Kennedy) befriends Joe Morgan (James Edwards) during their residence at an army rehabilitation facility, then rejects him when he learns Morgan is an African American, and finally seeks reconciliation when his blindness leads him to reevaluate his racial prejudice. Copyright © 2000 by Universal City Studios, Inc. Courtesy of Universal Studios Publishing Rights. All rights reserved. Frame enlargement courtesy of the George Eastman House Motion Picture Collection. The author gratefully acknowledges the cooperation of Laurie Kennedy.

of language. From the book's dedication to a blinded veteran and BVA founder ("To Lt. Lloyd Greenwood, USAAF, who has vision") and the acknowledgments (among them one to "the boys who have sacrificed their sight so that the people of the world might have another chance to see"), we know we are in for much clichéd, metaphorical manipulation of the imagery of vision and blindness, light and dark, black and white, and ignorance and insight. Like Joseph Conrad in *Heart of Darkness*, Kendrick necessarily reverses the associations of light, clarity, and truth, for Niven's blindness, his darkness, must lead to his enlightenment. Blindness brings him to understand, among other things, the insignificance of color as a marker of human difference, but he struggles mightily with himself and with his more tolerant comrades to reach this point.[19]

In searching for a hypothesis to explain these connections, one is naturally led to wonder if Kendrick has the story right. He embraces the stereotype of the blind gaining wisdom from their condition but sees this as a gradual process achieved through conflict. Perhaps the pilgrimage of Larry Niven is in some way representative of that of the BVA and its founding cohort toward their egalitarianism. Why not, then, proceed to let Kendrick dictate a hypothesis about the BVA's politics: that this politics was born in internal struggle, within and among men who shared their society's prejudices but who, in the process of rehabilitation, as they reached out to one another and came to understand the value of solidarity, had an experience of political enlightenment?

This hypothesis is given legitimacy by the fact that Kendrick was hardly an unknowing observer. His lifelong commitment to the blind began during World War I when, as a young American volunteer in the Canadian Army, he visited St. Dunstan's, Great Britain's recently founded and much-respected facility for the rehabilitation of blinded servicemen.[20] There he met with a former school classmate, who had been blinded in combat. As Kendrick later recalled, he left awestruck at the compensatory abilities of the blinded veterans he met, encounters that served as one foundation for the character of Duncan Maclain.[21] After returning from the war, he worked for a time for the management of an industrial firm in Florida, a state he loved for its natural beauty and hated for its reactionary racial politics. A business career, however, was not to Kendrick's liking, and he retired in 1931. He wanted to write and had begun to publish mysteries in the 1920s. It was not until 1937 that he produced the first of the crime novels involving Maclain, the writing of which required him to do extensive background research at blindness agencies and rehabilitation facilities.[22] His ingenious and commercially successful books as well as his frequent presence among them made him well known to professional blindness workers employed by the American Foundation for the Blind. Kendrick was too old to serve in World War II, but these men and women, many of whom shifted their attention during the war to the rehabilitation of blinded servicemen, recruited him to visit armed forces hospitals and give encouragement to these often despairing men. When, early in 1944, Old Farms opened, he was asked to serve as a full-time volunteer, teaching courses of his own innovative design in accounting, English, and creative writing.[23] Because the army sustained most of the American blinded casualties and almost all these men underwent rehabilitation at Old Farms, Kendrick came in contact in his classroom, the mess hall, and the recreation room with a large, representative sample of the blinded veterans. Old Farms is the setting for much of *Lights Out* and hence of *Bright Victory*. Kendrick's most effective writing is found in his evocation of place, both Florida in the preintegration era and Old Farms, and in his depictions of the daily life of the blind men undergoing rehabilitation.

The founders of the BVA believed that blinded veterans must control their own veterans organization. They believed they knew best what programs would serve their interests; moreover, they needed to prove to themselves that their disability would not prevent them from governing their own affairs. For these reasons, they refused to leave their interests to the larger and more powerful organizations like the American Legion. Moreover, they insisted that all the officers and board members of the BVA be blinded veterans.[24] Nonetheless, they felt a close enough friendship for and trust in Kendrick to appoint him to their first board of directors, on which he was the only sighted member, and to give him the title "Honorary Chairman." He worked for the BVA for a year, setting up its New York headquarters and producing its publications. From the start, his activities were aimed at training the blinded men to replace him and to run the office themselves, as they soon came to do. Kendrick thus initiated the BVA's commitment to the struggle for equal employment opportunity for blind people in its own offices. He continued to speak and lobby in behalf of the blinded veterans after leaving his BVA position.[25]

This detail about Kendrick is important for establishing his authority not only to speak about and for blinded veterans but to render their history with insight and accuracy. To be sure, Kendrick was an artist, and his writings sought to further his own high-minded and didactic purposes. His novel is certainly not history, and it is clear that he folded into it a number of disparate elements (his own Florida experience, hatred of segregation, liberal internationalism, and close identification with the blinded veterans) that were familiar to him and over which he believed he could easily take artistic control. Yet his vision of men transformed by devastating injury and learning to live with themselves and with each other in new ways, including mutual tolerance, is not implausible.

The greatest problem for this surmise is that the blinded veterans themselves do not remember their history as Kendrick rendered it in his novel or as screenwriter Robert Buckner formulated it for the Hollywood version. In interviews on one or more occasions with five significant members of the BVA founding cohort, I asked these men to identify the origins of the BVA's progressive politics. For them the question was surprising, because the answer seemed so obvious: blindness, I was told by Irvin Schloss, who was twice BVA president and for a decade a member of the board of directors, "overpowered all other distinctions between us."[26] Russell Williams, one of the BVA's founders who established the first permanent Veterans Administration Blind Rehabilitation Facility at the Hines, Illinois, VA Hospital in 1948 and then went on, from 1959 to 1976, to serve as director of Blind Rehabilitation Services for the Veterans Administration, added that blindness imposed "maturity" of judgment on the veterans and thus forced them to see that racial prejudice was as unreasonable as the prejudice against the blind.[27] Anyway, they say plausibly, but with a sly trace of irony, what possible difference does skin color, of all things, make when you are blind? In effect, they suggest that blindness was an instant, democratizing force in their lives. In their telling, it obliterated military rank and all of the fragmenting social categories and identities that divided them in civilian life and brought them together in experiences, perceptions, and needs. But they will also admit, when further and closely questioned (and this is a distinctly minor and reluctantly granted point in their re-creation of the BVA's early political history), to contradictory details. Yes, there were men at the hospitals and rehabilitation facilities where their cohort was formed, and even later in the BVA itself, who were not egalitarians and were slow to accept egalitarian principles. Indeed, struggle sometimes resulted from the clash of values and views.[28] The existence of such individuals hardly surprises an outside observer, given the practices and the attitudes of the larger society, of which the BVA, with all its regional and social diversity, was broadly representative. Clearly, however, the members of the founding cohort I interviewed seem to believe that blindness *should* have overwhelmed prejudice. They themselves appear to have been too immersed psychologically in the process by which this actually did occur, in real time and in daily life, to stand back and make sense of the transformation that took place in men's minds.

We move closer to understanding the meanings of their testimonies when we understand the grounds for their impatience with Kendrick's novel and the movie. Russell Williams spoke with me about Kendrick's narrative and its principal characters. Like many other BVA activists, Williams had had *Lights Out* read to him, and along with the BVA's first president, Ray Frey, he had served as a consultant to the makers of the movie. But Williams's intimacy with

Kendrick's materials did not bring about sympathy for the novelist's characters, particularly Niven, whom Williams found vacillating and indecisive. Niven and Judy, he said, did not know what they wanted, and they agonized endlessly about it at that.[29] I believe that Williams is not simply being impatient with the genre of melodrama here. In his suffering and confusion, the character of Niven, at least throughout most of Kendrick's story until, at the end, he achieves his psychological breakthrough, represented for Williams and his peers what they might become. If they surrendered themselves to isolation from their fellow blinded veterans, to the impulse to re-create the social hierarchies of the prewar experience in their postinjury lives, and, above all else, to self-pity and a self-imposed loss of personal autonomy, they, too, might vacillate and become powerless to take control of their lives.

Thus, with tremendous self-discipline, Williams and other BVA founders developed an ideology that insisted on solidarity and commitment to one another's welfare. They held a positive attitude that was open to rehabilitation and refused to allow the blinded veterans to trade indefinitely on public goodwill, to become wards of the government, or to indulge, at least in public, in regrets. How else, they reasoned, could they begin to face the challenge of their disability but by building solidarity and mutual support on the basis of their military comradeship and discipline and the collective experience of rehabilitation? Blindness incurred in adulthood, and in many of their cases as wounded combat veterans, with little warning or time for preparation, was as fundamental a challenge to autonomy, self-confidence, and self-respect as these men could imagine. That challenge was even stronger in a culture in which people with disabilities had to wage a constant struggle against the prejudices that limited their inclusion and autonomy. We need to recall that the founding BVA cohort was highly conscious of the lowly position of the civilian blind and anxious to resist being reduced to rolelessness and dependence. Mutual respect and solidarity, and hence drawing from the group the courage to go on with their individual lives, could readily have appeared to them the *sine qua non* for successful rehabilitation and reintegration, for these were values that preserved their sense of themselves as a distinct social group, different from the civilian disabled and possessed of singular claims to civic dignity for their sacrifices on behalf of their country.

To understand the BVA's early political history, we need to analyze the protean act of ideological construction by which the founding cohort of the BVA brought together its disability ethic from disparate sources. There were few precedents or models for them to call upon from either civilian or veteran experiences of disability, and especially of blindness. Initially, they had no contact with the National Federation of the Blind or its state affiliates. As far as they were aware, in the past these populations had largely been acted *upon* or *for* but had been able to exert little agency on behalf of their own interests. Begin with the veterans' embrace of the view that blindness incurred in adulthood can best be characterized as a series of psychological, physical, and social losses that constitute a virtual death of the adult personality. Adjustment and rehabilitation, therefore, constitute acts of rebirth, in which the old self must act willfully as the midwife for the new. This view of blindness is associated with two sighted men influential in the lives of the founding cohort: Dr. Alan Blackburn, a blindness specialist and wartime military medical official who was greatly responsible for the founding of Old Farms, and Rev. Thomas Carroll, a Catholic priest and for many years head of the Boston diocese's Guild for the Blind, who shared with a handful of sighted people, such as Kendrick, the confidence of the blinded veterans and served as a BVA chaplain.[30] In later years, the death-and-rebirth view of blindness would seem to men like Russell Williams an overdramatization of the situation of the blinded, which Williams came to understand more in terms of inconvenience than handicap. But especially in the BVA's early years, it was widely accepted as the fundamental psychological truth from which rehabilitation had to spring.[31]

In language rich in the gendered metaphors of their own experience and culture—metaphors of military endeavor, the masculine warrior, and manliness—the BVA founders would proceed over the years to analyze the terms of this rebirth and the ideal character of the new man who emerged from it. They would speak of waging a "concentrated attack" on blindness, describe the campaign to be waged as "our own fight" and as "a battle against darkness," seek the "fortification of knowledge" against the limitations imposed by the prejudices against the blind, and call for strategies that would "spearhead the advance" of the BVA and help it to take "command of the situation" of the blinded veteran.[32] The goal was "to be men again" and "men among men."[33] Williams also spoke of "respectability"—"striving to once again feel genuinely respected" in the community of men by being independent and possessing self-confidence and self-respect.[34]

The program the BVA created sought to win this campaign for masculine dignity[35] on two fronts. The first was the struggle to create a public context, characterized by opportunity, accessibility, and inclusion, for reintegration of the blinded veterans. The organization sought to marshal resources to ensure that they reentered society with the assistance they needed to compete effectively. The BVA engaged in a campaign of public education, lobbying, and lawsuits to oppose discrimination against the blind in employment and residence. It advocated for access to public accommodations for those using guide dogs. While it warned against dependence on government paternalism that would turn men who could work into retired pensioners, the BVA nonetheless understood the necessity of attaining safety nets for blinded veterans. It represented men in their efforts to acquire the best pension ratings as visual impairments and general health worsened over the years. Faced with the army's decision to close Old Farms, the BVA began calling in May 1945 for the creation of a permanent blind rehabilitation program within the Veterans Administration, an effort in which it worked closely with the Veterans Administration in an advisory role. This campaign culminated in the opening of such a facility under Russell Williams's direction at the Hines, Illinois, Veterans Administration Hospital in 1948.[36]

But the founding cohort of the BVA's aggressive campaign for the normalization of the blinded veteran did not stop with these public goals. From the beginning, in line with the view that blindness required a largely self-directed rebirth, the founding cohort placed a strong emphasis on a second front: the role of the transformed individual in achieving Williams's "respectability."

The ideal blinded veteran's character in this formulation of manhood consisted of three elements. The first was a willingness to be rehabilitated. Above all else, rehabilitation meant the courage to acquire orientation and mobility skills and to use them to be independent. While convalescing from their injuries at the Valley Forge Army Hospital at Phoenixville, Pennsylvania, many of the men who next would go to Old Farms were introduced to the use of the long, white metal cane for orientation and mobility. Cane technique was, in fact, greatly advanced during World War II through the work of Dr. Richard Hoover, who hoped to assist American blinded war veterans.[37] At Old Farms, however, cane technique was de-emphasized in favor of a soon-to-be discredited theory of facial vision: men were supposed to be taught to "braille" environments through messages that surfaces and spaces were believed to send to the nerves of the face. They were allowed the assistance of only some rudimentary handheld devices, finger snapping, and heel taps. They were allowed to use their canes only when they left the grounds of Old Farms. In addition to the belief that men taught facial vision could dispense with the encumbrance of the cane, the theorists of facial vision considered the white cane a stigmatizing marker of disability.[38] The blind men themselves soon came to understand that few, if any, of them possessed the nerve sensitivity that facial vision required and that, as an extension of the body and conductor of sound, the white cane was greatly superior. Moreover, they understood that the white cane was stigmatizing only to the extent that the public possessed prejudices about blind people. It was not consistent with their understanding of their dignity to attempt to mask their blindness, let alone make any concessions to prejudice.[39]

Out of the rise of consciousness about the white cane as both symbol and instrument, the BVA founding cohort embraced cane technique as the primary method of rehabilitation. Their campaign for a permanent blind rehabilitation center that led to the opening of the Hines, Illinois, facility was premised on the necessity of further training in the use of the cane for those whose exposure to it had been frustrated at Old Farms and whose cane skills were rudimentary or in decline. Williams's demanding eighteen-week rehabilitation program at Hines, the epitome of the sort of masculinized "tough love" approach to rebirth that characterized BVA ideology, placed cane technique at the center of its pedagogy. Men who signed up for the course were not allowed to see family or relatives for the entire four-and-a-half-month program, in the belief that contacts, particularly with wives, mothers, and girlfriends, were distracting and likely to be characterized by some degree of spoiling and pity. Instead, Williams's students spent their days learning typing, braille, the use of various electronic prosthetic devices, job skills, sports and recreation, and, above all else, the use of the cane. Completion of a special project was required in order to graduate: monitored by instructors who followed him at a distance, each man had to find his way from suburban Hines into the congested heart of downtown Chicago and back using public transportation, a journey that required taking a bus, transferring to a commuter train, and then reversing the process.[40] This program was too demanding for many men, and Williams would be criticized in later years for the uncompromising standards he set for reaching out for "respectability."[41] Even men who passed through the program successfully did not necessarily keep up their cane skills, which require periodic renewal to check the rise of bad habits. As men aged, they often became dependent on their wives, as they willingly admit when interviewed.[42]

The second of the elements of the ideal blinded veteran's character relates to this uncompromising requirement that men give themselves over to rehabilitation. The purpose of mastering cane technique was to be an independent traveler, particularly not dependent on female helpmates, in order to function normally in daily life. The BVA took pride in the fact that its field service, which was formed to help the organization reach isolated men who lacked the skills to travel and needed to be encouraged into rehabilitation, was composed of salaried blinded veterans, able and willing to travel vast distances to bring assistance to others. Above all else, normal functioning required that the blinded veterans return to the workplace and, even while possessing a generous pension, become self-supporting. Just as the BVA itself at first refused to engage in fund-raising, in order to avoid being perceived as a charity organization manipulating pity and guilt to rake in donations, it encouraged blinded veterans to refuse to live solely off public funds. BVA members were not to be members of "the sitters club" of bored pensioners. Armed with its motto "Jobs not pity," the early BVA placed a heavy emphasis on job counseling and placement. For the BVA cohort, work did not mean what were contemptuously called "blind jobs," for example, making brooms in sheltered workshops. Work meant a return to the civilian workforce in any respectable employment or profession that a visually impaired man could realistically hope to do. Of course, allowances were made for special opportunities given only to the blind; for example, beginning at Old Farms, many blinded veterans were taught to run newsstands in government buildings, to a great extent because they were given preference by law in the granting of concessions in these locations.[43] Ideology aside, these lofty goals for normalized employment, like those for completely independent mobility and orientation, were only partially met. Employer prejudices, declining health (many of the men had multiple war injuries that worsened over time), and the temptations of generous pensions conspired to keep many men out of the job market. By 1958, only half of the relatively youthful cohorts of World War II and Korean War blinded veterans were in the workforce, and as they reached their middle years, many left the labor market permanently.[44]

The third element, deemed essential for achieving all other group and individual goals—solidarity—brings us back to the subject with which we began our inquiry into the blinded veterans' embrace of egalitarianism. The intense solidarity that has characterized the BVA's understanding of the ideal character of the blinded veteran throughout the organization's history, and that has been expected of and practiced by its members, dates from the experience of cohort formation of the founding generation during and just after World War II. It was not simply that blindness as such created the intense fellowship shared by the members of the cohort. The practical progress of these men as a unit, from the battlefield to Old Farms and Hines, into civilian life, and then through the balance of the life cycle, conditioned them to support one another and draw strength from the group. Their sense of comradeship was reinforced by the masculine military ethos, which, as the BVA's language suggests, outlived the actual experience of being in the armed services.

Their intense solidarity was situationally reinforced. The number of blinded servicemen was not large. The policy of armed forces medicine was to concentrate men with similar injuries together to facilitate treatment in a cost-effective manner, but with the recognition of the psychological benefits to the men involved. In the case of the blinded men, this concentration proceeded without regard to race. Though stateside military hospitals and rehabilitation facilities were inconsistent during the war regarding the racial integration of wounded men, here maintaining segregated medicine but there refusing to do so, the small numbers of blinded men and of specialists to treat them and the great expense of maintaining blind rehabilitation facilities worked in favor of mixing men across all the lines that usually divided them.[45]

Within hospitals and rehabilitation facilities, intense friendships and networks of friends were formed. These provided an interpersonal foundation for the emergent cohort that became the BVA. It would seem that the intensity of these relationships grew in direct proportion to these men's perception of the severity of the challenge of blindness. Those observing the BVA from outside have been quick to comment on the strong solidarity that existed among its members. Comparing the BVA to other veterans organizations, Hector Chevigny and Sydell Braverman noted in 1950 that "there is every indication that it is the most strongly imbued with a sense of real relationship among its members."[46] To speak with the members of the founding cohort is to understand quickly that this solidarity did not end at Old Farms or Hines or even at the close of the annual BVA convention. It continued daily, throughout the life cycle, as these men married, became parents, went back to work, bought homes, and faced, with the added difficulties that blindness put in their path, the daily frustrations and triumphs that characterize the adult American life. For them, therefore, a belief of the "I never could have made it without my buddies" variety seemed just as valid in their seventies, when I interviewed them, as in their twenties, when the large majority of them were injured.

So deeply embedded in the consciousness of the BVA's founding cohort became these beliefs in solidarity and egalitarianism that at the time of these interviews, these veterans continued to minimize or to deny whatever ideological divisions existed in their ranks at the time the BVA was founded. Even differences that involved significant principles or deeply held beliefs, such as the superiority of the white race, were considered minor compared to the need to face blindness together. The official narrative of the BVA's history that one finds in its in-house publications tells much in this regard: while other narrative strategies, such as mastering techniques of rehabilitation and the struggle to maintain government benefits, are certainly explored, the most emotionally evocative and intensely depicted moments are those dedicated to the practice of the mutual assistance and solidarity that helped men confront self-pity, powerlessness, and despair.[47]

Equally telling are the veterans' memories of the men in their cohort whom they remember as inadequate role models. In some accounts, these are the men whom Williams calls "poor travelers"—veterans who lacked the courage for true rehabilitation, proved fearful of going out into the world and of working a regular job, and remained excessively dependent on their wives.[48] But even more often, the inadequate role model is the man who broke solidarity and turned his back on the cohort. Al Schmid, a blinded combat veteran who won the Congressional Medal of Honor for his conduct during a battle at Guadalcanal in 1942, provides an example. One of the first widely acknowledged American heroes of World War II, Schmid appeared frequently on the war bond circuit during the war and was the subject of the immediate postwar feature film *Pride of the Marines*. As a Marine he was not rehabilitated at Old Farms, but his notoriety and the BVA founders' desire to bring U.S. Navy and Marine veterans into the new organization made him an excellent choice for the first BVA board of directors. Yet Schmid never attended a BVA meeting and had little contact with blinded veterans or with blind people generally throughout his life.[48] As his wife told me in an interview, "Al didn't make a big deal of being blind." The same could hardly be said about the men who founded the BVA, who retained strong, negative feelings about Schmid for many years.[49]

Thus, the desire to maintain the symbol and the practice of solidarity led to both a formal organizational memory and an informal oral tradition that wrote the history of internal struggle—one aspect of which Kendrick attempted to capture—out of the BVA men's understanding of the collective past. The resulting understanding, which is more poetically consistent with the metaphor of rebirth than is the actual record of struggle, made it appear that the BVA was born egalitarian. But the matter was, of course, not *consciously* resolved in the minds of the veterans. Long-term autobiographical

David A. Gerber

memory is constantly semiconsciously filtered, accreting layers of add-ons and revisions.[50] In many ways, in later years the value of solidarity increased in the minds of the BVA's founders. As it did, the memory of what divided these men, which had formed part of Kendrick's narrative and which could be brought up to consciousness again only under rather insistent questioning, grew increasingly less accessible. In no way does this memory of how blindness changed them discredit the founders of the BVA; but then, neither does the more precisely accurate version of their story told by Kendrick.

NOTES

1. Portions of this essay were previously published as "Memory of Enlightenment: Accounting for the Egalitarian Politics of the Blinded Veterans Association," *Disability Studies Quarterly* 18 (Fall 1998): 257-63. I would like to acknowledge the assistance of Bruce Stave, Alice Hoffman, and a room full of enthusiastic auditors (whose names I could not learn under the circumstances) at the 1998 Oral History Association annual meeting, at which some of this essay was presented at a session on memory. The audience on that occasion; Professor Stave, who served as commentator; and Professor Hoffman, who gave a paper at the same session, asked me many challenging questions that pushed this essay along significantly toward its present form.

2. Kenneth Jernigan, "Blindness: Is Literature against Us?" in *Walking Alone and Marching Together: A History of the Organized Blind Movement in the United States, 1940–1990*, ed. Floyd Matson (Baltimore: National Federation of the Blind, 1990), pp. 356-58; "Metaphors We Could Do Without," *Disability Rag* (March/April 1992): 26-28.

3. In-person interview: Edward Huyczyk, member, BVA Board of Directors (1946-1948), August 7 and 14, 1990. Telephone interviews: Edward Huyczyk, December 9, 1992; Russell Williams, BVA Board of Directors (1945-1948), retired chief, Blind Rehabilitation Service, Veterans Administration (1948-1975), July 24, 1990, and December 11, 1992; Ray Frey, BVA president (1946-1948), July 24, 1990; Irvin Schloss, BVA president (1967-1968, 1968-1969), BVA employee (1948-1958), December 9, 1992; Dr. Ed Glass, participant in the BVA founding meeting, July 24, August 3, 1990. Also interviewed, by telephone, were these sighted BVA employees: Billie Jean Hill, July 23, 1990; Chris Brantley, BVA communications director, December 22, 1992; and these Veterans Administration (VA) blindness workers: in person, Elaine Powers, Visual Impairment Services coordinator, Buffalo VA Hospital, January 3, 1991; by telephone, Gloria Adalion, Visual Impairment Services coordinator (retired), Bay Pines VA Hospital, St. Petersburg, Florida, August 6 and 15, 1990, and June 13, 1992. Hereafter, interviews are cited only by name of the interviewee and the date of the interview.

Oral historians have questioned the efficacy of telephone interviewing in the practice of oral history, but their reservations cannot account for the special situation of the blind, for whom the telephone is an equalizing instrument in their interactions with the sighted. The blind cannot read body language and facial expression in conversation, the sort of nonverbal cues that personal encounters in oral history interviewing are supposed productively to factor into the relation of interviewer and interviewee. Indeed, in such an in-person encounter the blind may be said to be placed at a disadvantage, though they may possess compensatory abilities, such as an especially well-developed ear for verbal nuance, that provide an additional resource in knowing their interviewer.

4. *New York Times*, June 26, 1945, and April 13, 1948; Robert Brown and Hope Schutte, *Our Fight—A Battle against Darkness* (Washington, D.C.: Blinded Veterans Association, 1991), pp. 5-23; Lloyd Greenwood, "The Blinded Veteran," in *Blindness*, ed. Paul Zahl (Princeton: Princeton University Press, 1950), pp. 261, 269-70; Francis Koestler, *The Unseen Minority: A Social History of Blindness in America* (New York: McKay, 1976), p. 266.

5. Brown and Schutte, *Our Fight*, pp. 19-23, 30-33, 42-54; Greenwood, "Blinded Veteran," pp. 269-70; *New York Times*, January 20, June 9, August 9, and November 27, 1946; September 7, 1947; August 8, September 3 and 6, and October 20, 21, 22, and 28, 1948.

6. Brown and Schutte, *Our Fight*, pp. 2-3, 11; Dr. Howard Rusk, *New York Times*, June 9, 1946.

7. On racism and anti-Semitism in the United States in the 1940s, see Gunnar Myrdal, *An American Dilemma*, 2 vols. (New York: Harper and Row, 1944); Ulysses Lee, *The Employment of Negro Troops* (Washington, D.C.: Government Printing Office, 1966); Henry L. Feingold, *The Politics of Rescue: The Roosevelt Administration and the Holocaust, 1938–1945* (New Brunswick: Rutgers University Press, 1970); Leonard Dinnerstein, *America and the Survivors of The Holocaust* (New York: Columbia University Press, 1982); Corey McWilliams, *A Mask for Privilege: Anti-Semitism in America* (Boston: Little, Brown, 1948).

8. Congress of Industrial Organizations, Veterans Committee, *Veterans' Organizations* (Washington, D.C.: Congress of Industrial Organizations, 1946), pp. 1-4; Charles Bolte, *The New American Veteran* (New York: Reynal and Hitchcock, 1945), pp. 71-72; William Pencak, *For God and Country: The American Legion, 1919–1941* (Boston: Northeastern University Press, 1990), pp. 68-69, 81-82, 99; Ralph J. Bunche, *The Political Status of the Negro in the Age of FDR* (Chicago: University of Chicago Press, 1973), pp. 387, 392; "Celebrating Shavuot and Other War Tales: Museum Highlights Role of Jewish Veterans," *Forward*, January 1, 1993.

9. *BVA Bulletin* 1 (June 15, 1946): 7; 1 (August 1946): 8, 9; 2 (October 1947): 1; 2 (June 1947): 6; 2 (July 1947): 6; 2 (August 1947): 3; 3 (January 1948): 6; 3 (May 1948): 1; 4 (June-July 1951): 6; 4 (August-September 1951): 8; 7 (July-August 1952): 5; Rus-

sell Williams (December 11, 1992); Irvin Schloss (December 9, 1992); Edward Huyczyk (August 14, 1990, and December 9, 1992).

10. *New York Times*, April 13 and October 20, 21, 22, and 28, 1948.

11. Bernard C. Nalty, *Strength for the Fight: A History of Black American in the Military* (New York: Free Press, 1986), pp. 204-6, 235, 237; *New York Times*, August 9, 1946, and April 13, 1948; *BVA Bulletin*, 1 (August 1946): 14; 1 (December 1946): 5; 2 (March 1947): 6; 2 (April 1947): 6; 2 (May 1947): 6; 2 (August 1947): 6.

12. *BVA Bulletin* 3 (May 1948): 1; *New York Times*, April 13, 1948; Russell Williams (December 11, 1992); Irvin Schloss (December 9, 1992).

13. Alan Blackburn, "The Army Blind in the United States," in Zahl, ed., *Blindness*, p. 272.

14. Brown and Schutte, *Our Fight*; Robert Brown, *The Fight Goes On: Perspective on the Blinded Veteran Experience and the Work of the Blinded Veterans Association* (Washington, D.C.: Blinded Veterans Association, 1994).

15. *Bright Victory* (1951), dir. Mark Robson, screenplay by Robert Buckner, Universal Pictures.

16. Baynard Kendrick, *Lights Out* (New York: William Murrow and Company, 1946).

17. Obituary for Baynard Kendrick, *New York Times*, March 23, 1977; Irving Kenneth Zola, "'Any Distinguishing Features?': The Portrayal of Disability in the Crime-Mystery Genre," *Policy Studies Journal* 15 (March 1987): 489; Robert A. Baker and Michael T. Nietzal, *Private Eyes: One Hundred and One Knights—A Survey of American Detective Fiction, 1922–1984* (Bowling Green, Ohio: Popular Press, 1985), pp. 163-65; Baynard H. Kendrick, "Duncan Maclain," in *The Great Detectives*, ed. Otto Penzler (Boston: Little, Brown, 1978), pp. 128-40.

18. Peter Roffman and Jim Purdy, *The Hollywood Social Problem Film: Madness, Despair, and Politics from the Depression to the Fifties* (Bloomington: Indiana University Press, 1981); Thomas Cripps, *Making Movies Black: The Hollywood Message Movie from World War II to the Civil Rights Era* (New York: Oxford University Press, 1993), pp. viii-ix, 254, 257, 279.

19. Kendrick, *Lights Out*, ii, iv; Harold Isaacs, "Blackness and Whiteness," *Encounter* 21, 1 (1963): 8-21.

20. James H. Rawlinson, *Through St. Dunstan's to Light* (Toronto: Thomas Allen, 1919); Ian Fraser, "The Service War-Blinded in Great Britain," in Zahl, ed., *Blindness*, pp. 294-309.

21. Kendrick, "Duncan Maclain," pp. 131-36.

22. Obituary for Baynard Kendrick; Charles Shibuk, "Kendrick, Baynard H(ardwick)," in *Twentieth Century Crime and Mystery Writers*, ed. John M. Reilly (New York: St. Martin's Press, 1980), p. 892; Kendrick, "Duncan Maclain," pp.137-39.

23. Obituary for Baynard Kendrick; Koestler, *Unseen Minority*, pp. 280-82.

24. Brown and Schutte, *Our Fight*, pp. 12-13, 16-18.

25. Obituary for Baynard Kendrick; Brown and Schutte, *Our Fight*, p. 17; Koestler,

Unseen Minority, 281–82; "The BVA: Yesterday, Today, and Tomorrow," *BVA Bulletin* 45 (March/April 1990): 3–5.

26. Irvin Schloss (December 9, 1992).

27. Russell Williams (July 24, 1990, and December 11, 1992).

28. Russell Williams (December 11, 1992); Irvin Schloss (December 9, 1992).

29. Russell Williams (July 24, 1990); Ray Frey (July 24, 1990). The role of both men as consultants was limited largely to technical matters having to do with blind rehabilitation.

30. Koestler, *Unseen Minority*, p. 268; obituary for Thomas Caroll, *New York Times*, April 25, 1971; Brown and Schutte, *Our Fight*, pp. 35–36; Thomas J. Carroll, *Blindness: What It Is, What It Does, and How to Live with It* (Boston: Little, Brown, 1961), pp. 3–87. The desire to be separate from the civilian blind, which grew out of these negative stereotypes and the public valorization of the disabled veteran, may help to account for the fact that the BVA did not seek to make an alliance with the National Federation of the Blind, which stood for many of the same principles and goals as the BVA. The BVA, however, did work with the more conservative American Foundation for the Blind, which lent the BVA some resources (though not money) that were needed in the early years to attain organizational stability. This relationship, whatever goodwill may have existed on both sides, seems to have been a practical, not a political, arrangement.

31. Russell C. Williams, "Why Should I?" *VIS [Visual Impairment Services] View* (February 1987): 13; Russell Williams (July 24, 1990). Williams, however, has given Carroll credit for his clear exposition of the psychological context of the deficits that must be overcome in rehabilitation.

32. *BVA Bulletin* 1 (August 1946), quoted in Brown and Schutte, *Our Fight*, p. iv; Russell Williams, "Some Historical Perspectives on VIST and Blindness," *VIS View* (Winter 1984): 7–8.

33. Brown and Schutte, *Our Fight*, p. 91; Russell Williams, "Believers," *VIS View* (Winter 1989): 5.

34. Ellen Papadimoulis, "Editorial," *VIS View* (Winter 1989): 1–2, analyzing Williams's concept of "respectability"; Williams, "Some Historical Perspectives on VIST and Blindness," 7; Williams, "Believers," 4–6.

35. But as the military and the larger culture changed, so, too, would the BVA. The BVA now has female blinded veterans in its ranks and has had women in leadership positions. Its official language, moreover, no longer speaks in the heavily gendered metaphors of the masculine warrior. There is a marked difference in the tone of the two volumes of its in-house history: volume 1, which covers the years from World War II through the Vietnam War, speaks in the masculine language of Russell Williams and his cohort, but volume 2, mostly on the contemporary BVA, employs a much less gendered idiom. See Brown and Schutte, *Our Fight*; and Brown, *The Fight Goes On*, pp. 24–28, 45–46, which provide mention of women office workers and pro-

fessionals employed by the BVA and women veterans in leadership positions. No mention was made of the former in the first volume, while the latter have not been present until recent years.

There are moments when the contemporary reader may detect a note of misogyny in this heavily gendered language. Such a judgment is to some extent simply historical: these men did not live in a culture transformed by late twentieth-century feminism. Their understanding of manhood was pervasive throughout the culture in which they lived. The language of other veterans organizations, able-bodied or disabled, was not any different. More important, however, this language is less misogynist than a privileging of the masculine, which remained one of the few mental resources the blinded veterans of the founding cohort possessed for summoning up the will to overcome their own inner resistance to normalization. Such language served, therefore, as both a call to action and an expressive symbol of self-respect. It did not, however, provide much conceptual ground for moving beyond their experience and their masculine veterans' identity to expand their solidarity to embrace the civilian blind, male and female alike.

36. Koestler, *Unseen Minority*, pp. 282–83; Brown and Schutte, *Our Fight*, pp. 19–23, 42–54; *New York Times*, June 26, 1945; January 20, June 9, August 9, and November 27, 1946; September 3 and 6, 1948.

37. Richard E. Hoover, "The Cane as a Travel Aid," in Zahl, ed., *Blindness*, pp. 353–65; Brown and Schutte, *Our Fight*, pp. 6–7; *BVA Bulletin* 1 (November 1946): 2.

38. Brown and Schutte, *Our Fight*, pp. 13–15; Koestler, *Unseen Minority*, pp. 263–64.

39. Brown and Schutte, *Our Fight*, pp. 9, 15–16.

40. Koestler, *Unseen Minority*, pp. 276–77, 315–16; Brown and Schutte, *Our Fight*, pp. 46–50; Hector Chevigny and Sydell Braverman, *The Adjustment of the Blind* (New Haven: Yale University Press, 1950), pp. 245–46; Veterans Administration, *The Long Cane*, training film, 1952.

41. Williams, "Why Should I?" pp. 10–11, 13.

42. Gloria Adalion (June 13, 1992); Williams, "Why Should I?" p. 12; Milton D. Graham, *851 Blinded Veterans: A Success Story* (New York: American Federation for the Blind, 1968), pp. 74, 126–28.

43. Greenwood, "Blinded Veteran," pp. 268–70; Brown and Schutte, *Our Fight*, pp. 22, 78–91; Koestler, *Unseen Minority*, pp. 262, 282–83; *New York Times*, June 26, 1945; June 9, 1946; August 8 and September 3 and 6, 1948; August 25, 1950. The BVA resolved at first to support itself solely from dues and fees but soon came to accept unsolicited grants; see *New York Times*, June 26, 1945 and September 6, 1948; Koestler, *Unseen Minority*, pp. 280–82. The BVA now fund-raises aggressively among the general public.

44. Graham, *851 Blinded Veterans*, pp. 74, 126–28.

45. Clarence McKittrick Smith, *The Medical Department: Hospitalization and Evacuation, Zone of the Interior* (Washington, D.C.: Office of the United States Armed Forces

Surgeon General, 1956), pp. 110-12, 223-24; Brown and Schutte, *Our Fight*, pp. 5-8; *BVA Bulletin* 3 (May 1948): 1.

46. Chevigny and Braverman, *Adjustment of the Blind*, pp. 287-88.

47. Brown and Schutte, *Our Fight*; Brown, *The Fight Goes On*.

48. Russell Williams (December 11, 1992); Dr. Ed Glass (August 3, 1990).

49. David A. Gerber, "In Search of Al Schmid: War Hero, Blinded Veteran, Everyman," *Journal of American Studies* 29 (Spring 1995): 1-32; telephone interview, Ruth Schmid, August 3, 1990. My essay on Schmid is, in part, based on the same oral history interviews that informed the conception of the present essay.

50. Michael Ross, *Remembering the Personal Past: Descriptions of Autobiographical Memory* (New York: Oxford University Press, 1991); Eugene Winograd, "The Authenticity and Utility of Memories," in *The Remembering Self: Construction and Accuracy in the Self-Narrative*, ed. Ulrie Neisser and Robyn Fivush (Cambridge: Cambridge University Press, 1994).

CITATIONS FROM THE *NEW YORK TIMES*

June 26, 1945, sec. 4, p. 21, "Blinded Veterans to Join to Convince Public of Ability to Do 'Useful' Tasks"

January 20, 1946, sec. 4, p. 17, "Group Head Elected by Blinded Veterans"

June 9, 1946, sec. 4, p. 35, Dr. Howard Rusk, "Emphasis on Ability Rather Than Disability Is Said to Be New Concept in Training Blinded Veterans in Social Adjustment"

August 9, 1946, sec. 2, p. 18, "Woodard Greeted by Blinded Veterans"

November 27, 1946, sec. 7, p. 11, "BVA to Make Claims on Veterans' Behalf"

September 7, 1947, sec. 5, p. 14, "Blinded GIS Charge VA Fails to Give Aid"

April 13, 1948, sec. 7, p. 29, "Truman Honors Blind GIs"

August 8, 1948, sec. 3, p. 20, "BVA NYS Convention Here at Waldorf"

September 3, 1948, sec. 7, p. 40, "Blinded Vets Meet"

September 6, 1948, sec. 7, p. 15, "Blinded Vets Job Campaign"

October 20, 1948, sec. 1, p. 6, "Blinded Vet to Test New Law as Restaurant Bars Him and Dog"

October 21, 1948, sec. 5, p. 29, "Orders Complaint in Blind Law Test"

October 22, 1948, sec. 3, p. 24 [editorial], "Seeing Eye Dogs"

October 28, 1948, sec. 5, p. 31, "Blinded Vet Drops Action"

August 25, 1950, sec. 1, p. 25, "Blind Ask Employment"

13

Seeing the Disabled
Visual Rhetorics of Disability in Popular Photography

Rosemarie Garland Thomson

1.

Sander Gilman's landmark study *Seeing the Insane* charts a history of images of insanity ranging from classical art to clinical psychiatric photographs.[1] Gilman includes psychiatric photographs of insane patients taken by Hugh W. Diamond in the 1850s. These images are particularly arresting representations because of the sense of directness that the medium of photography confers on a human condition traditionally hidden from public view. Gilman analyzes the ways in which the insane have been portrayed in order to reveal the cultural work of these images: that is, to show what the pictures themselves, as well as the context of their presentation, try to say to their viewers about how we understand insanity and people who are labeled "insane."

Gilman's study thus excavates what Alan Sekula calls the "task" of these photographs.[2] Not only is the content of these pictures significant in understanding how the nineteenth-century British medical profession imagined insanity, but the medium of photography itself creates part of the message these images transmit. As a form of representation, photography carries more truth value than other images; in other words, we think of photographs as being closer to reality, as more reliable sources of truth than, say, drawings or even verbal representations. Maren Stange points out in her study of documentary photography that a photograph derives its status as "real" because it is an "index," that is, a symbol whose representative function is intensified because it refers to an object that exists.[3] Although photographs may seem to be transparent windows into reality, in fact, like all representations, they construct the object they represent as they depict it, shaping it through the conventions of presentation and through cultural ideas and expectations about such pictures. Perhaps the most characteristic aspect of photography is that it obscures its mediation between the viewer and the viewed. Photographs organize our perceptions of what we see without announcing to us what they are doing. The images we see seem to ensnare truth. Even though photographic images appear to capture the genuine, at the same time this representational medium arrests time, freezes motion, and prunes away space, which are the coordinates and the context of "real" life. Photographs thus evoke the familiar only to make it seem strange, eliciting a response Alan Trachtenberg describes as "astonishment mingling with recognition."[4]

Photographs of disabled people traffic in this "dialectic of strange and familiar" that Trachtenberg finds at the heart of the photographic effect. That effect has been put to many purposes. To extrapolate from Gilman's broad premise in *Seeing the Insane*, photographs of disabled people recapitulate cultural ideas about disability at the same time that they perpetuate those beliefs. In Gilman's words, "We do not see the world, rather we are taught by representations of the world about us to conceive of it in a culturally acceptable manner."[5] The role of seeing—both figuratively and literally—influences how modern America imagines disability and disabled people.

The photos Gilman includes in *Seeing the Insane* are among the first photographs of disabled people. These images belong to the genre of medical photography, one of the major photographic modes used to shape our modern notion of disability. Modern medicine and photography arose simultaneously in the nineteenth century, converging in the use of photography's supposed truth value to support the objective view of the body that medicine claimed to capture. The clinical photograph materialized what Michel Foucault calls modernity's "medical gaze," which defines the norm by picturing the deviant.[6] Over the last century and a half, photography has contributed substantially to the medicalization of disability through its extensive use in diagnosing, documenting, identifying, treating, and pathologizing disability.

Medicalization has perhaps been the primary lens used to interpret disability in the nineteenth and twentieth centuries. But as the image has proliferated, becoming what many cultural critics take to be the hallmark of postmodernity, disability has been increasingly articulated in other visual modes as well. This essay explores popular photographic images of disability rather than medical images, whose circulation was generally limited to textbooks and clinical studies aimed toward a specialized and often elite audience. While medical photography certainly has inflected and reflected what Gilman calls the "visual stereotypes" that govern perceptions of disability, the rhetorical purposes of popular disability photography have been more diffuse and complex.[7] Because disability has such potent cultural resonances, its visualization has been enlisted to manipulate viewers for a wide range of aims. This essay focuses on how that manipulation has operated and what meanings it has carried.

Modernity, as many scholars have shown, is ocularcentric.[8] The very development of photography in 1839 and its rapid flourishing thereafter testify to this urgent primacy of the visual. As Roland Barthes claims despairingly in his meditation on photography, "One of the marks of our world is [that] we live according to a generalized image repertoire."[9] In modernity, the image mediates not only our desires but who we imagine ourselves to be. Indeed, Alan Trachtenberg argues that photography has made us see ourselves as images.[10] Among the myriad, often conflicting and never disinterested images modernity offers us, the picture of ourselves as disabled is an image fraught with a tangle of anxiety, distance, and identification.

This is so for complex historical reasons that can receive only brief and speculative treatment here. In the Judeo-Christian tradition, disability functions as a symbol for the corruptible and suffering body, which western culture has both fetishized and denied. One might broadly historicize the representation of disability in this tradition as a shift from displaying the wounded, suffering, disabled body of Christ as the central icon of the premodern western imagination to sequestering disability within the discourses of science and medicine. Along with this representational shift came the literal confinement of some disabled people in institutions such as asylums and hospitals.[11] As a culture, we are at once obsessed with and intensely conflicted about the disabled body. We fear, deify, disavow, avoid, abstract, revere, conceal, and reconstruct disability—perhaps because it is one of the most universal, fundamental of human experiences. After all, we will all become disabled if we live long enough. Nonetheless, in representing disability in modernity, we have made the familiar seem strange, the human seem inhuman, the pervasive seem exceptional.

At the particular historical moment in America when photography enabled us to represent the body in new ways, many disabled people and their images were largely hidden from public view. Looking at disability became inappropriate in the same way that public executions and torture came to be considered offensive by the nineteenth century. The rise of sensibility and sympathy as marks of civilized, bourgeois status, as well as the imperative to discipline the body through self-control rather than punishment, shaped the notion of the middle-class man of fine feeling whose delicate sensibilities might be blunted by such spectacles.[12] In addition to segregating some disabled people in asylums and hospitals, so-called ugly laws codified the banishment of other disabled people from the public sphere. A Chicago ordinance, for example, forbade persons "diseased, maimed, mutilated or deformed in any way so as to be an unsightly or disgusting object or improper person to be allowed in or on the public ways or other public places."[13] This refusal to see the disabled was a kind of bowdlerizing of the body that enacted widespread consequences for people with disabilities. Among them were the slow and conflicted demise of publicly displaying disabled people as freaks, as well as institutionalizing, segregating, and medicalizing people with disabilities. Such a banishment of the image of disability is emblematized in the wounded Christ being removed from the Protestant cross. So, even though disabled people have always been a large and significant segment of any social order, those among us whose impairment could be enlisted to symbolize disability were often hidden from public view or their images ghettoized in medical textbooks.

Although modernity deemed disability an improper object to be looked at, the anxious, conflicted will to see disability persisted in the popular imagination. After the daguerreotype was launched in 1839, photography waxed in virtually every register of modern life, providing middle-class viewers with an immediate yet distanced way to contemplate the disabled body without actually having to expose themselves to visibly disabled people.

2.

Thus disability entered the public sphere as a highly mediated image shorn from interactions with actual people with disabilities. By circulating these images widely, popular photography has calcified the interpretations of disability embedded in the images. If the familiar experience of disability has been made to seem strange in western representation, then photography as a representational medium has made disability at once more familiar and stranger yet. Photography's immediacy and claim to truth intensify what it tells viewers about disability, at once shaping and registering the public perception of disability.

Rosemarie Garland Thomson

To look at the way we look at disability, this essay proposes a taxonomy of four primary visual rhetorics of disability: the wondrous, the sentimental, the exotic, and the realistic. Rhetoric is the art of persuasion. By formulating popular photographic images of disability as visual rhetorics, we can not only "read" the content, conventions, and contexts of the photographs but also probe the relationship the pictures seek to establish with the viewer. A rhetorical analysis such as this seeks to illuminate how and what the photographs intend to persuade their audiences to believe or do.

This template of visual rhetorics complicates an often restrictive notion of images as being either "positive" or "negative," as communicating either the "truth" of disability or perpetuating some oppressive stereotype. More analysis than evaluation, the discussion here does not suggest a progress narrative in which the culture marches invariably toward a state of egalitarian enlightenment. Instead, it suggests that visual images, especially photographic images, of disabled people act as rhetorical figures that have the power to elicit a response from the viewer. The wondrous, the sentimental, the exotic, and the realistic modes of representing disability converge and inflect one another within individual pictures as well as in all genres of disability photography across modernity. These rhetorics have arisen precisely because they are useful devices with which to manipulate the viewer for a variety of purposes, almost all of which are driven to a greater or lesser degree by the economic mandates of modern capitalism. These visual rhetorics wax and wane, shift and combine, over time as they respond to the purposes for which they are produced. Moreover, these four popular rhetorics constitute part of the context into which all representations of disabled people enter. Not only do they configure public perception of disabled people, but all visual images of disabled people either inadvertently or deliberately invoke these visual rhetorics and the cultural responses that have come to be associated with them.

Spatial metaphors help describe the relation between viewer and viewed that each of these four visual rhetorics establishes. Photography operates in a visual mode in which perception takes place across distance, in contrast, for instance, to modes of perception such as touch or taste that depend on contiguity. In this way, photography choreographs a space between the observer and what is observed. In other words, photographs instruct their viewers to see the object of perception from a certain position in relation to what is viewed. This inherent distancing within the photographic relationship replicates the social untouchability of disabled people, one of the most

Figure 13.1. This photograph invokes wonder by inviting the viewer to look up in admiration and awe at the person who can scale rocks while using a wheelchair. Courtesy of Greg Lais, Wilderness Inquiry.

oppressive attitudes directed at them. The disabled figure in western culture is the to-be-looked-at rather than the to-be-embraced. Consequently, the visual—whether it is looking toward or away—is the major mode that defines disability in modernity. Most important for this analysis is to recognize that none of these rhetorical modes is in the service of actual disabled people; indeed, almost all of them appropriate the disabled body for the purposes of constructing, instructing, or assuring some aspect of an ostensibly nondisabled viewer.

Briefly then, the first visual rhetoric is the wondrous. Historically the oldest mode of representing disability, the wondrous nevertheless continues to find a place in modernity's framing of disability. Monsters and prodigies of antiquity were imagined as inspiring awe and terror. Their different bodies were thought to augur the future or encode enigmatic omens from the gods.[14] The rhetoric of the wondrous stages a spatial relation in which the viewer occupies the position of the ordinary, looking up in awe at difference framed as distinction by the wonder. This mode of representation operates

Rosemarie Garland Thomson

according to a model of adulation that situates the spectator in a crowd of undistinguished commoners, while elevating the object of observation to a position of eminence. Modernity secularized the wonder—whether deified (Christ's broken body) or demonized (the cloven-hoofed Devil)—into the stereotype of the "supercrip." Such a figure amazes and inspires the viewer by performing feats the common folk cannot imagine themselves able to do, such as rock climbing while using a wheelchair (figure 13.1). Here the photographic composition literally positions the viewer to look up in awe at the climber dangling in her wheelchair. The rhetorical purpose of this contemporary figure is less to humble viewers who imagine themselves as nondisabled than to invoke the extraordinariness of the disabled body in order to secure the ordinariness of the viewer. The picture operates similarly to the figurative pedestal on which women have been placed so as to keep them out of circulation in the mundane world of political and economic power. By positioning the disabled figure as the exception to human capability rather than the rule, the wondrous estranges viewer from viewed, attenuating the correspondence that equality requires.

The second visual rhetoric is the sentimental. Whereas the wondrous positions the disabled figure above the viewer, the sentimental places the disabled figure below the viewer, in the posture of the sympathetic victim or helpless sufferer needing protection or succor. If the rhetoric of wonder enlarges the disabled figure, the rhetoric of sentiment diminishes that figure to evoke pity, inspiration, and frequent contributions. The sentimental disabled figure developed as a part of the larger nineteenth-century bourgeois culture of fine feelings.[15] This discourse of middle-class noblesse oblige operates on a model of paternalism, often trafficking in children and alluding to the cute, the plucky, the long-suffering, and the courageous. The poster child (figure 13.2) is the representative figure of sentimental rhetoric. This adorable little boy, for instance, transforms viewers into parentified adults by entreating them to deliver him from his impairment. In sentimentality, disability operates as the manifestation of suffering, a seemingly undeniable sign that makes what is internal and unnarratable into something external and narratable. In this way, the visibly disabled body operates as the spectacle of suffering rather than the reality of suffering, which is less representable.[16] In other words, visible disability acts as the stigmata of suffering. Such appeals use the sympathetic helpless child to contain the threat of disability and to empower the viewer to act on his or her behalf. By configuring the viewer as above and the object of sympathy as below, the sentimental

Figure 13.2. This poster boy appeals to the rhetoric of sentiment, which often employs pathetic, courageous, or cute children to elicit the viewers' sympathy and money. By permission.

constructs the viewer as benevolent rescuer and the disabled figure as grateful recipient. Such a model infantilizes the disabled figure—literally, in the case of the poster boy—and bestows authority and agency on the spectator.

The third visual rhetoric is the exotic. Although the exotic may coach the observer to look either up or down at the object in the photograph, the primary spatial arrangement it composes is one of distance. Whereas the wondrous and the sentimental create a spatial hierarchy by promoting a complex relation of identification and differentiation cemented by the emotions of admiration or pity, in contrast, the exotic presents disabled figures as alien, often sensationalized, eroticized, or entertaining in their difference. As such, the exotic reproduces an ethnographic model of viewing characterized by curiosity or uninvolved objectification and informed historically by western imperialism.[17] For example, a nineteenth-century freak photograph of "Spotted Boys" (figure 13.3) recruited the dermatological condition that

Figure 13.3. Early freak photography used the rhetoric of the exotic to transform the medical condition termed *vitiligo* into the ethnologically interesting "Spotted Boys" in this cabinet photograph. Courtesy of The Harvard Theatre Collection.

medical discourse termed *vitiligo* to fashion an engaging alien for the viewers' amusement and amazement—and for the showman's profit. The rhetoric of the exotic transforms spectators into tourists or ethnographers who imagine themselves as diverted, enlightened, or titillated by their encounter with the figure of the remote, alien body brought before them at the safe distance the image enforces.

The fourth visual rhetoric is the realistic. The realistic minimizes distance and difference by establishing a relation of contiguity between viewer and viewed. Whereas the wondrous, sentimental, and exotic modes of representation tend to exaggerate the difference of disability to confer exceptionality on the object in the picture, the realistic mode usually normalizes and often minimizes the visual mark of disability. To use the term "realistic" does not suggest that this visual rhetoric is more truthful, accurate, or real than the other modes discussed here. Realism's function is to create the illusion of reality, not to reproduce or capture its elusive and complex substance. Although more subtle perhaps, the rhetoric of realism is just as constructed and convention-bound as the rhetorics of the wondrous, sentimental, or exotic.

The rhetoric of the realistic trades in verisimilitude, regularizing the disabled figure in order to encourage a nonhierarchical identification between seer and seen. Realism in disability photography is the rhetoric of equality, most often turned utilitarian. The use of realism can be commercial or journalistic, and it can also urge the viewer to political or social action, as is suggested by the image of the African amputee (figure 13.4) . Presented as a victim of interethnic conflict, this man is portrayed completely without visual markers that particularize him—except his impairment, which is foregrounded but not exoticized or sensationalized. This presentation thus makes him a universal sign for human brutalization, with whom all viewers are encouraged to identify. As opposed to the rhetoric of diminishment invoked by the poster child or the rhetoric of distance in the exotic presentation, this image suggests that the viewer must become concerned or involved with postcolonial African politics because the disabled figure is like the viewers—socially level with them—rather than different from them.

Despite the identification with this man that the picture encourages, the photo's purpose, however, is to warn viewers against becoming disabled, suggesting that although he is similar to the viewers, he is separated from them

The Washington Post Magazine

Peace Without Justice
A Journey to the Wounded Heart of Justice By

Figure 13.4. Characteristic of documentary photography, this photo of a victim of African tribal conflict draws upon the rhetoric of realism to encourage identification between the viewer and the viewed and to normalize the disabled subject. © 2000, The Washington Post. Reprinted with permission.

by misfortune. Although the picture confers political support and social acceptance, it nevertheless marks the disabled man as the person the viewer does not want to be.

To recapitulate simply these rhetorics of disability: the wondrous mode directs the viewer to look up in awe of difference; the sentimental mode instructs the spectator to look down with benevolence; the exotic mode coaches the observer to look across a wide expanse toward an alien object; and the realistic mode suggests that the onlooker align with the object of scrutiny. A visible signifier of disability—that is, the physical impairment—is always apparent in photographic images. In representing disability, the visualization of impairment, never the functional experience of it, defines the category of disability. In this sense, disability exists for the viewer to recognize and contemplate, not to express the effect it has on the person with a disability.

An important caveat here is that these rhetorics seldom occur discretely from one another. Instead, they are typically co-present in individual images and inform in varying manifestations the representation of disability throughout modernity. Moreover, creating a taxonomy with which to probe the effects and operations of these visualizations of disability implies that these rhetorics are more distinct and oppositional to one another than they actually are when they blend into any single photograph. Before fully examining this taxonomy, however, it is useful to consider the relationship of looking and disability.

3.

As anyone with a visible disability knows, being looked at is one of the universal social experiences of being disabled. Even children learn very early that disability is a potent form of embodied difference that warrants looking, even prohibited looking. The dominant mode of looking at disability in this culture is staring. Staring is an intense form of looking that enacts a relationship of spectator and spectacle between two people. In the visual choreography of staring, the starer becomes the subject of the act of staring while the staree becomes the object acted upon. The dynamic of staring registers the perception of difference by the viewer and enforces the acceptance of difference by the viewed. As such, it manifests the power relations between the subject positions of "disabled" and "able-bodied."

In contrast to glancing, glimpsing, scanning, surveying, and other forms of casual or disinterested looking, staring estranges and discomforts both people engaged in this awkward partnership. Gazing—which has been highly theorized as the dominant visual relation in patriarchy between male spectators and female objects of their gazes—differs from staring in that it usually encompasses the entirety of the body, even as it objectifies and appropriates that body.[18] Staring at disability, in contrast, intensely telescopes looking toward the physical signifier for disability. Starers gawk with abandon at the prosthetic hook, the empty sleeve, the scarred flesh, the unfocused eye, the twitching limb, but seldom do they broaden looking to envelop the whole body of the person with a disability. Staring at disability is nevertheless a form of inappropriate looking in modernity; it is, after all, considered rude in our historical moment to stare. The disabled body thus becomes a visual paradox: it is at once to-be-looked-at and not-to-be-looked-at. This illicit aspect of staring further dramatizes the encounter by making the viewer furtive and the viewed defensive. In this way, the staring dynamic attenuates the bonds of civil intercourse between equal members of the human community.

Staring is the social relationship that constitutes disability identity and gives meaning to impairment by marking it as aberrant. Even if a disability is not apparent, the threat of its erupting in some visual form is perpetually present. Disability is always ready to disclose itself, to emerge as some visually recognizable stigmata, however subtle, that will disrupt social order by its presence. The staring dynamic constitutes the starer as normal and the object of the stare as different. The exchange between starer and object witnesses both the anonymity that confers agency on the starer and the singularity that stigmatizes the one who is stared at. In this context, then, staring is the ritual enactment of exclusion from an imagined community of the fully human. As such, it is one of the cultural practices that creates disability as a state of absolute difference, rather than as simply one more variation in human form.

This analysis of staring suggests that disability is not simply the natural state of bodily inferiority and inadequacy it has traditionally been taken to be. Rather, disability is a culturally fabricated narrative of the body, similar to what we understand as the fictions of race and gender. Disability, then, is a system that produces subjects by differentiating and marking bodies. Furthermore, this comparison of bodies legitimates the distribution of resources, status, and power within a biased social and architectural environment. As such, disability has four aspects: first, it is a system for interpreting bodily variations; second, it is a relationship between bodies and their environments; third, it is a set of practices that produce both the able-bodied and the disabled; fourth, it is a way of describing the inherent instability of the embodied self. The category of disability exists as a way to exclude the kinds of bodily forms, functions, impairments, changes, or ambiguities that call into question our cultural fantasy of the body as a neutral, compliant, and predictable instrument of some transcendent will. Moreover, *disability* is a broad term within which cluster ideological categories as varied as sick, deformed, ugly, old, maimed, afflicted, abnormal, and debilitated—all of which disadvantage people by devaluing bodies that do not conform to cultural standards. Thus disability functions to preserve and validate such privileged designations as beautiful, healthy, normal, fit, competent, intelligent—all of which provide cultural capital to those who can claim such status, who can reside within these subject positions. It is, then, the various interactions between bodies and world that make disability from the raw material of human variation and precariousness.

The history of disabled people in the western world is in part the history of being on display, of being visually conspicuous while being politically and socially erased. For example, the earliest record of disabled people is of their exhibition as prodigies, as "monsters" taken as omens from the gods or indexes of the natural or divine worlds. In religious thought, from the New Testament to the miracles at Lourdes, the lame, the halt, and the blind provide the spectacle for the story of bodily rehabilitation as spiritual redemption that is so essential to Christianity. From antiquity through modernity, the bodies of disabled people considered to be freaks and monsters have been displayed by the likes of medieval kings and P. T. Barnum for entertainment and profit in courts, street fairs, dime museums, and sideshows.[19] Moreover, medicine has from its beginnings exhibited the disabled body as what Michel Foucault calls the "case," in medical theaters and other clinical settings, in order to pathologize the exceptional and to normalize the ordinary.[20] Disabled people have variously been objects of awe, scorn, terror, delight, inspiration, pity, laughter, and fascination—but we have always been stared at.

Rosemarie Garland Thomson

Photography mediates between the viewer and the viewed by authorizing staring. After all, photos are made to be looked at. With the actual disabled body absent, photography tends to stylize staring, exaggerating and fixing the conventions of display and eliminating the possibility for interaction or spontaneity. Indeed, photographs of disabled people invite the viewer to stare without inhibition or contrition. They absolve viewers of responsibility to the objects of their stares at the same time that they permit a more intense form of staring than an actual social interchange might support. In other words, disability photography offers the spectator the pleasure of unaccountable, insistent looking. This license to stare that inheres in the medium of photography becomes a powerful rhetorical device that can be mobilized in the interest of persuasion. Disability photography hence manipulates its viewers, evoking an array of responses that have been harnessed—like all other images—primarily as commodities within late capitalism. In other words, these photographs appropriate the complex relations of the stare.

4.

A fuller elaboration of each of the four visual rhetorics of disability photography highlights these dynamics of the stare. The visual rhetoric of the wondrous, as was briefly suggested above, springs from a premodern interpretation of disability as either augury or a mark of distinction, whether representing good or evil. Oedipus, Tiresias, monsters, giants—even Shakespeare's Richard III—were imposing, if ominous, disabled figures. The exceedingly popular photographic portraits of the disabled people who were the elite entertainers in nineteenth-century freak shows exploited the notion of the wondrous in order to increase the circulation of freak figures and to make money. These widely disseminated photos served the dual purpose of creating a desire in the viewer to see the amazing spectacle and to re-create the satisfaction of viewing such a performance. The word *freak* meant whimsical more than monstrous to nineteenth-century popular audiences. This genre capitalized on physical differences in order to elicit amazement and admiration. This convention of presentation made freaks celebrities. For example, Charles Tripp, a famous "Armless Wonder" (figure 13.5), is pictured in a *carte*

Figure 13.5. Surrounded here by the products of his agile feet, the famous freak show entertainer, Charles Tripp, one of many "Armless Wonders," is presented as an amazing wonder. Courtesy of Robert Bogdan.

Rosemarie Garland Thomson

d'visite eating with his toes. This was only one of many images of the disabled performer sold to augment and promote his live appearances. This carefully choreographed portrait includes samples of Tripp's calligraphic skills, paper figures he has cut out, as well as the pen and scissors he used to accomplish such remarkable tasks. The silver tea set in the picture refers to other photos of him drinking from a cup with his toes. Here the composition acts as a kind of visual résumé documenting Tripp's accomplishments. The spectacle tries to elicit awe from the viewers, whose sense of their own clumsy toes makes Tripp's feet feat seem wondrous.

Like all disability photography, the *carte d'visite* of Tripp carefully choreographs a relationship of identification and differentiation between the subject and his viewer. In other words, it makes Tripp seem simultaneously strange and familiar. The typically exaggerated rhetoric that can be captured in nonphotographic renderings such as drawings of monsters or in verbal and textual expressions of wonder, for example, is somewhat tempered by the realism of photography, especially by the conventions of Victorian portraiture that necessarily inflect freak photos. What portraiture introduced into the rhetoric of wonder was the illusion of the ordinary that could be fused with the extraordinary. Viewers saw a regular man who engaged in the quotidian acts of writing, eating, and drinking tea, but—to those who had arms—he did these things in a most extraordinary manner. These wonder pictures thus invite viewers to identify with the mundane aspects of Tripp's presentation, which constitute almost the entire scene. But by spotlighting his unusual manner of eating, the portrait also encourages spectators to occupy the nondisabled position and differentiate themselves from Tripp. Only the single detail of eating with feet rather than hands marks this scene as distinctive. This departure from the normative expectations of the viewer creates the novelty and determines the meaning of the entire photograph. This is how disability operates visually: by juxtaposing the singular (therefore strange) mark of impairment within a surrounding context of the expected (therefore familiar), the picture coaches the viewer to understand impairment as the exception rather than the rule. Arresting time and space, the conventions of the photograph telescope the viewer's eye to the mark of impairment; in other words, the picture instructs the spectator to stare. The effect is that staring, the visual apprehension of the mark of impairment that is orchestrated and provoked by the photographic image, constitutes a particular relationship between the viewer and the viewed, thus producing disability.

The contemporary version of the wonder genre emphasizes admiration rather than amazement, in part because bourgeois respectability now deems it inappropriate to delight in staring at disabled people. The charity model of presenting disabled people has inflected the wonder model, producing the convention of the courageous "overcomer," contemporary America's favorite figure of disability. Even though armless calligraphers are no longer an acceptable form of middle-class entertainment, photos of disabled people who have adapted tasks to fit their bodies still ask their viewers to feel a sense of wonder. An advertisement for Habitat for Humanity, for example, pictures a volunteer worker with no fingers using a hammer (figure 13.6). Like Tripp, this man is portrayed as entirely ordinary except for the detail of the fingerless hand that holds the hammer, which the photo places as its center of interest. Such an arrangement at once invites and authorizes the stare. As is typical in disability photography, the text instructs the viewer how to respond to the picture by including a headline that says, "Extraordinary Volunteer, Unstoppable Spirit." The ad thus combines the narrative of admiration for "overcoming" disability with the narrative of empowerment characteristic of a post–Disability Rights movement consciousness. As in the photographs of the rock climber (figure 13.1) and of the "Armless Wonder" (figure 13.5), this carpenter places his viewer in the quotidian world, the one where prosaic people go about their business. But, by making these disabled subjects masters of ordinary activities such as climbing rocks, drinking tea, or using a hammer, the photos create a visual context that elicits adulation for accomplishing what the normalized viewer takes to be a superhuman feat. To varying degrees, these images thus lift their subjects out of the realm where ordinary people live typical lives and create them as distantly strange yet compellingly familiar.

5.

If the spatial rhetoric of wonder positions the disabled figure above the viewed, the spatial rhetoric of the sentimental places the disabled figure below the viewer in a position of supplication or impotence. Whereas the wonder mode makes its subjects the capable if exceptional agents of climbing, eating, and hammering, the sentimental mode makes its objects helpless, most often by presenting the disabled figure as a child or a woman so as to invoke other com-

Figure 13.6. This photograph of a Habitat for Humanity volunteer utilizes the narrative of overcoming to elicit admiration for the "Unstoppable Spirit" supposedly shown by his hammering regardless of having a disability. Courtesy of *Habitat World*.

Figure 13.7. This image of the famous 1863 wedding of two people of small stature, Charles Stratton ("General Tom Thumb") and Lavinia Warren, capitalizes on how these supposedly childlike adults arouse the sentiment of delight in their many viewers. Courtesy of Robert Bogdan.

plementary stereotypes that will intensify the equation of disability with diminishment, vulnerability, dependence, or incapacity. The sentimental is a hallmark of the rhetoric of charity and commerce alike. Most representations of disability promote the exchange of money, whether it is commerce or charity, buying or giving. Disability sells, for different reasons at different times.

The rhetorical element that charity introduces into the conventions of wonder is the sentiment of sympathy. Sympathy literally diminishes the wonderful, replacing awe with pity or the delight of the "cute."[21] The cute was a popular Victorian convention, as witnessed by the remarkable popularity of General Tom Thumb (figure 13.7) whose 1863 wedding, orchestrated by P. T. Barnum, was one of the major society events of New York City in the nineteenth century. Sympathy, which was largely absent from freak rhetoric, does not sell show tickets. But sympathy did flourish in the sentimental literature of nineteenth-century fiction, which often featured disabled characters intended to move their readers to political action or religious benevolence. The pathetic, the impotent, and the suffering confirmed Victorian bourgeoisie status by arousing their finest sentiments. As the increasingly empowered middle class imagined itself capable of capitalizing the world, it began to see itself as responsible for the world as well, a stewardship that launched humanitarian and reform movements that today's telethons are heir to.

The rhetoric of sentiment found an effective home in the photographic conventions of the charity poster child of the mid–twentieth century. The 1946 March of Dimes poster child (figure 13.2) clearly echoes Tom Thumb's spunky cuteness, but where the delight inspired by Tom Thumb was in his replication of adulthood in miniature—he is, after all, a "general"—this poster choreographs the boy's childlike vulnerability by showing him propped up in a corner of his crib in a before-and-after format. The poster child is the quintessential sentimental figure of twentieth-century charity campaigns. To catalyze the adult middle-class spectator to whom the photo addresses itself, this March of Dimes poster presents disability as a problem for the rescuer to solve, an obstacle to be eliminated, a challenge to be met. Such a logic transforms disability from an attribute of the disabled person to a project that morally enables the rescuer. The viewer's dimes, the poster suggests, will literally catapult the little boy who is unhappily trapped by his braces in the corner of his crib into a smiling and spirited little fellow striding determinedly toward the viewer. In this scene, disability becomes an occasion when the viewers' own narratives of progress, improvement, or heroic deliverance can be enacted.

Not only does the poster pack in the benevolent rescue and the overcoming narratives, but it suggests as well what is often called the cure-or-kill approach to disability. The logic of "cure or kill," accompanied by today's faith in technology, posits that if the disabled body cannot be normalized, it must be eliminated. If it does not respond to being improved, if it refuses to register the success of the rescuer's moral or technological efforts, the disabled body becomes intolerable, a witness to the human inability to perfect the world. This aspect of the relationship between the disabled and the nondisabled has led to such contemporary practices as aborting disabled fetuses, emphasizing elimination rather than accommodation of disability, and the sometimes excessive surgical procedures that normalize disabilities. By thwarting the narrative of heroic redemption, the permanently disabled body testifies to the impotence of its failed rescuer, a reminder that the body is ultimately not fully under the control of the human will. The disabled body moves from opportunity to rebuke if it will not be rehabilitated.

Thus the poster child of the 1940s and 1950s introduced two new elements into the rhetoric of sentiment that disability photography inherited from the nineteenth century. The first is that cure replaces suffering as the motivation for action in the viewer. Whereas the earlier sentimental literature accentuated suffering to mobilize readers for humanitarian, reform, or religious ends, the poster boy's suffering is only the background to his restoration to normalcy that results from "your dimes." Sentiment here, then, replaces the intensity of sympathy with the optimism of cure, testifying to a growing faith in medical treatment and scientific progress that developed as modernity increasingly medicalized and rationalized the body in the nineteenth and twentieth centuries. The second new element is what Paul Longmore describes as the self-serving opportunity that charity provides the giver for "conspicuous contribution."[22] What is clearest is that this rhetoric of sentiment diminishes the disabled figure in the interest of empowering, enhancing, and enlarging the viewers' senses of themselves.

The rhetoric of sentiment has migrated from charity to retail in late capitalism's scramble to capture markets. For example, the cover of a 1998 Benetton public relations brochure distributed in stores (figure 13.8) employs a chic sentimentality in documenting a school for developmentally disabled children that Benetton supports and outfits. The child featured has both Down's syndrome and a chic Benetton hat. Emblematic of the entire brochure, this cover girl fuses sentimental cuteness with high fashion to produce the conviction in the viewer/shopper that Benetton is humanitarian rather than crassly commercial. In anticipation of its patrons' skepticism and aptness to see this as "cynical advertising," Benetton devotes a whole introductory page to chiding the cynics and assuring its customers that this brochure is about "the gift of love." So, while commercial fashion marketing demands a certain sophistication and sleekness that preclude the gushy sentiment of the 1940s poster child, Benetton still assures its viewers of their tolerance and allows them to fantasize rescuing this child from the stigma of being disabled by dressing her smartly and supporting her school.

6.

The rhetoric of sentiment domesticates the disabled figure, making it familiar and comforting. In contrast, the visual rhetoric of the exotic traffics in

Figure 13.8. Sentimental cuteness and high fashion come together in this public relations brochure's presentation of a developmentally disabled child in a school supported and outfitted by Benetton. Courtesy of United Colors of Benetton. Photo by O. Toscani.

the alien, the strange, and the distant. Freak photography invoked the intensely exotic, which complemented the wondrous. Thus, even though the "Spotted Boys" (figure 13.3) were diminutive children, their presentation as primitives highlighted their foreignness. The boys' costuming and props suggest savagery and allude to the proliferation of popular ethnographic photography that accompanied the era of European imperialism.[23] The exotic demedicalizes, fascinates, seduces with exaggeration, and creates an often sensationalized, embellished alien. Even these domesticated "spotted boys" are distanced from the viewer by their setting, reducing their ability to elicit sympathy and making them objects of curiosity in a way the poster boy never could be.

Even self-presentation of people with disabilities can invoke the exotic mode of representation. Bob Flanagan, for instance, appropriates the rhetoric of exoticism in his live artistic performances, self-portraits, and autobiographical films. All of these seek to articulate a sensational, disturbing, but poignant connection among masochism, pain, and disability. In one self-portrait, Flanagan, who is famous for pounding a nail through his penis in one of his performances, presents himself as a "supermasochist" (figure 13.9). Creating a profane parody that fuses the cultural figures of the invincible superman, the porn star, and the sick person, he combines cape, chains, piercings, and the oxygen mask characteristic of cystic fibrosis to discomfort his viewers.[24] He deliberately provokes his viewers by rendering himself a contemporary freak figure. By hypersexualizing himself, cultivating exaggeration, and creating a radically transgressive persona, he aggressively enlists the exotic mode to counter unequivocally the rhetoric of sentimentality and renounce even the admiration of the wondrous. His self-presentation insists on the embodied dynamic of pain and its capacity to render one grotesque rather than transcendent—but never sympathetic. Regardless of how strenuously Flanagan's performances work against transcendence and toward establishing distance between himself and his spectators, there is nevertheless a strange nobility and attraction in the harsh character he creates. Perhaps that was his intent.

The introduction of disabled models has exploded the contemporary fashion world in the last several years, returning the rhetoric of the exotic to disability photography in newly acceptable, yet still controversial, ways—as the Benetton brochure (figure 13.8) suggests. Where the sentimental makes the disabled figure small and vulnerable, so as to be rescued by a

Figure 13.9. Bob Flanagan links pain, disability, and sex in his performance of the "supermasochist" role that calls on the hyperbole, sensationalism, and irony fundamental to the exotic mode. Courtesy of Vale Research.

benevolent agent, the exotic makes the disabled figure large, strange, and unlike the viewer. Ever straining for novelty and capitalizing on titillation, the fashion arm of the advertising world was sure to discover the power of disabled figures to provoke responses from viewers. Advertising has learned that disability sells in two ways. One is by making consumers feel good about buying from a company that is charitable toward the "disadvantaged," which is the Benetton brochure's pitch. The other is to capture the disability market, 54 million people and growing fast with the aging of the baby boomers, whose spending power is estimated to reach the trillion-dollar mark in 2000.[25]

Two venues for the exotic in advertising seem to have emerged in contemporary American culture. The first are ads that attempt to harvest the growing disabled market, which companies are beginning to recognize as both huge and affluent. The exotic serves here to upset the earnest, asexual, vulnerable, courageous image of disability that charity rhetoric has so firmly implanted. One image advertising wheelchairs (figure 13.10) presents a tattooed biker figure brandishing a hockey stick. The ad alludes to the strong men and tattoo kings of the sideshows and then inflects the image with a hyperphallic sexuality, completely rewriting the cultural script of the emasculated invalid and the male who becomes feminized by disability. As is typical with much popular disability photography, the text instructs the viewer to read this photo. The exaggeration characteristic of exoticization here marshals ironic hyperbole to mount a brazen, sensational parody similar to Flanagan's, provocatively challenging the viewer by lewdly commanding, "Lick this!" Such representations preclude even a trace of the sentimental or the wondrous, insisting instead on the empowerment of the transgressive, even at the expense of—or perhaps because of—distancing the spectator from the spectacle.

The second venue for disability as the exotic is emerging in the high-fashion market, always desperate to keep its edge. These advertisements and magazine features present disabled models in a dual attempt to capture a market and to novelize high fashion by introducing bodies that at once depart from and conform to the exhausted image of the high-fashion body. English fashion designer Alexander McQueen, known as "the bad boy of fashion design," recently designed a series of clothes and a shoot called "Accessible," featuring eight disabled models in the September 1998 issue of style magazine *Dazed and Confused*. McQueen's shots fold the models' dis-

Figure 13.10. The rhetoric of the exotic in this ad for wheelchairs "with an attitude" alludes to the tatooed biker/jock figure to create a transgressive, hyper-masculine image for the wheelchair user. By permission.

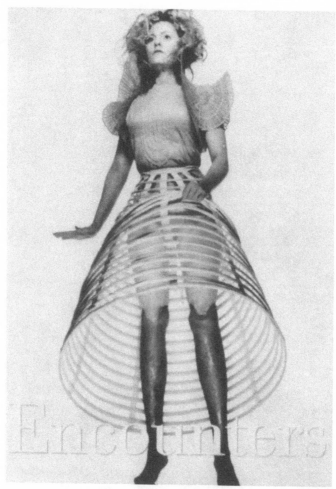

Figure 13.11. This high-fashion shot of model, sports star, and double-amputee, Aimee Mullins, emphasizes, rather than concealing, her prosthetic legs, exploiting the exotic mode to make disability seem chic. Used by permission of We media.

Rosemarie Garland Thomson

abilities into a context of exoticism that extends to the entire frame. The shot of Aimee Mullins, who is a double-amputee, champion runner, celebrity cover girl, renders her as a kind of high-tech bionic mannequin (figure 13.11).[26] No attempt is made to disguise her cosmetic prosthetic legs to pass for nondisabled; rather, the entire photo thematically echoes her prostheses and renders the whole image chic. As a gorgeous amputee, Mullins becomes an embodied contradiction. Her prosthetic legs parody—indeed, proudly mock—the very idea of the perfect body that has been the mark of fashion until today, even as the rest of her body conforms precisely to fashion's impossible standards.

Rather than concealing, normalizing, or erasing disability, these photos use the sensationalism and stigma traditionally associated with disability to quench postmodernity's perpetual search for the new and arresting image. Transgressive juxtapositions of disability and high fashion, such as our macho chair user and the athletic but legless Mullins, produce a fresh, attention-grabbing brand of exotic radical chic that redefines disabled identity for the disabled consumer.

7.

The final visual rhetoric of disability photography is the realistic. All photographic images employ the conventions of realism to some extent because of the verisimilitude the medium advances. Because looking at disability is at once forbidden and desired, it is always a highly charged scene that risks eclipsing the familiar with the strange. Whereas the exotic mode cultivates estrangement, the realistic mode often engages the rhetoric of realism in order to mobilize affiliation between the viewer and the viewed. Realism avoids differentiation and arouses identification, positioning the viewer and viewed on the same spatial plane, often as equals. Realism aims to routinize disability, making it seem ordinary. As such, it has the most political power in a democratic order, although one could argue that the transgressive most effectively achieves social change in democracies.

Realism emerged as a property of portraiture, documentary, and medical photography of the nineteenth century.[27] Freak photographs seem to recognize and capitalize on the way in which the mundane juxtaposed with the wondrous can capture viewers, as is suggested by the visual choreography of the portrait of Charles Tripp eating with his feet in a context of the quotidian (figure 13.5). Realism exploits the ordinary to set off Tripp's extraordinary body, at once calling attention to his startling disability and domesticating it. Documentary photography such as that made famous by Lewis Hine and Jacob Riis aimed photographic realism at the nineteenth-century obsession with social reform.[28] Documentary and journalistic photography differ from charity and commercial photography in that they do not solicit the exchange of money directly but rather aim to democratically disseminate information intended to shape the viewers' actions and opinions.

Documentation was a strategy of social reform, the sometimes religious, sometimes secular, but ever pervasive fantasy of perfecting American society. Hine tirelessly recorded the fabric of the American underclass, exposing the supposed truth of the conditions under which they struggled. Among those he photographed were wounded workers (figure 13.12). He focused his lens particularly on men, whose disabilities he concluded robbed them of the male privilege and duty of work, and on children, whose disabilities he felt stole their childhood. His captions instructed the viewers in the narrative of disability the images visualized: "The Wounds of Work," reads one; "When a man's hand is mutilated, he keeps it out of sight."[29] The implied message here is that the social mandate to hide disability precludes entry into the workplace. Ironically, Hine's photograph reveals plainly and undramatically the physical impairment society refuses to look at. Much like the photo of the African amputee (figure 13.4) that is heir to Hine, the picture of the wounded worker exposes the empty sleeve to protest this closeting of disability by surrounding it with the common. Nevertheless, the sociopolitical protest implied in the photograph, like that of the African amputee, frames disability as the threat of affliction and catastrophe that troubles the ordinary. Such protest or reform photos, then, enlist disability to tell a cautionary tale. Disability, they suggest, should and can be avoided in a world that works right.

In its urgency to capture ostensible truth, realism often fuses the sensational to the ordinary in a gesture of obstinate opposition to the supposed pretenses or evasions of other representational modes. For example, the photograph of the African man (figure 13.4) brutally foregrounds his handless stumps. In a similar register, the realistic portrayal of disability recently provoked controversy and roused political protests over what consti-

AN ARM GONE AT TWENTY
This young brakeman when last seen was studying
telegraphy in order to stay in the service

THE WOUNDS OF WORK
When a man's hand is mutilated he keeps
it out of sight

Photo by Hine

Figure 13.12. Lewis Hine documented the disadvantaged by using the rhetoric of realism as a form of social protest against excluding disabled workers from the privileges of labor.

tutes unacceptable looking at women's breasts. The Breast Cancer Fund, a San Francisco–based nonprofit organization dedicated to education about and funding of breast cancer research, mounted a public awareness campaign in January 2000 called "Obsessed with Breasts" that featured three posters showing women boldly displaying mastectomy scars. The posters parodied a Victoria's Secret catalog (figure 13.13), a *Cosmopolitan* cover, and a Calvin Klein perfume ad, all of which typically parade women's breasts in upscale, semi-pornographic modes that have become an unremarkable staple of commercial magazine advertising. The Breast Cancer Fund posters disrupt the visual convention of the female breast as sexualized object for male appropriation and pleasure by replacing the now-normative eroticized breast with the proscribed image of the amputated breast. The powerful visual violation produced by exchanging the spectacle of the eroticized breast, which has been desensationalized by its endless circulation, with the medicalized image of the scarred breast, which has been concealed from public view, was so shocking to viewers that many demanded the images be removed. Of course, censuring and censoring images that demand a recognition of the reality of breast cancer ignited a conversation and controversy that more than accomplished the goals of the initial campaign. The images mobilize the charge of this forbidden version of the disabled breast by ironically juxtaposing it with the commonplace but virulently sexist eroticized breast. In this way, the posters advance a potent feminist challenge not only to sexism in medical research and treatment for breast cancer but to the oppressive representational practices that make everyday erotic spectacles of women's breasts while erasing the fact of the amputated breast that one in eight women will have. By mocking the tired sensationalism of pornography, these pictures protest against the refusal of contemporary America, literally and figuratively, to look at breast cancer.

The visual rhetoric of the ordinary, unglossed by the sensational or sentimental, has emerged in a climate of integration and diversity created by the Disability Rights movement and resulting legislation, such as Americans with Disabilities Act of 1990 (ADA). While the post–ADA era is not without resistances and backlashes to the integration of people with disabilities, the social environment is filling with disability in the popular press. Disability now appears not only in the sensationalist or sentimental underbelly of the press, where it always has, but tucked in various degrees of inconspicuousness into the fabric of common visual culture. Department store and catalog advertising, for instance, has adopted the rhetoric of the ordinary simultaneously to appeal to disabled people as a market and to suggest an ethic of inclusion. L. L. Bean promotes a wheelchair backpack in its catalog; Wal-Mart and many other stores feature disabled models and mannequins in everything from frumpy jogging suits to evening gowns. Toy lines such as Barbie and the upscale American Girl have wheelchair-using dolls.

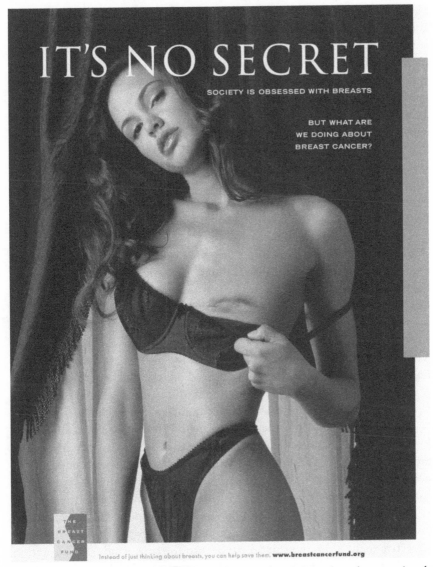

Figure 13.13. This controversial Breast Cancer Fund poster employs the sensationalism often characteristic of realism to protest inadequate breast cancer research and to expose the cultural effacement of mastectomies. Courtesy of the Breast Cancer Fund. Photo: Heward Jue.

For the most part, the conventions of realism govern the images of disabled figures in the world of commerce, the visual component of which is
advertising. Ads do not usually distinguish the presentation of disabled
models from nondisabled ones. In the aggregate, contemporary advertising
casts disabled people as simply one of many variations that compose the
market to which they appeal. Such routinization of disability imagery not
only brings disability as a common human experience out of the closet but
enables people with disabilities—especially those who acquire impairments
as adults—to imagine themselves as a part of the ordinary world, rather than
as a special class of untouchables and unviewables. Images of disability as a
familiar, even mundane experience in the lives of seemingly successful,
happy, well-adjusted people can reduce the identifying against oneself that is
the overwhelming effect of oppressive and discriminatory attitudes toward
people with disabilities.

This form of realism constitutes a rhetoric of equality radical in its refusal
to foreground disability as difference. A particularly vivid example is the upscale disability fashion photography featured in magazines that target the
disability market, such as We Magazine. Such ads reimagine disability by casting what has been culturally invisible—the disabled body—in the context of
what is culturally hypervisible—the fashion model. A shot of a classically
handsome, sophisticated dandy (figure 13.14) invokes the conventions of
high-end fashion photography but differs from the exoticized presentation
of Aimee Mullins (figure 13.11) in that it markets itself to a disabled, upscale
audience who are after the look of affluent authority and charm. The image
is entirely ordinary within the conventions of fashion photography except
for the highly unusual detail of the prosthetic hook that replaces the
model's amputated hand. Although the model looks like all models, who
never look like real people, the juxtaposition of a visual disability with this
conventional image is arresting, as is the restraint in its presentation. The
arrangement attempts neither to conceal nor to expose the hook, instead
presenting it as casually apparent, as one simple aspect of a conventionally
attractive man. Although this ad panders to the conspicuous consumption
that all advertising does, what makes the image radical is that it does not appeal to the conspicuous contribution associated with charity photography.
In other words, the conjunction of the visual discourse of high fashion,
which has traditionally trafficked exclusively in standardized, stylized bodies, with the visual discourse of disability, which has traditionally traded in

Figure 13.14. The Disability Rights movement has generated a rhetoric of the ordinary in contemporary advertising that appeals to the disability market and suggests an ideology of diversity and inclusion.

the pathetic, earnest, or sensational creates a visual disjuncture that calls previous cultural images of disability into question.

The most radical reimagining of disability offered by the realist mode is, ironically, the least visually vivid of the images discussed here, perhaps because it is the only type of photography with no commercial purpose. This genre of disability photography is the official portrait, exemplified by the Department of Education's simple photographic portrait of Judith E. Heumann, Assistant Secretary of Education during the Clinton Administration (figure 13.15). The conventions governing such pictures strive for the effect of the everyday, inflected with enough dignity and authority to communicate the importance of the position but not enough to separate the official from the constituency. In a democracy, official portraits depict public servants, after all, in no-nonsense black and white, with standard costuming and poses, and flanked unpretentiously by flags. As opposed to commercial photography, these portrayals are neither generalized nor stylized but rather particularized. The photo suggests that this is a real, recognizable person responsible for certain official duties. In this instance, her wheelchair particularizes this woman. It is clearly an aspect of her identity, an integral element of who and what the photograph says she is. The glimpse of her chair is descriptive, as fundamental to her image as the shape of her chin, the cut of her hair, or the tint of her skin. In its ordinariness, this photo discourages staring without prohibiting it. Indeed, this photo encourages forms of looking such as glancing, if the viewer is not very interested in the secretary, or perhaps beholding, if one is engaged by her. By depicting Secretary Heumann as an ordinary person who has a position of official status in the society, this photograph encourages viewers who consider themselves as either disabled or nondisabled to identify with her. The photo suggests neither that her accomplishments are superhuman nor that she has triumphantly overcome anything. She thus becomes more familiar than strange. Most important, the picture conveys the message that a woman with a disability can occupy such a position. Secretary Heumann's picture thus sits in bold historical opposition to the many now-controversial official photos of President Franklin D. Roosevelt which hide the wheelchair that he used daily.[30] Authorized by the cultural changes the civil right movements wrought, the official portrait is one of several genres in contemporary photography that familiarize disability rather than defamiliarize it. Indeed, such representations banish the strange and cultivate the ordinary, radically reimagining disability by installing people with disabilities in the realm of human commonality and dismantling the assumption that disability precludes accomplishment.

This taxonomy of four primary visual rhetorics of disability provides a way to see how we see disability. The dynamics of looking mounted by these rhetorics suggests that all visualizations of disability are mediations that

Figure 13.15. The contrast between this official portrait of Assistant Secretary Judith E. Heumann sitting in her wheelchair and the many photos of FDR that hid the wheelchair he used daily during his Presidency marks the difference between a pre- and a post–civil rights era.

shape the world people who have or do not have disabilities inhabit and negotiate together. All representations have social and political consequences. Understanding how images create and recreate disability as a system of exclusions and prejudices moves us toward the process of dismantling the institutional, attitudinal, legislative, and architectural barriers that keep people with disabilities from full participation in the society. Although this analysis has been more descriptive than prescriptive, it suggests that the realistic mode is most likely to encourage the cultural work the Disability Rights movement began. Imagining disability as ordinary, as the typical rather the atypical human experience, can promote practices of equality and inclusion that begin to fulfill the promise of a democratic order.

NOTES

1. Sander L. Gilman, *Seeing the Insane* (New York: J. Wiley, Brunner/Mazel Publishers, 1982).

2. Alan Sekula, "The Body and the Archive," *October* 39 (Winter 1986): 3–64.

3. Maren Stange, *Symbols of Ideal Life: Social Documentary Photography in America, 1890–1950* (New York: Cambridge University Press, 1989), xiii, 66. See also John Tagg, "A Means of Surveillance: The Photograph as Evidence in Law," in *The Burden of Representation: Evidence, Truth and Order* (London: Macmillan, 1988).

4. Alan Trachtenberg, *Reading American Photographs: Images as History, Mathew Brady to Walker Evans* (New York: Hill and Wang, 1989), 4.

5. Gilman, *Seeing the Insane*, xi.

6. Michel Foucault, *The Birth of the Clinic: An Archeology of Medical Perception*. trans. A. M. Sheridan Smith (1964; reprint, New York: Vintage Books, 1994), 29.

7. I do not want to draw too fine a line between medical and popular photography here. Medicalized photographs sometimes found their way into the larger public viewing world, as, for example, in the 1858 book of medical photos mentioned by Gilman, called *The Mind Unveiled; or, A Brief History of Twenty-two Imbecile Children*, published by Isaac Kerlin, superintendent of the Pennsylvania Asylum, for the purpose of raising funds for the asylum. See Gilman, *Seeing the Insane*, quote on xi.

8. Jonathan Crary, *Techniques of the Observer: On Vision and Modernity in the Nineteenth Century* (Cambridge: MIT Press, 1990); Guy Debord, *The Society of the Spectacle* (Detroit: Black and Red, 1983); Martin Jay, *Downcast Eyes: The Denigration of Vision in Twentieth-Century Thought* (Berkeley: University of California Press, 1993).

9. Roland Barthes, *Camera Lucida: Reflections on Photography*, trans. Richard Howard (New York: Hill and Wang, 1981), 118.

10. Trachtenberg, *Reading American Photographs*, 29.

11. Foucault, *The Birth of the Clinic*; David Rothman, *The Discovery of the Asylum: Social Order and Disorder in the New Republic* (Boston: Little Brown, 1971).

12. Karen Halttunen, "Humanitarianism and the Pornography of Pain in Anglo-American Culture," *American Historical Review* 100 (April 1995): 303-34; Michel Foucault, *Discipline and Punish: The Birth of the Prison*, trans. Alan Sheridan (New York: Vintage Books, 1979).

13. Marcia Pearce Burgdorf and Robert Burgdorf, Jr., "A History of Unequal Treatment: The Qualifications of Handicapped Persons as a 'Suspect Class' under the Equal Protection Clause," *Santa Clara Lawyer* 15 (1975): 855-910, quotation on 863.

14. Rosemarie Garland Thomson, "From Wonder to Error: A Genealogy of Freak Discourse in Modernity," in Rosemarie Garland Thomson, ed., *Freakery: Cultural Spectacles of the Extraordinary Body* (New York: New York University Press, 1996), 1-22.

15. Much is written on sentimental culture in general. For explications of the disabled figure's place in the rhetoric of sentiment, see Rosemarie Garland-Thomson, "Crippled Little Girls and Lame Old Women: Sentimental Spectacles of Sympathy within Rhetorics of Reform in Nineteenth-Century American Women's Writing," in Karen Kilcup, ed., *Nineteenth-Century American Women Writers: A Critical Collection* (Oxford: Basil Blackwell, 1998), 128-45; Rosemarie Garland-Thomson, "Narratives of Deviance and Delight: Staring at Julia Pastrana, the 'Extraordinary Lady,'" in Timothy Powell, ed., *Beyond the Binary* (New Brunswick: Rutgers University Press, 1999), 81-104; Rosemarie Garland Thomson, *Extraordinary Bodies: Figuring Physical Disability in American Culture and Literature* (New York: Columbia University Press, 1997). For a related analysis of the slave—who is often disabled—as sentimental figure, see Elizabeth B. Clark, "'The Sacred Rights of the Weak': Pain, Sympathy, and the Culture of Individual Rights in Antebellum America," *Journal of American History* 82 (September 1995): 463-93.

16. Elaine Scarry, *The Body in Pain: The Making and Unmaking of the World* (New York: Oxford University Press, 1985), argues that pain as a form of suffering is not narratable because it is not manifest in the body. Disability operates as pain's opposite in that it is visibly manifest in the body and therefore can be employed as the representation of suffering, even though it may not actually entail suffering.

17. Robert Bogdan uses the exotic mode to classify freaks in his pathbreaking study of freak shows, *Freak Show: Presenting Human Oddities for Amusement and Profit* (Chicago: Chicago University Press, 1988).

18. The exception here is sexualized staring at breasts, which are often the targets of staring if they are large. Much is written on the gaze in the context of gender. For some formulations, see, for example, Laura Mulvey, *Visual and Other Pleasures* (Bloomington: Indiana University Press, 1989); Edward Snow, "Theorizing the Male Gaze: Some Problems," *Representations* 0, 25 (Winter 1989): 30-41; E. Ann Kaplan, *Looking for the Other: Feminism, Film, and the Imperial Gaze* (New York: Routledge, 1997).

19. Leslie A. Fiedler, *Freaks: Myths and Images of the Secret Self* (New York: Simon and

Schuster, 1978); Richard D. Altick, *The Shows of London* (Cambridge: Belknap Press, 1978); John Block Friedman, *The Monstrous Races in Medieval Art and Thought* (Cambridge: Harvard University Press, 1981); Kathryn Park and Lorraine Daston, "Unnatural Conceptions: The Study of Monsters in Sixteenth- and Seventeenth-Century France and England," *Past and Present: A Journal of Historical Studies* 92 (August 1981): 20–54; Yi-Fu Tuan, *Dominance and Affection: The Making of Pets* (New Haven: Yale University Press, 1984); Robert Bogdan, *Freak Show*; Dudley Wilson, *Signs and Portents: Monstrous Births from the Middle Ages to the Enlightenment* (London: Routledge, 1993).

20. Foucault, *The Birth of the Clinic*, 59.

21. Lori Merish, "Cuteness and Commodity Aesthetics," in Garland Thomson, ed., *Freakery*, 185–206.

22. Paul Longmore, "Conspicuous Contribution and American Cultural Dilemmas: Telethon Rituals of Cleansing and Renewal," in David Mitchell and Sharon Snyder, eds., *The Body and Physical Difference* (Ann Arbor: University of Michigan Press, 1997), 134–60.

23. Christopher A. Vaughan, "Ogling Igorots: The Politics and Commerce of Exhibiting Cultural Otherness, 1898–1913," in Garland Thomson, ed., *Freakery*, 219–33.

24. Bob Flanagan, *Bob Flanagan: Supermasochist* (San Francisco: Re/Search Publications, 1993). For an analysis of Flanagan's performances, along with those of Orlan, the performance artist who repeatedly performs cosmetic surgeries on her face, see Linda S. Kauffman, *Bad Girls and Sick Boys: Fantasies in Contemporary Art and Culture* (Berkeley: University of California Press, 1999). The allusion in Flanagan's work to the figure of Superman has taken on new resonance since the actor Christopher Reeve, who not only has played Superman but is Superman in the cultural imagination, became disabled.

25. John M. Williams, "And Here's the Pitch: Madison Avenue Discovers the 'Invisible Consumer,'" *WE Magazine* (July–August 1999): 28–31.

26. Mullins has two types of prosthetic legs, functional sets for running and cosmetic sets for modeling. Part of her revision of the disabled role is that Mullins casts disability as a career advantage. For example, as a model, she had the advantage of choosing how tall she wanted to be. She was also featured as one of *People* magazine's "50 Most Beautiful People of 1999."

27. John Pultz, *The Body and the Lens: Photography 1839 to the Present* (New York: H. N. Abrams, 1995).

28. Jacob Riis, *How the Other Half Lives: Studies among the Tenements of New York* (New York: Charles Scribner's Sons, 1890); Walter Rosenblum, Naomi Rosenblum, and Alan Trachtenberg, *America and Lewis Hine* (Millerton, N.Y.: Aperture, 1977).

29. Stange, *Symbols of Ideal Life*, 60.

30. Hugh Gregory Gallagher, *FDR's Splendid Deception* (New York: Dodd, Mead, and Company, 1985).

American Disability Policy in the Twentieth Century

Richard K. Scotch

On January 22, 1907, the Committee on Pensions of the U.S. House of Representatives held a hearing on the subject of pensions for disabled veterans of the Civil and Mexican-American Wars. The hearing began with a statement from Robert Burns Brown, Esq., of Zanesville, Ohio, the commander in chief of the influential veterans lobby the Grand Army of the Republic. He testified:

> We are not here asking for that that [*sic*] we ought not to have, for we represent a class of men who in the days of their youth surrendered to this Government the best service they had. . . . And very good authority could be cited to show that every survivor of the war of three years' service gave up about thirteen years of his life. Many of them are maimed, and they have been handsomely provided for by the American Congress. Some are blind, and they have been cared for. Many are crippled by rheumatic troubles, but they have not been cared for as we think they ought to be.[1]

This statement, one of the first policy records of the twentieth century in the United States dealing with disability, has some interesting qualities worthy of comment.

First, Brown justifies assistance to disabled veterans not merely in terms of their need but also as repayment for past military service. He bases their claims before the government not on their impairments alone but also on the moral worth and social worthiness of these men. A survey of modern U.S. disability policy reveals that Brown is far from alone in this view. Many public disability programs were, and are, based on past contributions. For example, the largest federal program that provides cash payments to people who have a disability, Social Security Disability Insurance (SSDI), is a social insurance program available only to those who have participated in the paid workforce and have paid payroll taxes into the Disability Insurance trust fund. While Supplemental Security Income (SSI), a federal income maintenance program, provides cash benefits for those who have never worked, SSI benefits are significantly lower than payments made to most SSDI beneficiaries.[2] In every type of disability policy and program, from veterans pensions to vocational rehabilitation, from social insurance to civil rights, notions of moral worth and social worthiness have played a central role in determining what individuals have qualified for benefits or protections.

Brown also distinguishes among people who are "maimed" and blind, whom he says have been well provided for, and those with rheumatic difficulties, who have not. This kind of distinction has also appeared frequently in disability policy in the United States. Because of the often piecemeal and ad hoc manner in which public policy has been made, different levels of benefits may have been available to people with different types of impairments, even if those differences have not reflected severity of condition or the economic and social need with which it was associated. For example, blind people have long enjoyed special status in public policy, including vending opportunities in federal facilities and unique tax advantages. This disparity in part reflects the political mobilization of blind people, in which organizations such as the National Federation of the Blind (NFB) have played a pivotal role.[3] It may also relate to some special cultural meaning of blindness, because of which policymakers and the public have been more willing to extend assistance to blind people than to individuals with other disabilities.[4]

As these reflections on Brown's testimony begin to suggest, disability policy includes relevant public laws and regulations, government programs that provide various benefits and subsidies, and judicial rulings concerning those laws and programs. It involves programs that deliver disability-specific cash benefits, services, or legal protections. It also reflects and reveals deep-seated cultural values about work, worthiness, dependency, and much more.

Public policy has played an important role in shaping the lives of all Americans in the twentieth century, as state-related activity has become central to the functioning of all levels of the economy and most arenas of public life. Government has served as a major contextual factor in much of private life as well, by promoting technological development and establishing ground rules for many kinds of private transactions. People with disabilities, however, have had a larger stake than many other citizens in the expanding role of the state in economic and social life as, with the rise of the industrial economy, they came to be stigmatized and excluded. The accommodations people with disabilities may require for participation in public life have often depended on state subsidies or mandates. Political scientist Harlan Hahn, in his analysis of the barriers to participation faced by disabled people, writes that "all aspects of the environment [for people with disabilities] . . . are fundamentally molded by public policy."[5]

Of course, a truly comprehensive overview of disability policy would look beyond programs specifically targeting people with disabilities to examine more generic social and economic policy realms. The vast majority of public policies that affect people with disabilities (in both positive and negative ways) were not created specifically for them. Many aspects of education, employment, health, and transportation policy have disproportionate consequences for disabled people compared to their implications for people without disabilities. Other essays in this volume discuss the ways in which American social and cultural institutions have either ignored the existence of people with disabilities or stigmatized and excluded them and consider the consequences of such treatment. For example, non-disability-specific Medicare and Medicaid policies disadvantage many people with disabilities, while general issues of school finance and health insurance coverage touch many disabled children. Meanwhile, policies and programs specifically directed toward people with disabilities also impinge on their lives. They represent broader social and cultural patterns and serve as powerful forces that shape the lives of many people with disabilities.

According to the somewhat sparse ethnographic data on nonindustrial societies, people with disabilities typically have lived in the context of kinship networks and communities.[6] With the industrial revolution in the United States and northern Europe, however, provision for many persons with disabilities shifted from kin groups and neighbors to local governmental authorities. The social dislocation, rapid urbanization, and increasing geographic mobility of the early industrial era undermined the capacity of kinship- and community-based support systems. The rise of the asylum movement in mid-nineteenth-century Western Europe and North America, a far-reaching cultural and institutional development, accompanied these trends in political economy and demography.[7] By the beginning of the twentieth century, many people with disabilities had left or been removed from community settings to reside in institutions, for various reasons. These included people who were blind, deaf, mentally retarded, mentally ill, or had a variety of other impairments. While private religious or charitable groups supported some of these institutions, state governments created many others. Some institutions offered education and training. Many provided services to ameliorate the conditions associated with impairment. Others were essentially custodial. Many of these institutions remained in operation well into the twentieth century, although the countermovement of deinstitutionalization in the 1960s and 1970s led many of them to close. This recent development in part resulted from technological developments and cultural values that promoted community-based services, but it also reflected an overall legal shift toward procedural rights related to the growth of the civil rights movements, including the disability rights movement.

The earliest national disability programs in the United States provided pensions for disabled military veterans. At first limited to those who had sustained combat-related injuries and to their survivors, these pensions were justified in terms of moral obligation to those who had sacrificed in their service to the nation. Veterans pensions also served the political purpose of rewarding a substantial component of the adult population of Northern states in the late nineteenth century. The pensions were broadened substantially at the end of the nineteenth century to include any Northern Civil War veteran who became unable to work due to any disability. The pensions became the functional equivalent of old-age pensions for native-born Americans who had fought for the North, yet they still were justified in terms of the moral worthiness of beneficiaries rather than purely on the needs associated with impairment.

These veterans disability pensions constituted a "precocious" American welfare state that anticipated Social Security. They reflected what Theda Skocpol refers to as "institutional cultural oppositions between the morally 'undeserving' and the less deserving that run like fault lines through the entire history of American social provision."[8] By contrast, the first European social insurance and pension programs were offered as categorical entitlements to broad categories of workers and the indigent. Skocpol notes the distinctive moral component of the American disability pension programs: they were restricted not to those with the most need but to those who "by their own choices and efforts as young men had earned aid." She concludes that in American public policy, "no matter how materially needy, the morally undeserving or less deserving were not the nation's responsibility."[9]

Subsequent to the pension program for disabled Civil War veterans, workers' compensation, originally referred to as workman's compensation, became the first public policy initiative of the early twentieth century. Workers' compensation rested on the precept that an injured worker was entitled to redress by his or her employer. While this concept was not new in the twentieth century, the rise of industrial capitalism and the ideology of laissez-faire had led to an erosion in workers' common-law rights to compensation. With the increasing mechanization of industry and accompanying loss of workers' control over their working conditions, workplace injuries increased substantially. Yet, early in the twentieth century, many workers injured in industrial accidents typically could not obtain either medical assistance or financial compensation from their employers.

In response to this situation, Progressive Era reformers argued for the passage of workers' compensation laws. These laws required both medical and financial assistance to workers injured on the job. The statutes were modeled on the compensation already being provided to disabled military veterans. But, unlike disabled veterans' compensation programs, workers' compensation initiatives focused on the states rather than the federal government. This state-centered policymaking followed the pattern of pre–New Deal American social policy. It had appeared earlier in the asylum movement. The first state laws were passed in 1909. By 1921, forty-five states and territories had enacted workers' compensation laws.[10] Later in the century, after extended debate between advocates for workers and the business and insurance industries, industrial diseases were added to the list of conditions eligible for coverage.[11]

Workers' compensation programs aimed to provide an automatic benefit to eligible injured workers and to eliminate the need to seek redress through civil litigation. They led to improvements in support of injured workers. While the federal government has promoted model workers' compensation legislation, there remains considerable variation across states in program structure and operation.[12] Litigation and debate over program inconsistency have persisted despite periodic efforts to reform the system.

In the post–World War II prosperity of 1956, Congress amended the Social Security Act to create a federal cash-benefit program, Social Security Disability Insurance, for workers who acquired long-term disabilities. Though SSDI is a federal entitlement, the states have had the responsibility for determining eligibility for the program. Payments are provided to an individual whose impairment, in the language of the 1967 SSDI amendments, is of "such severity that he is not only unable to do his previous work but cannot, considering his age, education, and work experience engage in any kind of substantial gainful work which exists in the national economy, regardless of whether such work exists in the immediate area in which he lives or whether a specific job vacancy exists for him or whether he would be hired if he applied for work."[13]

Disability insurance had been a goal of earlier social insurance reformers in the 1930s and 1940s, but its potential cost and the opposition of business and medical interests had prevented its passage.[14] At first, Congress limited SSDI to disabled workers between the ages of fifty and sixty-four, but in 1960 it removed the lower age limit; nonetheless, to receive full SSDI benefits, individuals must have paid work experience of at least ten years. The attractiveness of the program increased as automatic eligibility for Medicare coverage was tied to SSDI enrollment. Despite its narrow definition of eligibility, participation in SSDI expanded rapidly from its creation on through the late 1970s. Attempts in the early 1980s to reduce the rate of increasing participation by making it more difficult to qualify for SSDI benefits proved controversial. Ultimately, those efforts failed, in part due to political pressures heightened by dramatic media accounts, and in part because the rate of program expansion leveled off in the 1980s.

Deborah Stone has sought to explain the growth of SSDI and parallel developments in the United Kingdom and Germany in her book *The Disabled State*.[15] She suggests that the consequences of impairment for different individuals are uncertain and largely subject to the interpretation and expectations of medical gatekeepers. She contends that it is impossible to determine medically the extent to which particular impairments mean that particular individuals cannot work; therefore, the process of certifying someone as too disabled to work cannot be determined objectively. She concludes that, for political reasons, the process typically is biased in favor of qualifying the applicant.

Some analysts have viewed the SSDI program as a ticket out of the workforce for displaced workers with limited educational credentials or technologically obsolete skills.[16] Many others have objected to the all-or-nothing work disincentives in the program's eligibility requirements that force applicants to choose, on the one hand, between receiving income support and medical insurance and, on the other, accepting employment, often at low-paying jobs without medical benefits.[17] (In 1999, some of these disincentives were reduced with the enactment of the Work Incentives Improvement Act, although the impact of this law remains unclear.)

In 1972, an additional federal cash-benefit program, Supplemental Security Income, was created under the Social Security Act amendments. SSI replaced previous federal-state welfare programs for people with disabilities (and a separate set of programs for blind people) because Congress considered them too inconsistent and, in some states, inadequate.[18] SSI provides cash benefits to eligible individuals with disabilities who have very low incomes, regardless of their work history (unlike SSDI). SSI's determination of work disability is similar to SSDI's, with many of the same ambiguities and problems. Because SSI beneficiaries have very low incomes and the cash benefits themselves are quite modest, individuals eligible for SSI also automatically qualify for Medicaid, the federal-state health program for low-income individuals and families. Like SSDI, few SSI beneficiaries enter the paid workforce after they are enrolled in the program. In recent years, an increasing number of SSI applicants have had psychiatric and addiction disorders, complicating issues of building work incentives into the program.

Other government initiatives sought to provide not pensions or income maintenance supporting retirement from the job market but rehabilitation to facilitate return to paid employment. In the wake of World War I, the federal government enacted the Smith-Sears Veterans' Rehabilitation Act of 1918. It established and subsidized state programs of vocational training for disabled veterans. Though a federal board would oversee these state programs, recently established state departments of vocational education would operate them. In 1920, through the Smith-Fess Act, Congress extended the veterans training program into a more general federal-state vocational rehabilitation (VR) program for disabled Americans. The law authorized limited services for individuals with physical disabilities, including vocational training, job placement, and counseling to be provided by state agencies. The federal government would assume half the cost. Rehabilitation clients were to be at least sixteen years of age, and their impairment had to be consistent with the potential for gainful employment (including homemaking). This VR program exists with largely the same structure today, although with major programmatic additions and greater fiscal contributions by the federal government.

In less than two years, thirty-four states had created state VR units, but not until 1935 did every state have an operational program. In 1933, at the height of the Great Depression, VR agencies began to provide modest living expenses for their clients, out of a federal appropriation totaling $840,000. In 1935, federal grants to the states were increased, and administrative responsibility for the program subsequently shifted to the new Federal Security Agency, which would ultimately become the Department of Health, Education, and Welfare. In 1940, services were extended to people with disabilities who worked in sheltered workshops, to severely disabled people who were homebound, and to individuals with disabilities in the paid workforce who required VR services to remain employed. Another significant expansion occurred in 1943 with passage of the wartime Barden-La Follette Act. It provided funding for medical and reconstructive services and made people with mental disabilities eligible for vocational rehabilitation.

The vocational rehabilitation program grew again in 1954, under the leadership of Mary Switzer, the first director of the newly established Office of Vocational Rehabilitation (OVR) in the new Department of Health, Education, and Welfare. In addition to creating OVR, the 1954 VR amendments expanded funding to the states, provided financial aid for professional training of medical and rehabilitation professionals, supported research and development in rehabilitative medicine and rehabilitative engineering, and created additional facilities for rehabilitation and sheltered employment. VR legislation in the 1960s increased the federal share of program funding to 80 percent. That made the federal-state VR system a model program within the emerging American welfare state referred to by President Lyndon Johnson as the Great Society. Vocational rehabilitation gained great popularity in the post–World War II era, in part because its beneficiaries were perceived as truly deserving of public assistance. Public and congressional support also resulted from the convincing arguments of advocates that the financial benefits of assisting people with disabilities to enter the paid, taxpaying workforce far exceeded the costs of VR services.[19]

Additional expansions of vocational rehabilitation in the 1970s included civil rights initiatives, discussed below, and funding for local centers for independent living (CILs). CILs expanded the VR program beyond its focus on an individually based rehabilitation process facilitated through professional assessment and counseling. The independent living approach promoted a new emphasis on self-help and consumer control, peer support, and environmental change.[20] This initiative also demonstrated the growing disability movement's impact on public policy, by building on the model of voluntary action in communities such as Berkeley, Houston, and Boston, and the influence of movement leaders such as Ed Roberts and Lex Frieden. The VR program of the 1970s reflected the CIL influence in its shift of service priorities from a nearly exclusive programmatic emphasis on individuals with less severe impairments, who were considered more capable of entry into paid employment, to a more inclusive position encompassing those with more severe impairments. With this shift, the objective of VR went beyond supporting paid employment by people with disabilities to the more general goal of promoting independence. While these major conceptual changes challenged long-held vocational rehabilitation practices, they nevertheless left the existing VR federal-state system of services largely intact.

Furthermore, while a key program for individuals with disabilities, vocational rehabilitation remained isolated from other federal disability programs such as workers' compensation and Social Security Disability Insurance. Despite congressional expectations that VR would help unemployed disabled individuals receiving cash benefits to reenter the workforce, effective relationships never developed among the various disability programs. As a result, few beneficiaries of income maintenance programs have gone to work through vocational rehabilitation programs.[21]

Beginning in the late 1960s, disability policy began to incorporate still another approach to the socioeconomic marginalization of disabled persons: antidiscrimination components. These redefined the problems and needs of people with disabilities away from those inherent in their impairments and toward those associated with inaccessible physical and social environments. This development marked a shift from policies based on a medical or economic definition of disability to those based on a sociopolitical definition.[22] In fact, this approach had historical antecedents dating back to the 1930s. Beginning in that era, local and state governments enacted statutes designed to protect the right of access to public places by blind people using white canes or service dogs. These statutes were effectively the first American civil rights laws protecting people with disabilities. More general antidiscrimination measures protecting all people with disabilities passed in several localities in the late 1960s, although enforcement of these laws was minimal and inconsistent at best.

Several federal laws passed in the 1970s provided broader protection. Among them were Title V of the Rehabilitation Act of 1973 and the Education for All Handicapped Children Act of 1974, later renamed the Individuals with Disabilities Education Act (IDEA). Title V prohibits discrimination in programs receiving federal grants and contracts. Its regulations, released in 1977, formed a broad statement of what constituted discrimination on the basis of disability and contained strong requirements for the elimination of such discrimination. These regulations required state and local governments, schools and universities, health facilities, and many other entities to make their programs accessible to people with physical or mental disabilities. The regulations were issued only after a change of presidential administration from Republican to Democrat and national demonstrations by the growing disability rights movement.[23]

Similarly, IDEA contained explicit requirements that all children with disabilities receive a free and appropriate public education and related services, regardless of the cost. Under IDEA, local districts could no longer deny disabled children access to public school programs or relegate them to generic, essentially custodial programs. Rather, each child must get services appropriate to his or her individual needs, and in a setting as close as possible to those provided to children without disabilities.

Both IDEA and Title V generated some controversy, but they were ultimately implemented. Still, adverse court rulings and weak enforcement limited the impact of Title V to some extent. These laws helped set the stage, however, for what was to be the broadest policy guarantee of nondiscrimination on the basis of disability, the Americans with Disabilities Act of 1990 (ADA).[24]

In the mid-1980s, a presidentially appointed advisory committee, the National Council on Disability, first proposed a bill that eventually became the ADA. That proposal became the focus of intense and prolonged lobbying by the disability community. Passage of the ADA at a time of increasingly conservative government in the United States demonstrated the maturity and effectiveness of the disability rights movement as a political interest group. A broad bipartisan majority of Congress approved the law, which President George Bush signed on July 26, 1990.

The ADA prohibits discrimination in private employment, public accommodation, and telecommunications. It draws on the precedents of Title V of the 1973 Rehabilitation Act, which helped define discrimination on the basis of disability, and the Civil Rights Act of 1964, which prohibited discrimination on the basis of race, religion, and, regarding employment, gender. At the time of its passage, supporters and observers hailed the ADA as a watershed in the quest of people with disabilities for equity. As a statement of policy, it is a powerful standard; its impact remains unclear, however, in the face of limiting judicial rulings and constraints on enforcement.[25]

This summary of the major elements of twentieth-century American disability policy raises several important conceptual issues. We may see public policies as expressions of consensus about what constitutes a public problem and what actions government may appropriately take to address that problem. While human beings have many problems, some are considered inevitable and not amenable to intervention or are viewed as personal misfortunes not worthy of public concern. But some personal troubles come to be regarded as public issues requiring public action.[26]

In the case of disability, public policies reflect assumptions about the nature of disability and the appropriate place of people with disabilities in our society. Our understanding of the meaning of disability for identity, work, and public life has been embedded in the availability of public benefits and in access to employment, public services, and public accommodation. Moreover, public policies not only reflect social status and cultural constructs; they also help create and reinforce them. This active governmental role has especially applied to disabled people, whose exclusion from much of mainstream economic life, along with the need by some for accommodation for their impairments, creates a greater need for public services and subsidies. Much of the social construction of disability and its consequences in the past hundred years has come through the medium of public policymaking and policy implementation. Especially in the latter decades of the twentieth century, public policies have defined who may work and who may receive public subsidies if they do not work; who may attend school and what services they will receive when they get to school; and whether people with disabilities have access to public transportation and private telecommunication systems.

By their very nature based on generalization, public policies deal with public issues through "wholesale" strategies rather than on a case-by-case basis. Any policy carries within it assumptions about the nature of the issue or problem to be addressed, about what is natural or unavoidable and what merits government action, and about the legitimacy of various intervention strategies. Many such assumptions are expressed through the creation of categories: of entitlement and nonentitlement, of what is permitted and what is prohibited, of who is required to perform certain activities and who is absolved from that requirement.

Public disability policies implicitly include or explicitly cover a wide range of physical and mental conditions. Some policies narrowly target benefits or services to people with a particular impairment, such as blindness, deafness, mental retardation, or end-stage renal disease. Other policies use functional definitions that, in theory, encompass a nearly infinite variety of impairments and etiologies. In each public program, assumptions about who deserves what kind of help shape the governmental response to disability.

The evolution of American disability policy reflects changing assumptions about the nature of the problems posed by impairment and what government should do about them. In the twentieth century, such assumptions appear to have shifted several times, as measured by the public policies the federal and state governments have created. Workers' compensation and SSDI assume that disability is incapacitating for paid employment. Vocational rehabilitation assumes that training and counseling can enable many individuals to overcome the functional consequences of their impairments and enter the workforce. Civil rights programs such as IDEA and the ADA assume that discriminatory environmental barriers create the marginal status of many Americans with disabilities.

Policy historian Edward Berkowitz notes the incongruities and lack of coordination among "two generations of ameliorative (or income-maintenance) programs [workers' compensation and SSDI] stemming from the Progressive Era and the New Deal and two generations of service (or corrective) programs [VR and civil rights], one originating in the 1920s and the other in the 1970s."[27] All of these programs, according to Berkowitz, encompass significant elements of litigation, which consumes resources and inhibits rehabilitation. Income maintenance and rehabilitiation policies do not effectively complement each other but rather operate largely independent of each other and often in opposition through the creation of work disincentives. One analysis, by economist Monroe Berkowitz, compiled the costs of all federal disability programs in fiscal year 1995, categorized by their broad purposes. Of the nearly $184 billion spent on all disability programs, over 90 percent went for health care ($91 billion) and income maintenance ($78 billion).[28]

Thus the vast majority of public dollars are spent in ways consistent with assumptions about disability linked to a medical model, in which impairment is associated with incapacity and, in particular, with the incapacity to support oneself through work. In this paradigm, if a person can work, that individual is not disabled. Disability policy compensates for the incapacity to work through the provision of cash benefits and custodial services, even though vocational rehabilitation seeks to help the client "overcome" assumed incapacity to regain the ability to function. Many programs make a dichotomous either-or distinction: those certified as incapable of work are thus disabled and eligible for benefits and services; those capable of work are therefore not disabled and are ineligible for benefits.

Recent judicial rulings have written this simplistic distinction into federal civil rights policy. For example, 1999 Supreme Court decisions exclude individuals from Americans with Disabilities Act's protection from discrimination if their impairments can be corrected with medication or devices. Chai Feldblum, a law professor and an author of the ADA, points out that the decisions "create the absurd result of a person being disabled enough to be fired from a job, but not disabled enough to challenge the firing."[29]

Certification as "disabled" takes place through an inherently uncertain gatekeeping process that combines medical and vocational assessment and is frequently systematized through complex policy regulations. Some programs utilize a unidimensional scoring system that specifies on a percentage basis how incapable of work an impairment renders a claimant and thus what amount of benefits that individual should receive. Other programs resort to more complex systems of scoring, whereby weighted assessments of an individual's ability to perform various everyday life activities are aggregated into an overall rating. Frequently, these processes make inferences about the consequences of particular physiological attributes, for example, an inability to walk or see. But they do so without reference to the ability of particular individuals to adopt strategies for coping with their impairments or to the context in which such activities might take place, such as the presence or absence of access features. However complex the determination criteria, they invariably reduce disability to a snapshot evaluation of capacity for economic performance. Such systems leave out the variability in how even similar forms of impairment affect different individuals. Such attempts to measure "disability," and thereby individual eligibility, have appeared in many programs throughout the twentieth century.

Another persistent theme in American disability policies has been their cultural constructions of worthiness and morality. This element has appeared in both their broad conception and their concrete criteria of eligibility. American disability policy traditionally has been framed primarily as a welfare benefit given to a segment of the "deserving" poor. In her discussion of social insurance programs for people with disabilities, Deborah Stone writes of the evolution of disability as a formal administrative category designed to differentiate between those who must work and those who are morally entitled to public benefits.[30] She describes how the framers of the SSDI program expressed concern about abuse and "malingering" by those claiming benefits due to an inability to work. SSDI policymakers hoped that the designation of physicians as program gatekeepers would ensure that objective medical standards would govern the determination of eligibility. They banked on this method despite the contention by most representatives of physicians that determining disability is inherently subjective. The underlying concern was that people able to work and thus undeserving might somehow successfully claim benefits. In concluding her analysis of disability definitions, Stone writes that "the label connotes a sense of moral worthiness or desert. The foremost element of consensus about the disability category is that its members are somehow deserving of social aid for some special reason."[31] She continues that the legitimacy of their claim to public support is based on innocence, the lack of personal responsibility for their condition, and suffering, or that their condition is particularly lamentable or pitiable. Embodying these characteristics may ultimately be far more important than the nature of one's actual impairment.

Comparable questions have been raised in the past decade over the ADA. Conservatives in Congress, academia, and the media have questioned the legitimacy of the ADA's mandates, expressing skepticism over the validity of the claims of those seeking protection under its provisions and the remedies they have sought. Critics have raised essentially moral objections to the deservedness of many claiming protection under the act and have sought to define disability narrowly in terms of those with obvious impairments who, they typically contend, are clearly incapable of functioning without societal support.

Yet disability embodies a vast and disparate set of circumstances that are dynamic and idiosyncratic for each individual. The consequences for everyday life of having a disability are both diverse and complex.[32] The variation in the meaning of disability is reflected in the variety of definitions utilized in public programs. Each policy realm adopts its own definition. Large-scale bureaucratic institutions, such as governmental agencies, may, of all social institutions, be the most resistant to dealing positively with individual variation. This is because of technologies and management systems that, in the pursuit of equity and efficiency, "rationally" emphasize standardized categories. Such institutions are less likely to easily incorporate the variability introduced by disability.

While there has been a tendency for large-scale systems to adopt "wholesale" rather than individualized solutions to problems, there have also been some countervailing trends. The Individuals with Disabilities Education Act, the vocational rehabilitation program, and a number of other public programs have mandated the development of individualized service plans based on the needs of each service recipient. Still, anecdotal evidence suggests that supposedly individualized plans based on individual characteristics have often constituted little more than boilerplates prescribing services dependent on established organizational routines and the availability of resources.

Edward Berkowitz notes the difficulty of such individualized assessment: "No one can predict the future course of an individual's impairment or make rules that take both individual differences and the future of the economy into account. Disability . . . resists precise measurement: it simply is not like poverty or old age."[33] He contends that disability policy has also failed to distinguish between younger people with disabilities who want to work but face a variety of policy disincentives and older workers who acquire impairments and seek income to support early retirement, in his view often justifiably.[34]

Industrialization brought policies that segregated disabled people, removing them from their indigenous communities, placing many of them in institutions, and, in effect, creating communities of people with disabilities. While the importance of institutions has waned over the past four decades, segregated programs persist and a separate community of people with disabilities continues to be reinforced by "special" service strategies and the stigma that pervades our culture. Sociologist Paul Higgins writes, "Policy that makes disability exceptional [as in the case of special education] also separates disabled people from nondisabled people."[35]

Such segregation persists. Policy incentives and the provision of services to targeted populations reinforce it. Even antidiscrimination policies that seek to reduce such exclusion appear to have limited impact on long-established assumptions and institutional arrangements that promote segregation. In an exhaustive analysis of ADA decisions in 1997, Robert Burgdorf, the author of the original 1988 bill that became the ADA, discusses how many decisions have perpetuated the incorrect concept that people with disabilities are some special group of individuals "drastically different from others and, therefore, should be treated differently and given special protection," rather than as "regular Janes and Joes" who, despite their impairments, are not essentially different from other people.[36] He concludes that "in the name of restricting this special treatment to the supposed truly deserving beneficiaries, obstacles have been erected that have kept many of the supposed core group along with many other citizens from the protection these laws were enacted to provide."[37]

Because of the diversity of disabling conditions and the variety of coping strategies of individuals who have them, many accommodations must be tailored to the individual involved. These may require periodic alterations to reflect changes in the individual's impairment or the environment in and outside the workplace. Truly accommodating people with disabilities may require a constant willingness to change; the periodic restructuring of expectations, tasks, and techniques; and a constructive communication between persons with disabilities and those responsible for their environments, such as employers. New forms of accountability may also be required to accommodate the complexity of disability with flexibility. Edward Berkowitz cautions:

> Federal policymakers hesitate to create grants that can be used for a wide variety of purposes, for fear that the money will be wasted or not reach the groups that Congress intends to aid. Consequently, regulation writers typically build in rules to limit the ways in which the money can be spent.... To gain the flexibility necessary to reach across programs, we must be prepared to sacrifice a bit of what policymakers call accountability.[38]

Disability policy has shifted in emphasis over the past hundred years, yet because it is an expression of the larger culture and social structure, it is a limited engine of social change. Advocates who seek to support people with disabilities and to eliminate barriers to their participation in public and private life need to confront the challenges of changing policy. They must also attend to the larger task of reorienting and redefining the disabling and institutionalized aspects of American culture and political economy.

NOTES

1. *Pensions to Certain Enlisted Men and Officers Who Served in the Civil War and the War with Mexico*, hearings before the United States House Committee on Pensions, 59th Cong., 2d sess., Jan. 22, 1907 (Washington, D.C.: GPO, 1907), p. 2.

2. Some individuals are eligible for both SSDI and SSI by virtue of their work history and low-income status.

3. Richard K. Scotch and Edward Berkowitz, "One Comprehensive System? An Historical Perspective on Federal Disability Policy," *Journal of Disability Policy Studies* 1:3 (1990): 1–19.

4. For a critical assessment of the cultural significance of blindness, see C. Edwin Vaughn, *Social and Cultural Perspectives on Blindness: Barriers to Community Integration* (Springfield, IL: Charles C. Thomas, 1998).

5. Harlan Hahn, "Towards a Politics of Disability: Definitions, Disciplines, and Policies," *Social Science Journal* 22:4 (1985): 95.

6. For a review of the general cross-cultural literature on disability through the 1980s, see Jessica Scheer and Nora Gross, "Impairment as a Human Constant: Cross-Cultural and Historical Perspectives on Variation," *Journal of Social Issues* 44:1 (1988): 23–38.

7. David J. Rothman, *The Discovery of the Asylum: Social Order and Disorder in the New Republic* (Boston: Little, Brown, and Company, 1971).

8. Theda Skocpol, *Protecting Soldiers and Mothers: The Political Origins of Social Policy in the United States* (Cambridge, MA: Harvard University Press, 1992), p. 149.

9. Ibid., p. 151.

10. For a critical history and review of recent issues in workers' compensation, see chap. 2 of Edward Berkowitz, *Disabled Policy: America's Programs for the Handicapped* (New York: Cambridge University Press, 1987).

11. The difficulties of achieving coverage of industrial diseases in workers' compensation is discussed in the case study of silicosis in Gerald Markowitz and David Rosner, "The Illusion of Medical Certainty and the Politics of Industrial Disability, 1930–1960," *Milbank Quarterly* 67, supp. 2, part 1 (1989): 228–54.

12. An analysis of variation across state workers' compensation plans is provided in Evangelos M. Falaris, Charles R. Link, and Michael E. Staten, *Causes of Litigation in Workers' Compensation Programs* (Kalamazoo, MI: W. E. Upjohn Institute for Employment Research, 1995).

13. Quoted in Berkowitz, *Disabled Policy*, p. 80.

14. Ibid., chap. 2.

15. Deborah A. Stone, *The Disabled State* (Philadelphia: Temple University Press, 1984).

16. Edward H. Yelin, *Disability and the Displaced Worker* (New Brunswick, NJ: Rutgers University Press, 1992).

17. See, for example, Berkowitz, *Disabled Policy*, chap. 4.

18. A critical account of the background and implementation of the SSI program is provided in Martha Derthick, *Agency under Stress: The Social Security Administration in American Government* (Washington, DC: Brookings Institute, 1990).

19. Berkowitz, *Disabled Policy*, pp. 163–67.

20. An early statement of the conceptual basis for independent living and its implication for services is presented in Gerben DeJong, "Independent Living: From Social Movement to Analytic Paradigm," *Archives of Physical Medicine and Rehabilitation* 60 (1979): 435–36.

21. The lack of coordination between vocational rehabilitation and other federal programs is addressed in the context of the program's history in Berkowitz, *Disabled Policy*, pp. 155–63.

22. Hahn, "Towards a Politics of Disability," pp. 87–101.

23. Richard K. Scotch, *From Good Will to Civil Rights: Transforming Federal Disability Policy* (Philadelphia: Temple University Press, 1984).

24. Jane West, *The Americans with Disabilities Act: From Policy to Practice* (New York: Milbank Memorial Fund, 1991).

25. A number of thoughtful discussions of the impact and significance of the ADA can be found in the special issue edited by William G. Johnson, "The Americans with Disabilities Act: Social Contract or Special Privilege?" special issue of *Annals of the American Academy of Political and Social Science* 549 (January 1997).

26. C. Wright Mills, *The Sociological Imagination* (New York: Grove Press, 1959), pp. 8–11.

27. Berkowitz, *Disabled Policy*, p. 229.

28. Monroe Berkowitz, "Federal Programs for Persons with Disabilities" (paper presented at Conference on Employment and Return to Work for People with Disabilities, Social Security Administration and National Institute on Disability and Rehabilitation Research, Washington, D.C., 1996).

29. Quoted in L. Greenhouse, "High Court Limits Who Is Protected by Disability Law," *New York Times,* June 23, 1999, p. A16.

30. Stone, *Disabled State.*

31. Ibid., p. 172.

32. Paul C. Higgins, *Making Disability: Exploring the Social Transformation of Human Variation* (Springfield, IL: Charles C. Thomas, 1992).

33. Berkowitz, *Disabled Policy*, p. 230.

34. Ibid., p. 239.

35. Higgins, *Making Disability*, p. 209.

36. Robert L. Burgdorf, Jr., "'Substantially Limited' Protection from Disability Discrimination: The Special Treatment Model and Misconstructions of the Definition of Disability," *Villanova Law Review* 42:2 (1997): 534.

37. Ibid., p. 585.

38. Berkowitz, *Disabled Policy*, p. 238.

Contributors

DOUGLAS C. BAYNTON is assistant professor of history and American Sign Language at the University of Iowa. He is the author of *Forbidden Signs: American Culture and the Campaign against Sign Language* (University of Chicago Press, 1996). His current project is a history of the concept of disability in the making of American immigration policy since the late nineteenth century.

JANICE A. BROCKLEY is a doctoral candidate in the History Department at Rutgers University. She is working on her dissertation, "Rearing the Child Who Never Grew: Parents, Experts, and Children with Intellectual Disabilities, 1910–1962."

SUSAN BURCH is assistant professor of history at Gallaudet University in Washington, D.C. Her areas of expertise include American and Soviet Deaf history as well as women's history in both countries. She is currently working on a book on American Deaf cultural history in the early twentieth century.

BRAD BYROM is on the faculty at Yuba College in northern California and is a Ph.D. candidate in history at the University of Iowa. He has previously published a biographical article on Joseph F. Sullivan and is currently completing a dissertation on the history of the rehabilitation movement.

NATALIE A. DYKSTRA recently completed a Ph.D. in American Studies at the University of Kansas. She is assistant professor of history at Hope College and is currently completing a book on autobiography, women's work, and the production of value in nineteenth-century America.

R. A. R. EDWARDS is assistant professor of history at the Rochester Institute of Technology in Rochester, New York. She received her doctorate from the University of Rochester in 1997.

ROSEMARIE GARLAND THOMSON is an associate professor of English at Howard University in Washington, D.C. Many of her scholarly publications and professional activities are devoted to developing the field of disability studies in the humanities. She is the author of *Extraordinary Bodies: Figuring Physical Disability in American Literature and Culture* (Columbia University Press, 1997) and the editor of *Freakery: Cultural Spectacles of the Extraordinary Body* (New York University Press, 1996). She is currently writing a book on staring and one on the cultural logic of euthanasia.

DAVID A. GERBER is professor of American history at the State University of New York at Buffalo. He is the editor of a collection of essays, *Disabled Veterans in History*, that will be published by the University of Michigan Press.

K. WALTER HICKEL received his Ph.D. from Columbia University and is currently a historian for the Digital Manuscripts Program in the History of Medicine Division at the National Library of Medicine.

HANNAH JOYNER is assistant professor of history at Gallaudet University and a doctoral candidate at the University of Pennsylvania. Her current research explores the experience of growing up Deaf in the American South during the nineteenth century.

CATHERINE J. KUDLICK is associate professor of history at the University of California, Davis. Her current research explores the historical origins of attitudes toward blind people and blindness in modern France and America.

PAUL K. LONGMORE is professor of history and director of the Institute on Disability at San Francisco State University. He is the author of *The Invention of George Washington* and numerous essays on disability history and disability studies, early American history, and the bioethics of disability.

KIM NIELSEN is assistant professor of Social Change and Development and Women's Studies at the University of Wisconsin–Green Bay. She has written *Women against Women: Anti-Radicalism, Anti-Feminism, and the First Red Scare*, forthcoming from Ohio State University Press. Her next book, *The Radical Lives of Helen Keller*, is in progress with New York University Press.

RICHARD K. SCOTCH is professor of sociology and political economy in the School of Social Sciences at the University of Texas at Dallas. He is the author of *From Good Will to Civil Rights: Transforming Federal Disability Policy* and, with Sharon Barnartt, the forthcoming *Social Movements in the Disability Com-*

munity. His current research interests include the impact of civil rights law on social and economic justice and developing a conceptual model of disability based on the concept of human variation.

JOHN WILLIAMS-SEARLE is a graduate instructor at the University of Iowa. His forthcoming dissertation, titled "Broken Brotherhood: Disability, Manliness, and Safety on the Rails, 1868–1908," builds on and seeks to integrate insights drawn from the history of disability, labor history, the history of manhood, and legal history.

LAURI UMANSKY is author of *Motherhood Reconceived: Feminism and the Legacies of the Sixties* and co-editor, with Molly Ladd-Taylor, of *"Bad" Mothers: The Politics of Blame in Twentieth-Century America*. She is associate professor of history at Suffolk University.

Index

Access: advocacy for, 1–2, 4, 10–11, 12, 323–324, 383; as difference in functioning, 19, 20; public policy and, 20, 383–384, 387; public transportation and, 1, 11; rehabilitation and, 134, 139, 145–146; statutes for, 20, 316, 324, 383. *See also* Advocacy; Public policy

Addams, Jane, 219

Advocacy: access, 1–2, 4, 10–11, 12, 19, 20, 316, 323–324, 383–384; advertising and, 366; consumer control and, 382; control of organizations/programs and, 3, 188–189, 193, 200, 208, 283, 320; cross-disability, 4–5; deinstitutionalization, 10–11; different functioning and, 19; disability-specific interests in, 20–21; education, 11–12, 17; Great Depression and, 281; health care, 12; impairment and, 20; independent living, 11, 382–383; minority consciousness in, 11, 16, 26n. 17; politicization of disability in, 4–5, 10–11, 12, 190, 208–209, 237–238, 273, 370; public policy, 1–2, 4–5, 10–11, 12, 190, 378, 382–383, 384; sociopolitical/minority-group model in, 16, 19, 190, 208, 237–238, 252, 253–254, 255, 273, 283, 382, 383–384. *See also* Blind people; Blinded Veterans Association (BVA); Deaf education, 1890s–1940s; Public policy; Veterans compensation

African Americans: attribution of disability to, 34, 37, 39, 237, 256–257; Blinded Veterans Association and, 315–316; "damage imagery" and, 41; disability benefits and, 255–258; disability justifying discrimination against, 33–34; *Drapetomania* and, 38; *Dysaesthesia Aethiopis* and, 38; disability justifying slavery of, 37–38, 53n. 11; education

causing disability in, 38; Freedmen's Hospital and, 241; freedom causing disability in, 38–39; images of, 39–41, 237; physically disabled, 37, 38, 39–40, 41, 98, 99–100; veterans, 237, 252–253, 255–258, 266n. 62, 314–316; white southern view of, 83, 98–100. *See also* Class; Ethnic minorities; Gender; Race

American Annals of the Deaf, 63, 72–73

American Association for the Promotion of Teaching Speech to the Deaf, 217, 219, 221

American Association of Instructors of the Blind, 188

American Association of Workers for the Blind (AAWB), 187–188, 189, 196, 199, 209n. 6

American Asylum for the Education and Instruction of Deaf and Dumb Persons, 59–60, 65, 73

American Blind Peoples Higher Education and General Improvement Association (ABPHEGIA): activism of, 3, 187, 189, 192–193; founding of, 187, 209n. 2; *The Problem* and, 187, 192; sighted professionals and, 3, 188–189, 193, 200, 283. *See also* Advocacy; Blind people; Blinded Veterans Association (BVA); Keller, Helen; *Outlook for the Blind; Problem, The*

American Coalition of Citizens with Disabilities, 11

American Deaf Citizen, 222

American Diabetes Association, 10

American Disabled for Accessible Public Transit (ADAPT), 11

American Disabled for Attendant Programs Today. *See* American Disabled for Accessible Public Transit (ADAPT)

American Foundation for the Blind (AFB), 188, 209n. 6, 276, 278–282, 284, 285, 319, 332n. 30

American Journal of Care for Cripples, 142, 151

American Legion, 3, 246, 254, 315, 320

American Otological Society, 227

American Sign Language. *See* Sign language

American Veterans Committee, 315

Americans with Disabilities Act (ADA), 1, 4, 14, 366, 384, 386, 387, 388, 389. *See also* Advocacy

Amputees, 46, 51, 133, 158, 159, 162, 164, 166, 176, 178, 179–180, 240, 244, 315, 344–346, 349–352, 362, 363, 368, 369

Architectural Barriers Act, 10

Association for Retarded Citizens, The, (ARC), 10

Association for the Severely Handicapped, The, (TASH), 10

Autobiography of the Neurasthene, The, 122

Baldwin, Barney, disabled railroader in sideshow, 157

Ballin, Albert, on oralist abuse of Deaf students, 222

Barden-La Follette Act, 382

Barnum, P. T., 40, 348, 354

Baynton, Douglas, 2, 6, 18, 58–59, 71

Beecher, Catharine, 117

Beggars: blind, 192; child, 136, 137; crippled, 136, 137, 139, 140. *See also* Charity; Dependence/Independence

Bell, Alexander Graham, 72, 216, 217, 282, 283, 284

Bellaire, Joseph, the "One-Fingered Fireman," 158, 179–180

Berkowitz, Edward, 386, 389, 390

Berubé, Michael, 13

Blackburn, Dr. Alan, blindness specialist, 323

Blind in the United States, 1910, The, 193

Blind people: activism of, 3, 4, 17, 187, 189, 190, 192, 193, 208–209, 209nn. 2, 6, 323–324; African American, 37, 39, 315; begging, 192; census and, 193; charity and, 314, 323; children as, 295, 304; citizenship and, 269–271, 272; community formation among, 187, 192, 193, 199–200, 207, 212n. 49; control of blindness organizations by, 3, 17, 188–189, 193, 200, 208, 209n. 6, 283,

320; cultural meaning of blindness and, 376; dependence/independence and, 202, 203, 205, 206, 207, 271, 317; disability and, 210n. 15; dog guide laws and, 20, 316, 324, 383; education of, 3, 4, 187, 191, 192, 193, 195, 197–200, 201, 203–204, 206, 207, 209n. 2; employment and, 193, 196–197, 202, 207, 271, 278–279, 288n. 14, 376; gender and, 18, 191, 201–207, 208; government's role regarding, 190, 193, 197, 200, 271, 278; historical agency of, 187–213, 268–290; history of, 187–213, 268–290, 313–334; homemaking and, 191, 202–207; identities of, 189–191, 199, 203, 206, 208–209; images of, 191–192, 194–199, 200–201, 202–204, 208–209, 271, 313, 314, 323, 324, 326, 348; immigration and, 34, 46, 50; institutions and, 195, 196–197, 378; Helen Keller and, 189, 194–195, 196, 200–201, 271, 276, 278–279, 288n. 14; marriage and, 202, 203, 204–205; masculinity and, 191, 202; medical treatment of, 196; mobility training and, 202; national college for, 197–199; politicization of, 190, 208–209; prejudice toward, 314; prevention of blindness and, 196; public policy and, 376; railroaders as, 162; residential schools and, 187, 192, 198, 199–200, 203, 204, 209n. 2, 212nn. 36, 49; sheltered workshops and, 195, 196–197, 314; sighted professionals and, 17, 188–189, 190, 191, 195–196, 197–198, 203–204, 208; society and, 192–194, 198; taxes and, 376; veterans as, 240, 244, 375; white canes and, 324–325, 383; white cane laws and, 20, 383; women as, 18, 191, 201–207. *See also* American Blind Peoples Higher Education and General Improvement Association (ABPHEGIA); Blinded Veterans Association (BVA); Keller, Helen; *Outlook for the Blind*; *Problem, The*

Blinded Veterans Association (BVA): African Americans in, 315–316; anti-semitism and, 314, 315, 316; blind civilians and, 314, 322, 323, 332n. 30; "blind jobs" and, 326; blind veterans' controlling, 320, 333n. 43; *Bright Victory* and, 320–322; cane technique and, 324–325; death-and-rebirth view of blindness and, 323, 324, 325, 332n. 31; dignity and, 314, 322, 323, 324, 325; disability ideology of, 314, 321–326; discrimination against blind people opposed by, 314, 316, 322, 323, 324, 325, 326; egalitarian politics of, 313–316, 319, 320–322, 326–329; employment and, 314, 316, 320, 324, 326, 327, 328; "facial vision" and, 324–325; field service of, 326; founding of, 313–314, 320; gender and, 323, 332n. 35; guide dogs and, 316, 324; health of members of, 324, 326; historical recollections of, 316, 321, 322, 327–329; images of blind people and, 313, 322, 323; independence and, 314, 317, 322, 323, 324–326, 328; integration of, 315; Jewish veterans in, 315; Baynard Kendrick and, 316, 319, 320, 328, 329; *Lights Out* and, 319, 320–322; masculinity and, 323, 324, 325–326, 327, 332n. 35; military metaphors and, 323; National Federation of the Blind and, 323, 332n. 30; newsstands and, 326; pensions and, 324, 326; racism and, 314–316, 321, 327–328; response to blindness by, 321–323, 327–328; rehabilitation and, 314, 316, 319, 322–326, 327, 328; Al Schmid and 328; sheltered workshops and, 314, 326; solidarity within, 314, 316, 319, 322, 326–328; Veterans Administration and, 314, 324; veterans organizations and, 314–315, 316, 320; women, relationships with, 317, 325, 327, 328; women veterans in, 332n. 35. *See also* Blind people; *Bright Victory*; Keller, Helen; Kendrick, Baynard; *Outlook for the Blind*; *Problem, The*; Veterans' compensation

Blodgett, William E., M.D., and rise of orthopedic surgery, 150–151

Body, cultural discourses of, 117–118, 157, 177, 179, 180–181, 269, 277, 278, 284–286, 293–295, 300–302, 337–338, 347–348. *See also* Images; Medical model

Booth, Frank, and oralism at Nebraska School for the Deaf, 221, 222

Boydston, Jeanne, 122

Braille: blind veterans learning, 325; competing tactile formats and, 188, 192, 199, 209n. 5, 211n. 18; publications in, 188, 209n. 5; signage and, 1. *See also* Blind people; Blinded Veterans Association (BVA); *Outlook for the Blind*; *Problem, The*

Bright Victory, 316–317, 320–322. *See also* Blinded Veterans Association (BVA); Kendrick, Baynard

Brotherhood of Locomotive Engineers (BLE), 161, 169, 171–177, 181n. 1

Brotherhood of Railroad Brakemen (BRB), 157, 158, 163, 167, 168–169, 181n. 1

Brotherhood of Railroad Trainmen (BRT). *See* Brotherhood of Railroad Brakemen (BRB)

Brown, Gillian, 121–122

Brown, James, supporting methodical signs, 73

Brown, Robert Burns, lobbying for veterans, 375

Bureau of War Risk Insurance, 240, 245–246, 250

Burgdorf, Robert, 389

Burke, Edmund, 34–35. *See also* Monsters/Monstrosities

Burnet, John, opposing methodical signs, 67–68, 73, 80n. 65

Bush, President George, 1, 384

Butler, Judith, 118

Calhoun, John C., 37–38

Campbell, Charles, F. F., editor of *Outlook for the Blind*, 188, 194–196, 207, 208, 209

Cancer, 107, 113–114, 120, 364–366, 367

Carnegie, Andrew, 217

Carroll, Rev. Thomas, BVA chaplain, 323

Census, U.S., 193

Cerebral palsy, 294

Charity: masculinity and, 169–171, 172, 200–201, 242; railroaders and, 169–171, 172, 176, 18nn. 56, 61. *See also* Beggars; Dependence/Independence; Fundraising; Moral appraisal; Rehabilitation

Children: blind, 3, 295, 304; families of, 83–84, 140, 217–218; fundraising and, 141, 341–342, 352, 355, 356; images of, 293–296, 297, 298–299, 300–302, 341–342, 352, 355, 356, 364; physically disabled, 3, 5; society's view of, 138–139. *See also* Deaf education, 1890s–1940s; Deaf education, mid-nineteenth century; Education; Families; Greenfield, Jerome; Rehabilitation; Repouille, Raymond

Citizenship: activism for full, 1–2, 3, 14, 281, 287n. 4; blind people and, 269–271, 272;

James, Alice *(continued)*
and, 110, 111–112, 113; female role and, 107, 108–109, 110, 111–113, 117–118, 122, 123; gender and, 18, 108–109, 110, 111, 114, 116–119, 121–122; illness as "work" of, 108–110, 113, 114–116, 118–122, 123, 125, 126, 128nn. 23–24, 129n. 39; illnesses of, 107, 110–111, 113–114, 116, 127n. 14; insanity and, 113; R. W. B. Lewis on family of, 120; Katherine Loring and 107, 110, 113, 114, 123, 126n. 2; market metaphors and, 120–121, 122; mother and, 111, 112, 113; neurasthenia and, 111, 113, 116; Ralph Barton Perry on, 129n. 50; Richard Rorty on, 125; spiritual value of illness to, 107, 113, 124–125; Jean Strouse on, 118; suicide and, 111, 113. *See also* Gender; Women

James, Henry, Sr., 110, 111–112, 113, 120

James, Henry, 107, 108, 113, 116, 121, 123

James, Mary, 111, 112, 113

James, William, 107, 108, 110, 111, 113, 116, 120–121, 123, 125, 128n. 28

Jewish Immigrants' Information Bureau, 50

Jewish War Veterans of America, 315

Johnson, Charles S., on linking African Americans with "defectives," 41

Keller, Helen, 268–290; American Foundation for the Blind and, 276, 278, 279–282, 284–285; American Rescue Ship Mission and, 279; autobiography of, 271; Alexander Graham Bell and, 282, 283, 284; birth control advocacy of, 268; civic fitness and disability of, 18, 269–270, 272–275, 276, 277, 280, 281, 283–286; civic fitness and work of, 271–272, 288n. 14; class and, 272–273; Committee to Purchase Products Made by the Blind and, 278–279; contributing to *Outlook for the Blind*, 189, 194–196, 200–202, 205; critics using disability to discredit, 274–275, 277; dependency of blind people and, 200–201, 271–272; disability as personal overcoming of adversity and, 273, 283–284, 286, 288n. 19; disability as political category and, 270–271, 272–274, 281–284, 285; disability discrimination and, 273, 282, 285; disability rights activists contrasted with, 273, 280–283; education of, 268, 284; eugenics and, 277, 282; euthanasia and, 282; Federal Bureau of Investigation and, 279; fundraising and, 276, 278, 280, 282, 284, 285; gender and, 201–202, 269–270, 272, 283–284, 285; Emma Goldman on, 276; House Un-American Activities Committee and, 279; images of blind men and, 200–202, 271, 272, 288n. 14; images of blind women and, 201–202, 269–270, 272, 283–284; Robert B. Irwin, criticizing politics of, 279–280; isolation of, 276, 282, 284; Robert La Follette and, 277; liberal individualism and, 284–285; livelihood of, 200, 271–272, 276–277, 278, 284; John Macy and, 268, 275; metaphorical use of disability by, 274; Military Intelligence Division file on, 279; motherhood and, 272; National Association for the Advancement of Colored People and, 275; "Negro-blind" and "deafblind," view of, 281; opposing Talking Books, 281; oralism and, 282, 286n. 2, 290n. 54; organized blind movement and, 282; *Out of the Dark: Essays on Physical and Social Vision* and, 273; origin of deaf-blindness of, 274; paternalism and, 281, 282; Westbrook Pegler on, 280; people with disabilities, relationship to, 213n. 52, 281–285; philanthropy and, 200–201, 271–272, 276, 282; political activities of, 268, 269–270, 272–273, 275, 276–277, 278, 279, 289n. 38; political cautiousness of, 276–279, 280–281, 283, 285; politics of downplayed/devalued, 268, 272, 285, 288n. 25; politics of the body and, 269, 277, 278, 284–286; professionals and, 282; public image and role of, 268, 274–278, 280, 282–285; racism, disability, and, 281; Radcliffe College and, 268, 276; radicalism and, 268, 272–274, 275, 276–277, 281, 284, 285; Eleanor Roosevelt and, 278, 279, 280; Franklin Roosevelt and, 278, 281, 283–284, 286, 289n. 40; Schenectady socialists and, 275; self-image of, 269, 275, 283–285; sexuality of, 278; sheltered workshops and, 282; social causes of impairment and, 273–274; Anne Sullivan and, 213n. 52, 268, 271, 275, 276, 279, 282, 283, 284, 289n. 35; vocational rehabilitation and, 271, 278–279, 288n. 14; Henry Wallace and, 279–280; women activists and, 276–277; women's suffrage advocated by, 268; work

Mongolism. *See* Down's Syndrome

Monsters/Monstrosities, 34–35, 37, 41, 348, 349. *See also* Images

Moral appraisal: blind people and, 192, 201; causes of disability and, 241; cripples and, 133, 139–140, 143, 153n. 23; developmentally disabled people and, 294, 295, 296–297, 299, 300; fraud and, 163, 164, 182n. 12, 185n. 56, 246, 250–251; manhood and, 158; medical explanations displacing, 241; "overcoming" and, 16; public policy and, 375–376, 378, 385, 387–388; railroaders and, 158, 163, 165, 167, 172, 182n. 12; rehabilitation and, 134, 137, 143; rescue and, 355; sexuality and, 204, 205, 206, 237, 250–251, 257, 266n. 61, 278, 295, 296–297, 299, 300; veterans and, 237, 240, 241, 242, 246, 250–251, 251–252, 253–254, 257, 266n. 61, 375–376. *See also* Religious views

Mothers: blind women as, 5, 203, 204–205, 206–207, 272; societal views of disabled children and, 295–296; societal views of disabled women as, 272. *See also* Children; Families; Greenfield, Jerome; Marriage; Repouille, Raymond; Women

National Association for the Advancement of Colored People, 194, 275

National Association of the Deaf (NAD), 10, 219, 221, 226, 281

National Conference of Union Labor Legionnaires, 315

National Council on Disability, 11, 384

National Easter Seal Society, 10

National Education Association, 217

National Federation of the Blind, 10, 189, 208, 209n. 6, 282, 283, 323, 332n. 30, 376

National Society for the Prevention of Blindness, 196

Natural, concept of, 35–36. *See also* Normality, concept of

Neilson, D., on disabled railroaders, 178–180

Neurasthenia, 111, 113, 116, 117, 118, 122, 128nn. 25–28. *See also* James, Alice

New York Hospital for the Ruptured and Crippled, 136, 149

New York School for the Deaf, 6, 64, 66, 67, 84, 87, 88, 91–93, 94–95, 222, 228

Nolan, Edward J., and blind advocacy, 188, 189, 199

Normality: concept of, 6, 35–36; Deaf people and, 36, 52n. 5, 71–72, 216, 218, 228; "cure or kill" and, 355–356; developmentally disabled people and, 307–308; Helen Keller and, 275, 285; race, disability, and, 39–40; railroaders and, 178, 180; staring and, 347. *See also* Medical model; Natural, concept of

North Carolina School for the Blind and Deaf, 94–95, 197

Not Dead Yet, 11. *See also* Euthanasia

Nursing homes. *See* Institutionalization

Old Farms, U.S. Army blind rehabilitation facility, 314, 319, 320, 323, 324, 325, 326, 327, 328

Oralism: abuse of students in, 222; academic achievement in, 223–224, 225–226, 229, 231; assimilationist goals of, 214, 216, 218; audiometer and, 225–226; Alexander Graham Bell and, 72, 216, 217; child-centered approach and, 225; Clarke Institution for Deaf-Mutes and, 59, 218, 219, 220, 232n. 9; classification and nomenclature in, 226, 234n. 24; combined method and, 221, 224, 225–226, 231; Darwinian thought in, 71, 74, 78n. 26, 81n. 82; day schools in, 217–218, 226; Deaf community opposing, 5, 17, 214, 217, 221–223, 224, 227–228, 231, 233n. 18; Deaf culture opposed in, 74–75, 227; Deaf men reacting to, 219–221; Deaf newspapers opposing, 222; Deaf teachers and, 80n. 65, 214, 219, 220, 221, 227–228, 229, 230–231; Deaf women displaced by, 219–221; educators supporting, 217; enrollment of young children in, 218; female dominion of reform and, 218–220, 221, 232nn. 7, 9; financial resources of, 217, 232n. 9; Georgia state school and, 223–224, 233n. 18; German, 59; hearing teachers in, 217, 218–221; hearing women teachers in, 215, 218, 219–221, 225, 229, 232nn. 7, 9; historical origins of, 58, 215; historiography of, 58–59, 214, 227, 229, 230; Samuel Gridley Howe and, 59, 71–72, 74; "humanizing power" of speech and sign and, 71–72, 228; images of deaf people in, 216, 222, 224, 226–227, 228–229, 230–231; Helen Keller and, 282, 286n. 2;

Physicians *(continued)*
model; Orthopedists; Public policy;
Rehabilitation
Politicization of disability, 4–5, 10–11, 12, 190,
208–209, 209nn. 2, 6, 237–238, 243, 244,
252, 375–392. *See also* Advocacy; History;
Public policy
Pope, Alvin, oralist superintendent of New Jersey School for the Deaf, 221–222, 223, 225
Porter, George, editor of *Silent Worker,* resisting
oralism, 222
Power: blindness professionals', 5, 187–189,
190, 191, 195–199, 203–204, 205–206,
207–208, 212n. 36; bureaucrats', 5, 237, 244;
class and, 5, 140–141, 147, 152n. 3, 254;
consumer control and, 382; control of
blindness organizations, 3, 188–189, 193,
200, 283, 320; Deaf education and, 3, 5, 17,
60, 61–62, 64, 65–66, 73–75, 214–215,
216–217, 218–220, 221–225, 229, 230–231,
232; female dominion of reform and,
146–147, 215, 218–221, 232nn. 7, 9;
fundraising images and, 341–342, 344–346,
352, 355–356; gender and, 5; material interests and, 5–6; physicians', 5, 37–40, 42–43,
134–135, 138, 236–237, 238, 245–246, 252,
254; rehabilitation and, 5–6, 147, 149–151,
152n. 3; white southern views of deaf people
and, 18, 83, 87, 95. *See also* Advocacy; Public
policy
Problem, The, 6, 283; activism and, 17, 187, 190,
192–194, 207, 208; American Blind Peoples
Higher Education and General Improvement Association and, 187, 192–193, 200;
blind people's forum in, 17, 187, 188, 189,
190, 192–194, 201, 207; class in, 191; education in, 191, 192, 203, 204; employment in,
192, 202; gender and, 191, 202–207; history
of, 187, 188, 189, 200; homemaking in, 191,
202–203, 204–205, 206–207; images of
blind people in, 189, 191, 192–194, 195,
202–203, 204–205, 207; identity in, 189,
190, 191, 202–203, 204–205, 207–209; marriage in, 202, 203, 204–205, 206–207; men
in, 191, 202; news in, 188, 192; *Outlook for the
Blind* contrasted with, 188, 190–191,
194–196, 201–209; perspective of, 187,
190–192, 193–194, 195, 196, 199, 201,
202–203, 204–205, 206–209; politicization

of blindness and, 190, 208–209; professionals and, 187–188, 188–189, 190, 191; Progressive Era and, 189–190, 194, 196; public
policy in, 192; readership of, 196; residential
schools and, 187, 192, 200, 203, 204; self-help in, 192, 207; sighted contributors to,
189, 193; success stories in, 192, 202, 203,
204–205; tactile formats and, 192, 194; sexuality of blind women in, 5, 191, 204, 205,
206; women in, 191, 202–207. *See also* American Blind Peoples Higher Education and
General Improvement Association (ABPHE-GIA); Blind people; *Outlook for the Blind*
Progress, concept of, 35–36
Professionals: academic study of disability
and, 7, 9; blind people and, 5, 187–189, 190,
191, 195–199, 203–204, 205–206, 207–208,
212n. 36, 282; disability studies and, 12; material interests of, 5–6; mothers of disabled
children and, 295–296, 297–298, 304–305,
306; people with disabilities and, 3, 5–6, 17.
See also Physicians; Power
Progressive Era: blind people in, 189–192, 194,
196; Deaf people in, 214, 216; disability and
industrial capitalism in, 236, 242; disability
definitions in, 190–192; education in, 214,
216; rehabilitation in, 135; social changes
in, 189–190; transformation of medicine in,
184n. 39; workers' compensation in,
242–243, 379, 386; veterans in, 236,
242–243, 251
Public policy: advocacy, 3, 8, 4–5, 10–11, 382,
383, 384; benefits in, 4, 236–237, 238, 376,
379–380, 385; Edward Berkowitz on, 386,
389, 390; blind people and, 4, 376, 383; categories of disability in, 21, 385; class in, 238;
complexity of disability versus standardized
categories in, 388–389, 389–390; contradictions in, 376, 380, 383, 386–387; cultural
values in, 376, 385, 388; disability definitions in, 4–5, 10, 12, 236–238, 240–241, 242,
251, 255, 258, 379–380, 385, 386; disability-specific interests in, 20–21; eligibility rules
in, 379–380, 386–388; expenditures under,
386; general overview of, 375–376, 384–385,
390; generic categorization of disability in,
4–5, 385; government's role in disability
and, 190, 193, 197, 200, 241, 271, 278, 281,
282, 376–377, 378–379, 385; Harlan Hahn

on, 377; historiography of, 7, 8, 21, 258n. 1; identity and, 4–5, 385; immigration and, 33, 34, 45–50; impairment-specific, 376, 385; individualized solutions under, 388–389, 389–390; medical definition of disability in, 7, 20–21, 236–238, 242, 258, 380, 383, 386–388; moral appraisal in, 375–376, 378, 385, 387–388; politicization of disability and, 4–5, 10–11, 190, 237–238, 258, 375–392; racism in, 237, 238; separation perpetuated by, 389; significance of disability in history of, 236, 238, 378–379; Theda Skocpol on, 378; social worthiness in, 375–376, 378, 385; sociopolitical model in, 383–384, 385, 386, 390; state and local government role in, 241, 378, 379, 381, 383–384; Deborah Stone on, 258, 380, 387–388; "ugly laws" in, 338

CIVIL RIGHTS: access in, 20, 316, 324, 383–384, 386, 387; advocacy for, 3, 8, 4–5, 10–11, 382, 383, 384; Americans with Disabilities Act as, 1, 4, 14, 366, 384, 386, 387, 388, 389; anti-discrimination, 4, 383–384, 386; blind people and, 4, 383; Robert Burgdorf on, 389; court rulings on, 384, 386–387, 389; deinstitutionalization and, 378; difference perpetuated by, 389; disability studies and, 12–13; dog guide laws as, 20, 316, 324, 383; education in, 377, 378, 383, 384, 385; employment and, 386, 387; Chai Feldblum on, 387; individualized solutions under, 388–389, 389–390; Individuals with Disabilities Education Act as, 383, 384, 386, 388–389; medical definition of disability in, 386–387; moral appraisal and, 388; Rehabilitation Act of 1973, Title V/Section 504, as, 10, 383–384; sociopolitical model in, 383–384, 385, 386, 390; state and local government role in, 383–384; white cane laws as, 20, 383

SOCIAL WELFARE: age, disability, and, 389; benefits in, 4, 236–237, 238, 376, 379–380, 385; blind people and, 4, 376; bureaucratic conception of disability in, 237–238, 243–244; custodial care in, 378; development of disability category in, 236–238, 242; eligibility rules in, 236–238, 242, 379–380, 386, 387–388; European social policies compared with, 378; expenditures for, 386; in-

come maintenance programs in, 236, 244, 258, 376, 379–380, 386, 387; measurement and rating in, 387; Medicaid as, 377, 381; medical definition of disability in, 7, 20–21, 236–238, 242, 258, 380, 383, 386, 387–388; Medicare as, 377, 380; moral appraisal in, 375–376, 378, 387–388; physicians as gatekeepers in, 236–238, 242, 380, 387–388; Progressive reformers and, 236, 242–243, 251, 379, 386; social insurance in, 4, 243, 376, 377, 378; Social Security and, 5, 378; Social Security Disability Insurance as, 236, 244, 246, 258, 376, 379, 380, 387; social worthiness in, 375–376, 378; state and local government role in, 241, 378, 379, 381; subjectivity of determining disability in, 380, 388, 389; Supplemental Security Income as, 376, 381; welfare and, 4, 236–237, 242; work disincentives in, 380, 381, 386. *See also* Veterans' compensation; Vocational rehabilitation; Workers' compensation

Race: analytical category of, 208, 211n. 29; citizenship and, 33–34, 37–41, 53n. 11; evolutionary theory and, 36–37, 40, 41; freak shows and, 36, 40, 343–344, 358; historiography of, 9, 14–15, 17; normality and, 39–40; veterans and, 237, 252–253, 255–258, 266n. 62, 327. *See also* African Americans; Class; Ethnic minorities; Gender; Immigrants

Rae, Luzerne, opposing methodical signs, 73, 74

Railroad Brakeman's Journal, 157, 163

Railroad Men's Home, 160, 169–170, 173, 175–180, 186n. 70

Railroad Trainman's Journal, 167, 169

Railroaders with disabilities: Joseph Bellaire as, 158, 179–180; charity and, 168–172, 176, 185n. 61; class consciousness and, 158–160, 165, 166, 180–181; companies employing, 159, 164, 166, 183n. 18; companies giving benefits to, 164; competing for jobs, 160, 162–163, 183 n18; employment and, 157, 158; families of, 160, 167, 168, 172–174; fraud by, alleged, 163, 172, 182n. 12, 185n. 56; freak show imagery and, 157, 177–179; heroes, 158; images of, 158–159, 160, 162–163, 164, 166, 167, 168, 170, 175,

CPSIA information can be obtained
at www.ICGtesting.com
Printed in the USA
JSHW021102260722
28563JS00001B/34